HARVARD ECONOMIC STUDIES

VOLUME LXII

FASCIST ECONOMIC
POLICY

FASCIST ECONOMIC POLICY

AN ANALYSIS OF
ITALY'S ECONOMIC EXPERIMENT

BY

WILLIAM G. WELK

PROFESSOR OF ECONOMICS IN THE COLLEGE OF ST. THOMAS
ST. PAUL, MINNESOTA

NEW YORK

Russell & Russell

TO

MY FATHER AND MY MOTHER

PREFACE

THIS study is the product of a long acquaintance with Italian Fascism. My interest in the subject dates back to the days when, as a youth living in one of the larger Italian cities, I had the opportunity to observe at close range the early beginnings of the Fascist movement and its gradual rise to power. Student days at an Italian university and, more recently, the preparation at Harvard of a doctoral dissertation on Fascist economic policy have provided the incentive for intensive scientific work in this field. A visit to Italy made in the summer of 1936 for the purpose of completing the present volume has greatly facilitated the interpretation of recent Italian events.

To a large number of persons, to many more than I can mention here by name, I am indebted for assistance in the completion of this book. To my teachers at the University of Trieste and at Harvard I owe the debt which every student owes to those who are the first to guide him on the arduous paths of learning. To Professors F. W. Taussig and Edwin F. Gay of Harvard University, in particular, I am grateful for encouragement and inspiration during the early stages of the present work. To a large number of Italian scientists, business men, and government officials I am indebted for generous help and much valuable information. To Professor Alvin H. Hansen, of Harvard University, to Professors Frederick B. Garver and Eugen Altschul of the University of Minnesota, and to my friends and colleagues at St. Thomas, to Professor Stephen W. Mamchur in particular, I owe much for the valuable criticism and the many helpful suggestions which they have offered. To several American and European publishers I am indebted for permission to quote from copyrighted material. Finally, I must acknowledge with gratitude the financial aid granted for the completion of this work by the Social Science Research Council of New York and by the Administration of the College of St. Thomas.

W. G. W.

The College of St. Thomas
St. Paul, Minnesota
February, 1938

CONTENTS

PART III

THE ECONOMIC DEVELOPMENT OF THE FASCIST STATE:
1922–1937

CHARTS

TABLES

CHAPTERS I–IV

CHAPTERS V–VI

CONTENTS   xv

CHAPTER VII

CHAPTER VIII

CHAPTER IX

APPENDICES

APPENDIX I

LAWS OF THE CORPORATE STATE: SUMMARIES AND EXCERPTS

APPENDIX II

Membership of the Fascist Syndical System: April 1926 to December 31, 1933

xviii *CONTENTS*

INTRODUCTION

JOHN MAYNARD KEYNES, the distinguished British economist, said over ten years ago in *The End of Laissez-Faire*: "Perhaps the chief task of Economists at this hour is to distinguish afresh the *Agenda* of Government from the *Non-Agenda*. . . . Our problem is to work out a social organization which shall be as efficient as possible without offending our notions of a satisfactory way of life." This statement is as significant today as when it was first made. Since the beginning of the World War institutions hoary with age have been swept away; old beliefs and old convictions have been abandoned or thoroughly revised; new and powerful streams of human aspirations, perplexing and intriguing in their unexpected novelty, have come into being. Yet, while plans and suggestions for the construction of an efficient, just, and stable social and economic organization continue to be made and to be experimented with on an unprecedented scale, the problem itself still remains far from solution.

During the last two decades three unusually interesting attempts at a solution have been made: one by Russian Communism, another by Italian and German Fascism, and a third by our own "New Deal." Differing greatly in their general creed and philosophy, these three attempts at reform nevertheless have one fundamental aim in common: the creation of a better social order, the realization of a new scheme for the social and economic advancement of the people. Lauded by some and bitterly criticized by others, the second of these experiments — Fascism — has gradually evolved on the Italian peninsula a new type of political, social, and economic organization. The liberal democratic Italian commonwealth of pre-war days has disappeared and a new state built upon new doctrines and novel ideals has taken its place.

To describe in some detail and to analyze objectively the characteristics of the new economic system evolved in Italy and some of the problems which confront it today is the main purpose of this book. No attempt is made to explore in detail the questions raised by Fascist political theory or the ethical problems involved in the existence of a dictatorial political regime. After a brief historical introduction and a discussion of the fundamentals of Fascist doctrine the greater part of this study is devoted to an analysis of the economic institutions and the economic ideology which Fascism has created, and to an evaluation of the results that have been achieved in the economic sphere.

No student can hope to approach new ideas and to study new movements without being in some way influenced by his own subjective valuations and opinions. Education, environment, personal creeds and convictions tend to bias the mind of the most impartial investigator. It can only be said that in the following pages a sincere effort has been made to combine a fair and accurate picture of the Fascist phenomenon in Italy with a critical estimate of it, uninfluenced, as far as possible, by personal sympathies and ideological preconceptions. It remains for the reader to decide whether or not this goal has been attained.

PART I

BACKGROUND AND IDEOLOGY

CHAPTER I

A CLEAR understanding of Fascism and of the changes which the new regime has wrought in Italy's social, political, and economic life demands some knowledge of the historical background from which the movement arose. In its first political manifestations, Fascism was a truly Italian phenomenon; it is in Italy's history that one of the principal keys to its understanding must consequently be sought.

THE HISTORICAL BACKGROUND OF FASCISM:
FIRST NATIONAL ASPIRATIONS AND THE "RISORGIMENTO"

During the second half of the eighteenth century, when other nations were striving for political freedom and unity, there was as yet little national consciousness among the Italians. In spite of the memories of Rome the Italian people were content, as they had been for centuries, with the loose assemblage of petty states which took the place of a nation. It was the age of Maria Theresa, of Joseph II, of Alessandro Volta and Cesare Beccaria — an age of comparative well-being and peace. It left the country well advanced in literature, science, and social legislation, but it also stamped Italy as a land whose life, as an English historian puts it, "was in its memories and its arts, the beautiful woman-land of poetry, to be sung and caressed and coveted, but debarred from liberty and independence." [1]

The first Napoleonic campaigns broke in suddenly upon this peaceful era of poetry and song. Within a few years after the appearance of the first war clouds on Europe's political horizon, the establishment, in 1796 and 1797, of Napoleonic republics and kingdoms on Italian soil had swept away, apparently forever, the old social and political order. In a sense

[1] Bolton King, *A History of Italian Unity* (London, 1899), I, 1.

Napoleon may be said to have been the real founder of modern Italy. Foreseeing that unity of traditions, language, and literature was bound, sooner or later, to weld the many Italian states into a single nation, he encouraged the rise of a strong spirit of nationalism among the Italians. Abolishing feudalism wherever it still existed, he was the first to give Italy enlightened and uniform laws, to open new roads to talent, and so to stimulate and enliven the whole structure of Italian society.[2]

But the Napoleonic regime was of short duration. Napoleon fell, and with him fell the institutions which he had created. In 1815 the Congress of Vienna partitioned Italy anew into a series of petty states; the princely privileges, the arbitrary laws, the clerical assertion of power, and the intellectual stagnation of the past made their appearance again.

The spirit of Napoleon's work, nevertheless, survived. The memories of a unified and well-ordered Italian kingdom remained in the hearts of Italian patriots. Throughout the first half of the nineteenth century theories and programs of constitutional liberty and political unity were being developed and were finding ardent and self-sacrificing supporters. Secret societies, to fight for freedom and independence, were being formed throughout the country. In Piedmont, in Naples, in Lombardy and Romagna the first martyrs for Italian liberty and unity shed their blood. A school of patriots and liberals, supplying the impetus and the enthusiasm for the first wars of the Italian *Risorgimento*, gradually arose.[3]

THE ITALIAN KINGDOM BEFORE THE WORLD WAR

When, on September 20, 1870, over twenty years after the struggle for Italian unity had begun, Rome was finally occupied

[2] Cf. King, *A History of Italian Unity*, vol. I, chap. i; and J. A. R. Marriott, *The Makers of Modern Italy, Napoleon—Mussolini* (Oxford, 1931).

[3] See the dramatic history of the Italian secret societies, particularly that of the Carbonari and of Giuseppe Mazzini's Giovane Italia, in King, *A History of Italian Unity*, vol. I, chaps. ii, vi, vii. For a more detailed account of the movement for Italian independence and of the wars of the Italian *Risorgimento*, cf., among other works, King, *op. cit.*, Luigi Villari, *Italy* (New York, 1929), and George B. McClellan, *Modern Italy* (Princeton, 1933).

by Italian troops and the unification of Italy accomplished, the young nation still faced numerous problems. The salient one was, perhaps, the prevailing poverty. Natural resources appeared to be scarce, in some essential fields practically non-existent. Public improvements such as harbors, railroads, reclamation works, were badly needed. Heavy taxation had to be imposed to meet the nation's most urgent financial needs.

In the political field conditions were nearly as bad. The mass of the Italian people, especially in the South, were poor and illiterate. Party organizations were everywhere weak and inefficient; candidates for office were selected by small local cliques rather than by strong political groups. Politicians were, in the opinion of a liberal journalist of the time, "the worst element in Italian life." [4]

Yet, as the years went by, the economic conditions of the country began to show encouraging signs of improvement. In part at least, Italy's poverty was found to be remediable. Fertile new lands were made available to agriculture through reclamation; with the help of German and Swiss financiers some of the country's strongest financial institutions were founded, and several important large-scale industries were established; trade and commerce began to show heartening signs of improvement. In 1889, after several years of war-fare, the first colony, Eritrea, was officially added to the young kingdom. At the turn of the century the colonial domain was further extended through the occupation of Somalia (1910), Tripolitania, and Cirenaica (1912). By the time of the World War, Italy was no longer the land of sentimentalism and *dolce far niente* but had gradually become earnest, practical, progressive, and ready to take her place among the larger powers of the world.[5]

[4] King, *A History of Italian Unity*, II, 308. On reaching Rome in 1870 to take over his ministerial duties Massimo d' Azeglio, the first head of the new Italian government, thus expressed himself to the King: "Your Majesty, we have made Italy. Now we must make the Italians" (quoted in Antonio Cippico, *Italy, the Central Problem of the Mediterranean*, New Haven, 1926, p. 67).

[5] For a more detailed account of Italian political, social, and economic conditions in the pre-war period, see, among other works, Bolton King and Thomas Okey, *Italy Today* (London, 1901); F. S. Nitti, *La Ricchezza dell' Italia*

Yet, though the country's economic progress during the decade immediately preceding the World War was unmistakable, her political life remained unstable and insecure. No strong political parties competed for power. Local cliques and groups led by astute politicians continued to dominate the political scene. These groups split and combined, shifted and changed with incredible ease. Italian politics was a game in which the most artful player won the prize.

THE RISE OF NATIONALISM AND THE WORLD WAR

This easygoing political maneuvering was suddenly confronted with the World War. The mass of the Italian people had no desire to fight; the majority of the country's middle classes and working men, the Catholic and the Socialist groups, did not wish to go to war; Parliament opposed participation in the conflict. Moreover, Italy had no actual obligation to enter it on either side. Although an ally of Germany and Austria through membership in the Triple Alliance, her obligations were limited to the support of her allies in a defensive war; she was in no way bound to assist them in a conflict which they themselves had provoked. That is why on August 2, 1914, Italy declared for neutrality.

Some groups of Italians, nevertheless, had long been preparing for battle. In a victorious war against Austria, Italian Nationalists saw an opportunity for completing the country's unification through the annexation of Trento, Trieste, Fiume, and Dalmatia, the Italian provinces still under Austrian rule. Inflamed with patriotism and perhaps hoping for the emergence of a new social order out of the general turmoil of a great conflict, a small group of Italian Socialists joined the Nationalists in their plea for war. D'Annunzio, the poet, Corridoni

---

(Naples, 1904); R. Benini, *I Fatti caratteristici del nostro risorgimento economico* (Milan, 1911); Eugenio Messeri, *Cinquant' anni di vita economica e finanziaria italiana* (Rome, 1912); Ernest Lémonon, *L'Italie économique et sociale, 1861–1912* (Paris, 1913); F. S. Nitti, *Il Capitale straniero in Italia* (Bari, 1915); Gioacchino Volpe, *L'Italia in cammino* (Milan, 1928); Benedetto Croce, *A History of Italy, 1871–1915* (Oxford, 1929); Luigi Villari, *Italy* (New York, 1929); Robert Michels, *Italien von Heute . . . 1860 bis 1930* (Leipzig, 1930); Herman Finer, *Mussolini's Italy* (New York, 1935), chap. iii.

and Mussolini, the labor leaders, Cesare Battisti, the Austrian Irredentist, and other volunteers toured the north and center of the peninsula making inflammatory war speeches. Soon the people's emotions were aroused to fever heat. To a reluctant Parliament there remained, in the end, but the choice between war or revolution.

At this crucial point in Italy's history, Benito Mussolini, then a thirty-year-old Socialist agitator, made his first independent appearance upon the scene of his country's national politics. He publicly disavowed his party's stand for neutrality, declared himself openly in favor of intervention, and became one of the foremost agitators for the interventionist cause.[6]

Early in 1915, largely as a result of the agitation of the interventionists, the Italian Chamber was forced to yield; on

[6] Benito Mussolini, the future leader of Italian Fascism, was born on July 29, 1883, in the small village of Predappio, in the province of Forlì, in Romagna. His father, the village blacksmith, was a man strongly imbued with revolutionary Socialist doctrines. After completing his education and qualifying as a grade-school teacher, young Mussolini went to Switzerland, where he studied at several universities while earning his living as a manual laborer. He was expelled from Switzerland because of his extreme Socialist tendencies and returned to Italy for his period of military service. Imprisoned there for his part in certain local labor agitations, he left Italy and went to the Austrian Tyrol, where he earned his living as a Socialist newspaper man and labor leader. From Austria he was expelled after a short stay because of his Irredentist agitation, and he returned to Italy, where he was attracted by the new doctrines of Socialist syndicalism evolved by Georges Sorel. When the World War broke out, Mussolini, imbued with Irredentist sentiments, began his agitation for active Italian participation in the war against Austria. Because of his interventionist propaganda, on November 25, 1914, he was formally expelled from the Italian Socialist party and was asked to resign the editorship of the Avanti, the official organ of Italian Socialism, which had been entrusted to him. He thereupon founded his own newspaper, the Popolo d'Italia.

It has been asserted that at the outbreak of the war Mussolini was given financial aid by the French and that he became an interventionist for financial reasons. Although he may have accepted financial aid to found the Popolo d'Italia and to champion his new cause, it seems quite likely that his conversion to interventionism was sincere. By nature a warrior and a man of action, and at heart a patriotic Italian despite his Socialist affiliations, Mussolini simply refused not to take advantage of the opportunity to complete Italy's unification, and to crush Austria, Italy's traditional enemy.

See, for a detailed biography, Benito Mussolini, My Autobiography (New York, 1928); Margherita Sarfatti, Dux (Milan, 1934). On the role of Italian nationalism immediately before the World War, see Herbert W. Schneider, Making the Fascist State (New York, 1928), pp. 1 ff.; Antonio Cippico, Italy, the Central Problem of the Mediterranean, p. 68; Herman Finer, Mussolini's Italy, chap. iv.

May 24 of the same year war was declared upon the Central Powers.

The popular movement which forced Italy's entry into the World War marks, in a sense, the beginning of Italian Fascism. Although not called Fascist, the interventionist movement inspired the mass of the Italian people with a new national ideal, and taught them how, even against the will of Parliament, national goals could be achieved under the leadership of a few determined men. The Fasci di Azione Rivoluzionaria, or groups of revolutionary action, organized to agitate for Italy's entry into the war were the forerunners of the Fasci di Combattimento, Mussolini's post-war Fascist fighting squads.

When Italy declared war upon Austria, Mussolini enlisted as a private and spent the following two years at the front. Badly wounded, and unfit for further combat, he returned to Milan in August 1917 and resumed his post as editor of the *Popolo d'Italia*, the newspaper which he had founded two years earlier to preach intervention to the Italian masses. Through the columns of that newspaper he continued to incite the Italian people to resistance, and when the end of the conflict drew near he sounded the first battle cry of what was soon to be the Fascist movement. "We, the survivors, we who have returned, demand the right of governing Italy," he wrote on May 24, 1918, "not, of course to precipitate it in dissolution and disorder, but to lead it ever higher and higher and always forward, to make it in ideas and works worthy of being among the great nations which will be the leaders of the world's civilization of tomorrow." [7]

The fortunes of war were, in the main, unfavorable to the Italians. While the army was fighting the Austrians, the Socialist party, behind the lines, was still working for peace. As a result, in October 1917, the poorly commanded and utterly demoralized Italian army broke at Caporetto, and the Austrians advanced far into the Venetian plains. Venice seemed lost, the entire valley of the Po threatened. In the face of this national calamity the entire peninsula roused itself to a gigantic

---

[7] Quoted by Finer, *Mussolini's Italy*, p. 110.

patriotic effort: the commanders of the army were changed, Socialist propaganda was suppressed by a sweeping wave of nationalist feeling, a line of resistance was established on the Piave and successfully upheld until a year later, when the war was won.[8]

POST-WAR DIFFICULTIES

Returning from the trenches at the conclusion of the armistice, Italy's soldiers found the country bordering on chaos. The stress and strain of the war were being deeply felt. A sense of growing disappointment and dissatisfaction pervaded all classes of the population. The fruits of victory, paid for by the lives of 600,000 soldiers, were few. Because of President Wilson's veto, Fiume and Dalmatia, promised to Italy in the Treaty of London in 1915, were denied her at the Paris Peace Conference. The country's whole social and economic structure had been thrown out of gear. A painful process of readjustment was required before the machinery of production, geared to the necessities of war, could be shifted back to the requirements of peace. The country's finances, subjected to an excessive burden during the four years of the war, were utterly disorganized; railroads were in confusion; trade and industry were dislocated and languishing. With the exception of war profiteers, nearly everyone in the kingdom was poorer after the conflict than before. Exasperated by the rise in the cost of living and by other post-war difficulties, and unwilling to go back to their monotonous jobs in factories and farms after four years of war life, the nation's laboring men were ready to lend a willing ear to the pleas of Socialist and Communist agitators. Ready to make the most of the situation, Communist leaders began to point to Russia, the country where the proletariat had won a decisive and lasting victory. Italian workers were incited to attempt to do likewise.

As an open expression of this feeling of unrest and general dissatisfaction, strikes began to break out in the country's

---

[8] For an exhaustive account of the events immediately preceding and following the Great War, see Villari, *Italy*.

leading industries and in its essential public services. Steamers in the harbors, ready to weigh their anchors, were held up at the last moment in an attempt to secure higher wages or to impose an increase in the numbers of the crew. In railroading, too, strikes broke out at the least pretext. On April 10, 1919, a twenty-four-hour general strike, which completely paralyzed the economic activities of the nation, was declared.

At this time the country's political scene presented an equally discouraging spectacle. The prestige and the authority of the old ruling class had vanished. Caught in the maelstrom of rapidly moving events, the old political classes — divided and gravely discredited by the war — proved utterly incapable of dealing with the situation. One weak government succeeded another, and radical and revolutionist elements were given an almost entirely free hand.

In June 1919 the Orlando cabinet was forced to resign, largely because of its disastrous failure at the Peace Conference negotiations. It was succeeded by a new government, headed by Francesco Nitti. The advent of the Nitti government resulted in a recrudescence of strikes and disorders. Officers and soldiers wearing war decorations were insulted and assaulted in the streets. Upon protesting to the government, they were advised to avoid provocation by dispensing with their decorations and wearing civilian clothes when off duty. The weakness of the Nitti regime was climaxed by its granting an amnesty to war deserters, an act which exasperated and embittered every patriotic Italian. As a result, in June 1920, the incumbent cabinet was in its turn forced to resign.

A government headed by Giolitti, the veteran Italian statesman who for a quarter of a century had been the unchallenged leader of the Democratic party, followed. Under the new regime the general situation showed little improvement. Riots and strikes continued. At Ancona disorders costing several lives broke out. In September 1920 the metal workers of Lombardy and Piedmont seized the factories in which they were employed, hoisted the red flag, and took control. In Romagna, too, a number of large farms and estates were seized by the workers. The government, trusting neither the army nor the police, nor the people themselves, remained inactive despite the turmoil.[9]

THE BIRTH OF THE FASCIST MOVEMENT

A reaction against this condition soon appeared. As early as the beginning of 1919 some political groups had begun to protest against the weakness and inefficiency of the Italian governments of the day, and to resist the maneuvers of the Socialist and Communist leaders. Among these were the Nationalists, who urged the annexation of Fiume and Dalmatia, and advocated the enlargement of Italy's colonial domain; the patriotic associations, such as the Italia Redenta, the Arditi, the Italia Nuova, and a small group of "national" Socialists led by Benito Mussolini. On March 23, 1919, Mussolini called a meeting of a few dozen friends and sympathizers at a small assembly hall in the Piazza San Sepolcro in Milan, and with them founded the Fasci di Combattimento, the first Fascist fighting squads.[10]

Inspired by a curious mixture of Nationalism and Socialist doctrine, Mussolini's new organization stood for the improvement of labor conditions under a system of economic democracy and "national" syndicalism. It planned the creation of a series of Fasci, or organs of agitation and propaganda, for the purpose of overthrowing the weak Italian governments of the day and substituting in their place a strong national government headed by "the men who forced the country into the war and into victory, and who alone have a right to the suc-

[9] Some writers assert that Giolitti, perfectly calm in the turmoil of events, purposely refused to act. In the episode of the occupation of the factories he is said to have refused to interfere, allowing the experiment to take place in order to convince the workers of the impossibility of reaching their goal. As a matter of fact, a few days after the factories were occupied it became apparent that the attempt was doomed to fail, for the engineers and the managers refused to coöperate with the workers. For a detailed discussion of this point, see Carlo Sforza's portrait of Giolitti in his *Makers of Modern Europe* (Indianapolis, 1930), pp. 236 ff.

[10] The word *fascio*, from which *Fascismo*, the Italian name of the new party, was derived, means "bundle" and signifies the close union of those associated in the movement. It also designates the fasces, or bundle of rods, of the Roman lictors, the emblem chosen by the new party.

cession." During the months immediately following, Mussolini, a renegade and an adventurer in the eyes of the official Italian Socialist party, which had expelled him in 1914, was in effect still fighting for an essentially Socialist cause. In the party's program for the elections of 1919 there were such patently Socialistic planks as those favoring the nationalization of the property of religious congregations, a capital levy upon the rich, and the confiscation of war profits.

At the outset, the Fascists made little headway at the polls. In the election of 1919 they secured not a single seat in the Italian Chamber, while the Socialists won 156 and the Popolari 101 seats. In Milan, Mussolini, who was a candidate, received but 5,000 votes out of a total of over 300,000.[11]

Gradually, however, the tide began to turn. From the end of 1919 to the end of 1920 Italy was in a state of continuous ferment. Strikes and other labor disturbances followed each other in rapid succession, and increasingly serious conflicts occurred between the Socialist and the Nationalist organizations. Animated by strong nationalist sentiments, the Fascists violently opposed the Socialists and bitterly criticized the weakness and inefficiency of the central government. In September 1919, in direct defiance of the constituted government authorities, they actively supported the poet and war hero, Gabriele d'Annunzio, in his occupation of Fiume, and lent their material and moral support to his *legionari*. As the months went by, strikes increased in number and intensity, and conflicts with the Socialist organizations became more and more frequent. Eventually, when Italian factories were seized by the workers, in the second half of 1920, the Fascists, actively aided by the now thoroughly aroused Italian bourgeoisie, reacted vigorously. Definitely abandoning his old Socialist convictions, Mussolini

[11] At the beginning of 1919 a new political party, consisting largely of Catholic members of the middle classes and of small independent farmers, was formed. It was called Partito Popolare, the people's party. (The veto of the Pope forbidding Italian Catholics to participate in active politics had been withdrawn shortly before the war.) In favor of the League of Nations, and advocating an elaborate program of social reform, this party, under the able leadership of the Sicilian priest, Luigi Sturzo, made rapid progress. Cf. Villari, *Italy*, pp. 154 ff.

dramatically rallied the Fascist forces "to save Italy from the communist peril." It is at this point that Italian Fascism really begins to grow.[12]

THE RISE OF FASCISM TO POWER

Definitely nationalist and anti-Socialist, the Fascist movement rapidly spread to all parts of the country and to all classes. An ever-increasing number and variety of followers, former soldiers and army officers, students, shopkeepers, landowners, industrialists, and professional men of every description, inspired by the desire to help the nation out of its *impasse*, joined its ranks. *Fasci* were formed in almost every Italian town and village. The characteristic black shirt worn by the Arditi (the Italian shock troops) during the war was adopted as the emblem of membership in the new party. Patriotic demonstrations were held everywhere, only to be broken up by the Socialists and Communists. The destruction of "labor chambers" by the Fascists was met with violent reprisals by the Socialists. Castor oil and the *manganello* (a heavy wooden bludgeon) were used ruthlessly in the Fascist black-shirt squads' "punitive expeditions." In a series of bitter and bloody battles, costing hundreds of victims on both sides, the power of the Socialist and Communist organizations was gradually broken. When a new election was held in the spring of 1921, a solid block of thirty-five Fascists, ten Nationalists, and several sympathizers faced the Socialists in the new Chamber. Mussolini, the Fascist leader, defeated in 1919 and now returned by a large majority, headed the national forces in the new Parliament.[13]

---

[12] It is indeed a moot question whether or not, after the failure of the Italian worker's attempts to run the factories which they had occupied, a real Communist danger existed in Italy. Some observers maintain, and their argument is somewhat cogent, that after the unsuccessful occupation of the factories the real Bolshevik peril in Italy was gone and the Fascist reaction was consequently unnecessary and unjustified. Yet in 1920 and 1921 the mass of the Italian people, and particularly the middle classes, evidently failed to realize that the danger had passed and continued to regard Fascism as their best weapon against Socialist radicalism and against a government too weak to be relied upon.

[13] Did Mussolini, the former Socialist turned Fascist, go over to the middle

Although during the early struggles of Fascism no detailed doctrinal program had been elaborated, its fundamental motives and driving forces were clear. These were intense patriotism and national fervor, the determination to resist at all costs the anti-national and defeatist maneuvers of the Socialists and Communists, and the desire to give Italy, as rapidly as possible, a strong and respected central government.[14]

Perhaps unconsciously, the Fascist movement seems to have struck a note appealing to the very instincts of the Italian people. True to Italy's political tradition, the new movement originated in the city, which had been the country's basic political unit since the Middle Ages. For centuries political power had been vested in the men who could rush to the *piazza*, the city square, and there take part in an election, a party demonstration, or a fight, openly expressing their enthusiasms or antipathies. Whenever their governments became intolerable, whenever there was cause for dissatisfaction, the Italian people settled their difficulties not, like Anglo-Saxon countries, by a

---

classes for purely selfish reasons as some of his opponents assert? I am inclined to believe that his motives were different. A nationalist and anti-Bolshevik at heart, initially he fought his battles to prevent a Communist regime in Italy; later, when the immediate Bolshevik danger no longer existed, his purpose was to give the country the strong and effective government to which, he thought, the sacrifices of the war entitled it. In that endeavor the middle classes became his natural allies. For a more detailed history of the early development of Fascism, cf. G. A. Chiurco, *Storia della rivoluzione Fascista* (Florence, 1929), and Finer, *Mussolini's Italy*, pt. II.

[14] "Fascism," writes Benito Mussolini, "was not the nursling of a doctrine worked out beforehand with detailed elaboration; it was born of the need for action and it was itself from the beginning practical rather than theoretical. . . . And yet if one were to re-read, in the now dusty columns of that date, the report of the meeting in which the *Fasci Italiani di Combattimento* were constituted, one would find there no ordered expression of doctrine, but a series of aphorisms, anticipations, and aspirations, which, when refined by time from the original ore, were destined after some years to develop into an ordered series of doctrinal concepts, forming the Fascist political doctrine — different from all others either of the past or the present day." Mussolini, "The Political and Social Doctrine of Fascism," authorized English translation of the article contributed by Mussolini to the *Enciclopedia Italiana* in 1932, reprinted in *International Conciliation* (a publication of the Carnegie Endowment for International Peace), January 1935, pp. 5–6, quoted here by permission of the Hogarth Press.

For further details on the early program of the Fascist party, see Schneider, *Making the Fascist State*, p. 58.

solemn election but by a noisy demonstration or a brawl in the city square. So it had been for centuries; so it had been during the days of the *Risorgimento* and on the eve of the World War; so it was again when Fascism was fighting for power. The kind of politics a Latin people has in its blood is that of the *piazza* rather than that of the ballot box and polling booth, noisy and dramatic demonstration rather than formally calm and dignified action. While the Englishman for centuries has turned to Parliament for relief and action, the Italian has been accustomed to look up to one man, to put faith and power in one individual. We see this in the long list of the Roman rulers, in the emergence of the *capitani del popolo* in the medieval towns, in the dictatorial connotations attached to the names of some of the leading men in the Italian *Risorgimento*, and, again, in the ease with which Mussolini conquered Italy, crushed all opposition and "banished," as he puts it, "the corpse of liberal democracy from the land." [15]

After the elections of 1921 civil disturbances continued unabated, while the government, weak and helpless, persisted in its policy of indecision and inactivity until, pressed from all sides, it gradually lost what little authority it still possessed. In August 1921, in an effort to stop the violence and bloodshed, Mussolini negotiated a truce with the Socialists. That act almost cost him his leadership. The local leaders of the Fascist squads — the Farinaccis, the Grandis, the Balbos — would have no peace. They were determined to crush their opponents completely. Disgusted with some of their excesses, Mussolini actually tendered his resignation, which was, of course, not accepted. On November 7, 1921, against the wishes of the extremists but with the support of the more moderate elements within the movement, he transformed what had thus far been the Fascist movement into a definite political organization, the Fascist party. This newly created party, its constitution said, was to be "a voluntary militia placed at the service of

---

[15] For a suggestive and more detailed discussion of this point of view, cf. G. M. Trevelyan, "The Historical Causes of the Present State of Affairs in Italy," Sidney Ball Memorial Lecture delivered at the University of Oxford on October 31, 1923, in *Barnett House Papers*, No. 8 (Oxford, 1923).

the nation." Its activity was to be based "upon these three principles: order, discipline, hierarchy." [16]

Determined to bring discipline into its ranks, the party now applied pressure to stop the worst excesses of the fighting squads. But the squads had tasted power, and the violence which the leaders had unleashed during the earlier battles could not now be restrained. The action of the squads grew more and more arbitrary. Socialist organizations such as the coöperatives and the labor chambers were destroyed mercilessly, and the leaders beaten and persecuted.

The central government, as usual, did nothing. In February 1922 the Cabinet was once more forced to resign, and a new government, headed by Facta, an honest but feeble man, succeeded. During that summer the civil disturbances within the country became deeply intensified. A general strike, with the object of crushing the Fascist opposition, was declared by the Socialists on August 1. The majority of railroad workers, streetcar conductors, firemen, street sweepers, and employees of the water, gas, and electrical plants all over Italy ceased work. Immediately the Fascists, assisted by all the patriotic elements within the country, organized a powerful anti-strike movement. Waterworks, gas, and electrical plants, trains and streetcars were set in operation again. The strike was broken two days after it was declared, and the Socialists lost, thereby, their most effective weapon. In Milan the Fascists invaded the town hall, expelled the Socialist administration, and raised the national flag amid great popular enthusiasm.

Urged on by the more impetuous elements within their own ranks and determined to change the prevailing state of affairs and to give the country a new and efficient central government, the Fascists now began preparations to secure governmental control. At the party congress held on October 24, 1922, in Naples, forty thousand armed black-shirts paraded the streets of the city. Mussolini made a speech foreshadowing immediate action. "Our program," he announced, "is that we want to govern Italy." Two days later, led by the Fascist *quadrumvirate* con-

---

[16] Finer, *Mussolini's Italy*, p. 310.

sisting of Balbo, Bianchi, De Vecchi, and De Bono, fifty thousand armed black-shirts began their historic March on Rome.

At the last minute, just before the black-shirts actually began their march, the Facta government made a frantic effort to act. It issued a decree proclaiming a state of martial law. Realizing that the decree would mean civil war, the King refused to sign it. After an unsuccessful attempt to form a government under Salandra with a majority of Fascist ministers, the King sent for Mussolini. The latter immediately left Milan (where he had been while the March on Rome was in progress), arriving in the capital on the thirtieth of October. On that day, while armed black-shirt columns were marching into the city, the first Fascist government was formed under the premiership of Benito Mussolini. The Fascist regime in Italy had begun.

Was the coming of Fascism unavoidable? Would the democratic state in Italy have been able to cure its own ailments? Was the King justified in placing the government exclusively in the hands of a revolutionary party, or should he have resisted? Was the March on Rome a true revolution? These are difficult questions to answer. Had the King signed the decree of martial law, his army might well have refused to march against the Fascists. Or, had it marched, there might have been such serious bloodshed that in the event of a Fascist victory the King could hardly have kept his throne. Nor does it seem likely, conditions in Italy being what they were in 1922, that the Italian democratic state would have been able to overcome its own difficulties successfully. Economic disorder, political confusion, parliamentary weakness, and, above all, the determination of a comparatively small but indomitable political group to seize power provided a series of unusual circumstances which would have caused, sooner or later, a serious political crisis. The March on Rome, was, in itself, no more than a *coup d'état*, the violent seizure of power by the most determined among several political groups. The true Fascist revolution and its ultimate product, the totalitarian Fascist state, evolved only gradually from that first violent upheaval.

THE BEGINNINGS OF THE FASCIST REGIME

Immediately after the fateful days of October 1922 there was no actual dictatorship. Mussolini's first cabinet included several non-Fascist ministers. In spite of the extra-parliamentary nature of the new government, the Italian Chamber, by a vote of 215 to 80, granted it full powers for a year, thus enabling it to carry out, unhampered by parliamentary formalities, a series of necessary reforms.

Despite the gradual improvement in Italy's economic condition and the economic reforms adopted by the new government, its efforts to restore order did not at first prove successful.[17] Reaction continued, tolerated, if not actually encouraged, by the new regime. Leading Italian intellectuals, men like Amendola, Nitti, and Salvemini, known to be bitterly opposed to Fascism, suffered persecution; their homes were sacked, their libraries burnt, and they themselves were finally driven out of the country. Persecution of the Socialists also continued. Workers were beaten for celebrating May Day; Socialist coöperatives were invaded and destroyed. A feeling of tension and uneasiness pervaded many quarters, and opposition to the regime increased in the press and among the intellectuals.

In the face of this situation the government began to take definite steps to strengthen its position. In 1923 the Guardia Regia, a police force created by Nitti, was abolished, and its place was taken by the newly organized Milizia Volontaria per la Sicurezza Nazionale, an armed voluntary Fascist militia, established for the protection of the regime and recruited largely from among the members of the black-shirt formations of early Fascism. In the summer of the same year, ostensibly to avoid the recurrence of coalition governments which had hitherto been one of the main weaknesses of the Italian parliamentary system, the government drafted a new electoral bill according to which the party securing the largest number

---

[17] For a discussion of Fascist economic reform during this period, notably the balancing of the budget, successfully accomplished by the new Minister of Finance, Alberto de Stefani, cf. Part III, chap. vii, pp. 160 ff.

of electoral votes in the country was to be entitled to two-thirds of the seats in the new Chamber. The remaining one-third were to be divided among the other parties in proportion to the number of votes received. This method was, of course, contrary to the simple numerical majority principle of governing contained in the country's constitution. In spite of violent opposition by Socialists and Popolari, the bill was passed by Parliament and became law. In January 1924 the old Chamber was dissolved. The new elections held on April 6, 1924 (not without violence and intimidation), gave the government sixty-five per cent of the recorded votes. Even without the new electoral law assuring it two-thirds of the seats, the government would thus have had a clear majority in the new Chamber. In the Senate, the attitude of which had been, on the whole, rather sympathetic from the beginning, a Fascist majority was assured by the appointment of a number of new senators proposed to the King by Mussolini.

In May 1924 the new session of the Italian Parliament was opened. On May 30 one of the leaders of the Socialist group in the Chamber, the able young deputy Giacomo Matteotti, vigorously attacked the government, denouncing the frauds and outrages allegedly committed by the Fascists during the elections. On June 10 Matteotti mysteriously disappeared from Rome. A few days later he was found murdered in a lonely spot of the Campagna Romana.

This cold-blooded crime created a sensation. Some of the highest Fascist officials, Mussolini not excepted, were accused of complicity in the murder. Though Mussolini defended his government and pledged himself to find the murderer and bring him to justice, his position appeared to be untenable. The government seemed to stand isolated and friendless. On June 15 the opposition deputies withdrew from Parliament in protest and formed a rival Chamber on the Aventino, thereby hoping to render parliamentary business impossible and to bring about the fall of the government.

"TOTALITARIAN" FASCISM AND THE BUILDING OF THE
FASCIST STATE

At this crucial time a significant change took place in the Fascist attitude. After repeated but unsuccessful efforts by the Fascists for a rapprochement with their opponents, Mussolini boldly attacked. In a vigorous speech on January 3, 1925, he affirmed that the utterly uncompromising attitude of the opposition had made further coöperation with it impossible, and that from then on Fascism would govern the country on a one-party system and without "the gentlemen of the opposition." That date marks the true beginning of the Fascist dictatorship in Italy. After January 1925 Italian Fascism became more and more exclusive, "integral and totalitarian" (*integrale e totalitario*), as the Italian formula ran. The Italian state, Fascists held, was to be transformed according to Fascist ideals and Fascist formulae. A new kind of political and economic life was to be evolved in Italy. A new state, distinctly different from the old liberal democratic one, was to be erected.

The philosophy upon which the new Fascist state was to be based was first set forth in detail by the able Italian jurist Alfredo Rocco (a former member of the Italian Nationalist party and then Minister of Justice in the Mussolini Cabinet) in a famous speech made at Perugia on August 30, 1925. Mussolini immediately gave full public endorsement to that speech, which contained the first authoritative and carefully elaborated statement of Fascist economic and political doctrine.[18]

Measures designed to build the totalitarian state envisaged by the Fascist leaders were now adopted in rapid succession. The resignations of several non-Fascist members of the Cabinet were accepted, and Mussolini himself took over their portfolios ad interim. The newly appointed secretary general of the Fascist party, Roberto Farinacci, entirely reorganized the party, imposing upon it the extremist, intransigent attitude of

---

[18] Cf. the detailed analysis of Rocco's speech in chap. ii, pp. 31 ff.

which he himself was an exponent, and making it the primary force which was henceforth to inspire and control all the organs of the Fascist state. Toward the end of 1925 Italian Masonic orders were dissolved, and all other associations were requested to submit their constitutions and membership lists to the government authorities. Greater powers of parliamentary initiative were conferred upon the head of the government, and penalties were provided for offenses committed against him. Early in 1926 municipal elections were abolished and the system of governmentally appointed *podestà* (heads of cities and communes) introduced. On April 3, 1926, the fundamental law on the reorganization of the country's economic system, including the introduction of government-supervised collective bargaining through a system of legally recognized workers' and employers' associations, was passed. In the same year laws were promulgated suppressing all seditious newspapers and all anti-national parties (mainly the Socialist and Communist parties), introducing the death ·enalty for attempts on the life of the King and the Premier, providing for the *confino* or imprisonment for political crimes, and adopting the *fascio* in conjunction with the shield of the reigning House of Savoy as the official emblem of the kingdom.

In May 1928 another law drastically reforming the country's system of political representation and instituting representation on an occupational basis was passed. In December 1928 the constitutional status and the official functions of the Fascist Grand Council, the highest advisory organ of the regime, were formally defined by law, thus welding the Fascist party and the Italian state into a unit and providing for the continuity of the regime. In 1930 the reorganization of the country's economic system was further advanced by the institution of a supreme economic council entrusted with the supervision and coördination of the nation's economic life. Finally, in 1934, the series of basic economic reforms was completed by the establishment of the "corporations," twenty-two boards of economic control to which important normative and advisory functions were assigned.

Through the determined action of an all-powerful political party, a new state thus gradually arose in Italy. The liberal and democratic state of the past ceased to exist, and a novel political and economic system, to be discussed in detail in the succeeding chapters, took its place.

CHAPTER II

FUNDAMENTALS IN FASCIST ECONOMIC AND POLITICAL PHILOSOPHY

FASCIST THOUGHT AND THE PRAGMATIC REVOLT IN CONTEMPORARY POLITICS

ITALIAN Fascists do not stand alone in their plea for reform. Over the entire continent of Europe an open revolt seems to have occurred against the political and economic rationalism of the nineteenth century. But two decades ago the Great War was fought "to make the world safe for democracy." Today, in a dozen countries, democratic forms of government have been more or less openly abandoned, and dictatorships dot the map of the continent on which the Wilsonian ideal of popular self-determination was expected to rule supreme. Apparently the pendulum of European politics has swung away from the older political philosophies toward a new conception, a new philosophy of political activity. A growing distrust of intellect alone as a builder of programs has arisen. Wilson's idealistic Fourteen Points have vanished, while the world is still struggling in the hopeless tangle created by the Treaty of Versailles. Discouraged by its experiences, a large part of the post-war world seems to have adopted a new political creed: action — not talk, "planks," or theory — alone matters. Programs, as Mussolini puts it, are endless: it is men, it is groups of men, that count.

The philosophical foundations for this pragmatic creed were laid long ago. Over thirty years ago William James, distinctly skeptical of the validity and effectiveness of purely rationalistic programs, affirmed that man cannot be regarded solely as a rational being. Even the most intellectual of men, he contended, are influenced by emotions, by passions, and by impulses; absolute truth, therefore, must be renounced in favor of a "working" truth, which, after all, is man's best guide to the problems of his daily existence. "Who," wrote James, "can decide offhand which is absolutely better, to live or to understand life? We must do both alternately, and a man can no more limit himself to either than a pair of scissors can cut with a single one of its blades."[1]

On the basis of James's pragmatism, new political and economic theories, rejecting as idle abstractions the traditional doctrines of the sovereignty of the constitutional state, have been evolved. New philosophies of activism and political pluralism have risen; quite independently, a series of new ideological programs in which the group, not the individual, is to form the economic and political unit have been devised.[2]

THE DOCTRINES OF GEORGES SOREL, LÉON DUGUIT,
G. D. H. COLE, AND HAROLD J. LASKI

Long before the World War, Georges Sorel, the father of French revolutionary syndicalism and one of the men who contributed most to the molding of Benito Mussolini's early social thought, used the kindly doctrines of William James's pragmatism as a philosophical background for his main work, the *Réflexions sur la violence*. In this book Sorel espoused the formation of powerful workers' trade associations called *syndicats* (syndicates) which through violent revolutionary action would weaken the resistance of capitalists and employers, gradually forcing the latter to surrender all means of production. A union of workmen's syndicates in control of the productive apparatus of the nation would then take the place of the present liberal democratic state, while the ablest leaders of the country's workers' organizations would replace the present government. To hasten the coming of the new syndicalist state the use of violence was regarded as legitimate and de-

---

[1] *The Philosophy of William James, Drawn from His Own Works* (New York, 1925), introduction by H. M. Kallen, p. 92. For a fuller statement of James's philosophical creed, see his works, in particular his *Principles of Psychology* (New York, 1890), and his *Pragmatism* (New York, 1907).

[2] For a detailed discussion and a critical analysis of the various pragmatic currents in contemporary political theory, see W. Y. Elliott, *The Pragmatic Revolt in Politics* (New York, 1928).

sirable. To sustain the hope of the masses and ultimately give them the courage and will to revolt, Sorel advocated keeping the vision of a final general strike of all the workers — the strike which would end capitalist domination — constantly before their eyes.

The dangers which threaten the future of the world [Sorel wrote] may be avoided, if the proletariat hold on with obstinacy to revolutionary ideas, so as to realize as much as possible Marx's conception. . . . Proletarian violence, carried on as a pure and simple manifestation of the sentiment of class war, appears thus as a very fine and very heroic thing; it is at the service of the immemorial interests of civilization. . . .[3]

While Sorel was evolving his theories of revolutionary syndicalist action, another Frenchman was launching a powerful attack against the very foundations upon which his own countrymen had erected, a century and a half ago, the doctrinal structure of the liberal democratic state. Professor Léon Duguit, dean of the Faculty of Law in the University of Bordeaux until his death in 1928, denied the validity of the traditional systems of jurisprudence based on such "metaphysical" assumptions as "natural rights" and absolute state sovereignty. According to his views, characterized by him as *positives et réalistes*, the metaphysical conceptions of eighteenth-century theorists should be discarded because of the existence of two undeniable facts: social solidarity (*solidarité sociale*) and consequent social obligations (*devoirs*). He argues that the fact of social interdependence [4] rather than highly disputable

[3] *Reflections on Violence*, translated by T. E. Hulme (New York, 1914), pp. 98–99, quoted here by permission of The Viking Press, Inc. For a more exhaustive statement of Sorel's theories, see also his *Matériaux d'une théorie du prolétariat* (Paris, 1921). The doctrines of French revolutionary syndicalism, the *nouvelle école* of French Socialism, were preached through Sorel's books and through his articles in *Le Mouvement socialiste*. Both books and articles found a sympathetic echo in the main organs of Italian Socialism. His *Réflexions sur la violence* (Paris, 1912) are a revised collection of articles which originally appeared in the *Divenire sociale, Rivista di socialismo scientifico*, an Italian Socialist review, published in Rome by Professor Enrico Leone. The Italian articles were collected in a brochure under the title *Lo Sciopero generale e la violenza*, with a preface by Enrico Leone.
[4] A fact well established and rooted in an organic division of social functions as described by Émile Durkheim in his famous *De la Division du travail social*

metaphysical assumptions should form the basis for a new and truly scientific system of jurisprudence. As the cells constituting an organism are subjected to the laws of that organism, so the individuals constituting a social group should be subjected to the law of that group, a law which governs the group's formation and development. The true nature of the obligation which should cause the rulers as well as the ruled to submit to the rule of law is to be found in the *solidarité sociale* — the necessarily existent social solidarity arising out of the organic interdependence of the different units in the social structure. Syndicalism or trade unionism, the organized expression of that interdependence, is, in Duguit's view, not primarily a labor movement. It is a much more important and a much wider phenomenon.

What is today called the syndicalist movement is the principal manifestation . . . of the vast associational movement which fills our epoch [Duguit writes]. This movement . . . is not restricted to the class of manual laborers. It is not, contrary to what revolutionary syndicalists pretend, the effort of the laboring class to attain self-consciousness in order to concentrate in itself power and wealth and to destroy the bourgeoisie. It is a much larger movement, and a much deeper one. It is not a means of war and social strife; it is, on the contrary, a powerful means of pacification and union. It is not a transformation of the working class alone; it extends to all classes of society and tends to coördinate them into a harmonious whole. It makes possible the constitution of a society of strong and coherent groups with a defined juridical structure, groups composed of men already united by community of social function and by professional interest.[5]

And elsewhere:

It is only when associations of employers and workers within a given trade possess a structure strong enough and a membership large enough to be able actually to organize themselves into legally recognized bodies, that collective labor agreements will reveal their

(Paris, 1893). For a fuller discussion of Durkheim's views, see among other works Charles E. Gehlke, *Émile Durkheim's Contribution to Sociological Theory* (New York, 1915); E. Conze, "Zur Bibliographie der Durkheim Schule," *Kölner Vierteljahrshefte für Soziologie*, VI (Munich, 1927), pp. 279–283; M. Mitchell, "Émile Durkheim and the Philosophy of Nationalism," *Political Science Quarterly*, XLVI, 1931, pp. 87–106.
[5] *Traité de droit constitutionnel*, II (Paris, 1923), p. 9.

full value and significance. Then the collective agreement between employers' and workers' associations will actually be the law of the organized profession. Coördination of social classes will then be achieved by a series of collective contracts among the different associations into which each class will have been organized.[6]

Strangely similar, in their pluralistic outlook, were the doctrines adumbrated in the chief tenets of British guild socialism and in the early writings of Harold J. Laski, one of the foremost British advocates of political pluralism. G. D. H. Cole, until recently the leading exponent of guild socialism, advocated the substitution of representative government by a new system of functional representation operating through a series of powerful industrial guilds which would own and control the country's apparatus of production.

Freedom for self-expression, freedom at work as well as at leisure, freedom to serve as well as to enjoy — that is the guiding principle . . . of National Guilds. We can only destroy the tyranny of machinery . . . by giving into the hands of the workers the control of their life and work. . . . Out of the Trade Union shall grow the Guild; and in the Guild alone is freedom for the worker and a release from the ever-present tyranny of modern industrialism.[7]

Harold J. Laski, at one time the leading advocate of political pluralism, openly challenged the state's sovereign authority. He maintained that the present state, anxiously protecting the abstract "rights" of individuals as defined by eighteenth-century rationalism, does not in itself possess any special right to command. The life of certain groups within the state — trade unions, professional and trade associations, etc. — has become a much more real thing in men's experience than their common political life as represented by the state. Men belong to other groups within the state as well as to the state, and a competition for allegiance exists, therefore, continually. The state, as such, is only one association among many. Ultimately, the traditional state, as an author of commands, will

---

[6] *Les Transformations du droit public* (Paris, 1913), p. 132 ff. In addition see R. Bonnard, "Léon Duguit — ses œuvres, sa doctrine," in *Revue de droit public et de la science politique en France et à l'étranger*, XLVI (Paris, 1929), pp. 5–51.

[7] Cole, *Self-Government in Industry* (London, 1920), pp. 45–47, quoted here by permission of G. Bell and Sons, Ltd.

disappear, and in its place the various component social groups will become the new units of political authority.

We are urging [Laski wrote] that because a group or an individual is related to some other group or individual, it is not thereby forced to enter into relations with every other part of the body politic. . . . I would urge that you must place your individual at the centre of things. You must regard him as linked to a variety of associations to which his personality attracts him. You must, in this view, admit that the State is only one of the associations to which he happens to belong and give it exactly that preëminence — and no more — to which on the particular occasion of conflict its possibly superior moral claim will entitle it.[8]

Even though Laski's later works reflect a considerable modification of his earlier views, and though he now no longer regards the occupational group as the one logical unit of political autonomy and recognizes and defends the sovereign and coercive powers of the state, one still finds this significant statement in one of his later books:

Within the framework of a general minimum set of conditions determined by the central legislature, there should be devised for industries a system of subordinate legislatures with rule-making powers which, under suitable safeguards, can be compulsorily applied. We should seek, that is, to develop, *mutatis mutandis*, the kind of self-government for industry which has been characteristic of professions like the bar and medicine.[9]

Essentially the same spirit of pragmatism, the same impatience with the current doctrines of parliamentarianism and representative popular government which inspired the work of several of the aforementioned contemporary political theorists, finds its very evident and original expression in Fascist thought and action. Upon a foundation of political and economic pragmatism, tempered by their daily experiences on

---

[8] *Studies in the Problem of Sovereignty* (New Haven: Yale University Press, 1917), pp. 10, 19, quoted here by permission of the Yale University Press. On Laski's pluralist doctrines see his earlier writings, in particular the introductory chapter of his *Studies in the Problem of Sovereignty*, and his *Authority in the Modern State* (New Haven, 1919).

[9] *Politics* (Philadelphia, 1931), p. 109, quoted here by permission of the J. B. Lippincott Company. See also his *A Grammar of Politics* (London), 1925). For a fuller discussion and criticism of Laski's views, see W. Y. Elliott, *The Pragmatic Revolt in Politics*, pp. 142 ff.

the Peninsula, Fascist leaders and thinkers have gradually evolved their own novel and challenging body of political, social, and economic ideas.

THE FORERUNNERS OF FASCIST POLITICAL THEORY: MACHIAVELLI, SISMONDI, ROMAGNOSI, PERSICO

Long before the first appearance of Fascism on the Italian political scene several of the underlying ideas of the new movement had been advocated by Italian writers. For centuries the theory of state unity and state authority had been kept alive in the minds of Italian thinkers by memories of imperial Rome. In his *De monarchia* Dante developed the theory of a strong and unitary state. Niccolò Machiavelli pleaded for the liberation of his "enslaved, torn, and pillaged" nation and for the formation of a strong, unified, and independent Italy. Gian Battista Vico, in his criticism of the rationalistic philosophies of the eighteenth century, called attention to the social nature of man and emphasized the importance of history, as opposed to rationalism, as his supreme *magistra vitae*. Early in the nineteenth century, while the aphorisms of the French Revolution were still popular, some distinguished Italian students of political theory expressed the view that, while the French Revolution had destroyed a social and political structure resting mainly upon the oppression of the lower classes, it had failed to replace it by anything substantially better. In their opinion, the thought generated by the Revolution had been arrested and immobilized in an exaggerated exaltation of the individual and had lost contact with such larger social realities as the existence of clearly distinguishable social and economic groups.

Thus, in the eighteen-thirties, Sismondo de Sismondi, one of the foremost Italian thinkers of the period, observed that "as to the way of electing representatives in various localities, their representation would be more real if deputies were to be elected by the already existing social bodies, rather than by the population at large." A decade or so later, Giandomenico Romagnosi, an acute critic of the contractualism of Rousseau, advocated the election to the national assembly of direct representatives of the various social classes, in order to secure a truer expression of the national interests. Shortly after the unification of the kingdom, another Italian, Federico Persico, attacked what he called the "political prejudice" of a state consisting solely of individuals, and proclaimed this prejudice to be the cardinal vice of the existing political organism. As a solution of the difficulty, Persico proposed an electoral system through which all organized groups would be organically represented within a state qualified to act as an arbiter among the conflicting interests of the various social and economic classes.[10]

THE BEGINNINGS OF FASCIST ECONOMIC THOUGHT: SERGIO PANUNZIO AND ALFREDO ROCCO

Early in the twentieth century these plans for class and group representation were further developed under the stimulus of the new associational or syndicalist movements generated by the theories of Georges Sorel and Léon Duguit. In 1910 Sergio Panunzio, a young Italian, later one of the leading Fascist theorists, began to call attention to the new doctrines. A few years later, at the outbreak of the war, he urged that "the social classes within the nation must come out of the war solidly organized."

Italy needs [he asserted] not only a new economic but also a new political organization. The old syndicalism of the workers must leave its false proletarian exclusivism and join the national cause. For, today, all homogenous interests are uniting and social classes are assuming primary importance within the realm of the nation as a whole. The state must, under new forms, be reborn.[11]

During the years immediately following the war, Panunzio, strongly sympathizing with the newly created Fascist party,

---

[10] Cf. Sismondo de Sismondi, *Studi intorno alle costituzioni dei popoli liberi* (Capolago, 1839); Giandomenico Romagnosi, *La Scienza delle costituzioni* (Bastia, 1848); Federico Persico, *Le Rappresentanze politiche e amministrative* (1885); all quoted in *Relazioni e proposte della commissione presidenziale per lo studio delle riforme costituzionali* (Rome, 1925), pp. 133 ff.

[11] *Stato nazionale e sindacati* (Milan, 1924), pp. 35 ff. This book is a collection of articles contributed by the author to various Italian publications during the period from 1915 to 1924. Representing, as Panunzio puts it, "a record of the battle for the ideal of national syndicalism," his book gives an excellent picture of the early development of Italian syndicalism and its doctrines.

continued his fight for the ideals of national syndicalism. "The social originality of Fascism," he wrote, "rests in the fusion of proletarian syndicalism and nationalism. Mussolini, the born statesman, has succeeded in obtaining the fusion of these two ideological forces and in turning them to the use of the new Italian state." [12]

Other Italians besides Panunzio had long been interested in similar ideologies. Mussolini himself, in his early Socialist days, had read William James, Sorel, Nietzsche, and Hegel, and studied the challenging new doctrines of the circulation of the *élites* and the use of myths and force in government which were being evolved at the University of Lausanne by the famous Italian sociologist, Vilfredo Pareto.

In May 1914 two other Italians, Filippo Carli, an economist, and the young jurist, Alfredo Rocco, who was later to become Minister of Justice in Mussolini's Cabinet, presented to the Congress held by Italian Nationalists in Milan a paper on economic nationalism. Criticizing the doctrines of both the liberals and the Socialists, Rocco and Carli evolved in that study the outlines of a national economic system almost identical, in its essential aspects, with those officially expounded eleven years later by Alfredo Rocco when a member of the Fascist government.[13]

[12] Panunzio, *Stato nazionale*, p. 118.

[13] For a concise and authoritative statement of the fundamentals of Fascist doctrine as first elaborated by Rocco, see his "The Political Doctrine of Fascism," in *International Conciliation* (a publication of the Carnegie Endowment for International Peace), Bull. 223, October 1926.

On August 30, 1925, Rocco, then Italian Minister of Justice and formerly dean of the Faculty of Law at the University of Padua, delivered an address at Perugia, of which the paper referred to is the English translation. This speech contains what was and still is one of the most complete and authoritative statements of the political doctrine of Fascism. After his address, a message was sent to Rocco by Mussolini, reading in part as follows: "Dear Rocco: I have just read your magnificent address which I endorse throughout. You have presented in a masterful way the doctrine of Fascism. For Fascism has a doctrine, or if you will, a particular philosophy with regard to all the questions which beset the human mind today. All Italian Fascists should read your discourse and derive from it . . . the clear formulation of the basic principles of our program . . ." (*ibid.*, p. 391).

On the fundamentals of Fascist philosophy, and in particular on the Fascist conception of the nation and the state, and the relationship of the individual

THE DOCTRINE OF "NATURAL RIGHTS" AND THE FASCIST
CONCEPTION OF STATE SOVEREIGNTY

Traditional political thought and practice, Rocco maintained, were inspired, and, in the main, are still controlled, by the philosophy of "natural law" associated with the English, the American, and the French revolutions. Society is conceived as the sum total of all the individuals who compose it at any particular moment. The state, an organized plurality made up of a number of definite individuals, such as the members of the generations living at any given time, exists primarily for the sake of its immediate components. Its ends are those of the individuals who participate in it; its final goal is the welfare and happiness of these same individuals.

The main theories of social and political action evolved during the eighteenth and nineteenth centuries, according to Rocco, were based primarily upon such a purely individualistic doctrine. Both liberalism and Socialism held that the ultimate goal of society is the welfare and happiness of the individual, and that the state is merely the instrument for the attainment of that end. The two schools differed only in their proposals of the methods through which that end was to be achieved. The liberals held that it could be secured through a minimum of state interference, the state's essential function being that of coördinating individual liberties to guarantee their coexistence. The Socialists, on the other hand, maintained that because of existing and unavoidably recurring inequalities the majority of individuals, left to themselves, cannot attain the maximum of possible well-being. Social and economic injustices are bound to occur; hence the state cannot confine itself to the passive role of defender of liberties. If its aim is the welfare of the individual it must directly and actively participate in the regulation of the community's social and economic life. Thus, in a Socialist society the role of pri-

---

to both, see also Benito Mussolini, "The Political and Social Doctrine of Fascism," in *International Conciliation*, January 1935; Giovanni Gentile, *Che cosa è il Fascismo* (Florence, 1925); Alfredo Rocco, *La Trasformazione dello stato: dallo stato liberale allo stato fascista* (Rome, 1927).

vate property would be substantially reduced, if not totally abolished, and all production would be controlled by the state in the interest of the individual members of the social group. While the methods advocated are thus diametrically opposed, in Rocco's view, the final aim of both liberalism and Socialism is essentially the same: both seek to achieve the greatest good for the greatest number of individual members of their respective communities.

Alfredo Rocco, and with him Italian Fascists, openly reject both the liberal and the Socialist points of view. They have a different conception of the state, of the nation, and of the relationship of the individual to each.

Their theory runs thus: Man is a social animal, and lives not in solitude but in groups; and such groups are numerous and diverse. Every group exists as a distinct biological and social entity, possessing, as Rocco puts it, unity of language, of culture, of traditions, and unity also of territory, of economic interests, and of living conditions. The national group, consequently, is something more than a mere aggregate of the individuals who compose it at any given moment of time. While individuals come and go, the nation and its tangible expression, the state, remain. Their interests and ends and those of their component individuals are not necessarily and always the same. The economic or political preservation of the group may demand, as it clearly does in time of war, the sacrifice of individual rights and interests. The needs and aspirations of the individual must, then, be subordinated to those of the social group as a whole.

The foundation of Fascism [Mussolini himself writes] is the conception of the State. . . . For us Fascists, the State is not merely a guardian, preoccupied solely with the duty of assuring the personal safety of the citizens; . . . it is also the custodian and transmitter of the spirit of the people as it has grown up through the centuries in language, in customs, and in faith. And the State is not only a living reality of the present, it is also linked with the past and above all with the future, and thus transcending the brief limits of individual life, it represents the immanent spirit of the nation.[14]

[14] In *International Conciliation*, January 1935, pp. 13–14, quoted here by permission of the Hogarth Press.

The Fascists, then, would reverse the classical relationship between the state and the individual. Society, they assert, is more than a mere aggregate of the individuals constituting the social group at any given moment of time. The life of society overlaps the existence of its individual components; society projects itself, as it were, back into the past and forward into the future. The importance of the social group as such by far transcends that of the individual; while individuals come and go, the social group remains as the living unit of a series of past, present, and future generations whose interests may be and often are opposed to those of the individuals who at any one time compose it. Organized society does not exist primarily and solely for the individual; it is the individual who exists for society. Consequently, the rights of the individual should be definitely subordinated to those of the social and national group of which he is, at any particular time, a component part. Individual advantages must, if necessary, be sacrificed to the welfare of the nation. The individual must be definitely subordinated to society; society is the end, the individual the means. In place of the old emphasis upon "rights" of the individual, stress is laid upon the individual's "duties" toward the nation and state, and thus implicitly toward the social group of which he is a member. In this conception, individual liberty evidently loses its traditional character of a "natural right" and becomes, in practice, a concession of the state. Freedom, and especially economic freedom, is granted by the state on condition that it be used in a manner not conflicting with the interests of the social group as a whole.

THE FUNDAMENTALS OF FASCIST ECONOMIC AND POLITICAL PHILOSOPHY

The application of these principles to the economic field is particularly interesting. Economic activity and economic development are regarded under Fascism as eminently social interests. Society as a whole has a direct and superior concern in all phases of the nation's economic life. A truly social conception of economic life must consequently be substituted for the individualistic theories still implicit in current economic science, and this new conception must be national, since the nation is today the largest homogeneous social group in existence.

Once these fundamental postulates are firmly established the classical problem of *laissez faire* versus "state intervention" ceases to be a problem of principle, and becomes, Fascist thinkers believe, simply a problem of method, of expediency. Generally speaking, Fascists say, the purposes of society as a whole are best served by a system of economic liberty and state noninterference in economic processes. The task of the nation's economic development, the processes of production and distribution, may ordinarily be left to individual initiative, for, it is argued, freedom of initiative and competition in the economic sphere will assure the best social results with the least effort.

By recognizing the institutions of private property, individual initiative, and freedom of competition, Fascism rejects the Socialist solution. But at the same time it also differs significantly from the traditional liberal view. Even though English classicists may not have always conceived economic liberty as a natural right of the individual which it is the duty of the state to safeguard and to protect, they have nevertheless regarded it as a fundamental principle which ought to guide and restrain the state when it seeks to regulate individual activity. Fascism, on the contrary, accepts economic liberty merely as an expedient method, a concession made to the individual by society in the interest of the social group as a whole, a concession which may, whenever necessary, be revoked.[15]

---

[15] Adam Smith opposed restrictions of trade as being "violations of natural liberty" and therefore unjust; "they were too," he adds, "as impolitic as they were unjust" (*The Wealth of Nations*, ed. Nicholson, London, 1891, p. 217). While the "natural right" justification of economic liberty advanced by Adam Smith has been considerably modified and stripped of its metaphysical supports, an element of it still remains in the current economic thought of the English tradition. It is this support of economic liberty as a matter of principle which Fascist thinkers reject; to them economic liberty is merely a concession, made to the individual by society in the interest of the social group.

Alfredo Rocco writes,

Fascism does not look upon the doctrine of economic liberty as an absolute dogma. It does not refer economic problems to individual needs, to individual interest, to individual solutions. On the contrary it considers the economic development, and especially the production of wealth, as an eminently social concern, wealth being for society an essential element of power and prosperity. But Fascism maintains that in the ordinary run of events economic liberty serves the social purposes best; that it is profitable to entrust to individual initiative the task of economic development both as to production and as to distribution; that in the economic world individual ambition is the most effective means for obtaining the best social results with the least effort. Therefore, on the question also of economic liberty the Fascists differ fundamentally from the Liberals; the latter see in liberty a principle, the Fascists accept it as a method. By the Liberals freedom is recognized in the interest of the citizens; the Fascists grant it in the interest of society. In other terms, Fascists make of the individual an economic instrument for the advancement of society, an instrument which they use so long as it functions and which they subordinate when no longer serviceable. In this guise Fascism solves the eternal problem of economic freedom and of state interference, considering both as mere methods which may or may not be employed in accordance with the social needs of the moment.[16]

While, then, Fascism maintains private property, individual initiative, and freedom of competition as expedient methods for the achievement of social and economic well-being and progress, it has no place for uncontrolled economic individualism. Centuries ago, state control and state justice were substituted for unlimited personal freedom and the individual right of self-defense. In a similar manner, Fascism holds, a system of state control and state justice must now be substituted for the unrestricted economic freedom of individuals, classes, and groups. To provide an adequate machinery for this state control and for the dispensation of this state justice the various economic classes in Italy have been organized into separate occupational groups, a system of government-supervised collective labor agreements and labor courts has been instituted, and the *stato*

[16] *International Conciliation*, October 1926, p. 404, quoted here by permission of the Carnegie Endowment for Internationl Peace.

corporativo Fascista, the new Fascist corporate state, of which more will be said in the following chapters, has been gradually called into being.

If the doctrine of state preëminence, as developed by the Fascists, has led to interesting results in the economic sphere, its practical application in the realm of politics has produced results even more far-reaching. Fascists maintain that the national state in Italy, because of the high mission entrusted to it, cannot remain what it has been under the democratic regimes of the past — a shifting and changing expression of a simple numerical majority. Its administration, rather, must be entrusted to an *élite*, to a carefully chosen few, whose action, in contrast to that of a wavering parliamentary democracy, will be "quick, sure, unanimous, conscious, and responsible." Benito Mussolini writes,

Fascism combats the whole complex system of democratic ideology . . . [it] denies that the majority, by the simple fact that it is a majority, can direct human society; it denies that numbers alone can govern by means of a periodical consultation, and it affirms the immutable, beneficial, and fruitful inequality of mankind, which can never be permanently leveled through the mere operation of a mechanical process such as universal suffrage. The democratic régime may be defined as from time to time giving the people the illusion of sovereignty, while the real effective sovereignty lies in the hands of other concealed and irresponsible forces.[17]

---

[17] *International Conciliation*, January 1935, p. 9, quoted here by permission of the Hogarth Press.

It is of interest to note the similarity of these ideas to those of Vilfredo Pareto, the Italian sociologist some of whose lectures Mussolini is said to have attended during his sojourn in Switzerland and whose doctrines on the use of force in government and on the circulation of *élites* are believed to have been influential in forming Mussolini's own views on these subjects.

"We need not linger on the fiction of 'popular representation,'" wrote Pareto; "poppycock grinds no flour. Let us go on and see what substance underlies the various forms of power in the governing classes. Ignoring exceptions, which are few in number and of short duration, one finds everywhere a governing class of relatively few individuals that keeps itself in power partly by force and partly by the consent of the subject class, which is much more populous. The differences lie, principally, as regards substance, in the relative proportions of force and consent; and as regards forms, in the manners in which the force is used and the consent obtained" (*The Mind and Society*, ed. Arthur Livingston, New York, 1935, vol. IV, par. 2244, reprinted here by permission of Harcourt, Brace and Company).

THE FASCIST PARTY AND THE FASCIST STATE

Democracy thus scornfully rejected, what, then, is the Fascist idea of the state and what is the essence of Fascist political doctrine? "Three conditions are necessary for the full, complete, integral, and revolutionary fulfillment of the Corporate State," states Mussolini: first, "a single party, which shall effect political as well as economic control, and which shall be, above the competing interests, a bond which unites all in a common faith"; second, "the totalitarian state, that is to say, the state which absorbs in itself, to transform and make them effective, all the energy, all the interests, and all the hope of a people"; and, third, and most important, "life in a period of the highest ideal tension." [18]

It is upon these three cardinal principles that the structure of the Fascist state has, in fact, been based. "High ideal tension" is provided by the fervid, passionate nationalism which is the essence of the Fascist creed, the central axis around which life under Fascism revolves.

The organization which constantly keeps that national ideal before the people, and continually gives them incentive to bend every effort to conform to it, is the Fascist party. The true significance of the transformation brought about by Fascism in Italian life cannot be understood without some knowledge of the functions of the party and its relations to the Fascist state. Made up of about 1,800,000 men and women solemnly pledged to absolute obedience to their leader and to unconditional devotion to the Fascist cause, the party is defined in its own constitution as "a voluntary militia at the order of the Duce and at the service of the nation." Its main objective is to propagate the ideas and ideals of Fascism and to ensure their acceptance by the Italian people. To assure "order, discipline, and authority" within its own ranks, the party is organized under strict military discipline. A solemn oath is required of all members, binding them to obey without question

[18] Speech delivered on November 14, 1933, quoted in Finer, *Mussolini's Italy*, p. 231.

the commands of the party's leader and, if necessary, to shed their blood for the Fascist cause. As the Fascist party extends its influence into all spheres of Italian life and cuts through all layers of Italian society, people and institutions in Italy are in effect submitted to constant party control and party discipline.

Rigid hierarchy of membership and the concentration of authority which are the cornerstones of the party's organization imply that the direction of all party activity ultimately rests with the party's supreme chief, Il Duce, who is, at the same time, the head of the Italian government. Since all party officers are appointed from above and no government appointments are made without the endorsement of the party, the leader of the party completely controls, in effect, both the party and the government. The consequence is that Italy is, at present, a militarily organized one-party state at the command of one all-powerful leader, a state where the Fascist doctrines of state preëminence, discipline, hierarchy, and authority have been substituted for the traditional principles of liberalism and democracy, not only in the field of politics, but, as our analysis will show, in the economic and social fields as well.

PART II

FASCIST SYNDICALISM AND THE RISE
OF THE CORPORATE ORDER

CHAPTER III

THE EVOLUTION OF THE FASCIST SYNDICAL AND CORPORATE SYSTEM

NATIONAL SYNDICALISM AND THE BEGINNINGS OF THE FASCIST LABOR MOVEMENT

THE new type of economic organization created by Fascism in Italy cannot be understood without some knowledge of the historical development of Fascist syndicalism, the system of occupational organization upon which Fascist economy is based.

Fascist syndicalism is, essentially, the product of a fusion of nationalistic ideals with a socialist program of action. Its origins go back to the years immediately preceding the World War when two labor movements, Socialism and the Christian trade unionism sponsored by the Roman Catholic Church, were competing for the support of Italian workers.

Socialism had had difficult beginnings in Italy. The nationalistic ideals of the *Risorgimento* and the slow industrial development of the new kingdom had, until the last decade of the nineteenth century, impeded the rapid diffusion of its ideologies. It was not until after 1890 that, under the able leadership of Arturo Labriola and Augusto Turati, the Socialist party began to make rapid progress.[1] This growth continued, until in the

[1] The following table, showing the number of votes cast for the Socialist ticket and the number of Socialist members elected to the Italian Chamber, gives a good picture of the development of Italian Socialism during the pre-war period:

Year	Votes Cast	Members Elected
1892	26.000	6
1897	135.000	16
1900	164.946	32
1904	301.525	23
1910	338.865	40

(Before the World War the Italian Chamber consisted of 508 members, and in 1911 there were about three million electors within the kingdom.)
Cf. Arthur Shadwell, *The Socialist Movement, 1824–1924* (London, 1925), I, 113.

early years of the present century two antagonistic factions developed, and a bitter strife for leadership ensued. As a result in 1906 Arturo Labriola, one of the former leaders, left the party and organized an independent labor movement. This movement, inspired by the writings of Sorel, called for the economic rather than the political organization of the Italian working classes; it held that the future stronghold of Italian labor must be the syndicate, the workers' trade association, rather than a primarily political labor party.

Although this early socialist syndicalist movement never reached sizable proportions, its mention is important, for out of it evolved the Fascist syndicalism of a decade or so later.[2] On the eve of the World War, in fact, the syndicalist movement founded by Labriola had attracted the attention of Italian nationalists. Inflamed with patriotism and with a desire for social regeneration, nationalist writers began to demand that Italian syndicalism "be freed from its Marxian leanings and be made to serve the national cause." When the world conflict broke out, a small company of patriotic syndicalists openly joined the nationalists in their pleas for Italy's entry into the war. In this group were Filippo Corridoni, a young syndicalist of intensely nationalistic sentiments, Edmondo Rossoni, the future head of Fascist syndicalism, and the present leader of Italian Fascism, Benito Mussolini.[3]

---

[2] For a more detailed discussion of Sorel's revolutionary syndicalism, cf. chap. ii, pp. 24 ff. The Italian terms *sindacato* (syndicate) and *sindacalismo* (syndicalism), originally used to describe a Socialist workmen's movement, are now employed by the Fascists to describe the associational movement of both workers and employers.

[3] Cf. chap. i, pp. 6 ff. Filippo Corridoni, the young pre-war national syndicalist, lost his life in the World War and is now hailed as the pioneer and the first "martyr" of the Fascist cause. Rossoni came to Fascism after his unsuccessful attempt to organize national labor unions among Italian workmen in the United States. His motto, *La Patria non si nega, si conquista* (one's country must not be denied — it must be won), later became the battle cry of Fascist syndicalism.

For the attitude of Italian syndicalists at the beginning of the World War, there is an interesting historical precedent. In the Italo-Turkish war of 1911, which culminated in the occupation of Tripoli by the Italians, the syndicalist group had maintained a distinctly nationalistic attitude in contrast to the anti-militaristic position taken by the Socialist majority. The explanation offered by syndicalist leaders was that the conflict was a "proletarian" one, a "class

After the armistice both Rossoni, who had served as secretary
to several workingmen's organizations during the war, and
Mussolini continued to show deep interest in the problems of
Italy's laboring men. In the columns of the *Popolo d'Italia*
Mussolini vigorously supported the workers in their fights
for higher wages and for an eight-hour day. While he maintained that the workers' personal and class interests should
be recognized and vigorously defended, in no case, he declared,
should such a defense be carried on, as was done by the Socialists and Communists, through violent disruption of the productive process and thus at the expense of the whole nation.

THE DALMINE INCIDENT

In the spring of 1919 an incident occurred which served to
make Mussolini's attitude on the labor problem abundantly
clear. On March 15, 1919, a group of two thousand workmen
of the Franco Gregorini Company in Dalmine, a large Italian
manufacturing concern, started an agitation for higher wages
and an eight-hour day. This agitation was unique in the history of Italy's troubled post-war period, for these workers
did not strike. They voiced their grievances vigorously, elected
a committee for negotiation with the management, and then,
after raising the national flag on the factory pole, returned to
work — in the interest, as their resolution said, of the nation's
industry and to the advantage of the Italian people.[4]

Mussolini strongly supported this patriotic action. He personally went to Dalmine and, speaking to the workers, said:

I have often asked myself if after four years of bloody war,
labor should continue to follow the old path or whether it should
summon the courage to tread a new one. You have answered my
query. The resolution you have voted is an immensely important

---

struggle" in which "poor" Italy was engaged against her wealthier European
neighbors in order to secure her rightful share in African colonial domains.
Cf. Arturo Labriola, in *La Scintilla* (Naples), Oct. 11, 1911, quoted by Schneider,
in *Making the Fascist State*, pp. 140–141.

[4] For a detailed account of the Dalmine incident, and of the various later
phases in the rise of Fascist syndicalism, see Edoardo Malusardi, *Elementi di
storia del sindacalismo fascista* (Turin, 1930).

document. You have been mindful of the interests of your class, but you have not forgotten those of the nation.[5]

When, a few days later, on March 23, 1919, the historic meeting at which the first Fascio was founded took place at the Piazza San Sepolcro in Milan and Mussolini outlined the program of the new party to the small group of friends who had assembled there, he again urged "the necessity of protecting the interests of Italy's workers," but also of calling to their attention "the realities of production and the needs of the nation as a whole." [6]

Soon after the foundation of the Fasci, and under the leadership of Edmondo Rossoni, the first Fascist labor groups, mainly in agricultural districts, were formed. After the failure of the Socialist occupation of the factories, however, nationally-minded labor organizations (such as the Fratellanza Colonica in Toscana, and the short-lived Confederazione Italiana dei Sindacati Economici in Romagna and Emilia) began to attract members from the industrial field as well. In January 1921 the first Fascist labor chamber was established at Bologna at the initiative of Dino Grandi, and on October 7, 1921, the first association of Fascist railroad workers was formed. In other provinces similar syndical groups were successively organized. As the new movement grew in scope and popularity, leading nationalists, such as Alfredo Rocco, Forges Davanzati, Enrico Corradini, and others, and former Socialists, such as Oliviero Olivetti and Sergio Panunzio, were attracted to it.

[5] Malusardi, pp. 24 ff.

[6] It is of interest to note that at the time of the founding of the first *Fasci* there existed in Italy the following labor organizations: the Confederazione Generale del Lavoro, which represented the strongest Socialist group in the country; the Confederazione Italiana dei Lavoratori, created in 1917 with a Christian-social program and based, in the main, upon *Rerum Novarum*, the famous encyclical of Pope Leo XIII; the nationalistic Unione Italiana del Lavoro, founded by Edmondo Rossoni as an outgrowth of the Comitato Sindacale Italiano, of which he had been the secretary during the war; and two lesser organizations: the nationally-minded Ufficio Nazionale del Lavoro and the more radical Unione Sindacale Italiana, representing various shades of revolutionary syndicalism. Italian employers in turn were grouped into two great organizations: the Confederazione Generale dell'Industria Italiana, and the Confederazione dell'Agricoltura, representing respectively the interests of industry and agriculture.

THE CARTA DEL QUARNARO

At this time an event occurred which added considerable prestige to the national syndicalist cause. On September 8, 1920, the Italian poet and soldier, Gabriele d'Annunzio, occupied and proclaimed the independence of Fiume, the town which was denied Italy in the peace treaties. The constitution of the new state, written by d'Annunzio himself, contained several of the leading ideas which were embodied, a few years later, in the official Fascist syndical system. Among other things, this constitution provided for the establishment of a system of ten "corporations" or guilds, to one of which each citizen had to belong, and which were entrusted with the regulation and supervision of the economic life of the new state.[7]

On January 24, 1922, less than three years after the beginnings of the Fascist labor movement, the first congress of the Fascist labor associations was held at Bologna. Representatives of 250,000 organized workers attended and a national confederation of all existing Fascist trade associations or labor syndicates (the Confederazione Nazionale delle Corporazioni Sindacali) was founded. Within the confederation itself there were to be five large separate vocational groupings of syndical associations, called corporations. These included a national corporation for industrial labor, one for agricultural labor, one for commerce, one for seamen, and one for the members of the intellectual and the middle classes. The congress appointed Edmondo Rossoni as secretary general of the confederation,

---

[7] Cf. chap. i, p. 12. The word "corporation" was derived from the old Italian term *corporazioni delle arti e dei mestieri*, the name for the medieval guilds of Italian craftsmen. Some of the articles of the Carta della Reggenza Italiana del Quarnaro, as the charter of the new state was called, are particularly interesting. Article XVIII, for example, says: "The State represents the common will and directs the efforts of the people toward a higher degree of material and spiritual well-being. Whatever the type of labor performed, manual or mental, common or skilled, all citizens shall be compulsorily inscribed in one of the ten Corporations constituted within the City." Article XX provides that: "Each Corporation shall be a legal person recognized by the state, and shall have the right and the duty of sending its representatives into the City Council." Article XXXIX provides for the institution of a labor tribunal, a forerunner of the Fascist labor courts. For additional details on the Carta, cf. Malusardi, *Elementi di storia*, p. 42.

and proclaimed the twenty-first of April, the "birthday" of Rome, as the anniversary of Italian labor. It also adopted a resolution which emphasized the importance of labor as an essential factor in national economic life, but insisted upon the importance of subordinating, whenever necessary, "the rights and aspirations of the various social classes to the superior interests of the nation as a whole."

This profoundly nationalistic attitude of the new Fascist labor organizations distinguished them clearly from all other contemporary Italian labor movements, notably the Socialist one. While the Socialists continued to preach the Marxian doctrines of the class struggle, Fascist labor leaders advocated class collaboration in the interest of the nation as a whole, their nationalism being in part the heritage of the interventionism of 1915 and in part the result of the bitter experiences of some of them in foreign lands.[8]

On April 1, 1922, a few months after the first congress of the Fascist labor associations, the first number of the Fascist labor daily, *Il Lavoro d'Italia*, directed by Edmondo Rossoni, appeared. On June 4–6 of the same year, a second national congress of all Fascist labor organizations was held in Milan. At that meeting the membership of the organization was found to have grown to 458,284 members, represented at the congress by 473 delegates from 52 Italian provinces.

Less than a year after the first Fascist labor convention, the March on Rome took place and the Fascist party came

[8] Edmondo Rossoni, for example, wrote about his conversion to nationalism as follows: "In 1912 when I was organizing Italian workers in North America, far from my country, I felt that it is absolutely necessary to spread class nationalism, for we must defend not merely workers but Italians. . . . We who for many years have lived in foreign countries and in our long and bitter exile have learned to know and to live the life of an Italian removed from his native land, have begun to understand and feel how the fortunes of Italian workers are indissolubly bound to the fortunes of the Italian nation. . . . We have seen our workers exploited and held in contempt not only by capitalists but even by their revolutionary comrades of other countries. Hence we know by experience that internationalism is but a fiction and hypocrisy. Therefore we must above all work for our country and love our country" (*Le Idee della ricostruzione*, Florence, 1923, pp. 10, 56, 59, quoted in Herbert W. Schneider, *The Fascist Government of Italy*, New York, 1936, p. 67, reprinted here through the courtesy of D. Van Nostrand Company, Inc.).

into power. Under the new regime the Fascist labor movement made rapid progress. In December 1922, in a message of its secretary general, Edmondo Rossoni, the National Confederation of Syndical Corporations formally expressed its loyalty to the new premier and its decision to add the word "Fascist" to its official name.

On June 30, 1923, the first national council of the National Confederation of Fascist Syndical Corporations (a body composed of ten representatives of the organizations affiliated with the confederation) met in Rome. At the meeting a resolution was adopted, stating that

the National Council of Fascist Corporations affirms the principle that labor contracts should be the result not of blind class struggle, which prevents the correct appraisal of the possibilities of the enterprise and of the merits of those who devote their activity to it, but that they should be concluded after an accurate and conscientious analysis of the conditions of production. This analysis is possible only through the institution of such new relationships between workers and employers as are provided for by the Fascist corporation. According to the principles of Fascist syndicalism, labor contracts should therefore be elaborated with the assistance and under the control of the central syndical organizations.[9]

With this explicit repudiation of the class struggle and the defense of "national" as opposed to individual and class interests, Fascist syndicalism broke definitely with Socialism and embraced the ideology which led it, inevitably, to the defense of the "strong" Fascist state. The clear definition of its aims, moreover, made any attempt at collaboration with the socialist labor movement impossible. Though during 1923 Mussolini several times extended the olive branch to the still powerful Socialist labor organizations, their leaders refused to coöperate. They saw in Fascist syndicalism not a movement aiming at the improvement of the economic and moral position of Italian labor but merely an instrument of Fascist propaganda among the labor class and a convenient means of subjecting labor to the discipline of the Fascist party.[10]

[9] Malusardi, p. 74.
[10] In fact, though functions of vital consequence for the welfare of the

THE PACT OF THE PALAZZO CHIGI

In December 1923, in line with the government's policy of "class collaboration in the national interest," a meeting of the representatives of Fascist workers' and employers' organizations was called by Mussolini at the Chigi Palace in Rome. At that important gathering, Fascist employers' and workers' representatives agreed that henceforth conditions of labor should be settled through peaceful negotiation, and after an accurate analysis of the conditions of production, rather than through the traditional methods of class struggle, and that the syndical organization of both employers and workers should be intensified and made more coöperative in order to assure both labor and capital of "the best possible conditions for the development of their functions and the most equitable compensation for their work." [11]

Besides representing the first expression of the willingness of Italian employers to collaborate with workers under the aegis of the Fascist government, the significance of the Pact of the Chigi Palace lies in the fact that Fascist corporations, which heretofore had been allowed to include among their members both workers and employers, from then on confined their membership to labor, leaving the organization of employers to the General Confederation of Italian Industry.

In June 1924, shortly after the new election which seated Rossoni and several other syndicalist leaders in the Chamber, the murder of the leading Socialist deputy, Giacomo Matteotti, occurred. As we have seen, there followed, for the Fascist party, a period of isolation, uncertainty, and political rearrangement. For several months the fate of the regime hung in the balance. Then Mussolini put an end to uncertainty and hesitation by announcing in his speech of January 3, 1925, the government's new political program: the end of parliamen-

---

Italian laboring classes are now entrusted to it, the Fascist syndical system is to this day in essence a political rather than an economic organism, clearly subordinated to the general political program and the political exigencies of the Fascist regime. For a fuller discussion of this point, cf. chap. vi, below.

[11] Malusardi, p. 85.

tary compromise and the beginning of a new era of "totalitarian and integral" Fascism.

THE "COMMISSION OF EIGHTEEN" AND THE PACT OF THE PALAZZO VIDONI

An important step in this direction was taken immediately. On January 31, 1925, a commission of eighteen members under the presidency of Senator Giovanni Gentile, the distinguished Italian philosopher, was appointed by the government to prepare the plans for the constitutional reform and the legal recognition of the Fascist syndical associations long advocated by Fascist theorists.[12]

This commission submitted its final report to the government on June 24, 1925. The report consisted of two parts. The first dealt with a series of reforms concerning the relations of the executive branch of the government to the legislative branch and intended mainly to check the weaknesses of Italian parliamentarianism by increasing the powers and strengthening the position of the executive.[13] The second contained a detailed discussion of the problem of syndical organization and an elaborate scheme for its solution. It was proposed that each

[12] This Commission of Eighteen, or the Commission of "Solons," as it was popularly called, was the official successor of a Commission of Fifteen which had been appointed in September 1924 by the Fascist party to study the legislative and constitutional reforms destined to lay the foundations for the new Fascist state. Also headed by Senator Giovanni Gentile, this first commission had been composed of five senators, five deputies, and five eminent specialists in legal, economic, and social questions. Its report, containing a discussion of its suggested reforms (inclusion of syndical representatives in the Chamber of Deputies so as to "complete and integrate the existing, purely political representation by a representation of the country's economic interests"), is reprinted as an appendix to the official report of the Commission of Eighteen. The Commission of Eighteen itself, the membership of which included many of the participants of the earlier body, held a total of twenty meetings from February 26 to June 24, 1925. Besides Senator Enrico Corradini as vice-president, its membership included three senators, four deputies, five university professors, two publicists, and two high government officials. Cf. Presidenza del Consiglio dei Ministri, *Relazioni e proposte della commissione presidenziale per lo studio delle riforme costituzionali* (Rome, 1925), p. 203.

[13] To this end the following concrete proposals were made: modifications in the composition of the Chamber, widening of the fields from which senators could be chosen, enactment of new rules relating to the vote on non-confidence, and increasing the powers of the executive to render it less dependent upon the legislative chambers. Cf. *Relazioni e proposte*, pp. 72 ff.

separate syndical association of employers or workers be recognized by law as an autonomous legal entity, and that all citizens within the nation be grouped according to their vocations into three large "orders" — agriculture; professional men, artisans, and public employees; and industry, commerce, and owners of property. Each province, according to these recommendations, should have three chambers (corresponding to the three orders) to which all the legally recognized syndical associations would elect representatives. The three chambers in each province would elect representatives to the National Corporate Council in Rome, which would supersede the Chamber of Deputies. In this council one-half of the representatives, elected by the provincial chambers, would represent the various economic classes of the nation, while the other half would be chosen through the existing methods of political election.

On the details of this plan, however, the members of the commission could not agree. A liberal minority objected to the increase in government power and to the purely economic hierarchy of interests which the plan in their opinion was certain to bring about. The more radical members, on the other hand, favored compulsory membership in the various syndical associations and their direct supervision and control by the government.

Professor Corrado Gini, the eminent Italian economist and statistician, disagreeing with the proposals of the other members on the commission, expressed his views in a dissenting opinion appended to the majority report. He held that the various occupational categories should be represented in the new chamber, not as the majority report proposed, in proportion to their members, but rather in proportion to the importance of these members in the economic life of the nation. "How can one admit," wrote Gini, "that in a national organism the owner of 100 acres should have the same influence as the owner of 1,000 acres, the owner of 50 spindles the same as the owner of 2,000?" He also recommended the membership of "economic deputies" in the Senate rather than in the Chamber. The Chamber, he thought, should continue to be primarily a political body. In order to increase the efficiency of the political parliament, however, Gini advocated the election of a committee, composed of its most competent members, to perform the routine work, while the approval of the state budget and the discussion of matters of broad governmental policy would be left to the parliamentary assembly as a whole.[14]

When published, the report of the Commission of Eighteen aroused widespread interest and comment and brought the whole problem of the proposed political and syndical reorganization of the state into the foreground of public discussion. A movement was started in Fascist circles urging on the government to grant legal recognition to the Fascist employers' and workers' organizations. This movement culminated in what became known as the Pact of the Palazzo Vidoni. At a meeting held at the Vidoni Palace in Rome on October 2, 1925, under the presidency of the Hon. Roberto Farinacci, then secretary general of the Fascist party, the leaders of the General Confederation of Italian Industry, representing Italian employers, and the leaders of the Confederation of Fascist Corporations, representing the workers, adopted a joint resolution recognizing each other as the exclusive representatives of employers and employees respectively, and stipulated that all future collective contractual relations between employers and workers should be carried on exclusively through their own affiliated organizations.

This important agreement received the immediate attention of the Fascist Grand Council, the supreme advisory and executive organ of the Fascist party.[15] After discussing it exhaustively at its meeting on October 6, 1925, the Council passed a resolution recommending that syndicalism, "an essential aspect of modern Italian life," be supervised and controlled by the state. Specifically, the Council recommended that one employers' and one workers' syndicate for each type of enterprise or class of work be legally recognized by the state and given

[14] *Relazioni e proposte*, p. 191.

[15] For a detailed discussion of the nature and functions of this council, cf. chap. vi, pp. 136 ff.

the exclusive right to stipulate collective labor agreements; that employers' and workers' associations not legally recognized be permitted to continue in conformity with provisions of existing laws and regulations; that labor conflicts and disputes on collective labor agreements be henceforth resolved, not through violent agitation and strikes and lockouts, but by submission of the difficulty to a judicial organ of the state for arbitration, the decisions of which should be binding upon both parties; and that strikes and lockouts called without a previous attempt at arbitration through properly constituted judicial authorities, and strikes of a purely political nature, should be forbidden and punished as criminal offenses.[16]

THE LAW ON COLLECTIVE LABOR RELATIONS

Based on the report of the Commission of Eighteen and the resolution of the Fascist Grand Council, a draft of the new Italian syndical law, prepared by the Minister of Justice, Alfredo Rocco, was finally submitted to Parliament. On December 18, 1925, this proposed law, known as the law on "the legal discipline of collective labor relations," was approved by the Chamber of Deputies; on March 11, 1926, by the Senate; and on April 3, 1926, by the King. On July 1, of the same year, detailed regulations for its application were issued by the government.[17]

With the enactment of the law of April 3, 1926, the legal foundations for the new Italian economic system were definitely laid. Through its provisions, which far exceeded the proposals made by the Commission of Eighteen, all Fascist syndical associations of workers and employers already exist-

[16] Ministero dell'Economia Nazionale, *Bollettino del lavoro e della previdenza sociale*, XLIV (Rome, 1925), p. 182.

[17] During the discussions on the law in the Chamber, the question was raised whether compulsory arbitration in labor disputes should be limited to the country's basic industries and public services or whether it should be extended to all classes of industrial enterprises. After declaring that no reason existed for fearing experiments under the Fascist regime, since the government was not afraid of rectifying its own decisions whenever necessary, Mussolini ended the deliberations by declaring himself in favor of an extension of compulsory arbitration through the labor courts to all branches of productive activity.

ing within the various occupational fields were recognized as separate legal entities and were given the exclusive legal right to represent the interests of their occupational group, thereby making superfluous any non-Fascist labor organizations still in existence.[18] Strikes and lockouts were prohibited and declared to be punishable as criminal offenses. A new scheme of collective bargaining and collective labor agreements, binding upon all members of a given occupational group, whether members of a syndicate or not, was established. Finally, the *magistratura del lavoro*, a new plan of governmental labor courts, was instituted for the peaceful settlement of all collective labor disputes in which no satisfactory agreement could be reached through the ordinary processes of syndical bargaining.

THE STRUCTURE AND DEVELOPMENT OF FASCIST SYNDICALISM
BEFORE 1934

In the spring of 1926, as a result of the new law, the productive forces of Italy emerged, organized with almost military precision, into thirteen national confederations of legally recognized syndical associations: six representing employers, an equal number representing the workers, and one representing professional men and artists.[19]

[18] The Catholic labor organizations were, in fact, merged with the Fascist syndicates during 1926; the Socialist organizations were dissolved in the course of 1927.

[19] In the course of this reorganization, it had been planned to dissolve the old Confederation of Fascist Corporations and to have its place taken by the six newly created confederations of Italian workmen. Actually, however, the title of the old Confederation of Fascist Corporations was changed to that of National Confederation of Fascist Syndicates (legally recognized on September 26, 1926); the old corporations were dissolved and their members grouped into six national federations corresponding to the six newly formed confederations for employers. According to the provisions of the statutes of the National Confederation of Fascist Syndicates, in each province of the kingdom the existing provincial federations of Fascist corporations were to be supplanted by the provincial offices of the new confederation and entrusted with the supervision and coördination of the activities of all provincial syndicates. On November 21, 1928, the National Confederation of Fascist Syndicates was dissolved by royal decree and its six national federations transformed into six independent national confederations, corresponding to the already existing confederations of employers. On August 5, 1926, five national associations were formed for the benefit of Italian government employees and the employees of other public or semi-public bodies whose organizations could not, according to the new syndical law, obtain legal recognition. Thus associa-

These groupings, with their official names, were the following:

A. *Employers' Organizations*
  The National Fascist Confederations of:
  1. Industry
  2. Agriculture
  3. Commerce
  4. Land Transportation and Internal Navigation
  5. Credit and Insurance
  6. Maritime and Air Transportation

B. *Workers' Organizations*
  The National Confederations of Fascist Syndicates in:
  1. Agriculture
  2. Industry
  3. Commerce
  4. Land Transportation and Internal Navigation
  5. Credit and Insurance
  6. Maritime and Air Transportation

C. *Organization of Professional Men and Artists*
  The National Confederation of Fascist Syndicates of Professional Men and Artists

At the base of the syndical pyramid of which these thirteen national confederations formed the apex, there was a large number and variety of individual syndical associations of employers and workers organized within the various occupational groups existing within the country. These syndicates, which were called "unitary" or "first-degree" syndical associations, were granted full legal recognition, and were local, provincial, regional, or national in scope. They in turn were organized into "federations" of syndicates, or "second-degree" associations, which also were provincial, regional, or national. All the federations of syndicates, and the few existing independent

---

tions for grade-school teachers, postal agents, state railroad workers and postal, telegraph, and telephone employees came into being. At the same time several non-Fascist labor organizations joined the Fascist ranks; the Confederation of Italian Industry added the word Fascist to its official name, and its president obtained a seat in the Fascist Grand Council.

national syndical associations, were then grouped into the afore-mentioned thirteen national confederations. In order to achieve greater unity and administrative efficiency in this syndical structure, all local unitary syndicates were transformed, in 1932, into branches or divisions of newly formed "territorial unions" of syndical associations. To these territorial unions (there was one union for workers' syndicates and one for em-ployers' syndicates in each territory) full legal recognition was

CHART I

THE ORGANIZATION OF A FASCIST CONFEDERATION BEFORE 1934

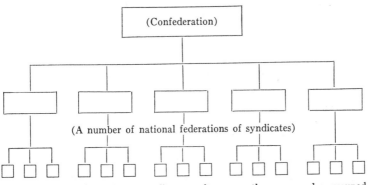

(Confederation)

(A number of national federations of syndicates)

(A large number 'of unitary syndicates; after 1932 these were also grouped territorially into a number of territorial unions)

given. The divisions of the territorial unions (which were, in effect, the unitary syndicates minus legal recognition) were then grouped vertically, according to the occupational group which they represented, into the legally recognized federations and confederations.

The organization of any one of the national workers' or employers' confederations, as it was before 1934, is repre-sented graphically by Chart I.

The detailed statistical tables, compiled from official Italian sources, given in Appendix II, pp. 330 ff., present a vivid picture both of the development and of the numerical strength of this syndical system until its complete reorganization in 1934.[20] The

---

[20] For details on that reorganization, and for statistical data on the mem-bership in the reorganized syndical system, cf. chap. v, pp. 121 ff.

tables show that on December 31, 1933, eight months before
the reorganization, there were in Italy 355 legally recognized
workers' organizations, 417 employers' organizations, and
1,036 associations representing professional men and artists;
on the same date there were 1,310,655 members in employers'
syndicates, representing a total of 4,151,794 employers; 4,369,-
772 members in the workers' syndicates, representing a total
of 6,059,941 workers; and 105,484 artists and professional
men, representing a total of 159,442 men belonging to that occupational group.

CENTRALIZED ECONOMIC CONTROL: THE CORPORATION

With the establishment of legally recognized employers' and
workers' syndicates and collective labor agreements and labor
courts,[21] the foundations for the new Fascist system of syndical organization were firmly laid. The next task before the
government was to devise an appropriate machinery for the
coördination and control of these new organs.

As we have seen, the ultimate aims of Fascist economic
reform far exceed the mere organization of the various occupational categories into large syndical groups. Syndical organization has never been conceived by the Fascists as an end
in itself, but rather as an instrument for the elimination of
open class warfare, the harmonization of the interests of
employers and workers with those of the national group, and
the ultimate establishment of an efficient and stable national
economic system. To achieve these aims, a central organization of coördination and control, based primarily upon, and
operating through, the existing syndical structure, but superior
to it in rank and authority, was gradually set up. This
organization comprised four new governmental organs: the
individual corporation, the Ministry of Corporations, the Corporate Chamber, and the National Council of Corporations.

After the transformation of the early corporations of workers
and employers into syndical associations,[22] the name "cor-

poration" reappeared in the syndical laws of 1926 as the official designation for a central governmental agency established as a connecting link, as it were, between employers' and workers' syndical organizations. The corporation was to be a board or council formed by the representatives of the higher employer and employee organizations existing within the major fields of national production; as such it was to be authorized to enforce regulations on collective labor relations and on the coördination of production whenever the necessary powers were delegated to it by the affiliated syndical organizations.[23]

THE MINISTRY OF CORPORATIONS

Up to 1930, however, no corporation as here defined was actually called into existence, although the Ministry of Corporations, the second of the four newly created governmental organs, functioned as a sort of *de facto* corporation through its action of coördination and control of the existing syndical organizations. This ministry, established by the royal decree of July 2, 1926, and somewhat similar to the Departments of Labor and Commerce in the United States, was and is the direct representative of the national government in the syndical structure and the chief governmental organ through which the Fascist state supervises and controls the operation of the existing syndical machinery. To it are delegated such important tasks as the supervision of the syndical associations of employers and workers, the registration and enforcement of national and provincial collective labor agreements, the general supervision of collective labor relations, the conciliation of collective labor disputes, the carrying out of programs of syndical education and instruction, the collection of statistical information on questions of production and labor and the supervision of Fascist welfare organizations.[24]

[23] The first explicit mention of the corporation as an organ of central coördination and control is found in Art. 3 of the law of April 3, 1926. A description of the essential functions of these "central connecting organizations" is given in the royal decree of July 1, 1926, Part III, and in Declaration VI of the Fascist Charter of Labor. Cf. Appendix I, pp. 259, 276, 288.

[24] Originally composed of two departments, that of corporations and that of syndical associations, the ministry was entirely reorganized in 1929. Since

In carrying out its activities locally, the Ministry of Corporations acts in coöperation with the prefects of the various provinces and with a number of local agencies in the various parts of the kingdom, functioning under its direct supervision.

On April 18, 1926, in fact, all chambers of commerce in Italy were transformed into new, semi-governmental organs called provincial economic councils. On June 16, 1927, provincial economic offices, in effect local offices of the Ministry of National Economy and now of the Ministry of Corporations, were established to act as secretariats for the provincial economic councils and as connecting links between the central and the local organs of economic control. Moreover, special inter-syndical committees, composed of representatives of local employers' and employees' organizations, were formed in each province and a central inter-syndical committee was established in Rome.

---

that year its work includes, besides syndical matters, all the affairs formerly under the jurisdiction of the Ministry of National Economy, which was dissolved after the transfer of its services to the Ministry of Corporations.

The following were the divisions of the Ministry of Corporations and their principal functions immediately after a further reorganization in 1933:

(*a*) The Secretariat. This also included the Secretariat of the National Council of Corporations and of the individual corporations. (*b*) The Division of Occupational Associations. This division was to deal with all questions relating to the legal recognition of syndical associations, to syndical dues, the financial administration of syndical associations, syndical propaganda and educational work among workers and employers, etc. (*c*) The Division of Labor, Social Welfare, and Social Insurance. This division was to draft legislation for the protection of labor and for social insurance, supervise unemployment, internal migration and emigration, assist in the arbitration of collective labor disputes and in the negotiation of collective labor agreements, etc. To it was also attached the Corporate Inspectorate entrusted with factory inspection and the supervision of labor conditions throughout the country. (*d*) The Division of Industry. This division was made responsible for all questions relating to the nation's industrial development. There were special sections dealing with the promotion and regulation of mining, petroleum research, trade marks and patents, etc. (*e*) The Division of Commerce. To this division were entrusted all questions relating to foreign trade treaties, tariff legislation, the development of foreign trade, etc. (The Division is now, 1937, a part of the new Ministry of Foreign Trade and Exchange.) (*f*) The Bureau of Insurance. This autonomous bureau was given control of the administration of insurance funds connected with the state and supervision of all private insurance companies doing business within the kingdom. Cf. *Sindacato e corporazione*, February 1933, p. 241.

The rapid development of the corporate system, however, soon called for a reorganization of these provincial organs. By the law of June 18, 1931, their name was changed to that of Provincial Councils and Provincial Offices of Corporate Economy, the powers of the councils were greatly increased, and the principle of equal representation of employers' and workers' associations in the councils was established. The councils were to be independent and autonomous corporate bodies while the offices were to be the local offices of the Ministry of Corporations.[25]

THE CORPORATE INSPECTORATE

Another agency which coöperates effectively with the Ministry of Corporations in its control of collective labor agreements, the work of local welfare organizations, and the gathering of information on local conditions of production and labor is the Corporate Inspectorate, the new governmental agency attached to the Ministry of Corporations, into which the preexisting organization for governmental factory inspection was transformed.[26]

The decree which in 1926 established the Ministry of Corporations also provided for the creation of the National Council of Corporations, an advisory organ made up of high governmental and syndical officials to assist and advise the Ministry of Corporations. As first established, this National Council was essentially a bureaucratic advisory board of comparatively small practical importance; it was only after its complete reorganization in 1930 that, as we shall see, it became for a while

[25] For a fuller account of the organization and functions of these provincial organs, cf. the condensed versions of the royal decrees of April 18, 1926, June 16, 1927, and June 18, 1931, given in Appendix I, pp. 317–319.

A detailed account of the functions and the internal organization of the Ministry of Corporations is given in the condensed versions of the royal decrees of July 2, 1926, and of March 17, 1927, in Appendix I, pp. 285, 286, and in the discussion of the reorganization of its services in *Sindacato e corporazione*, February 1933, p. 241.

[26] The organization and duties of the Corporate Inspectorate, first organized by the decree of November 14, 1929, were formally defined by the decree of December 28, 1931, converted into law on June 16, 1932.

The total number of inspections made by it during 1933 was 161,097; during

one of the most important organs in the Fascist corporate system.[27]

THE FASCIST CHARTER OF LABOR

Shortly after the establishment of these new institutions, the government decided to issue a formal declaration outlining the principles which had guided it in its work and the ideals and doctrines which were to inspire the economic and social policies of the Fascist state in the future. The plan having met with the approval of the Fascist Grand Council, the detailed elaboration of the document in question was entrusted to the Ministry of Corporations. Three months later, on April 21, 1927, a day

1934, 180,647. The number of "ordinary visits" normally made during the year to ascertain the observance of all industrial and labor laws has been as follows:

Year	Firms Inspected	Workmen Employed
1929	27,954	771,926
1930	32,017	827,326
1931	26,131	662,568
1932	27,567	787,035
1933	39,332	928,422
1934	51,353	1,079,957

The number of "extraordinary visits" made to ascertain the observance of individual labor laws has been:

Year	Firms Inspected	Workmen Employed
1929	91,352	176,892
1930	98,968	234,258
1931	94,336	279,248
1932	96,681	......
1933	121,755	......
1934	129,294	......

The total number of fines imposed for disregard of labor laws amounted to:

1929	12,918	1932	19,292
1930	17,182	1933	24,947
1931	17,938	1934	27,860

Data compiled from various issues of *Sindacato e corporazione*.

[27] For details on the membership and functions of the National Council of Corporations as first established, cf. the royal decree of July 2, 1926, Art. IV, in Appendix I, p. 285.

solemnized as the anniversary of Italian labor, the Grand Council of Fascism formally approved the final text of the declaration known henceforth as the Fascist Charter of Labor, and in a special message called the attention of the Italian people to "this fundamental document of the Fascist Revolution." [28]

Stripped of their solemn phraseology, some of the thirty declarations of the Fascist Charter of Labor contain novel and challenging ideas. The charter as a whole gives the best short description of the aims and aspirations of the Fascist syndical movement and undoubtedly represents the best single, authoritative statement of the Fascist attitude on the fundamentals of economic and social policy.[29]

PARLIAMENTARY REFORM AND THE CORPORATE CHAMBER

After the passage of the syndical laws of 1926 and the promulgation, on April 21, 1927, of the Charter of Labor, the next major step in the completion of the Fascist system of corporate economy was the enactment, on May 17, 1928, of the law on the reform of the Italian Chamber of Deputies. This new law, which substituted vocational or trade representation for the old system of political representation, fulfilled one

---

[28] To the first meeting of the committee of experts entrusted with the elaboration of the Charter of Labor (held on February 11, 1927, at the Ministry of Corporations) Mussolini himself sent the following detailed instructions outlining the fundamental principles which the charter must express and which must be the bases of the new Italian corporate structure: (*a*) Equality of rights and obligations among the various social classes and solidarity of all citizens with respect to the higher interests of the nation. (*b*) Foundation of semi-autonomous syndical groups through the transformation of occupational associations into semi-public institutions (syndicates) invested with normative powers over all members of their occupational category. (*c*) Direct responsibility of members of syndical associations toward their syndicate for the observance of all existing regulations on production and labor. (*d*) Responsibility of syndical associations to the state, for the organization and control of the professional categories which they represent and the duty of these associations to insure the means of such control through appropriate statutory provisions. (*e*) Collaboration of syndical associations with the Ministry of Corporations, thus insuring to the state the general direction of the social and economic forces within the nation. Cf. Augusto Turati and Giuseppe Bottai, *La Carta del lavoro illustrata e commentata* (Rome, 1929), pp. 15 ff.

[29] For a detailed discussion of the contents of the Fascist Labor Charter, cf. chap. iv, pp. 90 ff. For the full English text of the Charter, cf. Appendix I, pp. 287 ff.

of the major aspirations of Italian syndicalists.[30] According to its provisions, the composition of the Italian Senate (the members of which are not elected but nominated by the king for life) was to remain unchanged, while the Chamber of Deputies, the lower of the two branches of the Italian Parliament, corresponding to the House of Representatives in the United States, was to be entirely reorganized. After the reorganization, deputies were to be selected, not through the traditional political parties (which ceased to exist) but through the syndical organizations of workers and employers and a few other legally recognized cultural and welfare associations existing within the country.

The procedure for the selection of the members of the Italian Chamber is now, in fact, the following: the various Fascist syndical associations within the kingdom designate eight hundred candidates for the new Corporate Chamber, while some of the large national cultural and welfare organizations select two hundred candidates. This list of one thousand names is then presented to the Fascist Grand Council. The council selects four hundred candidates out of this total and their names are submitted in one single list to the electorate of the kingdom for approval or rejection.

As to the qualifications for voting in this national plebiscite, the electoral laws provide that anyone over twenty-one years of age, paying syndical dues or taxes of over 100 lire, or receiving a salary from the state or other public body, is entitled

[30] Requests for a reform of the system of political representation had, in fact, repeatedly been advanced by Nationalist and Fascist leaders. As early as March 1919, at the convention held by the Nationalist party in Rome, a plan of reform for the Italian Senate was proposed, according to which senators were to be designated by the various groups representing the intellectual, the administrative, and the economic interests of the nation. In the program of the first Fasci di Combattimento (March 1919) Benito Mussolini had included the demand for a "technical parliament." In the report of the Commission of Fifteen, appointed in 1924 to study the problem of constitutional reform in the new Fascist state, the proposal was made that half of the members of the Italian Chamber should be composed of representatives of trades and professions. The clearest and most definite proposal for the corporate reform of the Italian Parliament, however, was made in 1925 in the report of the Commission of Eighteen. For the details of that report, see the discussion on pp. 51 ff.

to vote. The underlying theory is that any citizen actively contributing to the productive process should have the right to participate in the choice of parliamentary representatives.

In the elections of 1929, the first elections held under the new electoral law, 200 candidates were chosen by such national associations as those of disabled ex-service men (75 candidates), state employees (28 candidates), the universities (30 candidates), the scientific academies (9 candidates), etc., while the remaining 800 names were supplied by the general councils of the confederations of Fascist syndical associations in the following proportions:

	Number of Candidates Named	Percentage
National Fascist Confederations		
Agriculture (employers)	96	9.6
Agricultural employees	96	9.6
Industry (employers)	80	8.0
Industrial employees	80	8.0
Commerce (employers)	48	4.8
Commercial employees	48	4.8
Maritime and air transportation (employers)	40	4.0
Employees in the field of maritime and air transportation	40	4.0
Land transportation and internal navigation (employers)	32	3.2
Employees in the field of land transportation and internal navigation	32	3.2
Banking (employers)	24	2.4
Banking employees	24	2.4
Professional men and artists	160	16.0
Cultural and welfare associations, etc.	200	20.0
Total	1,000	100.0

On February 27, 1929, from the list of 1,000 names thus formed the Fascist Grand Council selected the four hundred candidates whose names were to be submitted for popular approval. In the ensuing election, March 24, this list was approved by 98.34 per cent of the total votes cast. In the election held five years later (March 25, 1934) the percentage of favorable votes cast was even larger.[31]

Should the results of these popular plebiscites at any time show that the list of candidates selected by the Fascist Grand Council does not meet with the approval of the people, the electoral laws provide that the Court of Appeals in Rome, acting as a national electoral office, is to order new elections with alternative lists of candidates which may be submitted by all associations having among their members at least 5,000 persons qualified to vote in national elections.

The present Italian Chamber, the Corporate Chamber, as it is called, is thus composed of representatives drawn from the various major branches of national production, who represent, not a variety of political parties, but, Fascists contend, the interests, needs, and aspirations of the productive forces which carry on the work of the nation.

While a detailed critical appraisal of the Corporate Chamber and the other Fascist institutions here described must be postponed until our description of the principal organs of the Italian corporate state is complete,[32] it is of interest to note at this point the opinion on the present Italian electoral law expressed by the leader of the few remaining liberal members

---

[31] The complete official returns for the two elections are shown in the following table:

	1929	Per Cent	1934	Per Cent
Number of qualified voters	9,682,630	....	10,527,608	....
Votes cast	8,661,820	89.46	10,060,426	95.56
Favorable votes	8,517,838	98.34	10,043,875	99.84
Unfavorable votes	135,773	1.57	15,215	0.15
Voided votes	8,209	0.09	1,336	0.01

In spite of skillful governmental propaganda (the solution of the "Roman question," a subject which could not but stir deeply the feelings of a vast majority of Italians, was announced on February 11, 1929, six weeks before the first election) and of the pressure which in some instances was undoubtedly brought to bear upon electors, these votes, it would seem, can hardly be interpreted except as an endorsement of the regime by the mass of the Italian people.

Source: *Compendio statistico italiano*, 1934, p. 276.

[32] For a detailed critical discussion of the Fascist corporate system, cf. chap. vi, pp. 134 ff.

of the Italian Senate. While the new law was passed with little comment in the Chamber, it met with the most strenuous opposition on the part of the liberal group in the Senate. The leader of that group, Senator Albertini, stated:

> The existence of an elective Chamber does not suffice to take the absolute character from a regime . . . which defends the captured position by such means as are used by Fascism. . . . [In Italy] . . . but a single opinion is tolerated and regarded as worthy of respect, that of the Government, that is, of the head of the Government. . . . The opposition is not allowed to have newspapers, nor to hold assemblies, nor to found associations, nor to fight, nor, in conclusion, to exist. . . . Would it not be more logical to abolish the Chamber altogether?

To these remarks Mussolini answered by pointing out that Fascists and Liberals were evidently speaking different tongues and that a discussion between them could be but fruitless. Thereupon the Senate as a whole passed the new electoral law by a vote of 161 to 46.[33]

THE NATIONAL COUNCIL OF CORPORATIONS

In spite of its vocational representation the Italian Corporate Chamber performs functions essentially akin to those of any other legislative assembly. Therefore another agency was needed, Fascist theorists maintained, to synthetize the new syndical system and to coördinate and control Italy's economic life upon a national basis. This new agency came into existence through the law "on the reform of the National Council of Corporations," passed on March 20, 1930.

As we have seen, the syndical laws of 1926 provided for the organization of corporations and the establishment of the National Council of Corporations. Up to 1930, however, no corporation as defined by these laws had actually been formed, and the Council of Corporations had played a comparatively minor role among the other advisory bodies of the Fascist state. It is the law of March 20, 1930, therefore, which marks the

---

[33] See the text of Albertini's speech in *Atti Parlamentari, Senato del Regno, Legislatura XXVII — Sessione 1924–1928*, Rome, also quoted in Carmen Haider, *Capital and Labor under Fascism* (New York, 1930), pp. 254 ff.

real beginning of the corporations and of the Fascist corporate system.

This law provided for the establishment of a national economic council made up of seven separate sections, six of them composed of the representatives of the six pairs of confederations of Fascist employers' and workers' syndical associations and the seventh of the representatives of the thirteenth confederation of syndicates, that of professional men and artists, for which no distinction between workers and employers was possible. These seven sections were: (1) the section on liberal professions and arts, divided into two sub-sections, one for liberal professions and one for arts; (2) the section on industry and handicrafts, divided into two sub-sections, one for industry and one for handicrafts; (3) the section on agriculture; (4) the section on commerce; (5) the section on land transportation and internal navigation; (6) the section on maritime and air transportation, divided into two sub-sections, one for maritime and one for air transportation; (7) the section on banking and insurance.[34]

These seven sections and the various sub-sections of the council were to perform the functions of the corporations as first defined by Fascist leaders in 1926.[35] They were the organs through which representatives of employers' and workers'

[34] To illustrate the composition of membership in the various sections and sub-sections of the council, the complete membership of the sub-section of Industry in the section on Industry and Handicrafts is given below. Membership in that sub-section included: (1) the president of the General Fascist Confederation of Italian Industry; (2) seven representatives named by the General Fascist Confederation of Italian Industry, two representing managers of industrial enterprises; (3) the president of the National Fascist Confederation of Industrial Syndicates; (4) seven representatives of industrial employees and laborers named by the National Fascist Confederation of Industrial Syndicates, two representing industrial employees; (5) two representatives of the National Institute of Coöperation named by the Institute.

For full details of the membership in the seven sections of the council, cf. the table showing the distribution of membership in the various sections and sub-sections of the National Council of Corporations, appended to the condensed version of the law of March 20, 1930, in Appendix I, pp. 311 ff.

[35] Article 13 of the law of March 20, 1930, states explicitly that "upon the proposal of the Minister of Corporations, the attributions and powers of the corporations as described in Art. 3 of the law of April 3, 1926, may be conferred upon the various sections and sub-sections of the Council."

syndical associations within each one of the seven large fields of national productive activity would be brought together for the peaceful settlement of economic disputes, for the regulation of collective labor relations, and for the discussion of all other matters of common interest.[36]

The sub-sections of the council which had, within their own sphere of competence, powers equal to those of the sections, were allowed to function independently. When the questions at issue were of general interest, the sections and sub-sections could combine and hold their sessions jointly. A general assembly of the National Council of Corporations, which consisted of the members of the seven sections drawn together in common council, meeting twice a year in ordinary session, and in special sessions whenever a written request was made by the president or by one-third of the membership, was provided for the discussion of the larger questions of economic policy, such as the regulation of the syndical system, the problems of collective labor relations, and the national and regional coördination of employment. Moreover — and this provision was possibly the most significant one in the new law — this assembly was empowered to formulate binding rules for the coördination of the activities of the various branches of national production and thus, in effect, to regulate the economic life of the nation according to plans and programs which the assembly would work out and approve.[37]

---

[36] During the first meetings of one of the seven sections of the council (that of industry), for example, there was discussion of such questions as the promotion of industrial exports, new industrial salary and wage rates, the stipulation of industrial collective labor agreements, the position to be taken toward the new legislation on industrial accidents proposed by the government, the use of electric power in agriculture, etc.

[37] According to the new law, the following high government officials, in addition to the representatives of the syndical confederations of employers and workers included in the various sections and sub-sections of the council, were to be members of the General Assembly of the National Council of Corporations: the Minister of Corporations, the Minister for Agriculture and Forestry, the Secretary General of the National Fascist Party, and the Under-Secretaries of State for Corporations. The law provided further that some other high government officials should be included also, as well as two representatives of Italian economic interests abroad and ten technical experts in questions of syndical organization, corporate law, and economics. The General Assembly of

For the discussion of topics of a very technical character, special and permanent commissions, consisting of especially qualified members of the general assembly, were to be established. In addition, there was to be a Central Corporate Committee, composed of high government officials and the presidents of the thirteen syndical confederations, to coordinate the work of the council and to serve in the place of the general assembly during the intervals between the regular meetings.[38]

---

the council was to be, in effect, more than a purely technical body made up of syndical representatives; its scope was widened considerably by the inclusion of a number of high public officials and the representatives of some of the large cultural and welfare organizations.

[38] The actual work performed by the National Council of Corporations during the period immediately following the official beginning of its activities on April 21, 1930, is interestingly illustrated by the following figures, showing the number of meetings held by its various organs from May 1930 to September 1932:

The Central Corporate Committee	31 meetings
The Section on Industry	16
The Section on Agriculture	26
The Section on Commerce	11
The Section on Maritime Transportation	11
The Section on Land Transportation	10
The Section on Credit and Insurance	3
The Section on Professional Men and Artists	5
The General Assembly	8

Total   121 meetings

The following abridged list of the major topics discussed during these meetings gives a still more precise idea of the actual work performed by the various organs of the council:

The Central Corporate Committee, during its thirty-one meetings, held mostly under the presidency of the head of the government, discussed the establishment of new syndical associations for special groups of producers (workers in coöperatives, insurance companies, etc.) ; the formation of a new corporation, the corporation of the stage; the problem of adjustment of salaries, wages, costs of production, and prices to the new economic situation created by the stabilization of the lira; the regulation of collective labor contracts; the organization and regulation of national employment offices; questions of foreign trade policy, etc.

The Section on Industry discussed questions relating to Italian exports, the regulation of industrial salaries and wages, the use of electric power in agriculture, the reform of the law on industrial accidents, etc.

The Section on Agriculture discussed, among other things, problems arising in connection with the exportation of agricultural produce; various problems of agricultural technique; the labor problem in the Po valley; wage scales for

Composed of the direct representatives of all the major productive forces within the nation, the National Council of Corporations was destined to be, as Mussolini put it, the "general staff," the supreme regulator of Italian economy, the highest economic authority, which would be ready and able to act — through the almost military organization of the national syndical system which the council would control and of which it would be, at the same time, the highest expression — on the major problems of the nation's economic life.

In the speech made on April 21, 1930, during the solemn inauguration of the council on the Capitol in Rome, Mussolini himself stated the background, the aims and purposes of the council as follows:

It is in the corporation that the Fascist State finds its ultimate expression. Syndicalism as such, except for variations in method, has a similar life in all its schools. It begins with the education of individuals in associational activities, it continues with the stipulation of collective labor agreements, the organization of social welfare and assistance, and the perpetuation of professional ability. But while socialist syndicalism, moving along the road of class struggle, seeks its ultimate end in the political sphere — its final program being the suppression of private property and of freedom of individual initiative — Fascist syndicalism, with its doctrine of class collaboration, seeks its goal through the corporation. According to the Fascist conception, the corporation is the organ which makes collaboration systematic and harmonic, on the one hand by safeguarding private property and elevating it by insuring its performance of a social function, and, on the other, by respecting individual initiative within the boundaries set by the economic life and the

-----

workers engaged in the work of land reclamation, the use of electricity and power in agriculture, the regulations for the sale of milk in Rome, etc.

The Section on Commerce discussed such topics as the opening and closing hours of stores, the formation of groupings among Italian exporters, the negotiation of a collective labor agreement between insurance agents and insurance companies, etc.

The Section on Maritime and Land Transportation discussed the proposal of a new law on industrial accidents, the elaboration of uniform national characteristics for public vehicles (taxicabs, etc.), various collective labor agreements, etc.

For a more detailed chronological account of the activities of the various organs of the National Council of Corporations, cf. the 1931, 1932, and 1933 issues of *Sindacato e corporazione*.

economic interests of the nation. Syndicalism cannot be an end in itself; it either exhausts itself in political socialism or is bound to converge toward the Fascist corporation. For it is in the corporation that unity of the various economic elements — capital, labor, technique — is realized; it is only through the corporation — that is, through collaboration of all forces converging to one single end — that the vitality of syndicalism is assured. It is only through an increase in production, and consequently of wealth, that the collective labor agreement can assure constantly improving conditions to the laboring classes. Syndicalism and the corporation are thus interdependent and mutually conditioning; without syndicalism the corporation is not possible; but, without the corporation, syndicalism exhausts itself in its preliminary phases — in actions of detail foreign to the productive process.

This is what is happening in all western countries, where syndicalism, unable to arrive either at the so-called socialization of the means of production and exchange, or, as in Italy, at the corporation, marks time or starts battles which regularly end in disaster. For syndicalism necessarily reaches a point at which it must either transform itself into something else or confine itself to administrative "routine." It is because of these considerations that . . . I proclaim the originality and strength of this institution (the National Council of Corporations) in which the corporation finds not only its economic, but its political and moral expression.[39]

The foregoing account of the historical development of the Fascist syndical and corporate system may best be brought to a close with the presentation of a chart showing the system as it existed in Italy before its reorganization in the summer of 1934.

[39] Translated from Mussolini's speech at the inauguration of the National Council of Corporations on the Capitol in Rome, on April 21, 1930, as reprinted in the Ministry of Corporations' *Bollettino del lavoro e della previdenza sociale*, April–May 1930, p. 340.

CHART II

THE FASCIST SYNDICAL AND CORPORATE SYSTEM BEFORE 1934

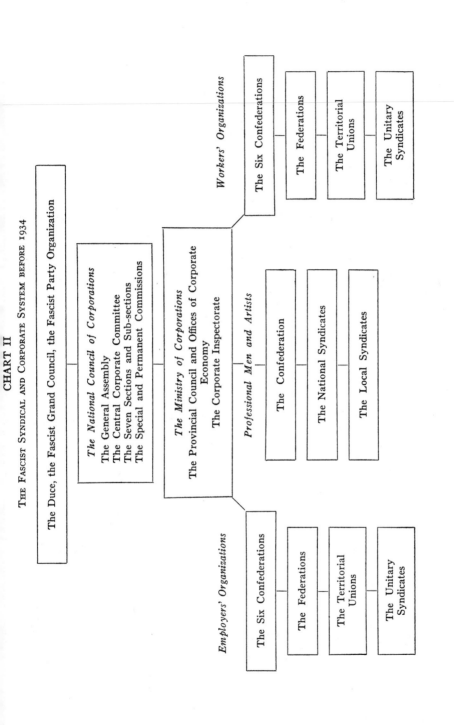

The Duce, the Fascist Grand Council, the Fascist Party Organization

The National Council of Corporations

The General Assembly
The Central Corporate Committee
The Seven Sections and Sub-sections
The Special and Permanent Commissions

The Ministry of Corporations

The Provincial Council and Offices of Corporate Economy
The Corporate Inspectorate

Workers' Organizations

The Six Confederations

The Federations

The Territorial Unions

The Unitary Syndicates

Professional Men and Artists

The Confederation

The National Syndicates

The Local Syndicates

Employers' Organizations

The Six Confederations

The Federations

The Territorial Unions

The Unitary Syndicates

CHAPTER IV

SYNDICAL ORGANIZATION, COLLECTIVE LABOR AGREE-MENTS, LABOR COURTS, AND SOCIAL WELFARE

ORGANIZATION AND FUNCTIONS OF FASCIST SYNDICAL ASSOCIATIONS

THE law on collective labor relations passed on April 3, 1926, fundamentally altered the labor situation in Italy. After its enactment all privileges of organization were reserved by law to the Fascist syndical associations and Italian workers were no longer free to choose between labor organizations of varying political faiths. It was natural therefore that only individuals decidedly opposed to Fascism and determined to show their opposition at the price of manifest disadvantages to themselves should continue to be hostile to the Fascist associations, and that the rest should join the associations in ever-increasing numbers.

LEGAL RECOGNITION

The conditions for the legal recognition of the Fascist syndicates, the requirements for membership in them, their functions and internal organization, were all minutely provided for in the new law and in the royal decree of July 1, 1926, which contains the regulations for its application. To obtain legal recognition by the state and thus the right to exist as separate legal entities, the law provided that syndical associations must conform to the following conditions: (1) The total membership of each employers' association must include employers of at least one-tenth of the workers in a given occupational group within the territorial jurisdiction of the organization. (2) The total membership of each workers' association must include at least one-tenth of the workers in the given occupational group within the territorial jurisdiction of the organization. (3) Syndical associations must attempt to advance not only the economic but also the educational and moral interests of their members. (4) The directors and officers of each association must give evidence of competence, character, and strong national convictions.[1]

CONDITIONS FOR MEMBERSHIP

While Fascist syndicates are the only ones eligible for legal recognition, membership in them is not compulsory. The only qualifications required of members are that they be at least eighteen years of age, that they be of good moral and political character, and — if foreigners — that they prove residence within the kingdom for at least ten years.[2]

The law further endows the legally recognized syndical associations of workers or employers with the following rights and duties: (1) to represent every employer or worker within the occupational group for which the association is formed, whether or not he is a member of the syndicate; (2) to defend the interests of a given occupational group against other groups and the state; (3) to negotiate collective labor agreements which shall be binding upon all members of a given occupational group; (4) to levy syndical dues upon members; (5) to exercise such other functions of public interest as may be delegated to the association by law.[3]

[1] Cf. Art. 1 of the law of April 3, 1926, on the "legal discipline of collective labor relations," Appendix I, p. 258. While these quantitative requirements assure the legally recognized syndical association of a certain minimum membership, the qualitative ones tend to impress upon it an orthodox national and Fascist character. The provision that only 10 per cent of the members of a given occupational group are needed to form an association that may obtain the legal right to represent the whole group is justified by the Fascists by reference to the fact that, in many sections of the country and in many types of activity, the Fascist syndicate represented the first attempt at a systematic organization of employers and workers ever made, and that, had the required percentage been higher, the task of uniform syndical organization would have been rendered much more difficult, if not well-nigh impossible. Cf. Carlo Costamagna, *Diritto corporativo italiano* (Turin, 1928), pp. 102 ff.

[2] Cf. royal decree of July 1, 1926, Arts. 1–9, in Appendix I, pp. 266 ff.

Besides the legally recognized syndical associations, however, the syndical laws admit the existence of *de facto* associations, viz., associations established for educational or social purposes; these do not require official recognition by the state. But, since they cannot represent their members in collective bargaining or perform any of the other functions of representation entrusted to the official Fascist syndicate, their scope and influence are extremely limited.

[3] For a concise statement of these rights cf. especially Declaration III of the Fascist Labor Charter. The official text of this charter (of which more

LEGAL REPRESENTATION OF MEMBERS

The first of these rights, that of existing as a separate legal entity and of representing all the members of a given occupational group whether they belong to the syndicate or not, is the fundamental prerogative of the Fascist syndical association. It implies the syndicate's power to assume, as a separate legal person, well-defined contractual rights and obligations. One of the most important of these is the appointment of its official representatives to those councils and organs of the state where such representation is required. This right includes, as we have seen, that of nominating candidates for membership in the Corporate Chamber, the corporations, and the National Council of Corporations.

The second function of the syndicates, that of protecting the economic interests of the occupational groups which they represent, is similar to the chief function of the old Socialist workers' syndical association. But while the Socialist syndicates endeavored to attain their aims by open class warfare, that is, by exerting constant pressure upon employers and by attempting to wrest from them, often by force, all the advantages that could possibly be obtained, Fascist associations must seek to protect the interests of their class through bargaining and negotiation. Controversies in which no agreement is reached are resolved not through strikes or lockouts (which according to the Fascists are wasteful and socially harmful expressions of class warfare) but through the verdicts of high administrative or judicial authorities of the state.

COLLECTIVE BARGAINING AND COLLECTIVE LABOR AGREEMENTS

One of the most important functions, if not the most important, of the Fascist syndical association, consequently, is that of collective bargaining and the negotiation of collective labor agreements. It is through collective labor agreements, concluded between the syndical associations of workers and

---

is said on p. 90) was published in the *Gazzetta ufficiale del regno* on April 30, 1927.

employers existing within the various major occupational groups, that labor relations are settled in Italy today. The collective agreements concluded by Fascist associations are binding upon all the members of the given occupational group, whether they are members of the syndical associations within that group or not. In addition to detailed provisions on wage rates and working hours, all collective agreements must contain precise regulations on disciplinary matters, trial periods, and such Fascist innovations as the indemnity to be paid to the worker if discharged through no fault of his own, and the annual paid vacation, usually a week or more, to which every steadily employed worker in Italy is entitled by law.[4]

To be valid, collective labor agreements must be made in writing, must be signed by the proper representatives of the contracting associations, and must specify their occupational and territorial jurisdiction and the period of their duration. If they apply to a province, they must be published in the official provincial or national *Gazzette* and filed with the prefect; if their validity is regional or national, they must be filed with the central government authorities. Labor agreements concluded between individual employers and workers must conform to the provisions of the collective agreements in that specific occupational field. Only those clauses in the individual agreements which are to the worker's advantage are exempt from this necessity to conform with the collective agreement.

Employers and workers, whether members of a syndical association or not, must abide by the provisions of collective labor agreements, and in case of failure are civilly liable to the syndical associations through which the agreement was negotiated.[5] The syndicates, in turn, are responsible for the faithful execution of the provisions of such agreements negotiated by them. In this connection, the by-laws of the syndical associations of higher rank (federations and confederations)

---

[4] For the full texts of the most important collective labor agreements, cf. the collection of such agreements contained in: Ministero delle Corporazioni, *Contratti collettivi di lavoro* (Rome), a supplement to the *Bollettino ufficiale* of the same ministry.

[5] Cf. law of April 3, 1926, Art. 10, in Appendix I, p. 261.

may require that collective labor agreements negotiated by their affiliated associations shall be previously approved by them. Agreements negotiated without proper authorization may be declared void.[6]

Tables 1 and 2 give the numerical distribution of these collective labor agreements in different occupational fields. Up to the end of 1936, as the tables show, 16,026 provincial and 1,420 inter-provincial and national collective labor agreements had actually been concluded.

With the introduction of the collective labor agreement as the principal regulator of the working conditions of the Italian population, the old-time higgling and bargaining between individual employers and workers has, in large measure, disappeared. Hours, wages, conditions of work are now regulated, for almost every occupational group, through national, provincial, and local collective agreements. Though the system which, like everything else in Italy, operates under the political control of the government and the party, has obvious weaknesses,[7] it has undoubtedly brought about a more detailed and precise definition of the working conditions of Italian labor and the determination of certain minimum standards as to wages, hours, and conditions of work to which all Italian employers must now conform.

No matter what difficulties or what disputes may arise in the negotiation of collective labor agreements, strikes and lock-outs are prohibited. The law of April 3, 1926, states explicitly that employers who close their factories, enterprises, or offices without justifiable reason and for the sole purpose of compelling their employees to modify existing labor agreements shall be punished with a fine from 10,000 to 100,000 lire. Employees and laborers who, in groups of three or more, cease work by agreement or work in such a manner as to disturb

---

[6] Cf. royal decree of July 1, 1926, Arts. 50 and 55, Appendix I, pp. 278, 279. For a more detailed discussion of collective labor agreements from the legal point of view, see Costamagna, *Diritto corporativo italiano.* Cf. also, on the same subject, the studies by Giuseppe Bottai and Luigi Spinelli in the issues for 1932 of *Il Diritto del lavoro,* the official monthly review published by the Ministry of Corporations in Rome.

[7] Cf. the critique of the Fascist syndical system in chap. vi.

TABLE 1

DISTRIBUTION OF NATIONAL AND INTER-PROVINCIAL COLLECTIVE LABOR AGREEMENTS FILED WITH THE MINISTRY OF CORPORATIONS, BY OCCUPATIONAL FIELDS AND YEARS, 1926–1936 *

Occupational Field	April 1926–Dec. 31, 1928	1929	1930	1931	1932	1933	1934	1935	1936	Total
Industry †	40	29	31	38	36	20	100	119	201	614
Agriculture	7	6	4	5	2	4	5	15	25	73
Commerce	17	18	18	6	10	10	21	66	59	225
Maritime and Air Transportation	3	4	1	12	15	15	14	..	..	64
Land Transportation and Internal Navigation	15	3	19	49	52	33	68	..	..	239
Banking and Insurance	25	11	30	9	46	8	6	16	35	186
Professional Men and Artists	..	..	..	..	5	1	1	9	3	19
Total	107	71	103	119	166	91	215	225	323	1420

* Compiled from various issues of *Bollettino del lavoro e della previdenza sociale*, *Sindacato e corporazione*, and *Annuario statistico italiano*.

† After 1935 the figures include agreements in the field of Maritime and Air Transportation and Land Transportation and Internal Navigation.

TABLE 2

Distribution of Provincial Collective Labor Agreements, by Occupational Fields and Years, 1926–1936*

Occupational Field	April 1926–Dec. 31, 1927	1928	1929	1930	1931	1932	1933	1934	1935	1936‡	Total
Industry †	2064	1012	615	816	762	893	828	720	894	974	9578
Agriculture	371	227	221	210	196	222	223	202	165	189	2226
Commerce	238	218	188	231	246	153	215	302	256	174	2221
Maritime and Air Transportation	5	4	19	8	..	1	3	2	..	..	42
Land Transportation and Internal Navigation	116	254	110	255	271	217	216	213	..	..	1652
Banking and Insurance	27	29	3	15	9	20	12	35	12	45	207
Professional Men and Artists	..	..	..	..	..	11	48	30	1	10	100
Total	2821	1744	1156	1535	1484	1517	1545	1504	1328	1392	16,026

* Compiled from various issues of *Bollettino del lavoro e della previdenza sociale*, *Sindacato e corporazione*, and *Annuario statistico italiano*.

† After 1935 the figures include agreements in the field of Maritime and Air Transportation and Land Transportation and Internal Navigation.

‡ Data for some provinces for December are missing.

the continuity or regularity of the work in order to compel employers to change existing labor agreements shall be punishable with a fine of from 100 to 1,000 lire. Moreover,

employees of the State and of other public organizations and employees of public service and public utility enterprises who, in groups of three or more, shall cease work by agreement or perform it in such a manner as to disturb its continuity or regularity shall be punishable by imprisonment from one to six months, and shall be barred from public office for six months.[8]

ARBITRATION OF COLLECTIVE LABOR DISPUTES

Strikes and lockouts being thus barred by law as criminal offenses, all labor disputes in Italy must be settled by arbitration. The first attempt at arbitration is made by the highest organs of the syndical system itself, by the federations and the national confederations of syndical associations. If no settlement is reached, the controversy is taken to the Ministry of Corporations for further debate and for a further attempt at solution. It is here, before the high officials of this government department acting as mediators, that most controversies are settled and most collective labor agreements of national importance are actually concluded, sometimes only after prolonged disagreement and discussion.

It may be well to analyze briefly what the Ministry of Corporations has done in the field of conciliation and arbitration of collective labor disputes. From 1927 to 1933, 498 disputes, involving collective labor agreements, were brought to the ministry for arbitration.[9] Sixty-eight per cent were settled at the ministry; 19 per cent were left for further consideration (many were later composed privately), while 13 per cent remained undecided and were carried to the courts for decision. A settlement of these disputes, usually involving questions of wage regulation, especially wage reductions made necessary by

[8] See Arts. 18 and 19 of the law of April 3, 1926, in Appendix I, pp. 264, 265.
[9] The annual figures were: 9 disputes in 1927, 54 in 1928, 87 in 1929, 87 in 1930, 94 in 1931, 65 in 1932, and 102 in 1933. Of the total, about two-thirds, or 347, concerned industry, 74 agriculture, 25 commerce, 21 land transportation. Cf. *Sindacato e corporazione*, February 1934, p. 298.

the depression, was ordinarily reached through a compromise between the demands of the workers and those of the employers, frequently after a detailed inquiry had been made by the ministry into the conditions of the industry. During 1934 and 1935, 273 disputes were submitted to the ministry. As Table 3 shows, 181 of these were settled at the ministry; 20 could not immediately be resolved, and 72 were withheld for settlement pending further investigation.

TABLE 3

CONCILIATION OF COLLECTIVE LABOR DISPUTES BY THE MINISTRY OF CORPORATIONS, BY OCCUPATIONAL FIELDS, 1934 AND 1935 *

	NUMBER OF DISPUTES DEALT WITH							
	1934				1935			
Occupational Field	Total	Con-ciliated	Not Con-ciliated	Pend-ing	Total	Con-ciliated	Not Con-ciliated	Pend-ing
Agriculture	7	4	1	2	5	3	..	2
Industry	120	79	14	27	126	87	5	34
Commerce	2	2	..	..	9	5	..	4
Credit and Insurance	1	1	..	..	1	..	..	1
Professional Men and Artists	1	..	..	1	1	..	..	1
Total	131	86	15	30	142	95	5	42

* *Annuario statistico italiano*, 1937, p. 170.

If, even after an exhaustive discussion of the controversy at the Ministry of Corporations, a collective labor dispute cannot be settled by arbitration, the Italian syndical laws provide that it be brought for adjustment before the newly established governmental labor courts.

THE FASCIST LABOR COURTS

These courts in Italy had antecedents in other countries. France had instituted *conseils des prud'hommes* (boards of employers' and workers' representatives for the arbitration of labor disputes) as early as 1806. German governmental *arbeitsgerichte*, very similar to the Italian labor courts, were established in 1926. The English-speaking countries, however, until recently, have made little progress in this general movement for judicial arbitration of labor disputes. England has maintained the principle that arbitration should be resorted to only if spontaneously requested by the parties involved, without compulsory government intervention, while the United States has regarded compulsory arbitration of labor disputes as conflicting with the principles of individual liberty of contract set down in the Constitution.[10]

In Italy the competence of the labor courts has been limited exclusively to the field of collective disputes. Jurisdiction on individual controversies arising out of the interpretation of collective agreements belongs to the ordinary magistrates assisted by two experts on questions of production and labor.[11]

Fascist labor courts were first established, as we have noted, through the law of April 3, 1926. They are organized as separate sections of the sixteen courts of appeal and consist of three magistrates of the Court of Appeals and two experts in the problems of production and labor who are chosen by the president of the court from a carefully prepared list of eligible citizens. Before a judicial decision is made by a labor court, the law prescribes that a last attempt at conciliation be made by the president of the court. Employers or workers may be represented in court only through their legally recognized syndical associations. Appeals from the decisions of the labor courts may be carried to the Supreme Court of the Italian kingdom.[12]

The work of the labor courts may best be illustrated by a brief description of one of the cases, now classical, tried by

[10] For a somewhat more detailed discussion of the international antecedents of the Italian labor court, see Fausto Pitigliani, *The Italian Corporative State* (London, 1933), pp. 61 ff.

[11] See in this connection the detailed provisions of the royal decree of May 21, 1934 (published in the *Gazzetta ufficiale* of July 14, 1934), on the regulation of individual labor disputes and on the rules of court procedure applying to them. This decree takes the place of the royal decree of February 26, 1928, which up to September 1, 1934, when the new decree went into force, provided for the regulation of individual labor disputes. Cf. *Sindacato e corporazione*, July–August 1934, p. 44.

[12] Detailed provisions as to the composition and the powers of the Fascist labor courts are given in Section II of the law of April 3, 1926, and in Part V of the royal decree of July 1, 1926. Cf. the texts of these laws in Appendix I, pp. 262, 280 ff.

them. In March 1927 a collective labor agreement regarding wages of the workers in the rice fields of the valley of the Po, was concluded between the Confederation of Fascist Syndicates of Agriculture, representing the workers, and the Fascist Confederation of Agriculture, representing the employers. Because of the economic difficulties resulting from the revaluation of the lira and the reduction in the price of rice in world markets, the agriculturalists asked for a revision of the agreement and for authority to reduce the wage rates by 30 per cent. The representatives of the workers' syndicates flatly refused to consider such a proposal, and, various attempts at conciliation having failed, the dispute was ultimately carried to the labor court for decision. After a careful study of the case and after hearing representatives of both sides as well as the opinion of its own expert advisers, the court decreed a reduction of 5 per cent in the average rice workers' daily wage in addition to the 10 per cent general national wage reduction which had been previously decreed by the government. The decision was apparently made on the theory that the consequences of the country's economic difficulties were to be equitably born by employers as well as workers.

The experience of the Italian courts (both labor courts and the ordinary civil tribunals) in dealing with individual and collective labor disputes during the period from April 1926 to November 30, 1933, may be briefly summed up by a few figures. During this period a total of 145,289 labor disputes were submitted to the courts. Of these, 29,144 were settled through the powers of conciliation of the magistrates; 86,505 were decided by sentences of the courts; 20,191 were withdrawn from the court by consent of the parties involved; and at the end of the period 9,449 were left undecided. Of the total mentioned, however, 145,255 represented individual controversies (which may be settled before the ordinary civil courts), and only 34 were collective disputes involving the Magistratura del Lavoro, the governmental labor courts proper. Of the 34 collective disputes only 14 were decided by a sentence of the labor courts, the remainder being settled through the court's conciliatory efforts.[13] During 1934 four collective disputes were brought before the labor courts; two of these were later voluntarily withdrawn, and the remaining two were settled by conciliation. In 1935 two controversies were brought before the courts, but in both cases the courts declared themselves incompetent to pronounce judgment. In 1936 no disputes at all were brought before the labor tribunals.[14]

In reading the decisions of the Italian labor courts one gains the impression that the decisions are fair and that the courts are inclined to consider sympathetically every legitimate demand of the workers. Among Italian workers and employers, too, the impression seems to prevail that the courts are equitable and impartial. The question of course remains whether, under the present regime, the courts are in a position to judge a case solely on its merits or whether their decisions do not, at times, necessarily represent but a compromise, not uninfluenced by the political situation of the moment, between the demands of the workers and those of the employers. Some observers believe that the process of judicial settlement of labor disputes in Italy rests primarily upon a political basis and that, besides, the courts would seldom be

[13] Of the 14 decisions actually rendered, those of the labor court of Rome are of particular importance, since that court decides not only controversies arising within its own district but also those involving residents within the districts of two or more labor courts. The decisions of the Roman labor court related to the following questions: settlement of wage rates for the rice cleaners in the provinces of Pavia, Milan, Novara, Cremona, and Vercelli for the year 1927; settlement of the wages and allowances to be paid to persons engaged in maritime transportation; conditions of employment for officers serving with the Italia and Cosulich steamship companies; new working conditions for persons engaged in the silk industry; settlement of wage rates for rice cleaners in the provinces of Milan, Pavia, Vercelli, Alessandria, and Cremona for the year 1931. The Labor Court of Naples delivered two important decisions, one relating to the establishment of new working conditions for the workers and employees of the firm operating the Naples aqueduct, and the second relating to the conditions of employment of persons engaged in the canned foods industry. In these decisions the court determined conditions as to salary and wage rates as well as conditions relating to methods of hiring, probationary periods, disciplinary measures, etc. The Labor Court of Milan has rendered one decision only, relating to the wages of textile workers in the provinces of Como, Varese, and Milan. For additional details, see *Sindacato e corporazione*, January 1934.

[14] *Annuario statistico italiano*, 1937, p. 286.

able, even with the expert assistance at their disposal, to determine with absolute accuracy all the economic factors involved in the cases brought before them. In most instances, it is believed, a "judge-made wage" is of necessity but a compromise between the demands of the workers and those of the employers. Strikes, according to this view, are the only really effective means of forcing the employer to make the maximum concession.[15] Indeed, while in a society in which the principles of class war are definitely laid aside the ideal of class coöperation may appear logical and desirable, the sudden and complete deprivation of the laboring classes of one of their most cherished rights cannot but be open to serious question. Even if the reduction of industrial disputes to a minimum is clearly in the national interest, there can be little doubt that the complete abolition by one stroke of the pen of the right to strike, for which generations of workers had fought and which had become one of the most sacred rights of the laboring masses, deprived Italian workers of one of the most effective weapons at their disposal for the improvement of their economic position. Moreover, as Tables 4 and 5 show, even under a system of drastic legal restriction it has been impossible completely to eliminate strikes and lockouts in Italy.[16]

The foregoing analysis of collective labor relations in Italy reveals clearly the importance of the syndical associations in the corporate system of the Fascist state. To enable these associations to carry out their tasks effectively, detailed provisions for their internal organization and sources of revenue have been made.[17]

[15] Louis Rosenstock-Franck, *L'Économie corporative fasciste en doctrine et en fait* (Paris, 1934), p. 184, and *passim*. The same writer believes, possibly not without some justification, that in Italy strikes were abolished primarily because of political reasons, because of "the political necessity in which the government found itself to prevent all mass movements of any importance" (p. 53).

[16] It must be recognized, however, that while before 1926, the year in which the prohibition of strikes and lockouts became effective, the total number of laborers involved in such disturbances amounted to several hundred thousand every year, after 1926 the number shrank to almost negligible proportions.

[17] For a detailed description of the internal organization of the various types

INTERNAL ORGANIZATION OF SYNDICAL ASSOCIATIONS

As to internal organization, the law provides that the administrative boards and the presidents and secretaries entrusted with the executive work of each association shall be elected according to the associations' by-laws. All appointments must, however, be approved by the government. While in the beginning these officials were almost invariably appointed by the government, they are now elected by the various syndical associations themselves, usually at annual conventions which have now become the rule.[18]

SYNDICAL DUES

The principal source of income of each syndical association is the dues, legally authorized, which each employer or worker in a given occupational group pays, whether or not he is a member of the syndicate. The payment of dues by non-members as well as members is justified by the argument that non-members, too, reap the benefits from all that collective bargaining implies. The principal difference between members and non-members is, therefore, that the latter are not eligible to vote in any syndical elections and that their participation in the syndical educational and welfare programs is limited.

---

of Fascist syndical associations, cf. Arts. 6–9 of the law of April 3, 1926, and Sections II and IV in Part I of the royal decree of July 1, 1926, in Appendix I, pp. 260, 269, 272.

[18] In this connection, a passage taken from a speech made by a former president of the National Fascist Confederation of Merchants, at the fourth congress of that confederation, held on April 9, 1931, in Rome, is of interest. During his address at the congress, the president of the confederation, Lantini, said: "Through the syndical elections held last January, the territorial organization (the presidents and other officers of regional, provincial, and local syndicates) of the Confederation has been entirely renewed. The Confederation of Commerce has been the first to hold these elections, which proved completely successful. Over 450,000 merchants, active members of the Confederation and representing 60 per cent of all Italian merchants, were called upon to participate in the election. 300,000, representing 68 per cent of the members of the Confederation, took an active part in them. In order to appreciate the significance of these figures, it must be remembered that in the elections of the old Chambers of Commerce the percentages of actual votes usually amounted to about 10 per cent." See *Commercio* (the monthly review of the Fascist Confederation of Commerce), March–April 1931, p. 176. For a more detailed description of the internal organization and selection of officers in the syndical associations today, cf. chap. v, pp. 122 ff.

TABLE 4
DISTRIBUTION OF STRIKES AND LOCKOUTS IN AGRICULTURE AND INDUSTRY, BY YEARS, 1919–1926 *

Year	NUMBER OF STRIKES			NUMBER OF STRIKERS			Number of Lockouts	Number of Laborers Involved in Lockouts
	Agriculture	Industry	Total	Agriculture	Industry	Total		
1914	82	782	864	49,379	173,103	222,482	12	9,367
1915	68	539	607	47,798	132,136	179,934	2	56
1916	61	516	577	14,892	123,616	138,508	3	424
1917	27	443	470	6,191	168,626	174,817	2	180
1918	10	303	313	675	158,036	158,711	3	740
1919	208	1663	1871	505,128	1,049,438	1,554,566	8	4,822
1920	189	1881	2070	1,045,732	1,267,953	2,313,685	16	18,113
1921	89	1045	1134	79,298	644,564	723,862	66	60,279
1922	23	552	575	25,146	422,773	447,919	37	18,829
1923	1	200	201	110	66,103	66,213	14	7,145
1924	6	356	362	2,713	181,012	183,725	6	3,417
1925	10	604	614	2,693	304,551	307,244	4	989
1926 1st Sem....	1	125	126	16	23,379	23,395	1	70

* Bollettino del lavoro e della previdenza sociale, July–August 1931, p. 72.

TABLE 5
DISTRIBUTION OF CRIMINAL STRIKES AND LOCKOUTS * IN AGRICULTURE AND INDUSTRY, BY YEARS, 1926–1934 †

Year	STRIKES						INDUSTRIAL LOCKOUTS	
	Number Reported to Judicial Authorities			Number of Persons Indicted			Number Reported to Judicial Authorities	Number of Persons Indicted
	Agriculture	Industry	Totals	Agriculture	Industry	Total		
1926	2	44	46	114	677	791	3	14
1927	5	149	154	1881	16,752	18,633	15	27
1928	6	63	69	59	2,905	2,964	8	35
1929	6	68	74	180	3,042	3,222	9	30
1930	9	66	75	201	2,629	2,830	7	33
1931	15	48	63	746	3,376	4,122	4	19
1932	7	14	21	280	313	593	2	5
1933	8	22	30	101	723	824	4	17
1934	2	30	32	100	445	545	6	31

* Since the enactment of the law of April 3, 1926, on the judicial discipline of collective labor relations, strikes and lockouts are criminal acts in Italy.

† *Bollettino del lavoro e della previdenza sociale*, July–August 1931, p. 72, and *Compendio statistico italiano*, 1935, p. 162.

The law provides that each employer's annual dues shall not exceed a sum equal to one day's compensation for each worker employed, and that the worker's annual dues shall not exceed the amount of his wage for one full working day. Further, a part of the fund from dues so collected must be set aside by each association to meet its obligations assumed in collective labor agreements.[19]

The last of the previously enumerated rights of Fascist syndicates, that of "exercising such functions of public interest as may be delegated to them by law," is related, in part, to the ways in which they may spend their funds. The law makes certain financial obligations mandatory. For example, each association has to meet the expenditures incurred in the promotion of the economic and the social welfare interests of its members. Moreover, each syndicate must provide facilities for the education, especially professional, both of members and non-members. The social welfare obligations include contributions to such organizations as the National Institute for Maternal and Infant Welfare, which cares for thousands of poor children, the Opera Nazionale Dopolavoro, a semi-governmental national "leisure time" organization established for the promotion of recreational activities among the workers, and the National Institute for Social Insurance, which provides insurance against accidents, sickness, old age, and unemployment, all of which every Italian worker is forced by law to carry.[20] The importance of all these syndical expenditures may be gauged from the fact that in 1936 the dues paid by members and non-members amounted to over 313 million lire. (Cf. Tables 6 and 7.)

THE CHARTER OF LABOR ONCE MORE

We must now turn to a brief discussion of the Fascist system of social insurance and social welfare. The principles govern-

[19] Cf. the law of April 3, 1926, Art. V. For a detailed discussion of the method of collection of syndical dues, of the supplementary dues which may, in certain cases, be imposed, etc., compare the detailed provisions of the royal decree of July 1, 1926, Section III, Arts. 23–28, in Appendix I, pp. 271 ff.

[20] Cf. the more detailed account of the organization and activities of the various Fascist social welfare organizations, given in this chapter, pp. 96 ff.

ing action in this field are set forth in detail in the Fascist Charter of Labor.[21] The official text of that charter begins with a terse definition of the relationship between the nation, the state, and the individual as the Fascists see it.

The Italian nation [we are told in Declaration I] is an organism endowed with purposes, a life, and means of action transcending in power and duration those of the separate individuals or groups of

TABLE 6

DUES PAID TO FASCIST SYNDICAL ASSOCIATIONS, BY YEARS, 1928–1933 *

(*In thousands of lire*)

	1928	1929	1930	1931	1932	1933
Employers' Associations						
The National Fascist Confederations of:						
Industry	74,719	61,054	78,997	66,988	67,473	62,726
Agriculture	54,034	61,020	64,370	54,470	63,259	76,419
Commerce	13,542	43,011	37,921	42,736	39,937	44,220
Maritime and Air Transportation ...	1,877	3,788	2,430	2,450	2,784	2,387
Internal Communications Enterprises ..	5,847	6,074	6,698	7,232	6,942	6,979
Credit and Insurance	3,590	1,976	5,675	4,255	4,882	3,363
The Autonomous Fascist Federation of Italian Artisans' Communities	3,541	8,243	8,036	8,985	9,505	10,648
Workers' and Professional Men and Artists' Associations						
The National Confederations of Fascist Syndicates in:						
Industry	..	38,790	40,194	39,296	31,712	31,215
Agriculture	..	12,629	11,112	13,568	19,593	23,728
Commerce	..	5,896	8,907	9,401	10,069	10,317
Maritime and Air Transportation ...	3,082	2,831	2,707	2,457	2,115	2,141
Internal Communications	..	4,192	5,415	5,067	4,552	5,494
Credit and Insurance	..	1,001	2,000	1,350	1,314	1,562
Professions and Arts	..	5,104	6,967	9,388	7,913	8,723
Total	223,576†	255,619	281,429	267,643	272,050	289,922

* Compiled from various issues of *Compendio statistico italiano*.

† Includes a total of 63,344,000 lire paid by members of the first National Confederation of Fascist Syndicates, dissolved in 1928.

[21] For a more detailed account of the events which led to the publication of the Fascist Labor Charter, cf. chap. iii, p. 62. Its full English text is given in Appendix I, pp. 287 ff.

TABLE 7

DUES PAID TO FASCIST SYNDICAL ASSOCIATIONS DURING 1934, 1935, AND 1936 *

(*In thousands of lire*)

Associations	1934		1935		1936	
	Totals Collected	Amounts Redistributed to Confederations and Affiliated Associations	Totals Collected	Amounts Redistributed to Confederations and Affiliated Associations	Totals Collected	Net Amounts Redistributed to Confederations and Affiliated Associations
Employers' Associations						
The Fascist Confederations of:						
Agriculturists	61,175	44,046	61,487	44,270	72,016	51,852
Industrialists	75,546	56,263	82,045	60,983	90,967	67,796
Merchants	40,898	29,446	42,358	30,505	45,559	32,802
Credit and Insurance	4,357	3,400	5,885	4,567	5,883	4,620
Total	181,976	133,155	191,775	140,325	214,425	157,070
Confederations in Liquidation						
The Fascist Confederations of:						
Maritime and Air Transportation	2,044	1,472	....	....	....	....
Internal Communication Enterprises ..	6,558	4,722	....	....	....	....
Total	8,602	6,194				
National Institute of Coöperatives	2,952	2,125	5,706	4,108	4,672	3,364
Grand Total (Employers)	193,530	141,474	197,481	144,433	219,097	160,434

Workers' Associations

The Fascist Confederations of Workers in:						
Agriculture	28,091	20,225	23,608	16,998	27,135	19,537
Industry	32,611	23,472	41,325	29,791	43,546	31,400
Commerce	12,898	9,287	13,047	9,387	10,692	7,699
Credit and Insurance Enterprises	961	692	2,436	1,754	2,182	1,571
Total	74,561	53,676	80,416	57,930	83,555	60,207
Confederations in Liquidation						
The Fascist Confederations of:						
Sea and Air Men	2,125	1,564	....	....	....	....
Workers in Internal Communication Enterprises	4,737	3,411	....	....	....	....
Total	6,862	4,975	....	....	....	....
The Fascist Confederation of Professional Men and Artists	8,572	6,172	7,728	5,564	10,520	7,574
Grand Total (Workers)	89,995	64,823	88,144	63,494	94,075	67,781

* *Annuario statistico italiano*, 1934, 1935, 1936.

individuals which compose it. It is a moral, political, and economic unity which realizes itself completely in the Fascist state.

The Fascist viewpoint on economic production is set forth in Declaration II: "From the national point of view, the productive process is unitary: its aims coincide with individual well-being and the development of national power." The principles which govern economic life in the Fascist state are further elucidated in Declaration VII. "The Corporate State," that declaration states, "considers private enterprise in production the most efficacious and useful instrument for the furtherance of the nation's interests." But, it continues, "private organization of production being a function of national interest, the entrepreneur is responsible to the state for the direction of the productive process." Declaration IX, finally, tells us that in the Fascist view, "the state intervenes in economic production only when private initiative is lacking or insufficient or when the political interests of the state are at stake. Such intervention may take the form of encouragement, regulation or direct management."

After this introductory restatement of some of the fundamental principles of Fascist economic philosophy (analyzed in detail elsewhere),[22] the Charter of Labor deals with the basic principles which should regulate labor relations, wages, social insurance, and social welfare.

WAGES IN THE FASCIST STATE

A definition of the Fascist concept of labor is given in the second declaration of the charter. "Labor in all its forms, intellectual, technical, and manual," we are told, "is a social duty. . . . As such, and only as such, it is safeguarded by the state." According to the Fascist conception, labor loses its traditional character of a "commodity" freely bought and sold in a market, and becomes a solemn duty of the individual towards society, a duty which must be performed under the safeguard and the protection of the state. This attitude toward

---

[22] Cf. the discussion of Fascist social and economic doctrines in chap. ii, pp. 32 ff.

labor helps to explain why strikes and lockouts have been prohibited in Italy and why collective labor agreements and peaceful conciliation of labor disputes have been substituted for individual bargaining and class warfare.[23]

The Fascist theory of wages, given in Declaration XII of the charter, is equally interesting. Wages, we are told, must not be fixed according to a general standard but must be determined by agreement between the parties through collective labor contracts. The action of syndicates, the conciliatory efforts of corporate organs, and the decisions of the labor courts must insure "the adjustment of wages to the normal requirements of life, the possibilities of production and the productivity of labor." Declaration XIII of the charter states that statistical data on the conditions of production and labor and the standard of living as compiled by official governmental agencies shall furnish the basic criteria "for the conciliation of the interests of the various economic classes with each other and with the superior interests of national production."

The Fascist official view, then, regards human labor as a social duty, as a contribution which the individual must make to the economic life of the nation. But, if labor is a duty toward society, society in turn has definite and inescapable obligations toward all those who perform this duty. The first and foremost of these obligations is to see that all labor receives a fair reward. A "fair" reward implies, according to Declaration XII of the Charter of Labor, that wages be adjusted to "the normal requirements of life, the possibilities of production, and the

[23] It is interesting to note that, besides collective labor agreements and the decisions of the labor courts, direct regulation by central corporate organs is also mentioned in the Fascist Labor Charter as one of the channels for the settlement of collective labor disputes. The syndical laws provide that regulations may be issued by corporate organs (corporations) whenever the necessary power is delegated to them by their affiliated associations. Such regulations have the legal status of collective labor agreements. (Cf. Art. 10 of the law of April 3, 1926; Arts. 56 and 57 of the royal decree of July 1, 1926, and Declaration VI of the Charter of Labor in Appendix I, pp. 261, 279, 288.) Even in the opinion of the Fascist theorists themselves, however, regulations of corporate organs must be limited to regulations of a broad character, affecting large occupational groups, and must not be extended to the determination of wages, a task best left to the individual syndical associations. For an authoritative statement of this view, see Costamagna, *Diritto corporativo italiano*, p. 586.

productivity of labor." There can be little doubt that the expression "normal requirements of life" includes the idea of a minimum upon which further wage discussion must rest. According to the charter, wages must be at least sufficient to provide for what is considered a "fair" standard of living. If employers pay less, it is the duty of the state, the supreme guarantor of the welfare of all members of the community, to step in and to remedy the situation. Moreover, wages must vary with the "possibilities of production and the productivity of labor." Here again it is the state which, acting through the semi-autonomous syndical system, must see that the proper adjustments are made. If times are good, production large, and the productivity of labor high, wages must be allowed to rise; if the opposite occurs, it is the duty of the state itself to bring about the required all-round downward adjustment.[24]

SOCIAL INSURANCE AND SOCIAL WELFARE

We turn now to a more detailed analysis of the elaborate program of social insurance and social welfare devised by the Fascist regime. There are two main channels through which this program is carried out in practice: the welfare provisions included in collective labor agreements and the social welfare institutions maintained by the state.

All collective labor agreements must provide for the following benefits to all classes of Italian workers: (1) An annual vacation with pay. "After a year of uninterrupted service the employee of enterprises whose work is continuous," Declaration XVI of the Labor Charter states, "is entitled to an annual vacation with pay" (usually a week or more). (2) An indemnity at death and upon discharge through no fault of the worker. "In concerns where work is continuous, the employee, discharged through no fault of his own, is entitled to an indemnity proportioned to his years of service. A similar indemnity must also be paid in the case of the worker's death"

---

[24] For a more detailed discussion of this interesting principle of rapid adjustment of wages to the course of the business cycle through state action and for numerical data on the wage situation in Italy, see chaps. vii and ix.

(Declaration XVII). (3) Provisions as to tenure and conditions of work. Declaration XVIII of the Charter of Labor states that

transfers of ownership of concerns whose work is continuous do not affect labor contracts; employees of such concerns retain all their rights and claims toward their new employers. Illness of an employee not exceeding a specific period likewise does not lead to cancellation of the labor contract. A call to arms or to service in the Fascist Militia is no valid cause for dismissal.

Declaration XXI of the Charter states that

the benefits of collective labor agreements shall also apply to workers in the domestic trades. Special regulations shall be passed by the state to assure proper control and hygienic conditions for such home workers.

Besides these three important benefits, all Fascist collective labor agreements must contain explicit provisions as to disciplinary matters, periods of probation, salary and wage schedules, assistance in case of sickness, and all such other matters as may be specified in new Fascist labor legislation.[25]

GOVERNMENT EMPLOYMENT EXCHANGES

In addition to these provisions favoring the workers, which must be included in every collective labor agreement, Declarations XXII and XXIII of the Charter of Labor state that it is the duty of the state "to ascertain and supervise the employment and unemployment situation — a comprehensive indicator of the general conditions of production and labor." To that end, "free governmental employment exchanges organized on the basis of equal representation for employers and workers shall be operated under the control of the corporate organs of the state." "Employers shall select their workers from among those enrolled in these offices; but, while they have the right of selection from among all the registered applicants, preference must be given to members of the Fascist party and of the Fascist syndicates according to priority of registration."

[25] Cf. the royal decree of May 6, 1928, published in the *Gazzetta ufficiale* of June 15, 1928.

These general provisions of the Charter of Labor were elaborated in detail in the royal decree of March 29, 1928, on the national regulation of the demand and the supply of labor, and in the subsequent decrees giving the rules for its application.[26]

On October 18, 1934, another decree provided that in lieu of the various provincial employment offices mentioned in Art. I of the decree of March 29, 1928, a central employment office should be established in each province of the Italian kingdom, its headquarters to be located at the Provincial Office of Corporate Economy; that this central provincial employment office should be subdivided into "sections" located at the offices of the various workers' syndical associations, and that it should be headed by a commission presided over by the provincial secretary of the National Fascist Party and composed of an equal number of representatives of the workers' and employers' syndical associations.[27]

Through these decrees then, a series of free national, provincial, and municipal employment offices, under the control of the Ministry of Corporations and the sections of labor and social welfare of the various provincial economic councils, have been created. Wherever such employment offices exist, private mediation is prohibited by law and registration with the governmental employment office made compulsory for the workers. Employers in their turn are forced by law to select their workmen from among those registered at these governmental employment exchanges.

Among the first free employment offices established were the National Employment Bureau for workers engaged in rice cleaning and the harvesting of olives and wheat and a free National Employment Bureau for the workers of the stage. The central offices for the first bureau are in Rome at the headquarters of the National Confederation of Fascist Syndicates of Agriculture, while offices of the latter have been opened in all the principal cities of the Peninsula.[28]

[26] Cf. the condensed versions of the royal decrees of March 29, 1928, and of December 6, 1928, in Appendix I, pp. 292, 298.

[27] *Sindacato e corporazione*, December 1934, p. 986.

[28] Ministero delle Corporazioni, *Bollettino del lavoro*, July–August 1932, pp. 145 ff.

The activity of these two national employment offices and the work done by provincial, district, and municipal offices are illustrated by Table 8.

An interesting recent addition to Italian legislation on labor and employment relations must finally be mentioned here. On January 10, 1935, a law was passed requiring the possession

TABLE 8
BUDGET AND ACTIVITY OF NATIONAL, PROVINCIAL, DISTRICT, AND MUNICIPAL EMPLOYMENT OFFICES, 1934–1935 *

A. NATIONAL OFFICES

Names of Offices	Cost of Offices 1934–35 Budget (*lire*)	Placements Effected during 1934
National Employment Office for Rice Cleaners, Olive Pickers, and Grain Cutters	400,000	762,614
National Employment Office for Workers of the Stage	950,000	836,728

B. PROVINCIAL, DISTRICT, AND MUNICIPAL OFFICES

Offices in	Provincial Offices	District Offices	Municipal Offices	Cost of Offices, 1934–35 Budget (*lire*)	Number of Cases Handled by Offices	Cost per Case
Agriculture ..	93	...	1,981	7,679,545.30	9,435,964	.81
Industry	93	279	..	6,611,079.15	1,461,737	4.52
Commerce ..	93	59	..	2,834,084.15	192,626	14.71
Total	279	338	1,981	17,124,708.60	11,090,327	

* *Sindacato e corporazione*, March 1935, p. 764.

of a *libretto di lavoro* (work book) by all wage earners gainfully employed or seeking gainful employment. Registration at government employment offices is now possible only if such a work book (a laborer's passport, as it were, stating his background, training, experience, and past connections) can be produced.[29]

"DOPOLAVORO": THE NATIONAL LEISURE TIME ORGANIZATION

In addition to free governmental employment offices, other welfare organizations have been created by the Fascist government. The law of May 1, 1925, established the Opera

[29] *Sindacato e corporazione*, November 1934, p. 829; March 1935, p. 736.

Nazionale Dopolavoro, the National Leisure Time Organization. This institution, which represents one of the most characteristic achievements of the Fascist regime, is a semi-governmental organization combining thousands of clubs and societies of a sporting and educational nature, and aiming, as its name implies, at the promotion of activities which make

TABLE 9

ACTIVITIES AND MEMBERSHIP OF THE NATIONAL LEISURE TIME ORGANIZATION (OPERA NAZIONALE DOPOLAVORO), BY YEARS, 1926–1937 *

Year	Number of Dependent Cultural, Educational, and Welfare Organizations	Number of Educational, Cultural, and Sporting Events Organized	Total Membership
1926	1,064	6,337	280,584
1927	4,067	23,364	538,337
1928	7,254	52,876	882,589
1929	11,084	154,134	1,445,226
1930	14,427	525,117	1,622,140
1931	16,192	701,702	1,772,085
1932	17,809	946,173	1,775,570
1933	19,029	1,155,365	1,927,557
1934	20,322	1,394,993	2,108,227
1935	19,996	1,175,320	2,377,538
1936	19,554	1,288,174	2,785,779
1937	....	....	3,159,687

* Compiled from various issues of *Compendio statistico italiano*, *Sindacato e corporazione*, *Annuario statistico italiano*, and *Bollettino mensile di statistica*.

for a better utilization of the leisure time of Italian workers. The program of the organization, which has become increasingly popular, is carried out by providing, for a nominal membership fee, a wide variety of recreational facilities, ranging from significant reductions on railroad rates for week-end excursions to the organization of popular festivals, open-air motion picture programs, classes of physical and vocational education, and the organization of home-building societies and community restaurants.

The constant growth of the national Dopolavoro organization is illustrated by Table 9.

THE INSTITUTE FOR MATERNAL AND INFANT WELFARE

Another important social welfare institution, created by the law of December 10, 1925, is the Opera Nazionale per la Protezione della Maternità e dell' Infanzia, the National Institute for Maternal and Infant Welfare. The chief aim of this institute is to render assistance to mothers in the care of their young children. The help given ranges from free medical and hygienic assistance to the distribution of subsidies to the families of the poor. In 1936 a total of 126.8 million lire was spent for this work, and assistance of some form was given to over 1,600,000 persons.[30]

Finally, mention must be made of what is perhaps the most important institution of social welfare in Italy, that of social insurance.

Declarations XXVI and XXVII of the Charter of Labor state that

social insurance being another instance where the principle of class collaboration finds application, employers and workers must proportionately share its cost. In this field, the Fascist state proposes to achieve: the improvement of accident insurance; the improvement and extension of maternity insurance; the institution of insurance against occupational disease and tuberculosis as an approach to a general system of health insurance; the further improvement of unemployment insurance and the adoption of special forms of dowry insurance for young workers.

A great part of this program has already been put into effect. At present, every Italian worker is forced by law to carry accident, sickness, old-age, tuberculosis, and unemployment insurance. Women workers are, moreover, required to carry maternity insurance.

THE FASCIST INSTITUTE FOR SOCIAL INSURANCE

Beside the government-owned Istituto Nazionale delle Assicurazioni (National Insurance Institute) which underwrites life insurance in competition with commercial companies and occupies a preëminent position in the Italian insurance world,

[30] *Annuario statistico italiano*, 1937, p. 256.

two other governmental insurance institutions have been organized to carry out the government's program of compulsory social insurance: the Istituto Nazionale Fascista della Previdenza Sociale and the Istituto Nazionale Fascista per l'Assicurazione contro gli Infortuni sul Lavoro (the National Fascist Institute for Social Insurance and the National Fascist Institute for Accident Insurance).

The rapid development and present magnitude of the work of these government insurance organizations is shown by Table 10.

TABLE 10

DEVELOPMENT OF GOVERNMENT LIFE, OLD AGE, UNEMPLOYMENT, MATERNITY, TUBERCULOSIS, AND ACCIDENT INSURANCE, BY YEARS, 1922–1936 *

A. NATIONAL INSURANCE INSTITUTE (LIFE INSURANCE)

Year	Life Insurance in Force (*million lire*)	Year	Life Insurance in Force (*million lire*)
1922	4,150	1930	11,326
1923	4,595	1931	11,355
1924	5,474	1932	11,465
1925	6,674	1933	11,505
1926	7,935	1934	12,065
1927	9,071	1935	12,802
1928	10,044	1936	14,144
1929	10,726		

B. NATIONAL FASCIST INSTITUTE FOR SOCIAL INSURANCE

1. OLD AGE AND INVALIDITY INSURANCE

Year	Pensions in Force at End of Specified Year Number	Annual Amount (*in thousands of lire*)
1922	59,461	16,546
1923	69,856	21,105
1924	85,052	30,764
1925	104,822	40,718
1926	129,474	57,974
1927	150,464	72,132
1928	176,202	88,219
1929	207,065	144,355
1930	244,246	176,573
1931	275,505	212.066
1932	313,885	252,696
1933	353,553	293,765
1934	394,155	343,814
1935	427,683	365,366
1936	464,588	399,509

2. UNEMPLOYMENT INSURANCE

Year	Number of Persons Receiving Subsidies	Number of Daily Subsidies Paid (*in thousands*)	Amount (*thousands of lire*)
1922	....	16,175	67,357
1923	....	12,062	42,058
1924	154,290	6,156	24,110
1925	98,301	4,019	14,087
1926	167,752	6,331	22,365
1927	445,509	19,971	69,793
1928	419,232	18,971	65,345
1929	387,017	17,231	59,086
1930	594,686	29,547	101,874
1931	790,220	49,627	168,725
1932	931,414	55,468	186,212
1933	814,732	38,939	130,072
1934	774,583	36,441	116,814
1935	644,406	29,095	90,033
1936	858,419	39,271	122,496

3. MATERNITY INSURANCE

Year	Number of Persons Insured	Number of Subsidies Paid	Amount of Subsidies Paid (*thousands of lire*)
1923	675,465	34,991	3,499
1924	725,268	35,214	3,521
1925	822,028	37,187	3,719
1926	887,790	39,526	3,953
1927	873,502	40,343	4,034
1928	902,940	39,779	3,978
1929	955,485	41,273	4,127
1930	962,929	44,030	4,753
1931	1,220,035	35,839	5,323
1932	757,825	36,504	5,433
1933	839,770	35,212	5,235
1934	892,152	38,633	5,738
1935	990,921	42,792	6,610
1936	1,072,239	51,876	7,506

4. COMPULSORY TUBERCULOSIS INSURANCE

Year	Number of Persons Assisted	Amounts Paid (*thousands of lire*)
1929	18,421	31,529
1930	49,100	94,316
1931	62,693	124,246
1932	60,116	134,052
1933	57,268	138,074
1934	58,517	139,196
1935	61,159	140,257
1936	57,646	167,597

C. National Fascist Institute for Accident Insurance

Year	Average Number of Persons Insured (thousands)	Number of Accidents (thousands)	Indemnities Paid (thousands of lire)
1922	889.1	140.3	76,167
1923	941.2	141.9	63,059
1924	1,063.5	158.1	67,189
1925	1,167.6	182.0	83,537
1926	1,148.7	193.9	97,100
1927	1,216.9	212.4	120,801
1928	1,427.7	239.4	131,335
1929	1,890.8	323.7	167,291
1930	1,949.8	330.8	176,141
1931	1,917.7	302.0	160,471
1932	1,875.6	299.6	154,875
1933	1,973.2	323.3	173,114
1934	2,833.9	466.6	238,195
1935	3,150.8	512.0	275,185
1936	3,386.9	503.3	340,325

* Tables compiled from various issues of *Bollettino del lavoro e della previdenza sociale, Compendio statistico italiano, Annuario statistico italiano,* and *Sindacato e corporazione.*

THE NATIONAL INSTITUTE OF COÖPERATION

Mention must finally be made of the National Fascist Institute of Coöperation, a government organization established by the royal decree of December 30, 1926, for the purpose of assisting, coördinating, and developing the work of the coöperative and mutual aid societies, many of which, however, were begun and developed under Catholic and Socialist auspices long before 1922 and then simply taken over by the regime.

In 1934 this institute included 11,771 coöperative societies and 2,493 mutual aid societies, a total of 14,264 organizations embracing over 2 million members. The number and the relative importance of the several types of coöperative societies may be seen in this data: there were, in 1934, 3,860 consumers' coöperative societies whose annual sales totaled 1,600 million lire; 1,817 coöperatives "of production and work" with annual profits of 550 million lire; 835 agricultural coöperatives for purchases and sales with total sales of 1,120 million lire; 2,763 coöperatives for the processing of agricultural produce; 399 agricultural coöperatives with 115,000 hectares of land under cultivation; 1,239 building coöperatives with buildings valued at 2 billion lire; 305 coöperatives in the field of transportation with payrolls amounting to 50 million lire. In the same year there were also 553 agricultural mutual aid and insurance societies and 2,493 mutual aid societies.[31]

While several among the now existing Italian social welfare institutions were begun long before Fascism came into power, and while it is, of course, impossible to say what the trend of development of the social welfare and assistance activities would have been under a different political regime, it must be recognized that under Fascism social welfare has been in the forefront of public attention and that institutions of considerable benefit to the mass of the Italian people have been perfected or created *de novo*.

[31] *Sindacato e corporazione*, March 1935, p. 767.

CHAPTER V

THE REFORM OF 1934 AND THE PRESENT STRUCTURE OF THE ITALIAN CORPORATE STATE

PRELIMINARIES TO THE ESTABLISHMENT OF THE CATEGORY CORPORATIONS

FASCISM, till 1934, though tending clearly toward a "corporate" organization, was still in what Mussolini termed "the syndical phase." Until March 20, 1930, when the law on the reform of the National Council of Corporations was passed and the sections of the council were given the attributions and powers of corporate organs, no "corporation" as defined by the syndical laws of 1926 actually existed. After that date, even though empowered to act as corporations, the sections of the council continued to function primarily as council organs and did not have the autonomy and independence which were to be the main attributes of the true corporations. It was not until May 1933, when Mussolini declared that the time had come for the creation of the autonomous organs of economic coördination long provided for by Fascist legislation, that detailed plans for the establishment of the corporations were submitted by the government to the Central Corporate Committee. After discussion by the committee, the Fascist Grand Council, and the Parliament, the government's plans were formally enacted into law on February 5, 1934.[1]

[1] Cf. the condensed version of the law, in Appendix I, p. 323 ff. On November 13, 1933, the General Assembly of the National Council of Corporations signified its approval of the government's proposals by unanimously adopting the following resolution:

"The National Council of Corporations defines the corporation as the instrument which, under the aegis of the state, shall exercise organic and unitary control over the nation's productive forces with a view to furthering the growth of the wealth, the political power and the well-being of the Italian people; it declares that the number of corporations to be established within the various branches of national production shall be adequate to meet the needs of the national economy; it establishes that the directing organs of the corporations shall include representatives of the state, the Fascist party, capital, labor, and technical experts; it invests the corporations with powers of conciliation and

THE LAW OF FEBRUARY 5, 1934

The new law provides that a number of "category corporations" be established by governmental decree within the leading branches of national production. These category corporations are boards or councils composed of an equal number of representatives of workers' and employers' syndical associations and a small number of technical experts and representatives of the Fascist party.

THE OBJECTIVES OF THE CORPORATIONS DEFINED

The corporations have consultive, conciliatory, and normative powers. Whenever asked to do so by a government department, they offer advice on any economic matter within the field of their competence. All collective labor disputes which cannot be settled by syndical bargaining are brought before a corporate conciliation board for a further attempt at amicable settlement before being carried to the labor courts for final decision. Corporations are also empowered to enact rules "for the collective regulation of economic relations and the unitary discipline of national production." This includes not only the power to devise regulations for the control of production and the determination of rules of "fair" competition, but also "the fixing of rates for services rendered and of prices for articles of consumption sold to the public under noncompetitive conditions." [2]

The law provides, further, that all rules, rates, and agreements elaborated by the individual corporations must be approved by the National Council of Corporations before they

---

of consultation, and, through the National Council of Corporations, with the right to propose laws for the regulation of the economic life of the nation; it entrusts to the Grand Council of Fascism the task of deciding upon the constitutional changes which may be made necessary by the actual creation and functioning of the corporations."

[2] The chief object of this last sweeping provision was to extend the price control of the corporations to labor and to those services whose remuneration could not be determined by syndical agreement (such as services rendered directly to consumers) and to prices of commodities produced under conditions of special privilege, in which cases adequate protection of the interests of consumers is particularly necessary.

can assume the character and binding force of law. The presidency of the corporations is assigned to the Minister of Corporations; in practice, however, another presiding officer usually acts in behalf of the Minister, giving the latter freedom to take personal charge of the meetings only when exceptionally critical situations arise. Finally, Article 7 of the new law provides that the syndical associations united in a corporation shall become autonomous in their particular syndical field, but that they must still retain membership in their respective syndical confederations.

THE TWENTY-TWO CATEGORY CORPORATIONS ESTABLISHED

After a three months' period of preparation during which administrative details were being worked out by the Ministry of Corporations, the Central Corporate Committee met to consider the steps to be taken for the actual establishment of the new corporate organs. It decided that corporations be organized vertically, namely, that they include representatives of all economic activities involved in a complete production cycle, beginning with the processing of the raw material to the marketing of the finished product.

In accordance with this principle, a plan was drawn up for the establishment of twenty-two category corporations, divided into three groups, as follows:

    I.   Corporations representing branches of economic activity which involve agricultural, industrial and commercial operations.

   II.   Corporations representing economic activities involving industrial and commercial operations only.

 III.   Corporations representing enterprises established for the performance of services.

In May and June 1934, soon after formal approval for the establishment of the corporations had been given by the Central Corporate Committee, the royal decrees creating the new corporate bodies were published. These decrees provided for the establishment of twenty-two corporations divided into three major groups. These are listed below, and their membership indicated.[3]

GROUP I

I. *The Corporation of Grains*

A president and 36 members, including representatives of the Fascist Party (3); Grain Growers (7 employers', 7 workers'); Threshing Industry (1 employers', 1 workers'); Milling, Rice, Pasta, and Sweetmeat Industry (3 employers', 3 workers'); Bread-making Industry (1 employers', 1 workers'); Grain Trade (3 employers', 3 workers'); Consumers' Coöperative Societies (1); Agricultural Technicians (1); Artisans (1).

The number of employers' representatives includes three representatives of business executives, one for agriculture, one for industry, and one for commerce.

II. *The Corporation of Vegetable, Flower, and Fruit Growing*

A president and 32 members, including representatives of the Fascist Party (3); Vegetable, Flower, and Fruit Growing (6 employers', 6 workers'); Canned Vegetable Foodstuffs Manufacture (2 employers', 2 workers'); Manufacture of Citrus Fruit Derivatives and Essences (2 employers', 2 workers'); Trade in Flowers, Fruits, Vegetables, and their Derivatives (3 employers', 3 workers'); Agricultural Technicians (1); Chemists (1); Vegetable, Flower, and Fruit Exporters' Coöperatives (1).

The number of employers' representatives includes three representatives of business executives, one for agriculture, one for industry, and one for commerce.

III. *The Corporation of Viticulture and Wine Production*

A president and 32 members, including representatives of the Fascist Party (3); Winegrowers (6 employers', 6 workers'); Wine, Vinegar, and Liquor Industry (2 employers', 2 workers'); Beer and Allied Industries (1 employers', 1 workers'); Alcohol, 2nd category (1 employers', 1 workers'); Traders in Wine and Spirits (3 employers', 3 workers'); Agricultural Technicians (1); Chemists (1); Coöperative Winegrowers and Wineshops (1).

The number of employers' representatives includes three representatives of business executives, one for agriculture, one for industry, and one for commerce.

[3] The royal decrees establishing the eight corporations in Group I were issued on May 29, 1934; those establishing the eight corporations in Group II on June 9, and those establishing the six corporations in Group III on June 23, 1934. See *Sindacato e corporazione*, June 1934, pp. 1205 ff.

IV. *The Corporation of Edible Oils*

A president and 25 members, including representatives of the Fascist Party (3); Growers of Olives and Other Oil Producing Plants (5 employers', 5 workers'); Pressing and Refining of Olive Oil (2 employers', 2 workers'); Pressing and Refining of Seed Oils (1 employers', 1 workers'); Sulphur Oil Manufacture (1 employers', 1 workers'); Oil Merchants (1 employers', 1 workers'); Agricultural Technicians (1); Chemists (1).

The number of employers' representatives in agriculture and that of employers' representatives in industry includes one representative of business executives.

V. *The Corporation of Sugar Beets and Sugar*

A president and 15 members, including representatives of the Fascist Party (3); Beet-growing Industry (2 employers', 2 workers'); Sugar Industry (1 employers', 1 workers'); Alcohol Industry, 1st category (1 employers', 1 workers'); Trade in Beets, Beet Sugar, and Alcohol (1 employers', 1 workers'); Agricultural Technicians (1); Chemists (1).

VI. *The Corporation of Animal Husbandry and Fishing*

A president and 43 members, including representatives of the Fascist Party (3); Cattle Ranchers (8 employers', 8 workers'); Sea and Fresh Water Fisheries and Fish Curing Industry (2 employers', 2 workers'); Milk Industry (for direct consumption) (1 employers', 1 workers'); Dairy Products (2 employers', 2 workers'); Sausages and Canned Animal Foods Industry (2 employers', 2 workers'); Cattle Trade (1 employers', 1 workers'); Milk and Milk Products Trade (2 employers', 2 workers'); Agricultural Technicians (1); Veterinarians (1); Coöperative Dairies (1); Coöperative Fishermen's Societies (1).

The number of employers' representatives includes three representatives of business executives, one for agriculture, one for industry, and one for commerce.

VII. *The Corporation of Wood and Wood Products*

A president and 33 members, including representatives of the Fascist Party (3); Agriculturalists (2 employers', 2 workers'); Forestry and Timber Industry (2 employers', 2 workers'); Manufacture of Furniture and House Furnishings (2 employers', 2 workers'); Manufacture of Fixtures and Floors (1 employers', 1 workers'); Cork Manufacture (1 employers', 1 workers'); Miscellaneous Woodworking Industries (2 employers', 2 workers'); Wood Merchants (3 employers', 3 workers'); Forestry Experts (1); Artists (1); Artisans (2).

The number of employees' representatives in industry and that of employers' representatives in agriculture includes one representative of business executives.

VIII. *The Corporation of Textile Products*

A president and 58 members, including representatives of the Fascist Party (3); Cotton Industry (3 employers', 3 workers'); Wool-growing Industry (1 employers', 1 workers'); Woolens Industry (2 employers', 2 workers'); Silkworm Seed Industry (1 employers', 1 workers'); Mulberry Growing and Silkworm Breeding (1 employers', 1 workers'); Silk-drawing and Silk-throwing Industry (1 employers', 1 workers'); Rayon Industry (2 employers', 2 workers'); Silk and Rayon Weaving Industry (2 employers', 2 workers'); Production of Flax and Hemp (2 employers', 2 workers'); Flax and Hemp Working Industry (1 employers', 1 workers'); Jute Industry (1 employers', 1 workers'); Cloth Dyeing and Printing Industry (2 employers', 2 workers'); Miscellaneous Textile Industries (2 employers', 2 workers'); Wholesale and Retail Trade in Textile Products (3 employers', 3 workers'); Agricultural Technicians (1); Chemists (1); Textile Experts (1); Artists (1); Artisans (2); Cooperative Dyeing Establishments (1).

The number of employers' representatives includes three representatives of business executives, one for industry, one for agriculture, and one for commerce.

GROUP II

IX. *The Corporation of Building and Construction*

A president and 31 members, including representatives of the Fascist Party (3); Building Industry (private and public buildings) (4 employers', 4 workers'); Brick Industry (1 employers', 1 workers'); Cements Products Industry (1 employers', 1 workers'); Cement, Lime, and Chalk Industry (1 employers', 1 workers'); Fireproof Materials Industry (1 employers', 1 workers'); Trade in Building Materials (2 employers', 2 workers'); Real Estate Owners (1 employers', 1 workers'); Engineers (1); Architects (1); Surveyors (1); Building Experts (1); Artisans (1); Building Coöperatives (1).

The number of employers' representatives includes a representative of business executives.

X. *The Corporation of Metallurgy and Machinery*

A president and 67 members, including representatives of the Fascist Party (3); Iron-working Industry (3 employers', 3

workers'); Other Metal Industries (2 employers,' 2 workers');
Manufacturing of Transportation Material (motor cars, motorcycles, aeroplanes, railroad materials, shipbuilding) (5 employers', 5 workers'); Manufacturing of Radio Apparatus, and
Machinery for the Generation, Transformation, and Utilization
of Electricity (2 employers', 2 workers'); Manufacturing of
Industrial and Agricultural Machinery (3 employers', 3 workers'); Foundry and Metal-working Industry (4 employers', 4
workers'); Construction of Optical and Measuring Instruments,
Instruments of Precision, and Arms (2 employers', 2 workers');
Manufacture of Rubber Products (for industrial purposes)
(1 employers', 1 workers'); Manufacture of Leather Products
(for industrial purposes) (1 employers', 1 workers'); Manufacture of Cables and Insulating Cords (1 employers', 1 workers'); Goldsmiths and Silversmiths (1 employers' 1 workers');
Trade in the above-mentioned products (5 employers', 5 workers'); Engineers (1); Artisans (2); Agricultural Coöperatives
(1).

The number of employers' representatives includes two representatives of business executives, one for industry and one for
commerce.

XI.   *The Corporation of the Clothing Industry*

A president and 49 members, including representatives of the
Fascist Party (3); Clothing Industry (3 employers', 3 workers'); Fur Industry (1 employers', 1 workers'); Hat Manufacture (1 employers', 1 workers'); Boot and Shoe and Leather
Novelty Industry (2 employers', 2 workers'); Glove Manufacture (1 employers', 1 workers'); Manufacture of Rubber Goods
used in the Clothing Industry (1 employers', 1 workers'); Knit
Goods and Hosiery Manufacture (2 employers', 2 workers');
Lace, Embroidery, and Ribbon, Elastic Fabric, and Trimmings
Manufacture (2 employers', 2 workers'); Button Industry (2
employers', 2 workers'); Miscellaneous Clothing Accessories
(1 employers', 1 workers'); Umbrella Manufacture (1 employers', 1 workers'); Trade in products named above (4 employers',
4 workers'); Artisans (3); Artists (1).

The number of employers' representatives includes two representatives of business executives, one for industry and one for
commerce.

XII.   *The Corporation of Glass and Ceramics*

A president and 33 members, including representatives of the
Fascist Party (3); Artistic Pottery Industry (4 employers', 4

workers'); Bottles Industry (1 employers', 1 workers'); White Glass Industry (1 employers', 1 workers'); Window-pane Manufacture (1 employers', 1 workers'); Mirrors and Crystals Manufacture (1 employers', 1 workers'); Scientific and Optical Glass Manufacture (1 employers', 1 workers'); Artistic Glass and Beads Industry (1 employers', 1 workers'); Electric Lamp Industry (1 employers', 1 workers'); Trade in products mentioned above (2 employers', 2 workers'); Artisans (2); Artists (1); Coöperative Societies (1).

The number of employers' representatives includes one representative of business executives.

XIII. *The Corporation of the Chemical Industries*

A president and 68 members, including representatives of the Fascist Party (3); Inorganic Acids Industry and Manufacture of Alkalis, Chlorine, Compressed Gases and Other Inorganic Chemical Products (3 employers', 3 workers'); Manufacture of Chemicals Used in Agriculture (3 employers', 3 workers'); Organic Acids Industry and Manufacture of Other Organic Chemical Products (3 employers', 3 workers'); Explosives Industry (1 employers', 1 workers'); Phosphorus and Match Industry (1 employers', 1 workers'); Plastic Materials Industry (1 employers', 1 workers'); Synthetic Dyes, Synthetic Medicinal Products, and Chemicals Used in Photography (2 employers', 2 workers'); Mineral Colors, Varnishes, Inks, Shoe and Leather Polish Manufacture (2 employers', 2 workers'); Soap, Stearine, and Glycerine Industry (2 employers', 2 workers'); Tanning Extracts Industry (1 employers', 1 workers'); Tanning Industry (1 employers', 1 workers'); Synthetic Oils and Perfumes Industry (2 employers', 2 workers'); Mineral Oils Industry (2 employers', 2 workers'); Coal and Tar Distillation Industry (1 employers', 1 workers'); Pharmaceutical Industry (2 employers', 2 workers'); Trade in products named above (4 employers', 4 workers'); Chemists (1); Pharmacists (1); Agricultural Coöperatives (1).

The number of employers' representatives includes two representatives of business executives, one for industry and one for commerce.

XIV. *The Corporation of Paper and Printing*

A president and 30 members, including representatives of the Fascist Party (3); Paper Industry (2 employers', 2 workers'); Manufacture of Paperware (1 employers', 1 workers'); Printing Industry (2 employers', 2 workers'); Publishing Industry (2 employers', 2 workers'); Newspaper Industry (2 employers', 2 workers'); Trade in products named above (2 employers', 2 workers'); Artists (writers and authors, musicians, fine arts, journalists) (4); Artisans (1).

The number of employers' representatives in industry includes one representative of business executives.

XV. *The Corporation of the Extractive Industries*

A president and 26 members, including representatives of the Fascist Party (3); Metallic Minerals Industry (2 employers', 2 workers'); Sulphur and Pyrites Industry (2 employeers', 2 workers'); Coal Industry (1 employers', 1 workers'); Quarrying Industries (2 employers', 2 workers'); Marble and Stoneworking Industry (1 employers', 1 workers'); Trade in Mineral Products (2 employers', 2 workers'); Mining Engineers (1); Industrial Mining Experts (1); Artisans (1).

The number of employers' representatives in industry includes one representative of business executives.

XVI. *The Corporation of Water, Gas, and Electricity*

A president and 25 members, including representatives of the Fascist Party (3); Waterworks and Aqueducts (3 employers', 3 workers', of which one employers' and one workers' representative are from municipalized enterprises); Gas Works (3 employers', 3 workers', of which one employers' and one workers' representative are from municipalized enterprises); Electrical Industries (4 employers', 4 workers', of which one employers' and one workers' representative are from municipalized industries); Engineers (1); Coöperative Societies (1).

The number of employers' representatives includes one representative of business executives.

GROUP III

XVII. *The Corporation of the Professions and Arts*

A president and 40 members, including representatives of the Fascist Party (3); Counsellors-at-Law (3); Doctors in Economics (1); Notaries (1); Barristers (1); Commercial Experts (1); Accountants (1); Physicians (2); Pharmacists (1); Veterinarians (1); Trained Nurses (1); Midwives (1); Engineers (2); Architects (2); Agricultural Experts (2); Surveyors (1); Industrial Experts (1); Chemists (1); Actors and Writers (2); Painters and Sculptors (2); Journalists (1); Musicians (1); Private Educational Institutions (1); Private Teachers (1); Industrialists and Artisans in the Applied Arts (4, of which one is an employers' representative, one a workers' representative, and two representatives of artisans); Art Dealers (1 employers', 1 workers').

XVIII. *The Corporation of Internal Communications*

A president and 50 members, including representatives of the Fascist Party (3); Railways and Suburban Tramways (3 employers', 3 workers'); Urban Tramways (1 employers', 1 workers'); Cableways and Funicular Railways (2 employers', 2 workers'); Internal Navigation (2 employers', 2 workers'); Autobus Lines (2 employers', 2 workers'); Automobile Renting Agencies (1 employers', 1 workers'); Taxi Service (1 employers', 1 workers'); Motor Trucking Enterprises (1 employers', 1 workers'); Forwarding Agents (2 employers', 2 workers'); Harbor Forwarding Services (1 employers', 1 workers'); Horse Cart Transportation Services (1 employers', 1 workers'); Miscellaneous Supplementary Transportation Services (2 employers', 2 workers'); Telegraph, Telephone, Cable and Radio Communication Services (2 employers', 2 workers'); Artisans (couriers, drivers, etc.) (2); Transportation Coöperatives (1); Municipalized Transportation Enterprises (1 employers', 1 workers').

XIX. *The Corporation of Sea and Air Transportation*

A president and 24 members, including representatives of the Fascist Party (3); Merchant Marine: Passenger Transportation (4 employers', 4 workers'); Merchant Marine: Merchandise Transportation (3 employers', 3 workers'); Merchant Marine: Sailing Vessels (1 employers', 1 workers'); Air Transportation (2 employers', 2 workers'); Coöperatives (1).

The number of employers' representatives includes one representative of business executives.

XX. *The Corporation of the Tourist and Hotel Trade (Hospitality)*

A president and 20 members, including representatives of the Fascist Party (3); Hotels and Boarding Houses (2 employers', 2 workers'); Tourist Agencies and Bureaus (1 employers', 1 workers'); Restaurants, Coffee Houses, Bars, etc. (2 employers', 2 workers'); Artisans connected with Hospitality Services (1 employers', 1 workers'); Private Hospitals (1 employers', 1 workers'); Thermal Establishments and Spas (1 employers', 1 workers'); Physicians (1).

The number of employers' representatives for commercial enterprises includes one representative of business executives.

XXI. *The Corporation of Credit and Insurance*

A president and 52 members, including representatives of the Fascist Party (3); Ordinary Credit Institutions (2); Provincial Banking Institutions (1); Financial Institutions (1); Private Bankers (1); Foreign Exchange Dealers (1); Stock Brokers (1); Bank Executives (1); Bank Employees (7); Foreign Exchange Dealers' Employees (1); Ordinary Savings Banks (4); Public Credit Institutions subject to the supervision of the Finance Ministry (2); Agricultural Credit Institutions (1); "Monti di Pietà" — public pawnbrokers (2); Public Credit Institutions' Employees (3); People's Coöperative Banks (1); Agricultural Banks (1); Employees of People's and Agricultural Banks (2); Private Insurance Companies (2); Insurance Company Executives (1); Employees of Insurance Companies (3); Insurance Agents (1); Insurance Agents' Employees (1); Employees of Public Insurance Institutions (1); Mutual Insurance Enterprises (1); The Governor of the Bank of Italy (1); The President of the Industrial Reconstruction Institute (1); The President of the Istituto Mobiliare Italiano (1); The President of the Association of Italian Joint Stock Companies (1); The President of the National Insurance Institute (1); The President of the National Fascist Institute of Social Insurance (1); The President of the National Fascist Accident Insurance Institute (1).

XXII. *The Corporation of the Theater and of Public Entertainment*

A president and 34 members, including representatives of the Fascist Party (3); Theater and Motion Picture Theater Operators (2 employers', 2 workers'); Producers: Opera and Operetta Producers (2), Concert Managers (1), Dramatic Producers (1), Radio Broadcasting (1); Workers: Singers (1), Dramatic Artists (1), Orchestra Players (1), Band Players (1), Stage Directors and Technicians (1); Allied Industries (stage equipment, recording, etc.) (1 employers', 1 workers'); Motion Picture Producers (1 employers', 1 workers'); Film Renting Establishments (1 employers', 1 workers'); Producers of Sporting Events (1 employers', 1 workers'); Publishers (2); Musicians (2); Playwrights and Motion Picture Script Writers (2); The President of the Italian Society of Authors and Publishers (1); The President of the National Institute L. U. C. E. (1); The President of the Opera Nazionale Dopolavoro (1).

The number of industrial employers' representatives includes one representative of business executives.

A summary of the numbers and the different classes of members in each corporation described above is given in Table 11. An interesting feature of this new organization is the fact that out of a total of 824 members in all these corporations, five are women. They represent the silk and cocoon workers, dressmakers, glove factory workers, trained nurses, and midwives. This is the first instance in the history of Fascist syndicalism of the admission of women to membership in a body of national importance.

The establishment of the twenty-two category corporations undoubtedly represents the most important step taken so far toward industrial self-government in Italy. Composed of the direct representatives of employers, workers, and the Fascist party, the category corporations, Fascists maintain, are destined to become the agencies through which organic self-discipline in the productive process, in thorough harmony with the political and economic interests of the Italian nation, will ultimately be achieved.

The fundamental functions with which the corporations are invested are described in some of the addresses of the head of the Italian government. On November 14, 1933, at the conclusion of the debate on the corporations in the General Assembly of the National Council of Corporations, Premier Mussolini referred to the new corporate organs as the agencies which will aid in expanding "the wealth, the political power, and the well-being of the Italian people" and as the instruments "through which Italy's laboring classes will improve their standard of living." [4] On October 6, 1934, about four months after their establishment, Mussolini told several thousand Fascist workers gathered at Milan that

the present crisis means the end of liberal capitalism, the economic system which emphasizes the individual profit motive, and marks the beginning of a new economy which stresses collective interests. These collective interests [the Premier said] will be achieved . . . through the corporate system which is based upon the self-regulation of production under the aegis of the producers. . . . When I say producers, I do not mean only employers, I mean workers

---

[4] *Sindacato e corporazione*, November 1933, p. 671.

TABLE 11

ORGANIZATION AND MEMBERSHIP OF THE TWENTY-TWO CATEGORY CORPORATIONS, DECEMBER 31, 1936 *

CORPORATIONS	NUMBER OF REPRESENTATIVES								
	Employers	Workers	Technical Experts	Artisans	Coöperatives	Public Institutions	Professional Men and Artists	Fascist Party	Total
Group I									
1. Grains	15	15	1	1	1	.	.	3	36
2. Vegetable, Flower, and Fruit Growing	13	13	2	.	1	.	.	3	32
3. Viticulture and Wine Production	13	13	3	.	.	.	.	3	32
4. Edible Oils	10	10	2	.	.	.	.	3	25
5. Sugar Beets and Sugar	5	5	2	.	.	.	.	3	15
6. Animal Husbandry and Fishing	18	18	3	.	1	.	.	3	43
7. Wood and Wood Products	13	13	2	2	.	.	.	3	33
8. Textile Products	24	24	4	2	1	.	.	3	58
Group II									
9. Building and Construction	11	11	4	1	1	.	.	3	31
10. Metallurgy and Machinery	30	30	1	2	1	.	.	3	67
11. Clothing Industry	21	21	1	3	.	.	.	3	49
12. Glass and Ceramics	13	13	1	2	1	.	.	3	33
13. Chemical Industries	31	31	2	.	1	.	.	3	68
14. Paper and Printing	11	11	.	1	.	.	4	3	30
15. Extractive Industries	10	10	2	1	.	.	.	3	26
16. Water, Gas, and Electricity	10	10	1	.	1	.	.	3	25

Group III

	C1	C2	C3	C4	C5	C6	C7	C8	Total
17. The Professions and Arts									
Legal Section							8	3	41
Medical Section							6		
Technical Section			3‡				9		
Arts Section	2			2			8		
18. Internal Navigation									
Section of Tramways and Internal Communication	8	8						3	50
Section of Motor Transportation	5	5							
Section of Transportation Auxiliaries	6	6	2	2	1				
Section of Telephone, Radio, etc.	2	2							
19. Sea and Air Transportation	10	10						3	24
20. The Tourist and Hotel Trade	8	8	1		1			3	20
21. Credit and Insurance									
Section of Banking	8	8				4		3	52
Section of Savings Institutions	5†	2				9			
Section of Insurance	5	5				3			
22. Theater and Public Entertainment	11	11				3	6	3	34
Total	318	316	34	19	11	19	41	66	824

* *Annuario statistico italiano*, 1937, p. 167.

† Three represent public employers.

‡ Two are representatives of workers in the Arts section and one of workers in professional men's offices. The latter is a member of each of the four sections and was included by decree of the Head of the Government dated March 20, 1936.

also. . . . Speaking to the people of Bari I said that the economic objective of the Fascist regime is greater social justice for the Italian people. What do I mean by greater social justice? I mean the guarantee of work, a fair wage, a decorous home, I mean the possibility of evolution and betterment. . . . If modern science has solved the problem of multiplying wealth, science, spurred on by the state, must now solve the other great problem, that of the distribution of wealth, so that the illogical, paradoxical, and cruel phenomenon of want in the midst of plenty shall not be repeated. Toward this great goal all our energies and all our efforts must be bent.[5]

On November 10, 1934, in a solemn ceremony in the great hall of Julius Caesar on the Roman Capitol, the members of the twenty-two corporations were officially inducted into office. On that occasion Mussolini again described the inadequacy of the present distributive system and defined social justice as the fundamental aim of the Fascist corporation.

In this age of ours [the Premier declared] the inevitability of material misery can no longer be admitted . . . ; the absurdity of artificial famines must last no longer . . . ; the existence of these is incontrovertible proof of the inadequacy of the present distributive system. . . . The past century has proclaimed the equality of all citizens before the law — and that was a tremendous conquest. To this cardinal principle Fascism adds another: that of the equality of all men with respect to labor, understood as a duty and as a right, as joy in creative effort destined to expand and ennoble man's existence rather than to embitter and depress it. . . . Today a great new system begins its work. No immediate miracles must be expected from it. We must, rather, prepare ourselves for a more or less lengthy experimental period . . . ; as for actual results, we shall ultimately have to count not only upon the efficacy of institutions but also on the changes which will be wrought in man's mentality. . . .[6]

THE CATEGORY CORPORATIONS AT WORK

Soon after their establishment, agenda listing the first subjects for discussion by the new corporate bodies were prepared. The following list indicates the nature of the topics included:

Corporation of Grains: Discussion of a standardized contract for the sale of flour; regulations for the distribution and sale of bread; regulations for wheat markets, the flour industry, etc.

[5] *Sindacato e corporazione*, October 1934, p. 469.
[6] *Sindacato e corporazione*, November 1934, p. 733.

Corporation of Textile Products: Encouragement of the silk industry with special regard to exports; changes in the cotton industry necessitated by Japanese competition; use of hemp and other national textile fibres in place of imported materials; new regulations on the retail trade in yarns, etc.

Corporation of the Clothing Industry: Regulations on apprenticeship in the clothing business; home work in the clothing trades — the hat- and glove-making industries and their position in the export field; coöperation between the clothing and the textile industries with a view to increasing the use of domestic raw materials, etc.

Corporation of the Professions and Arts: Regulations on accountants' fees, publishers' fees, etc.

Corporation of Sea and Air Transportation: The mercantile marine and the development of export trade; ratification of the conventions of Brussels on the responsibility of shipowners; coördination of air transport with transportation by sea, rail, and motor; establishment of vocational schools for pilots, etc.

Corporation of Edible Oils: Relations between the olive oil and seed oil industries; discussion of an official classification of olive oils, etc.

Corporation of Vegetable, Flower, and Fruit Growing: Limitation and localization of cultivation; standardization of vegetable products; grading and packing of vegetables and exhibition on export markets; new industrial uses of citrus fruits; producer and dealer contracts, etc.

As these agenda indicate, the Fascist corporations, when they actually began to function, were, in practice, little more than advisory organs bringing together representatives of the employers, workers, and the Fascist party for the discussion of the problems affecting the various branches of national production. The regulation of economic relations on a national scale which was to be the fundamental objective of the new corporate organs was, at the time, not attempted.[7]

THE REORGANIZATION OF THE FASCIST SYNDICAL SYSTEM

Immediately after the establishment of the category corporations, the government made detailed plans for a reorganization of the syndical system. This was made necessary by Art. 7 of the law of February 5, 1934, which, as we have

[7] More recently, however, interesting steps have been taken in that direction. For a more detailed discussion of the work of the category corporations and a critique of their activities, cf. chap. vi, pp. 144 ff.

noted, provided that syndical associations united in a corporation should become autonomous in the syndical field, though continuing to be members of their respective syndical confederations. This meant essentially that all collective labor contracts and other agreements formerly negotiated through the confederations were now to be concluded freely and independently among the various workers' and employers' federations. The detailed plans made for the syndical reorganization by the Ministry of Corporations and by the various employers' and workers' confederations were approved by the Central Corporate Committee on June 30, 1934. On August 16, 1934, a series of royal decrees was published, specifying the legal norms upon which the syndical reform was to be based.

PRESENT FUNCTIONS AND ORGANIZATION OF SYNDICAL ASSOCIATIONS

The leading features of this reform and the present organization of the Fascist syndical system may be briefly summarized as follows: [8]

(1) The federations of syndical associations (national associations grouping together individual syndicates within the larger occupational groups) are granted full legal recognition and autonomy. In any deliberations affecting the interests of the occupational group which they represent, federations may consequently participate as independent legal entities rather than as members of a given confederation, as was the case previously. Local, provincial, and inter-provincial syndical associations, through which national federations carry on their local activities, are not given any legal recognition. They are now regarded merely as local organs of the national federations with which they are affiliated and under whose immediate jurisdiction they are now placed.

(2) All collective labor contracts and other agreements formerly negotiated through the confederations are now concluded directly by the workers' and employers' federations.

[8] For an exhaustive discussion of the details of the reorganization of the Italian syndical system, see *Sindacato e corporazione*, September 1934, pp. 309 ff.

The law provides, however, that a copy of an agreement already made must be sent to the competent confederation, which must provide for its transmission to the proper government authorities and for its publication. Workers' and employers' federations are thus free to negotiate collective labor agreements independently, to provide educational and social assistance to their members, and, in general, to deal directly with all problems and questions of interest to the occupational groups which they represent.

(3) Although shorn of many of their former powers, the confederations of syndical associations continue in existence, primarily as organs for the coördination of the work of the autonomous federations. This coördination, exercised particularly in the field of social welfare, social assistance, and education, is effected by the offices of the confederations (to which legal recognition is given) in the capital, and by the provincial and inter-provincial unions of syndical associations (which have lost their autonomy and legal recognition and have become local offices of the confederations) in the various provinces of the kingdom. Confederations are also empowered to represent the collective interests of the large branches of national production within which they have been formed, to organize such economic and other services as can be used in common by the various syndical associations within their field, and to control the financial administration of all the syndical associations affiliated with them.

To facilitate the efficient performance of these new functions the number of confederations was reduced from thirteen to nine. Workers' and employers' confederations of land transportation and sea and air transportation were eliminated and the whole syndical system rearranged into the following five broad groups: industry, commerce, agriculture, credit and insurance, and professional men and artists. Syndical associations within the first four groups were organized into separate employers' and workers' confederations. In the fifth group, that of professional men and artists, no division into employers and workers is possible. No change was made, consequently, and the status of the large number of syndicates enjoying full autonomy and legal recognition affiliated with this confederation remains unchanged.

(4) The internal organization of the autonomous federations of syndical associations now consists of a general assembly, a council, an executive committee, and a president or secretary.[9]

The general assembly is constituted as follows: local assemblies of the members of all affiliated syndical associations elect representatives; within each province the provincial assembly of these representatives elects the president or the secretary of the provincial syndicate; the secretaries or presidents of all provincial syndicates in turn constitute the general assembly of the national federation. This general assembly (a large body ordinarily convened only once every three years) is empowered to discuss and express opinions on all questions of interest to the members of the federation, to approve the policies of the leaders of the organization and to elect the members of the federation's council.

The council meets once a year and is composed of a number of members sufficient to permit adequate representation of all syndical and occupational groups included in the federation. It elects, from among its own members, the members of the executive committee and, for each fiscal year, a board entrusted with the auditing of the federation's accounts. The council discusses the annual reports of the executive committee and gives its opinion on such questions as the committee chooses to submit to it for consideration.

The executive committee of the federation is composed of a limited number of members. It is entrusted with the active management of the federation, the preparation of the annual budget, the discussion of policies in negotiation of collective labor agreements, and the appointment of representatives to all organizations and bodies (such as the corporations) in which the federations have a legal right to be represented.

---

[9] The official title of the chief executive of a national federation of employers' associations is "president"; that of the chief executive of a federation of workers' associations is "secretary," a title which has long been traditional for executives of workers' syndicates.

The chief executive officer of the federation is the president or secretary; he is elected by the general assembly and, like all other members of the council and the executive committee, holds office for a period of three years.

(5) The internal organization of the confederations of syndical associations is similar to that of the national federations. The confederation also has a council, an executive committee and a president. The council, which ordinarily meets only once a year, is composed of the presidents or secretaries of the affiliated national federations. It nominates the president of the confederation (whose final appointment, however, is made by the government), elects the members of the executive committee and the board of auditors, and discusses and approves the annual reports of the president and the executive committee.

The executive committee, a small body elected by the council, advises on all questions of ordinary administration and nominates the representatives which the confederation is entitled to send to other administrative bodies within the syndical structure.[10]

(6) As in the past, the elections and appointments of all officers of syndical associations, federations, and confederations must be approved by the Ministry of Corporations. This ministry maintains a close contact with the national and provincial organizations of the Fascist party, and, through the information thus obtained, is in a position to prevent the appointment of persons lacking the moral and political qualities (faith in Fascist ideals and devotion to the Fascist cause) which, according to Fascist law, are required of anyone holding office in the syndical system.

[10] Most federations elected their councils and presidents in October 1934. During that month were also selected the presidents of several national confederations. At the meeting of the council of the Confederation of Italian Industry, held during that month, the government-appointed commissioner, Signor Pirelli, resigned, and Count Volpi di Misurata, former Italian Finance Minister and one of the leading figures in Italian industry, was selected by the members for the presidency of the confederation. See *Sindacato e corporazione*, November 1934, p. 764.

ITALIAN SYNDICALISM TODAY

After the enactment of the decrees of August 16, 1934, providing for the reorganization of the syndical structure, the total number of legally recognized syndical bodies, which on September 1, 1934 (when the August decrees went into force), was 1,805, was reduced to 1,201. It is of interest to note that of this total, 1,052 associations belonged to the Confederation of Professional Men and Artists. The distribution of the total number of legally recognized syndical associations existing in Italy on December 31, 1936, is shown by Table 12.

The legally recognized syndical associations established by the royal decrees of August 16, 1934, and altered somewhat since but still in existence, are the following: [11]

I. *The Confederation of Agriculturists*, including the national federations of: (1) landlords and tenant farmers; (2) landlords with leased lands; (3) landowners and tenant cultivators on own account; (4) managers of farming enterprises.

II. *The Confederation of Workers in Agriculture*, including the national federations of: (1) technical and administrative employees on farms and forestry enterprises; (2) share-tenants and métayers; (3) wage earners and day laborers; (4) specialists in agriculture, animal husbandry, and forestry.

III. *The Confederation of Industrialists*, including the national federations of: (1) clothing manufacturers; (2) boot and shoe manufacturers and producers of leather goods; (3) hat manufacturers; (4) tanners; (5) manufacturers of cotton goods; (6) manufacturers of woolen goods; (7) manufacturers of silks; (8) manufacturers of artificial textile fibres and their products; (9) manufacturers of miscellaneous textile fabrics; (10) building contractors; (11) real-estate owners; (12) manufacturers of cement, lime, chalk, and cement ware; (13) manufacturers of earthenware and bricks; (14) manufacturers of glass and glassware; (15) manufacturers of chemical products; (16) manufacturers of foodstuffs and allied

[11] Cf. *Sindacato e corporazione*, September 1934, pp. 309 ff., and Ministry of Corporations, *News Notes on Fascist Corporations* (Rome), August–September 1934.

TABLE 12

NUMBER OF LEGALLY RECOGNIZED SYNDICAL ASSOCIATIONS IN EXISTENCE, DECEMBER 31, 1936 *

Fascist Confederations	LEGALLY RECOGNIZED ASSOCIATIONS					INTERNAL ORGANIZATION (AS OF NOVEMBER 1, 1934) Occupational Associations (Syndicates)		
	National Associations		Syndi-cates	Local Associations (Syndicates)	Provincial & Inter-provincial Unions	National	Inter-provincial	Provincial
	Confedera-tions	Federa-tions						
Employers								
The Fascist Confederations of:								
1. Industrialists	1	45	..	..	92	..	38	3,600
2. Agriculturists	1	5	..	..	92	..	..	343
3. Merchants	1	37	..	..	92	..	..	2,652
4. Credit and Insurance	1	13	..	..	13	..	52	..
Total	4	100	..	..	289	..	90	6,595
Workers								
The Fascist Confederations of Workers in:								
5. Industry	1	20	9	..	92	..	31	4,024
6. Agriculture	1	4	..	..	92	..	..	368
7. Commerce	1	5	..	..	92	8	..	1,309
8. Credit and Insurance enterprises ..	1	4	..	..	13	11	52	125
Total	4	33	9	..	289	19	83	5,826
Professional Men and Artists								
9. The Fascist Confederation of Professional Men and Artists	1	..	22	1,043	92	..	..	..
Grand Total	9	133	31	1,043	670	19	173	12,421

* *Compendio statistico italiano*, 1934, p. 169, and *Annuario statistico italiano*, 1937, p. 167.

products; (17) manufacturers of soft drinks, beer, malt, and ice cream; (18) millers, manufacturers of alimentary paste, and persons engaged in the rice and threshing industries; (19) persons engaged in the fishing industry; (20) manufacturers of wine, liquors, and similar products; (21) manufacturers of sugar, candy, and similar products; (22) metallurgical industries; (23) the timber industry; (24) electrical engineers; (25) gas and water works; (26) paper manufacturers; (27) printers and allied industries; (28) the publishing industry; (29) the hydro-thermal industry; (30) the rubber industry and manufacturers of electrical cables, plastic substances, and similar products; (31) manufacturers of artistic objects and of wearing apparel and house-furnishing accessories; (32) the mining and quarry industry; (33) newspaper publishers; (34) theatrical producers; (35) municipalized industrial enterprises; (36) maritime transportation and auxiliary services; (37) air transportation; (38) railway, tramway, and internal navigation enterprises; (39) motor transportation; (40) municipalized transportation enterprises; (41) electrical communication industries; (42) auxiliary transportation industries; (43) private educational institutions; (44) industrial business executives; (45) artisans.

IV. *The Confederation of Workers in Industry*, including the national federations of workers in: (1) the clothing industry; (2) the water, gas, and electricity industries; (3) the food-products industry; (4) the house-furnishing industry; (5) the paper and printing industry; (6) the chemical industry; (7) the building industry; (8) the mining and quarrying industry; (9) the mechanical and metallurgical industry; (10) the fishing industry; (11) the textile industry; (12) the glass and ceramics industry; (13) the electrical communications industry; (14) the national federation of motor, railroad, and street car workers and of workers in internal navigation enterprises; (15) the national federation of motor car and truck drivers; (16) the national federation of longshoremen; (17) the national federation of workers in auxiliary transportation enterprises; (18) the national federation of seamen; (19) the national federation of aviators; (20) the national federation of workers in the theater and motion-picture industry. Affiliated with this national federation (20) are the legally recognized national syndicates of: (a) the operatic stage; (b) the dramatic stage; (c) light opera and vaudeville; (d) sports professionals; (e) motion-picture actors and technicians; (f) stage technicians; (g) orchestra and band players; (h) administrative and technical theater workers; (i) stage hands.

V. *The Confederation of Merchants*, including the national federations of: (1) grain, vegetable and fodder merchants; (2) bakers and allied lines; (3) dealers in fruits and vegetables; (4) coal and other solid fuel merchants; (5) dealers in arts and crafts products; (6) hotel and tourist agencies; (7) restaurants and allied enterprises; (8) commercial representatives and agents; (9) retailers of monopolized articles; (10) flower merchants; (11) wine merchants and dealers in allied products; (12) oil merchants; (13) druggists; (14) cattle and meat merchants; (15) dealers in milk and its by-products; (16) fish dealers; (17) dealers in preserved meats and allied foodstuffs; (18) dealers in wood, furniture, and allied products; (19) dealers in textile products; (20) clothing merchants; (21) book dealers and paper merchants; (22) goldsmiths and silversmiths; (23) dealers in motor cars, motorcycles, and accessories; (24) dealers in iron, other metals, machinery, and allied products; (25) dealers in furs, leather, and allied products; (26) dealers in chemical products; (27) dealers in fertilizers and agricultural machinery; (28) dealers in building materials; (29) dealers in glass and earthenware; (30) dealers in mineral oil, carburants, and lubricants; (31) forwarding agents; (32) auxiliary commercial services; (33) general public warehouse owners; (34) firms engaged in overseas trade; (35) private hospitals; (36) peddlers and street vendors; (37) managers of commercial enterprises.

VI. *The Confederation of Workers in Commercial Enterprises*, including the national federations of workers in: (1) warehouses and retail and forwarding establishments; (2) the foodstuffs trade; (3) the hotel and tourist trade; (4) the national Fascist federation of employees of professional men; (5) the national Fascist federation of janitors and superintendents.

VII. *The Confederation of Credit and Insurance Enterprises,* including the national federations of: (1) national credit institutions; (2) provincial credit institutions; (3) private bankers; (4) financial institutions; (5) stock exchange brokers; (6) foreign exchange brokers; (7) insurance brokers and agents; (8) insurance companies; (9) tax collectors; (10) contractors for the collection of excise and similar taxes; (11) people's banks; (12) agricultural and land banks and auxiliary organizations; (13) executives of banks and insurance companies.

VIII. *The Confederation of Workers in Credit and Insurance Enterprises,* including the national federations of: (1) executives of credit, insurance, and tax collecting enterprises; (2) workers in credit institutions; (3) workers in insurance companies; (4) workers employed by tax collectors.

IX. *The Confederation of Professional Men and Artists,* including the national Fascist syndicates of: (1) physicians (with 92 provincial syndicates); (2) pharmacists (with 92 provincial syndicates); (3) veterinarians (including an inter-provincial syndicate for the provinces of Ancona and Zara and 90 provincial syndicates); (4) midwives (with 92 provincial syndicates); (5) engineers (with 92 provincial syndicates); (6) architects (with 18 inter-provincial syndicates); (7) surveyors (with 92 provincial syndicates); (8) industrial experts (with 18 inter-provincial syndicates); (9) commercial experts (with 18 inter-provincial syndicates); (10) chemists (with 18 inter-provincial syndicates); (11) attorneys and counsellors-at-law (including 137 syndicates with jurisdictions corresponding to those of the respective courts); (12) notaries (with 24 district syndicates); (13) legal advocates (with 24 district syndicates); (14) doctors of economics and commercial science (with 18 inter-provincial syndicates); (15) accountants (with 18 inter-provincial syndicates); (16) journalists (with 11 inter-provincial syndicates); (17) private

TABLE 13
REPRESENTATION AND MEMBERSHIP OF FASCIST SYNDICAL ASSOCIATIONS, DECEMBER 31, 1934, 1935, 1936 *

Confederations	DECEMBER 31, 1934		DECEMBER 31, 1935		DECEMBER 31, 1936	
	Number Represented	Number of Actual Members	Number Represented	Number of Actual Members	Number Represented	Number of Actual Members
Employers						
Industrialists	157,596†	86,855†	158,704†	83,059†	157,334	82,380
Artisans	723,605	211,263	765,073	282,796	731,562	272,065
Owners of Real Estate (Buildings) .	3,520,000	120,948	4,289,350	91,980	4,343,510	91,557
Agriculturists	2,658,266	712,697	3,828,254	845,171	3,850,352	873,500
Merchants	724,574	390,684	907,065	550,829	886,024	590,136
Credit and Insurance Enterprises ...	15,560‡	8,269‡	15,158‡	8,571‡	15,036	8,367
Total	7,799,601	1,530,716	9,963,604	1,862,406	9,983,818	1,918,005
Workers						
Industry	3,313,382	2,086,951	3,376,229	2,204,275	3,570,462	2,387,521
Agriculture	2,744,072	2,023,750	2,790,145	2,197,199	2,790,145	2,392,748
Commerce	868,196	431,633	868,196	404,495	537,164	431,530
Credit and Insurance Enterprises	54,573	37,823	61,918	45,755	61,019	47,678
Total	6,980,223	4,580,157	7,096,488	4,851,724	6,958,790	5,259,477
Professional Men and Artists	170,564	117,862	171,249	121,553	188,478	119,107
Grand Total	7,150,787	4,698,019	7,267,737	4,973,277	7,147,268	5,378,584

* *Sindacato e corporazione*, February 1935, p. 336, April 1936, p. 425, April 1937, p. 729.

† These figures include industrial business executives, viz., total number of executives in 1934: 10,255; actual members, 6,500; in 1935: 10,255 represented, 7,011 actual members.

‡ These figures include bank and insurance executives, viz., total number of executives represented in 1934: 1,318; actual members, 662; in 1935: 1,323 represented, 849 actual members.

teachers (with 18 inter-provincial syndicates); (18) trained nurses (with 9 inter-provincial syndicates); (19) agricultural technicians (with 92 provincial syndicates); (20) authors and writers (with 18 inter-provincial syndicates); (21) musicians (with 18 inter-provincial syndicates); (22) fine arts (with 18 inter-provincial syndicates).

The national Fascist federations of coöperative societies named below belong to the National Fascist Coöperative Group as well as to the confederations of enterprises of their kind: (1) the federation of coöperatives among farm workers; (2) the federation of coöperative societies for the processing of agricultural products; (3) the federation of coöperatives for production and work; (4) the federation of coöperative building enterprises; (5) the federation of coöperative transportation enterprises; (6) the federation of farmers' coöperatives for purchasing and marketing; (7) the federation of consumers' coöperatives; (8) the federation of agricultural coöperatives for live-stock insurance.

The number of employers and workers represented and the actual membership in the reorganized syndical system described in the preceding pages are shown by Table 13, which gives the latest available statistical data on the subject.[12]

A convenient summary of the organization and structure of the Italian corporate system, finally, is given in Chart III, which indicates graphically the relative position of its various organs as they exist in Italy today.

---

[12] Cf. the data on the membership of the Fascist syndical system from 1926 to 1933, in Appendix II, pp. 330 ff.

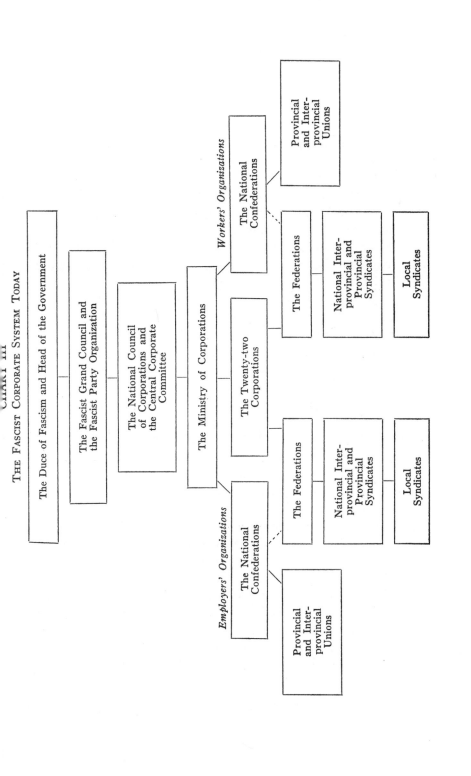

CHART III

THE FASCIST CORPORATE SYSTEM TODAY

The Duce of Fascism and Head of the Government

The Fascist Grand Council and the Fascist Party Organization

The National Council of Corporations and the Central Corporate Committee

The Ministry of Corporations

The Twenty-two Corporations

Employers' Organizations

The National Confederations

Provincial and Inter-provincial Unions

The Federations

National Inter-provincial and Provincial Syndicates

Local Syndicates

Workers' Organizations

The National Confederations

Provincial and Inter-provincial Unions

The Federations

National Inter-provincial and Provincial Syndicates

Local Syndicates

CHAPTER VI

A CRITIQUE OF THE FASCIST SYNDICAL AND CORPORATE SYSTEM

THE CORPORATE SYSTEM IN ACTION: THE POLITICAL ATMOSPHERE

OUR description of the growth of the Fascist syndical and corporate system is now complete, and we must turn to a critical evaluation of it as it functions in Italy today. We may best begin by describing the political atmosphere in which the system actually operates.

As we have noted, in 1925, after the Matteotti affair, the Fascist state became "totalitarian," that is, thoroughly, integrally Fascist.[1] All political parties at variance with Fascism were suppressed; freedom of speech in things political was prohibited; anti-Fascist newspapers and periodicals were silenced, and the loyal press was placed under the close supervision of the government press bureau; at the same time all individual or collective attempts at publicity unfavorable to the government were forbidden, anti-Fascist associations dissolved, and anti-Fascist individuals who caused annoyance to the regime were imprisoned or sent to the *confino*. It was made quite plain to the people at large that the Fascist state, as one author puts it, "will stand no nonsense from its adversaries." [2] In return for this surrender of individual freedom the Fascists promised the people a strong and energetic government, which, unhampered by political opposition, would deal ably and aggressively with the problems confronting the nation.

While opposition to the regime has been thus effectively silenced, every effort is now made to strengthen the people's faith in Fascism and their willingness to support the Fascist government. "High ideal tension," as Mussolini calls the Italians' collective enthusiasm for the Fascist cause,[3] is kept

---

[1] Cf. chap. i, pp. 19 ff.
[2] Finer, *Mussolini's Italy*, p. 243. [3] See chap. ii, p. 38.

alive by constant preaching of the Fascist gospel of fervid nationalism and "faith" in the Fascist state; all the modern means of propaganda — the press, the radio, the cinema — are constantly and liberally used in reminding the masses of the virtues of the Duce and of the merits and achievements of the Fascist regime.

THE FASCIST PARTY

The Fascist party, an organization whose importance in present-day Italy can hardly be overestimated, is the agency entrusted with the direction of this unceasing propaganda.[4] Its general functions and relations to the Fascist state are fundamental for a clear understanding of the transformation brought about by the new regime in contemporary Italian life.

Party and state are, in present-day Italy, indissolubly linked. The one cannot exist in its present form without the other. The party is the dynamo, as it were, from which the state derives its energies and its power; and it, in turn, is responsible for the proper management of the state. As one author puts it: "Mussolini would not possess the State if he could not possess the Party and he would lose the Party if, possessing the State, he governed it incompetently. The leadership of the Party and the management of the State are indissolubly connected." [5] The leader of the party, then, holds supreme and absolute authority in Italy today. All the governmental, syndical, and corporate machinery which we have so far described is, in

---

[4] Cf. chap. ii, pp. 38 ff. Training for membership in the party begins at an early age. Grade-school children are encouraged to join the Balilla and the Piccole Italiane organizations, which instruct them in patriotic songs and in the elements of Fascist discipline. At fourteen the boys graduate into the Avanguardia and the girls into the Giovani Italiane, the former being taught military drill and the use of the rifle, the latter how to become good housekeepers and mothers. All, of course, are trained, above all else, to be good Fascists. At twenty-one the recruits take the solemn oath of allegiance to Fascism and obedience to the Duce, and are formally admitted into the Fascist party as full-fledged members. Since the enthusiasm of the young is easily aroused by national ideals, and since membership in the Fascist party is essential for most careers in Italy, there is little that the average ambitious young Italian can do but join. Consequently, the Fascist party, through its present active membership of almost two million men and women pledged to unlimited devotion to the regime, is able to reach all classes and strata of Italian society and influence directly all phases of Italian life.

[5] Finer, *Mussolini's Italy*, pp. 287 ff.

fact if not in law, subject to his will. All the members of the Chamber, all the officials of the syndicates, the corporations, and the governmental bureaus of any importance must be party members bound to him by the party oath of obedience. In practice no step of any consequence can be taken by anyone, no law can be passed, no governmental plan approved and carried out, without the explicit sanction or at least the tacit consent of the leader of the party, who is at the same time the head of the government.

This absolute concentration of authority is admitted and defended by the Fascists. It expresses, they say, their ideal of the strong totalitarian state — a thoroughly united, efficient commonwealth at the command of an able and trusted leader who works for the present and future greatness and power of the Italian nation.

THE HEAD OF THE GOVERNMENT

Mussolini, the leader of the party and head of the government, then, is in effect the center of the system. He is the axis, as it were, around which everything in Italy revolves. In his capacity as head of the government he has been since 1926 responsible not to Parliament but solely to the King, who appointed him and who has the power, theoretically, to dismiss him. His position in the Cabinet is supreme; Cabinet members are not his colleagues but his subordinates. He is their chief who appoints and dismisses them. In actual practice he asks for resignations rather often and suddenly. Whenever he feels that new blood and fresh minds are needed, a "change of the guard," as the procedure is called, is announced. Some of the ministers or undersecretaries are informed that they are ministers no more; as loyal and obedient Fascists they withdraw without comment, and new men take their places — for how long only the leader knows.

THE FASCIST GRAND COUNCIL

Since the head of the government is not responsible to Parliament and only nominally to the King, his only responsibility is, in effect, to the Italian people and to his own conscience. Actually, if the Premier should fail or be unsatisfactory, it is the party, of which he is the leader and chief exponent, which would, most probably, bring pressure for his removal. The party organ from which that pressure would most likely emanate is the Fascist Grand Council, the highest organ of political control in the Fascist state. Established as the supreme council of the party immediately after the Fascist revolution, it has been, since December 9, 1928, a constitutional organ of the state.[6]

The law which established the Council as a state institution defined it as "the supreme organ which coördinates and integrates all the activities of the regime which issue from the revolution of October 1922." The head of the government is, ex officio, its chairman, and as such it is he who "calls its meetings whenever he considers it necessary and determines their agenda." On constitutional questions the Council must be consulted, but in all other matters it is dependent upon the will of the head of the government, at whose discretion it is assembled.[7]

In practice, besides expressing opinions on all questions of a constitutional character (prerogatives of the Crown, functions of Parliament, powers of the head of the government, modifications in the syndical and corporate order, etc.), the Council discusses matters of party organization, passes on all important current legislation, proposes new legislation, draws up the final list of deputies for every new Chamber,[8] sanctions international treaties, and keeps up to date a list of possible

[6] Cf. the law of December 9, 1928, on the organization and functions of the Fascist Grand Council, in Appendix I, p. 301.

[7] The Grand Council consists of the following members: the secretary general of the Fascist party and the quadriumvirs of the March on Rome whose tenure is "without limit of time"; the presidents of the Senate and the Chamber of Deputies, all the Cabinet ministers, the presidents of all the confederations of syndical associations, and several other high government and party officials who are members for the duration of their terms of office, and, finally, persons "who have rendered distinguished service to the nation," who are appointed for three-year periods by the head of the government. Il Duce may appoint, then, to gain personal support within the Council or for any other reason, personal friends in thorough sympathy with his plans and ideas.

[8] Cf. chap. iii, p. 64.

successors for the premiership. This last function is, in fact, one of the most important. Should the post of the head of the government and leader of Fascism become vacant, the King would have to select the successor from the list kept up to date by the Grand Council.[9]

THE KING

While the powers of the Council are thus quite extensive, those of the King are distinctly limited. Besides the formalities of "selection" of the premier and the signing of the laws passed by Parliament there is, officially, not much that he can do. Nevertheless, he is a personage of great dignity, who is looked up to by all Italians, Mussolini included, with the greatest outward respect, for he represents — and this is really his chief function — the unity and continuity of the Italian nation.

THE PARLIAMENT

The governmental organ next in importance in the present hierarchy of Fascist institutions is the Parliament. The lower house, the Chamber, is composed of 400 members selected by the Fascist Grand Council from a list of 1,000 names submitted to it by the syndical associations. The Senate, the other branch of Parliament, consists of members who, at the recommendation of the Premier, are appointed by the King for life.

Since political parties have been abolished, the Italian Parliament has lost much, if not all, of its real importance. All questions of any significance are now decided in their essentials by the Fascist Grand Council, the head of the government, and his ministers long before they reach Parliament. Made up, as Parliament now is, of hand-picked Fascists sworn to obedience to the party leader, its chief function is to discuss, rather academically, and to approve, usually amid assurances of Fascist "faith" and cheers to the leader, the laws submitted to it by the executive. Rejection or even severe criticism by Parliament of any important measure presented to it by the

---

[9] It is the council, then, which would designate who should fill the all-important post of prime minister; how much freedom of choice the King would actually have under normal circumstances is not difficult to imagine.

executive is, under present conditions, absolutely unthinkable. The Parliament, and particularly the Chamber, is little more than a forum of loyal and obedient Fascists before whom government spokesmen and the chairmen of parliamentary committees elucidate the legal measures which the government intends to take or has already taken.[10]

In view of the Parliament's impotence, it really matters little how its members are selected. Even though the members of the Corporate Chamber are the representatives of the nation's workers and employers and even though they may be technical experts thoroughly familiar with the problems and the desiderata of the economic groups which they represent, there is little that they can actually do with the knowledge they possess. No real clash of opinion, no real battle over any issue is ever permitted to arise. Controversial questions are settled by the executive and the Fascist Grand Council; all that is left for the Parliament is to approve their decisions. It

[10] Many of the lesser laws in Italy are first enacted in the from of *decreti-legge*, or "decree laws" promulgated by the government without any discussion in Parliament. The Parliament, however, must approve these decrees, if they are to be valid, within two years of their promulgation. Since many decrees are issued thus, they are usually approved by Parliament in wholesale fashion and in most cases without any discussion.

Among the most important Parliamentary discussions are the annual debates on the state budget. On that occasion it is customary to review and debate the work done by each government department. Even on that occasion, however, frank criticism of the government is never heard: all that the average member of Parliament may venture to do is to express his views upon questions of detail in which the government then may or may not follow his advice.

An interesting summary of the work done by the Italian Corporate Chamber in recent years is given by the following figures taken from official Italian sources. As the data indicate, the activity of the Chamber has of late consisted almost wholly in endorsing the laws and decrees presented to it by the Fascist government.

Work of the Chamber of Deputies *
(April 20, 1929–December 31, 1936)

Laws introduced by the government	3,556
discussed and passed	3,502
withdrawn	29
pending	25
Laws introduced upon the initiative of Parliament	11
discussed and passed	5
withdrawn	5
pending	1

* *Annuario statistico italiano*, 1937, p. 293.

is therefore impossible to tell from the Italian experience how a parliament organized on the principle of occupational representation would actually function in an atmosphere of free speech and free discussion.

Why then does the Parliament exist at all? Why are not its functions transferred to some other large Fascist assembly which could probably accomplish them just as well?

There is in practice considerable duplication of work as it is divided among the Corporate Chamber, the National Council of Corporations, and the General Assembly of the councils of the twenty-two corporations. The latter assembly is, clearly, a much more representative organ than the Chamber. Its membership, which consists of the representatives of all the major syndical associations, is more truly representative of the nation's productive forces than the members of the Chamber, who, though nominated by the syndical associations, are in fact chosen by the Grand Council. It would seem, then, that under these circumstances little inconvenience would result from the elimination of the present Chamber.

That such an elimination is considered, even by the Fascists themselves, a not unlikely development in the future is shown by several passages in some of Mussolini's recent speeches. On November 14, 1933, while commenting on the future functions of the National Council of Corporations and on the proposals which had been made to endow this body with legislative powers, Mussolini said that, although no immediate changes were contemplated, "it is quite conceivable that the National Council of Corporations may, at some later date, replace in toto the present Chamber of Deputies."

In the address on the establishment of the category corporations delivered by Mussolini on January 13, 1934, before the Senate, the same suggestion is made. "When this law is passed," the Premier stated, "we shall proceed to the actual constitution of the individual corporations . . . we shall follow closely their working, which should be speedy and not excessively weighted by bureaucracy . . . and when we shall have seen, followed and studied the practical working of the corporations, we shall

reach the third phase, the phase of constitutional reform. . . .
It will be at this stage that the fate of the present Chamber of
Deputies will be decided."

The "phase of constitutional reform" is now, apparently,
about to be reached. At a recent meeting (March 11, 1938)
the Fascist Grand Council issued the following resolution after
discussing the report submitted to it by the commission which
it had appointed to study the procedures for the replacement
of the present Chamber of Deputies by a new Chamber, to be
known as the "Camera dei Fasci e delle Corporazioni": "The
Fascist Grand Council resolves that the Chamber of the *Fasci*
and Corporations — the new legislative and representative assembly of the nation — shall be formed by bringing together
two existing bodies, the National Council of the Fascist Party
and the National Council of Corporations as reorganized under
the law of February 5, 1934." The new Chamber, it is expected,
will consist of some six hundred members. The present Chamber of Deputies will cease to exist on the expiration of the term
for which it was elected, and the new Chamber will begin its
work on March 23, 1939. The law embodying these proposals
is now being drafted by the commission on whose report the
Fascist Grand Council acted.[11]

THE MINISTRY OF CORPORATIONS

We turn now to a critical discussion of the various organs of
the syndical and corporate system proper.[12]

While the Fascist party, as we have seen, exercises general
political control over the syndicates and corporations, the

[11] Cf. *Sindacato e corporazione*, January 1934, p. 31, and Fascist Confederation of Industrialists, *Business and Financial Report*, May 1938, p. 4.

[12] Again attention must be called to the all-pervading importance of the
Fascist party. As we have noted, all appointments in the syndical structure must
be passed upon by the party before they are officially confirmed by the government. It is its task to see that all appointees are, as the syndical laws put it,
"men of character and strong national convictions." In addition, its secretary
general appoints three members (representing, the Fascists say, the party, the
consumers, and the general public) to the Council of each one of the twenty-
two newly established category corporations. The purpose of this strict party
control over the syndical and corporate system is, as we have repeatedly noted,
to make that system, like everything else in present-day Italy, "integrally" and
thoroughly Fascist.

Ministry of Corporations [13] has the more specific supervision over them. The ministry is entrusted with such tasks as the approval of the by-laws and the legal recognition of individual syndical associations; the confirmation in office of all syndical officials; the supervision of the general activities and the financial administration of all syndical associations; the dismissal of syndical officials and the appointment of government commissioners for the reorganization of syndical associations; the determination of the amounts and the distribution of compulsory syndical dues; the drafting of labor and social security legislation; the registration of collective labor agreements and the arbitration of collective labor disputes; the planning and direction of the work of the individual corporations, the National Council of Corporations, and the Central Corporate Committee, in each of which the Minister of Corporations is ex officio chairman, and the exertion of such persuasion and informal political pressure as may be necessary to insure collaboration of individual groups of workers or employers with the government. The ministry also supervises governmental unemployment exchanges, social insurance and social welfare organizations, and coöperative societies, collects and elaborates statistical information on questions of production and labor, edits several official periodical publications, and carries out such activities of the former Ministry of National Economy as registration of patents and copyrights, inspection of factories, control of weights and measures, supervision of state and private insurance concerns, etc. In its essence, it may well be said that the Ministry of Corporations is the government agency which keeps the entire syndical and corporate machinery functioning smoothly and in thorough harmony with the government's general economic and political plans.

THE NATIONAL COUNCIL OF CORPORATIONS

Among the syndical and corporate organs proper, the first in rank is the National Council of Corporations.[14] After its

---

[13] For a more detailed discussion of the work and of the internal organization of the Ministry of Corporations, cf. chap. iii, pp. 59 ff.

[14] Cf. the detailed description of the organization and of the work of the National Council of Corporations in chap. iii, pp. 67 ff.

reorganization in March 1930 this council was to be the supreme organ of economic coördination and control in the Fascist state, "the general staff," as Mussolini called it, of Italian economy. All major questions of economic policy confronting the nation were to be submitted to it for discussion; its general assembly was to deal with such problems as the organization of the syndical system, the national and regional coördination of employment, the adjustment of collective labor relations, and the formulation of rules for the coördination of the economic relations between the various branches of the nation's productive organism. In addition, after the establishment of the twenty-two category corporations, the general assembly was given power to approve the rules, regulations, and price scales enacted by the twenty-two corporations, while through its seven sections and their sub-sections the council was empowered to deal specifically with a variety of economic problems arising within any one of the seven economic groups which the sections represented.

In practice some useful work of economic coördination was done by the sections of the council and by its central corporate committee during the first four years of the council's existence.[15] After the establishment in 1934 of the twenty-two category corporations, however, these new corporate bodies took over practically all of the work of the council's sections. The large and rather unwieldy general assembly never did do more than pass resolutions of a very general nature. An actual control of the Italian economic system as a whole, which the assembly was empowered by law to exercise, was never attempted.

Actually, the most effective organ of the Council of Corporations was and still is the Central Corporate Committee. The powers of this committee, established to coördinate the work of the council and to serve in the place of the general assembly during the intervals between the latter's meetings, have been recently greatly expanded. Through the law of April 18, 1935, the committee was given full power to act in the place of the general assembly and thus to give final approval to all

[15] Cf. chap. iii, pp. 68 ff.

rules and regulations adopted by the twenty-two corporations. Since then this committee, which includes most of the members of the Cabinet and the highest officials of the party and the syndical organizations, has been taking the place of the general assembly of the National Council of Corporations.[16] The committee is the corporate body which exercises the highest authority and is empowered to make the final decisions. Many well-informed Italians believe that in a not too distant future it will replace the National Council of Corporations in law as it now takes its place in practice.

THE CATEGORY CORPORATIONS

The corporate organs next in importance are the twenty-two category corporations. As we have pointed out, it was not until 1934 that the corporations actually came into existence.[17] The Fascist syndical system since 1926 had grouped workers and employers into separate associations and provided a machinery for the regulation of collective labor relations and the settlement of collective labor disputes; the law of 1934 now entrusted the task of achieving "the collective regulation of economic relations and the unitary discipline of national production," the ultimate aims of the Fascist corporate state, to the newly established category corporations.

Like all the other organs of the state, the corporations are, in practice, under the complete control of the Fascist party. The membership of each corporation is composed exclusively of party members sworn to absolute obedience to the leader and to the party hierarchy. Since all the corporations are presided over by the Minister of Corporations, who has the power to determine their agenda, and all their decisions and

[16] The Central Corporate Committee consists of the Ministers of Corporations, Interior, Justice, Finance, National Education, Public Works, Agriculture and Forests, and Communications; the secretary general of the Fascist party; the undersecretaries of corporations and any other ministers or undersecretaries who may be serving as presidents of corporations: the secretary general, the vice-secretaries, and the administrative secretary of the Fascist party and the party representatives in the individual corporations; the presidents of the nine Fascist confederations and of the National Institute of Coöperatives, and the secretary general of the National Council of Corporations.

[17] Cf. chap. iii, pp. 58 ff., and chap. v, pp. 106 ff.

recommendations must be approved by the Central Corporate Committee before they become effective, there is ample certainty that no discussion will ever arise within a corporation that is not welcomed by the party and the government, and that no decision will ever be taken which the government does not approve. Such all-pervasive political control is, of course, completely justifiable according to the Fascists. In a truly totalitarian state, they maintain, no individual force or agency can be permitted to exist which may ever be out of harmony with the general plans and objectives of the supreme central political authority. Despite the independent normative powers conferred upon the corporations by law, they are, in actual fact, little more than advisory organs whose recommendations may or may not be accepted by a central government with which all final decisions ultimately rest.

Within these important limitations the work of the corporations promises, nevertheless, to be both useful and productive. As previously indicated, besides advising the government, corporations must attempt to settle collective labor disputes before they are carried to the labor courts for final decision. Some useful work has already been done by the corporations in this field. The first major dispute ever to be brought before the conciliation board of a corporation occurred in the early part of 1935. At that time the workers of the large automobile factories of the Fiat Company in Turin demanded the discontinuance of the Bedaux system of scientific management, which they had long opposed. The management of the Fiat refused the workers' request and the matter was brought before the conciliation board of the Corporation of Metal Working and Machinery. In its decision, made public on February 19, 1935, and arrived at after a careful study of the points at issue, the board recommended the discontinuance of the Bedaux system. Soon afterwards this pronouncement was accepted by the Fiat and the dispute declared closed.[18]

The normative powers of the corporations, as a series of recent instances indicate, have also been successfully exer-

[18] *Sindacato e corporazione*, February 1935, p. 327.

cised. In February 1936 detailed "norms" for the regulation of the economic relations between actors and theater owners and theatrical producers, and between motion picture producers and motion picture house operators, were published. These norms, elaborated by the Corporation of the Theater and Public Entertainment and duly approved by the Central Corporate Committee, now represent a "code" to which all dealings between the occupational groups in question must conform. Similar codes (closely resembling, in fact, the codes of fair competition adopted in the United States under the N.R.A.) have been drafted by the corporations concerned for the regulation of the book trade, the sugar trade, the relations of publishers with authors, and the professional fees of physicians and surgeons.[19] These codes have defined and prohibited certain unfair trade practices, and have fixed price scales and minimum prices for the commodities or services in question.

In the much more difficult field of "collective regulation of production" — the main objective of which is the maintenance of national economic equilibrium — some interesting beginnings have also been made.

Several years ago the national association of Italian sugar beet growers and the national association of sugar manufacturers began to experiment with agreements which would determine at the time of the planting of the beets the quantities the manufacturers would need and the price which could be paid to the producers. These agreements, satisfactory to both growers and manufacturers, were, after 1935, subjected to the scrutiny and approval of the Corporation of Sugar Beets and Sugar and transformed into corporate norms, which, after approval by the Central Corporate Committee, automatically acquired the binding force of law. These norms now bind Italian sugar beet growers to a certain volume of production, for which, in turn, they are assured a ready market at a satisfactory price.[20]

[19] Ministero delle Corporazioni, *L'Attività degli organi corporativi* (Rome, 1936), pp. 12 ff.
[20] Marco Fanno, *Introduzione allo studio della teoria economica del corporativismo* (Padua, 1936), pp. 143 ff.

More recently, important additional powers of economic control have been given the corporations. By the decree of January 14, 1937, they were entrusted with the task of passing upon applications for the building of new industrial plants or the enlargement of existing ones, formerly attributed to a special government commission.[21] Thus, while hitherto authorizations for plant expansion had been given by a body in which civil servants predominated, these authorizations are now given by the various corporations which consist mainly of representatives of the employers and workers of the already existing factories. It will indeed be interesting to follow the results of this change.

By the royal decree of April 28, 1937, the Central Corporate Committee and, in part, the individual corporations were invested with the powers of direct commodity price control held, until then, by special political price control committees established during the Ethiopian campaign and the League of Nations' sanctions.[22] Finally, the pursuit of economic autarchy now being, admittedly, one of the Italian nation's important ultimate economic goals, the twenty-two corporations were recently entrusted with the preparation of detailed plans for increased national economic self-sufficiency. Shortly after Mussolini had defined, in a speech delivered on May 15, 1937, before the 800 members of the Third General Assembly of the corporations convened on the Roman Capitol, a maximum of economic autarchy as "the guaranty of the nation's political independence and power" and a goal that must be unrelentingly pursued,[23] the councils of the various corporations met to consider plans for increased economic self-sufficiency within their particular fields. Among others the corporations of the extractive industries, of metal working and machinery, and of the chemical industry presented plans for the fullest utilization of domestic coal and mineral resources and for a thorough reorganization

[21] Cf. chap. vii, p. 170.
[22] Cf. chap. vii, p. 174. For a more detailed account of these new powers given the Fascist corporations, cf. Gerolamo Bassani, "Sviluppi corporativi," *Giornale degli economisti* (Milan), August 1937, pp. 576–592.
[23] *Sindacato e corporazione*, May 1937, p. 873.

of the Italian iron and steel industry intended to reduce the industry's reliance on foreign scrap iron and to provide a fuller utilization of domestic ores. The Corporation of Paper and Printing studied methods recently perfected by Italian chemists for the production of cellulose from wheat and rice straw, hemp husks, and chestnut wood waste.[24]

These first instances of production and price control through corporate norms are hailed by the Fascists as the initial steps in a movement of regulation which will gradually be extended to all branches of national production. Their ultimate goal is economic self-sufficiency, planned production and distribution, and the elimination of economic disequilibria caused by periodic overproduction and by recurring shortages of supply.

There can be little doubt that through the controls exercised by the Fascist corporations much can be done to prevent and to minimize economic maladjustment and to achieve short-run economic stability. But such stability, as seen from the experience of the German *Kartell*, can be achieved only at the price of greater rigidity in the national economic structure and at the constant risk of monopolistic combinations at the expense of the consumer. The danger that the Italian codes might lead to monopolistic agreements seems to be a very real one — and the fears of thoughtful observers are hardly allayed by the assurance, confidently given by the Fascists, that monopolies will be made impossible by the constant vigilance of the government and the three representatives of the party in each corporation.

Moreover, even though the dangers of rigidity and monopoly should be overcome, there would still remain the more general problem of how far coördination and planned control can actually be extended in a capitalist economy. Whenever economic control ventures out from such relatively safe domains as the regulation of collective labor relations or the supervision of production and attempts to deal with the fundamental problems of general economic stability, it finds itself confronted

[24] The Fascist Confederation of Industrialists, *Business and Financial Report* (Rome), August and November 1937.

with a twofold difficulty: first, the almost total absence of guidance from past experience and, second, a disconcerting abundance of plans of attack, ranging from controlled production and consumption to management of the price level through centralized control of the monetary and credit system. Furthermore, even though a workable method for economic control should be found and applied within one nation, the vital problem of how to maintain national economic stability in an eminently unstable world of independent nations would still remain. It seems safe to say, therefore, that, though the Fascist corporation represents a powerful instrument for the achievement of economic autarchy and a promising and novel mode of attack upon the problem of economic instability, it is not, as some of its most ardent supporters would claim, a universal panacea for the economic ills of the capitalist system.

THE SYNDICAL ASSOCIATIONS

The basic organs of the Fascist corporate state, to a critical discussion of which we now turn, are the syndical associations. As pointed out in detail elsewhere,[25] three important changes in the relations between Italian labor and capital took place with the passage of the law of April 3, 1926: first, legally recognized syndical associations, to which the exclusive representation of employers and workers was entrusted, were established; secondly, collective bargaining and the conclusion of collective labor agreements were made the principal avenues for the regulation of collective labor relations, and, finally, decisions of governmental labor courts were substituted for strikes and lockouts as the ultimate means of settling industrial disputes.[26]

[25] Cf. chap. iv.

[26] Today the Fascist syndical system consists, as we have noted, of nine confederations of syndical associations, a number of autonomous federations, and a great many individual syndical associations. The nine confederations coördinate the activities of the federations, organize all services which can be used in common by individual syndicates, and supervise and control the financial administration of the syndical system. Their work is carried on locally by the inter-provincial and provincial unions of syndicates.

The federations of syndical associations are at the present time the most important constituents of the syndical structure. They are empowered to represent officially all the workers or employers within a given occupational

We need not repeat in detail what has been said in earlier chapters about the historical development, the structure, and the functions of the Italian syndical system. Our remarks here will be confined to a brief critical discussion of it as it exists today.

One of the charges most commonly made against the Fascist syndical system is that it is but a tool used by the capitalist class and by a dictatorial political regime to preserve the *status quo* and to keep the mass of the Italian workers in subjection. In some respects such a charge is not unjustified. The bonds which previously tied the Italian laborer to the labor movements of the world have been definitely severed. Socialism, Social Catholicism, and all other non-Fascist labor movements have ceased to exist in Italy. In their place a national syndical system has been created, in the direct management of which the mass of workers have had, until recently, comparatively little to say. If it be true that today many Italian workmen sympathize with the regime because of its nationalistic aspirations, it is equally true that there always will be workers in Italy who will remain diffident and reserved, if not openly hostile, toward a regime which has restricted their freedom of speech and assembly and has suppressed their right to elect their leaders and representatives freely. Non-Fascist workmen may be paying their syndical dues because forced to do so by law, but they are likely to show slight interest in a system over which they have no control, and which has been arbitrarily imposed upon them with little regard for their own individual likes and preferences.

To these objections Fascists answer that non-Fascist workers constitute, more and more as the system is perfected, the exception and not the rule. Within the totalitarian state whose existence is necessary for the achievement of Italy's national aspirations there can clearly be room only for organizations

---

group, to nominate the candidates for membership in the Corporate Chamber, the National Council of Corporations, and the twenty-two category corporations, and to negotiate collective labor agreements binding upon all the members of a given occupational class. Their functions are carried on locally through interprovincial, provincial, and local syndicates which have no legal recognition.

of a thoroughly Fascist character. All others not in sympathy with Fascist doctrine would impede the achievement of the goals that the Fascist movement has set for itself. All "loyal" Italians are free to coöperate, however, in the work of the Fascist organizations. Inasmuch as since the reform of 1934 most Italian syndical officials have been elected by the members of the various syndicates or federations, the latter, Fascists say, now can and do express the desiderata of the class of producers whom they represent.

Such arguments may be answered, however, by pointing out that though, formally, officials in the syndical system are now freely elected, their election must be ratified by the government and no one elected can be confirmed in office without the full and unqualified endorsement of the Fascist party. In practice this means that every syndical official, whether appointed or elected, must be a loyal party member bound to obey the party leader. No matter what pressure may be brought to bear upon him by the members of his syndicate, no Fascist syndical official is ever able to begin a movement, say, for higher wages or shorter hours, without the approval of the superiors in the party.[27]

While, then, real freedom can scarcely be said to exist within the Italian syndical system, there are some factors which tend, in part at least, to compensate the worker for its loss. Through the elaborate system of collective labor agreements, labor courts and social insurance and welfare activities which we have described, some measure of economic security and more equitable working conditions are being provided for the Italian workman. Moreover, any impartial observer must admit that a new attitude toward labor and its problems has gradually developed in Italy. Under Fascism, labor is regarded as a social duty, as a duty toward the nation and the state, and, clearly, as something more than a mere factor of production

[27] In the summer of 1936, the president of the Fascist Confederation of Workers in Industry, Cianetti, himself told the author that before beginning his recent successful agitation for higher wages affecting several hundreds of thousands of Italian industrial workers he went to Mussolini and obtained the leader's approval for his plans.

bought and sold in a competitive market. According to this conception, the worker is a member of the national group engaged with the employer in the campaign for economic and social progress which the state is conducting in the interest of the nation as a whole; a campaign in which, through his syndical organization, the nationally-minded worker is gradually called to take an increasingly direct and active part.[28]

Fascism, furthermore, is in practice much less of a movement to the right than is commonly believed. Mussolini, a former Socialist, is far from having become, as is often thought, a mere guardian of the interests of the capitalist class. There is ample proof both in his speeches and in his actions that he is not unmindful of the worker. Besides, there is a militant and not uninfluential minority of Fascist leaders whose sympathies are openly directed to the left. One of the leading younger Fascist intellectuals, Professor Ugo Spirito, has recently gone so far as to advocate the taking over by the corporations of the full control of the means of production. In exchange, Spirito suggested that the corporations should issue shares of ownership to the former owners and to their workers and carry on production with the aid and in the interest of both. The plan has never been seriously considered by the Fascist majority, but the very fact that it could be openly presented and discussed at an important Fascist congress is a significant indication of the trend of some recent Fascist thought.[29]

A PROVISIONAL EVALUATION OF THE ITALIAN CORPORATE STATE

Yet, whatever may be the future course of Fascism in Italy, it is certain that at the present time all organs of the state are completely dominated by the Fascist party and the Fascist government and that everywhere the party's and the government's plans and wishes are bound to prevail. Workers' and

[28] Cf. on this point the speech delivered by Achille Loria, the noted Italian economist, in the Italian Senate on March 13, 1930, in support of the new law on the National Council of Corporations, reprinted in abridged form in Gaspare Squadrilli, *Il Consiglio nazionale delle corporazioni* (Rome, 1930), p. 360.

[29] For the details of Dr. Spirito's proposal, see the minutes of the Second International Congress of Syndical and Corporate Studies or the shorter account given in Ministero delle Corporazioni, *Bollettino del lavoro*, May 1932, p. 309.

employers' assemblies exist — but they are not free; syndicates and corporations may make plans and recommendations, but only those approved by the government will ultimately be put into effect. No free and open clash of interests, or even of opinions, is possible. Italian syndicalism and corporatism actually represent in practice only the means through which the productive forces of the nation are made to coöperate with the Fascist government and the Fascist party in the achievement of the latter's ultimate economic and political ends.

In the attainment of these ends the organs of the *stato corporativo* have actually played a comparatively minor role so far. Except in the field of collective labor relations, no fundamental changes have been put into effect regarding the basic rules for the conduct of Italian economic affairs; economic life in Italy has been managed fundamentally as it is being managed in other Western European countries. Autonomous coördination of the national economy through syndical groups and corporations has not been attempted on any really significant scale, and with very few exceptions the role of Fascist syndicates and corporations has been limited to giving support, assistance, and advice to a central government which almost entirely alone has maintained the prerogative of initiating positive action in the economic sphere.

Yet, if few fundamental changes have been made in Italian economic life, it must nevertheless be recognized that a surprisingly complete and effective system for the centralized control of the Italian economy has been evolved. For the old doctrines of individualism and laissez-faire a new philosophy of economic control in the national interest has been substituted. An elaborate system of syndical organization of employers and workers has been perfected. Strikes and lockouts, viewed as socially harmful manifestations of class warfare, have been abolished; a new system of collective labor agreements and labor courts has been created for the regulation of national labor relations, and a number of new corporate organs have been established for the collective control of the national economy. Should economic planning on a national scale ever be attempted by the Fascist government in Italy, as it may well be in a not too distant future, a serviceable machinery for such action would be ready for use.

The fact that such machinery has been established, and that through it a new pattern for the organization of a capitalist economy is gradually evolving on the Peninsula, makes the study of the Italian economic experiment particularly interesting at this time. On our continent and in Europe faith in traditional economic individualism has of late been severely shaken. Although during the last century a prodigious revolution occurred in the circumstances of existence, there has been as yet little change in our basic rules of social and economic life. Only slowly are we beginning to realize that some reorientation of our traditional theories of social and economic organization is needed, that economic individualism is not in itself sufficient for the attainment of lasting economic progress, and that the social group as a whole must be called upon to control and supervise intelligently certain fundamental economic functions if a minimum, at least, of economic security and justice is to be achieved. Future development seems to point toward an economic organization that is neither laissez-faire capitalism nor the complete state ownership of the means of production advocated by the Socialists; a system in which economic self-government through occupational groups, under the restraining and coördinating influence of the state, may possibly play a part.

In the world at large, ideas such as these are gradually gaining ground. Systems of corporate organization, more or less patterned after the Italian model, have been established in Austria, Germany, and Portugal. The introduction of a system of democratic "corporatism" pledged to the maintenance of fundamental individual liberties is being advocated, especially by Catholic social action groups, in France, Belgium, Switzerland, and the United States.[30] In our own New Deal

---

[30] For an authoritative statement of the Catholic position with regard to the problems confronting the United States, cf. the pamphlet, *Organized Social Justice* (New York, 1935), issued by the Social Action Department of the National Catholic Welfare Conference and based, in its essentials, upon the recent encyclical of Pope Pius XI: *Quadragesimo Anno*.

legislation, and especially in the N.R.A., the A.A.A., and the Guffey Coal Act, surprising parallels with some of the forms of economic organization discussed in this book are found. If economic self-government under the aegis of the state were ever to become a possible pattern for the organization of a democratic capitalist society, the Italian corporate experiment, though developed in a political atmosphere displeasing to most of us, may have some interesting suggestions to offer.

PART III

THE ECONOMIC DEVELOPMENT OF THE FASCIST STATE: 1922–1937

CHAPTER VII

FASCIST ECONOMIC POLICY: A PRELIMINARY SURVEY

FEW subjects have roused more discussion and controversy in recent years than the economic progress made by Italy under the Fascist regime. Yet personal and political biases have so often colored even firsthand accounts of Italian economic conditions that there seems to be justification for a fresh attempt at an objective study of fact.[1] Before a final evaluation of Fascist economic policy can be attempted, an answer must be given to such questions as: What have been the policies of Fascism in the fields of population, agriculture, industry, trade, and finance? What have been the effects of these policies upon the economic welfare of the Italian people? Have Italians gained or lost, economically, under the Fascist regime?

TYPES OF FASCIST ECONOMIC POLICY

Since the advent of Fascism in 1922 several clearly distinguishable types of economic policy have been successively adopted by the Fascist regime. The period from 1922 to 1926 was one of general economic readjustment and gradual industrial and commercial expansion; that from 1927 to 1929 a period of currency stabilization and industrial consolidation. During the four years of the depression (1930 to 1934) there was active state intervention intended to lessen the detrimental effects of the world crisis. From the middle of 1935 to October 1936 there was growing economic autarchy, culminating, during the recent Ethiopian war and the League of Nations' sanctions, in a period of almost complete economic isolation.

---

[1] In the following analysis official Italian statistics have been used whenever possible, and conclusions have been based primarily upon such data. Even though official sources tend to present statistical materials in a light favorable to the Fascist regime, the numerical data which they contain have been found to be generally accurate, and are believed to be, on the whole, the most reliable bases for an objective account of Italian economic conditions.

The period from October 1936 to the present may be best described as one of currency realignment followed by domestic economic readjustment and the gradual resumption of international economic activity.[2]

1922–1926: ECONOMIC READJUSTMENT AND INDUSTRIAL AND COMMERCIAL EXPANSION

When the Fascists came into power in October 1922 Italy was slowly emerging from the grave economic depression and disorder which followed the World War.[3] The advent of Fascism brought with it a quickening of that convalescence. Business confidence, shaken by three years of intensive socialist agitation and by the collapse in 1921 of the Ilva and the Ansaldo (two of the country's largest metallurgical enterprises) and the Banca Italiana di Sconto (one of the country's four largest banks), gradually revived. Mussolini's first Minister of Finance, Alberto de Stefani, reformed the tax system, enforced a program of drastic economy in government expenditure, and balanced the budget, the deficit of which had amounted during 1922–23 to over three billion lire. To increase its efficiency and reduce its cost, governmental bureaucracy was thoroughly reorganized; some former government monopolies (such as the telephones) were turned over to private enterprise, and some Socialist legislation, notably that providing for inheritance and other direct taxes, was repealed. Efforts were made at the same time to stimulate industry and agriculture. Agricultural education was brought to the farmers' doors by means of the Cattedre Ambulanti d'Agricoltura, traveling agricultural lecturers. Competitions were inaugurated and tempting prizes and honors given to the most efficient farmers. To reduce the importation of grain, an item weighing heavily on the debit side of the country's

[2] While critics of the Fascist regime are inclined to regard, not without some justification, such shifts and changes in policy as sheer economic opportunism, Fascists call their apparent lack of consistency "a courageous steering of their ship on troubled economic seas." Storms, they point out, are not rational and must be fought as best they can when they arise.

[3] For a more detailed description of Italy's economic and political conditions during the immediate post-war period, cf. chap. i, pp. 9 ff.

commercial balance, the *Battaglia del Grano*, the "battle" for a larger wheat crop, was instituted and a vigorous impulse given to land reclamation and improvement. In the industrial field an aggressive campaign for the rationalization of plants and the introduction of more scientific and efficient methods of production was launched. Mussolini and the Minister of National Economy at the time, G. Belluzzo, continually urged Italian industrialists to "rationalize" their productive apparatus in order to increase its effectiveness. Attention was directed to the methods of scientific management in America, and the work of the ENIOS, the newly established Italian Scientific Management Institute, was encouraged. The ultimate aim of all these measures was to stimulate domestic production and to bring about lasting economic revival.[4]

The effects of these policies of economic expansion soon became apparent. Under the stimulus of new capital investment and a liberal credit policy, industry made rapid strides forward, production grew, exports increased; from 1923 to 1926 Italy experienced a period of continuous industrial growth and prosperity. The country's textile, electrical, mechanical, and chemical industries made particularly swift progress. The output of artificial silk (rayon), of which in 1926 Italy produced more than any other European country, increased from 2.6 thousand tons in 1922 to 24.4 thousand in 1927. Iron and steel production rose from 1.0 million tons in 1922 to 1.9 million in 1926; the production of sulphur grew from 167.3 thousand tons in 1922 to 305.7 thousand in 1927. Electrical power output rose from 6.9 billion kilowatt hours in 1925 to 8.4 billion in 1927. The total net tonnage of the Italian merchant marine increased from 835 thousand tons in 1920 to 1.877 thousand in 1926, while the country's exports grew from 9.5 billion lire in 1922 to 15.6 billion in 1926.

Yet, though some of this industrial gain was sound, much of it was the result of an overexpansion of credit and of specu-

---

[4] For a detailed account of government activity in this field during the period under discussion, cf. G. Belluzzo, *Economia fascista* (Rome, 1928), and François Perroux, *Contribution à l'étude de l'économie et des finances publiques de l'Italie depuis la guerre* (Paris, 1929), pp. 151 ff.

lative activity. As Table 14 indicates, between 1922 and 1926 the number of Italian joint stock companies and the capital investment therein were almost doubled. The number of Italian joint stock companies increased from 6,850 in 1922 to 12,134 in 1926, while the total share capital of these enterprises grew from 21,395 million lire in 1922 to 40,413 million in 1926. The heaviest overexpansion occurred in the artificial silk, the

TABLE 14

NUMBER AND CAPITALIZATION OF ITALIAN JOINT STOCK COMPANIES, BY
YEARS, 1922–1937 *

(*Situation at the end of the year*)

Year	Number of Companies in Existence	Total Share Capital (*million lire*)
1913	3,069	5,643
1922	6,850	21,395
1923	7,898	23,523
1924	9,078	28,418
1925	10,737	36,481
1926	12,134	40,413
1927	13,201	42,253
1928	14,609	44,952
1929	16,170	49,596
1930	17,384	52,281
1931	17,718	50,853
1932	18,518	49,602
1933	17,375	47,782
1934	18,735	44,319
1935	19,228	44,095
1936	19,352	44,805
1937	20,018	47,695

* Compiled from various issues of *Compendio statistico italiano*, *Annuario statistico italiano*, and *Bollettino mensile di statistica*.

chemical, and the shipbuilding industries. In these fields huge "billion lire" industrial combines, such as the Snia Viscosa company in the artificial silk industry and the Montecatini company in the chemical industry, grew up.

When the Finance Minister, De Stefani, attempted to check this expansion by restricting the activities of the banks and by endeavoring to limit stock exchange speculation, he became unpopular and was forced out of office. The task of restricting speculation, securing a favorable settlement of the war debts, and stabilizing the currency was left to his successor, Count Volpi di Misurata, an able financier and a leading exponent of "big business." Volpi continued, for a while, to support a rather liberal credit policy. But when toward the middle of 1926 credit sank seriously and currency showed alarming signs of weakness, Mussolini himself called a halt to the movement of expansion and in a dramatic speech, delivered at Pesaro on August 18, 1926, pledged the country to a policy of defending the stability of the lira "to the last drop of blood."

As soon as a more rigid credit policy was adopted, in accordance with these new monetary plans, signs of uneasiness spread throughout the country's economic structure. It became apparent that in many fields the advance had been too rapid, and disproportionate in relation to the available capital resources and the real potentialities of domestic and international markets. To well-informed Italians it became clear that the Pesaro speech marked the end of the first period of Fascist economy and that an era of inflation and industrial expansion would be succeeded by a period of monetary stabilization and economic consolidation.

Throughout these first four years the action of the Fascist government in the economic sphere differed little on the whole from the type of intervention current under traditional liberal political regimes. Perhaps too much occupied with the problems of internal political consolidation, the Fascist government did not go much beyond the point of stimulating private agricultural and industrial activity and remedying such patent weaknesses in the country's economic structure as a badly unbalanced budget. Although Fascist organization of labor and capital had begun, corporate economy had not as yet made its appearance on a national scale.

1927–1929: CURRENCY STABILIZATION AND INDUSTRIAL CONSOLIDATION

The second period of Fascist economic policy is marked by a much more active and direct intervention of the government in national economic affairs. At the outset severe measures were taken to protect the currency and to prevent further inflationary excesses. The total note circulation, which had reached a peak of 21.4 billion lire in 1925, was reduced to 16.8 billion in 1929. The privilege of note issue which had been given to three banks (the Banks of Italy, Naples, and Sicily) was restricted to the Bank of Italy exclusively. Denied easy credit accommodation by the central bank, the large commercial banks were, in their turn, forced to restrict industrial and commercial loans. Helped by these deflationary measures, Italian currency, which in the previous two years had wavered between 25 and 26 lire to the dollar, rose in value and could finally be stabilized, on December 21, 1927, at 27.25 per cent of its pre-war value and at a rate of 19 lire to the dollar.

This currency stabilization was carried through at too high a level. Though calculated to increase the country's prestige, to benefit savers, and to help the country as a large importer of raw materials, the stabilization of the lira marked the beginning of a period of serious deflation and of industrial and commercial stagnation. Higher costs and export prices and the consequent rapid falling-off of foreign markets forced serious curtailment of operations in the industries working for export and a very painful process of general internal economic readjustment. Heavy losses were incurred by the industries which had led in the movement of expansion, and capital reserves which might have been used to advantage during the years of the world depression were depleted long before its beginning. The government, however, did not shrink from the responsibilities of its monetary program. The unpleasant task of reducing wages and other costs was not left to private enterprise alone. By a series of governmental decrees, an all-around reduction of wages, rents, interest, and taxes was put into effect in the effort to reduce industrial costs and to put Italian prices back into line with the world price structure.

Despite drastic measures to restore equilibrium, the revaluation of the lira occasioned, on the whole, a not insignificant amount of unemployment, suffering, and distress.[5] Only gradually and through a widespread program of industrial reorganization and the energetic "rationalization" of production techniques did Italian industry succeed in regaining its former competitive position in international markets. It was not until 1929, a year which, with few exceptions, marks a high point in Italian industry, that the difficulties inherent in the revaluation of the currency were definitely overcome and that the country's economy adapted itself to the new monetary situation.

While Italian industry was, on the whole, still left to fight its own way within the general limits set by the government's monetary program, government intervention increased considerably in the fields of labor relations and agriculture. Through the law of April 3, 1926, as we have seen, Fascist syndical associations were recognized as the sole representatives of their respective occupational groups, strikes and lockouts were prohibited, and collective bargaining and the decisions of governmental labor courts were recognized as the sole media for the adjustment of labor disputes. Although early collective labor contracts did little more than define prevailing labor conditions, an important beginning in a new field had nevertheless been made. In agriculture, too, a rapid increase in government intervention took place. The "Battle of Wheat," the national campaign for the increase of wheat production, was intensified, and a spectacular program of land reclamation, involving large government investments, was launched.[6]

1930–1934: ACTIVE GOVERNMENT INTERVENTION AND THE
STRUGGLE AGAINST THE DEPRESSION

When the world depression came, Italy's economic system was just emerging from the crisis occasioned by the revaluation of the lira. Weakened by this experience, Italian economy could offer little resistance when the depression began to make

---

[5] The annual average of the number of persons totally unemployed grew from 113,901 in 1926 to 278,484 in 1927 and to 324,422 in 1928. Cf. Chap. IX, p. 231.

[6] Both programs are described more in detail in chap. viii.

its effects felt. As in all other countries, conditions rapidly went from bad to worse. Prices fell, markets dwindled, production lagged, unemployment rose. Industrial production declined from 109.2 in 1929 (1928 = 100) to 73 in 1932. Unemployment mounted from 300,787 in 1929 to a total of 1,018,953 persons in 1933. Exports were reduced from 14,884 million lire in 1929 to 5,224 million in 1934. Imports dropped from 21,920 million in 1928 to 7,432 million in 1933. As Tables 15 and 16

TABLE 15

VALUES OF PRINCIPAL ITALIAN EXPORTS, BY YEARS, 1924–1937 *

(In million lire)

Year	Raw Silk	Cotton Cloth	Citrus Fruits	Artificial Silk (Rayon)
1924†	1,654	1,429	253	?
1925†	1,687	1,751	358	?
1926†	1,647	1,403	509	393
1927†	1,397	1,296	695	553
1928	1,171	1,363	493	530
1929	1,276	1,382	490	498
1930	994	966	468	466
1931	597	664	402	407
1932	251	466	329	298
1933	209	371	332	249
1934	97	259	275	299
1935	116	238	278	265
1936	143	301	245	248
1937	190	755	530	565

* Compiled from various issues of *Compendio statistico italiano*, *Annuario statistico italiano*, and *Bollettino mensile di statistica*.

† Values converted into 1927 gold standard lire for purposes of comparison.

show, exports of artificial silk, cotton cloth, and raw silk declined in the course of three years to one-half, one-third, and one-sixth, respectively, of their former value:

The Italian government, like the governments of most other countries, was soon compelled to lend active assistance to those parts of the country's economic structure whose stability was most severely threatened by the crisis. This intervention was effected not through the syndical and corporate machinery but, primarily, through a series of government institutions and decrees, due, in many instances, to the prompt personal action of the head of the government.

One of the devices to which Italian governments had resorted ever since the World War in dealing with emergencies of an economic nature was the creation of semi-governmental bodies, called *istituti* or *enti nazionali*. These *istituti* and *enti* were usually entrusted with the task of bringing together the responsible heads of a particular type of national economic ac-

TABLE 16

VALUES OF PRINCIPAL ITALIAN IMPORTS, BY YEARS, 1924–1937 *

(*In million lire*)

Year	Wheat	Cotton	Coal	Wood	Petroleum Products
1924†	2,051	2,321	1,268	?	452
1925†	2,909	2,531	1,325	?	478
1926†	2,613	2,220	1,492	632	557
1927†	2,894	1,699	1,849	674	654
1928	2,955	2,184	1,180	595	605
1929	1,718	2,201	1,546	630	654
1930	1,567	1,444	1,336	606	613
1931	836	772	1,084	393	420
1932	505	738	686	285	251
1933	206	840	677	260	198
1934	185	721	857	270	227
1935	199	577	1,024	290	274
1936	310	448	767	145	275
1937	1,393	1,050	1,728	317	455

* Compiled from various issues of *Compendio statistico italiano, Annuario statistico italiano*, and *Bollettino mensile di statistica*.

† Values converted into 1927 gold standard lire for purposes of comparison.

tivity and organizing them to meet, usually with the help of some direct government aid or subsidy, such emergency situations as had arisen. Examples of such *istituti* and *enti* are numerous. Ever since 1926 there had been in existence an Istituto Nazionale per l'Esportazione (to promote exports), an Ente Nazionale Serico (to reorganize the silk industry, threatened by the competition of rayon, and to promote exports of silk manufactures), and an Ente Nazionale Italiano per l'Organizzazione Scientifica del Lavoro (ENIOS, to introduce to Italian business the methods of Taylorism and scientific management).

In 1927, at the time of the currency revaluation, the Ente Nazionale Italiano per le Industrie Turistiche (ENIT) was established to coördinate and develop the tourist trade; the Ente Nazionale per l'Unificazione dell'Industria, to promote "rationalization" and "standardization" practices, and the Ente Nazionale per l'Artigianato e le Piccole Industrie, to encourage the work of the smaller industries and of independent craftsmen and artisans. In 1928 the Istituto per il Credito Navale was

TABLE 17

DEVELOPMENT OF THE ISTITUTO MOBILIARE ITALIANO, BY YEARS, 1933–1936 *

(*In million lire*)

	1933	1934	1935	1936
Owed by Subscribers of Capital	385.7	385.7	385.7	385.7
Loans Granted	532.2	627.2	621.1	534.7
Capital Subscribed to	551.0	551.0	551.0	551.0
Outstanding Bonds	179.9	566.2	483.7	394.4

*Compiled from various issues of *Annuario statistico italiano*.

formed to subsidize shipbuilding and aid in the reorganization of the merchant marine.

When the detrimental effects of the world depression began to be seriously felt a number of additional *enti* and *istituti* were established. On November 13, 1931, the Istituto Mobiliare Italiano was formed for the purpose of providing financial assistance to those branches of the nation's economy which had suffered most severely during the depression. The authorized capital of this *istituto* amounted to 500 million lire; its main function was to extend to commercial and industrial enterprises credits secured by negotiable collateral (mainly stocks and bonds). Against this, the institute could in turn issue its own bonds, guaranteed by the government, up to an amount equal to ten times that of its authorized capital. The financial condition and the magnitude of the operations of the Istituto Mobiliare are revealed by the figures of Table 17.

Shortly after the establishment of the Istituto Mobiliare Italiano, the Sofondit (Società Finanziaria Italiana), a government-controlled concern which was to aid the country's banks (in particular the Banca Commerciale Italiana, the country's largest commercial banking institution) in maintaining their solvency by taking from them large blocks of heavily depreciated industrial securities, was created. In January 1933 the Istituto di Ricostruzione Industriale (Industrial Reconstruction Institute), a body similar to the Reconstruction Finance Corporation in the United States, was formed to pro-

TABLE 18

DEVELOPMENT OF THE CONSORZIO PER SOVVENZIONI SU VALORI INDUS-
TRIALI, BY YEARS, 1930–1936 *

(In million lire)

	1930	1931	1932	1933	1934	1935	1936
Loans on Securities ..	109.1	210.2	268.5	619.1	888.3	859.6	798.8
Industrial Bills Held .	395.9	439.9	348.2	135.2	133.9	144.9	248.6
Short-term Bonds Issued	238.2	462.9	494.5	691.2	515.0	479.8	404.1
Capital	125.0	125.0	125.0	125.0	125.0	200.0	200.0

* Compiled from various issues of *Annuario statistico italiano*.

vide financial assistance to industrial enterprises through long-term loans financed through the issue of government guaranteed bonds. Finally, there existed the Consorzio per Sovvenzioni su Valori Industriali, a government-controlled consortium for industrial financing originally established in 1914, the recent development of which is shown by the data of Table 18.

While these organizations were established mainly to strengthen the capital structure of industrial and financial enterprises, two important measures were adopted by the government in an attempt to achieve better coördination of effort in the industrial system. With the coming of the depression a number of *consorzi* (voluntary associations, similar in nature to the German *Kartell*) were spontaneously formed among Italian producers for the purpose of combating collectively the increasingly severe hardships imposed upon them by the crisis. On June 16, 1932, a law was passed which placed these *consorzi* under the control of the government and authorized compulsory membership under certain conditions.[7]

A good example of such a compulsory *consorzio* is the Istituto Cotoniero Italiano (the Italian Cotton Institute). This institute, established among cotton-spinning enterprises as a voluntary organization in 1933, was transformed into a compulsory *consorzio* in March 1934. It was to combat, under direct government supervision, the hardships suffered by the Italian cotton industry by effecting a reduction in the domestic output of cotton yarn, by systematic allocation of production quotas among producers, and by studying ways and means of reducing production costs and increasing sales abroad.[8]

On January 12, 1933, another important law was passed in an effort to curb industrial overproduction. It required all Italian business organizations wishing to establish new plants, or to expand their old ones, to obtain a license from a special government commission established at the Ministry of Corporations, the commission rendering a decision after hearing the representatives of the competent syndical and corporate organizations. Up to the end of 1934, the commission received 811 such applications; 549 of these were granted, 227 refused, and 35 deferred for later decision.

While through the institutions and legal enactments described in the preceding pages the Fascist government attempted to stem the tide of financial deflation and to provide the necessary aid for businesses in distress, much also was done through a series of other measures to relieve unemployment and to alleviate the suffering among the working classes.

The government's program of public works, already large

---

[7] The new law provided that compulsory *consorzi* may be established whenever a request to that effect is presented by a majority (over 70 per cent) of the concerns engaged in a given branch of production and approval of the project is obtained by the competent corporate organizations. A provision of particular interest in this new law is that which subjects to the previous authorization of the government the building of new plants manufacturing products dealt in by the *consorzio*, or the extension of existing ones.

[8] Cf. Giorgio Mortara, *Prospettive economiche* (Milan, 1934), p. 291.

For further details on the law of June 16, 1932, on the establishment of compulsory *consorzi*, cf. the condensed version of the law itself, given in Appendix, I, p. 320.

before the depression set in, was expanded considerably. Land reclamation, hydroelectric power developments, the electrification of railroads, the construction of highways and public buildings were greatly intensified. Expenditures for public works increased from 1.676 million lire during the fiscal year 1928–29 to 2.877 million in 1931–32. The unemployed were assisted further through unemployment insurance (compulsory for agricultural laborers operating machines and for factory workers), through strict government control of internal migration, through a shortening of the work week in industry, and through special grants made by the government for the relief of particularly distressed areas.

As in most other countries, so in Italy the depression occasioned a heavy unbalancing of the government's budget. The shrinkage in the volume of general business reduced revenues greatly, while expenditures increased because of the expansion of public works, large subsidies, and increased military outlays. The budget deficit consequently rose from about one-half billion lire in 1930–31 to over three billion and a half in 1933–34. (This figure does not include an added expenditure of about three billion lire made during that year for a public debt conversion operation.)

While the syndical organizations (federations and confederations of workers and employers) were increasingly active during this whole period, their action was limited in the main to making recommendations to the government and endeavoring to obtain from it benefits and aid for their hard-pressed members. In the vast majority of instances the measures taken by the government to combat the depression were due, during this period also, not to the action of the syndical or corporate organs but, primarily and almost solely, to the laws and decrees enacted at the initiative of the central government.

1935–1936: ECONOMIC AUTARCHY, WAR FINANCE, WAR TRADE,
AND LEAGUE OF NATIONS' SANCTIONS

An analysis of the next period of Fascist economic policy may best be begun by a brief discussion of the effects of the world depression upon Italy's international economic position.

As in most other countries, the depression caused a remarkable shrinkage in the volume of foreign trade and a growing deficit in the commercial balance. While imports declined from a peak of 21.920 million lire in 1928 to a low of 7.432 million in 1933 and exports fell from 14.884 million in 1929 to 5.224 million in 1934, the country's trade deficit increased from 1.433 million in 1931 to 2.552 million in 1935. Under normal circumstances such trade deficits are not a cause for alarm in Italy. Commercial deficits, which were quite large in predepression years, were then made up through such "invisible" items of the country's balance of international payments as tourist expenditures and emigrant remittances. During the recent depression, however, these automatic adjustments failed to appear. Commodity exports as well as "invisible" exports were severely reduced. The result was a progressive widening of the gap between exports and imports, an increasing strain on the foreign exchange markets, frequent outflows of gold, and a consequent serious threat to the stability of the currency.

This precarious situation led in 1934 to a complete reversal of the comparatively liberal commercial policy which the government had up to then pursued and to the adoption of the same elaborate system of import licenses, quotas, exchange controls, and other trade restrictions which had been in force for some years in other European countries. In April 1934 wool, copper, oil seeds, and coffee ceased to be admitted into the kingdom without a special import license. In March 1935 the importation of a wide variety of commodities was placed under definite license and quota restrictions. In July 1935 a complete governmental import monopoly was established for coal, coke, tin, nickel, and copper, and henceforth these commodities could be imported only by a specially delegated government authority. When League of Nations' sanctions, on November 18, 1935, were applied against Italy in an effort to stop the Ethiopian war and fifty-two nations suddenly ceased their purchases of Italian commodities, Italy had at her disposal a well-developed machinery for the complete control of her foreign trade.

Besides the prohibition of commercial credits and an embargo on such war materials as rubber, tin, nickel, iron ore, scrap iron, and aluminum, sanctions consisted mainly in the total suspension, by fifty-two of the world's leading nations, of all imports from Italy. The chief objective of this suspension was so to weaken Italy's international economic position as to make it impossible for the country to buy indispensable supplies and war materials abroad and thus to force her to abandon her East African campaign. The sanctions' drastic curtailment of Italy's exports, it was hoped, would either force her to reduce voluntarily her imports of needed raw materials and war supplies, or else cause a severe unbalance in her international trade, a rapid depletion of her gold and foreign exchange reserves, and, ultimately, a suspension of her foreign purchases because of a lack of acceptable media of payment.

When the threat of sanctions became a reality, none of these alternatives occurred rapidly enough to make the sanctionist countries' plans effective. Italy already had an elaborate system of import restrictions which she could use on the one hand to retaliate against the restrictions imposed by the sanctionist countries and on the other to avoid increasing deficits in her own international trade. After November 18, 1935, only essential imports were admitted; all imports from sanctionist nations were prohibited except under special government permits; in practice such permits were granted only for such essential commodities as could not be obtained from non-sanctionist nations. The result of this policy of rigid import restriction was, as the Italian Minister of Finance announced in May 1936, that for some time during the period of the sanctions the total deficit of the Italian balance of trade was actually less than that which had existed during the corresponding months of the preceding year.[9]

---

[9] Speech made by Finance Minister Thaon de Revel on May 19, 1936. Cf. Fascist Confederation of Industrialists, *Business and Financial Report* (Rome), June 1936.

While stringent import restrictions thus helped Italy to defeat, in part, the most immediate purpose of the sanctions, that of causing a severe unbalance in her international trade, the payment for needed imports without an immediate, ruinous depletion of the country's gold reserve was made possible by the elaborate system of foreign exchange regulations adopted by the government. To prevent too rapid and continuous a drain upon the country's gold reserves (the gold reserve of the Bank of Italy declined from 3.936 million lire on October 20 to 3.027 million on December 31, 1935) and to safeguard the stability of her currency, the importation and exportation of lire were prohibited, all dealings in foreign exchange were concentrated in the hands of a newly created government department (the office of the Undersecretary for Trade and Exchange), and all Italian citizens were forced to surrender to the government, against payment in Italian treasury bonds, all their holdings of foreign securities and foreign exchange. While no precise official figures exist, the Italian government's purchases of foreign exchange and of foreign securities made in this manner, and the gold obtained through the donations of the Italian people (the exchange of their golden wedding rings for steel ones, for example, became a patriotic duty to which the vast majority of the Italian people spontaneously responded) are estimated to have yielded the Treasury an added reserve of several billion lire.

To lessen the effect of the sanctions upon the Italian consumer, a system of strict governmental price controls extending to most commodities of wide popular consumption was adopted and rigidly enforced; large stocks of raw materials, accumulated by the government and the leading industries in anticipation of the country's war needs long before sanctions went into effect, were drawn upon, and an intensive drive for the fullest exploitation of all available domestic resources and for the production of substitutes for leading imports was begun. During this drive for substitutes, a new textile fiber, "Lanital," obtained from the casein contained in skimmed milk, was developed as a substitute for wool; cellulose and paper stock were produced from straw; and wool, jute, and cotton fiber were successfully replaced by rayon and hemp. Alcohol distilled from wine, rice, and sugar beets was used as motor fuel in a mixture with gasoline; and castor oil, of which Italy is an important producer, was widely used as a lubricant of gasoline engines. Scrap iron, copper, lead, and brass were collected, melted, and used again. While the search for substitutes was going on, the drive for the fullest exploitation of the country's domestic resources, notably domestic petroleum and coal, was greatly intensified. A new company, the Azienda Italianà Carboni, was created for the encouragement of the production and distribution of domestic coal found in fairly large quantities in the Arsa basin and in Sardinia. Some industries, forced to curtail productions based exclusively on imported raw materials, branched out into the production of substitutes obtainable from materials produced at home. In the chemical industry in particular, notable progress was made in the production of articles which had formerly been imported. *Preferite il Prodotto Italiano*, "Buy Italian," became a slogan to be encountered everywhere, from the smallest village to the nation's capital.

To facilitate the more efficient organization of certain sectors of Italian industry, special "corporate committees," boards representing workers and employers within a given occupational group, and a number of *enti* and *consorzi*, organizations of producers similar to the German *Kartell*, were created. Notable among them were the corporate committees on national fuels, on glass and ceramics, on wool and silk, and the national *enti* for silk, cellulose, paper, and leather. Of great importance also were the National Cotton Institute, the government office for mineral oils, and the *consorzio* for scrap iron, to which organizations the mass purchase of the respective commodities abroad and their allotment to domestic consumers were entrusted.

The cumulative effect of these defensive measures adopted by the government was that the actual, immediately visible impact of the sanctions upon Italian economy was much less severe than had been generally anticipated. When the author arrived in Italy at the beginning of July 1936, eight months after the sanctions had begun, the average Italian consumer hardly realized that sanctions were in effect. Italian markets and stores were well stocked with goods, and with the exception of a few commodities (such as gasoline, for example, the price of which was purposely increased by the government in order to lessen consumption by civilians, and meat, which was not sold on "meatless" days twice a week) practically everything could be had by the average consumer at prices that were the same as those which had prevailed before sanctions went into effect, or only slightly higher. While certain export industries were undoubtedly hard hit by the sanctions (during sanctions Italian exports were reduced to 56 per cent of their former value), Abyssinian war orders and larger sales to domestic consumers, who were forced by the stringent import restrictions to turn to the home market, greatly increased the activity of other industrial units. Official statistics recently made available show that the total volume of industrial activity declined only slightly during this period. The national index of industrial production (1928 = 100) stood at 87.8 in 1934, at 102.4 in 1935, at 95.5 in 1936, and at 108.7 in 1937.

In surveying the sanctionist experiment one is thus forced to conclude that, while it is of course impossible to say with assurance what would have happened in Italy if sanctions had remained in force over a longer period, it is certain that while sanctions actually lasted they failed to do irreparable damage to the Italian economic system. Sanctions failed. They failed because of the aid which, throughout their duration, Italy was able to obtain from the twenty-seven non-sanctionist nations, because of the remarkable speed and success of the country's military operations in Africa, and because of the determined resistance to the sanctionist measures by the Italian government and by the Italian people.[10]

Immediately after the abandonment of sanctions (July 15,

[10] Although it is true that while sanctions lasted they failed to achieve their objective, the damage done by them to Italy's international economic position was, nevertheless, considerable. For additional details on the effect of the sanctions and the Ethiopian war upon Italy's trade and her international economic position, see chap. viii, pp. 209 ff. and chap. ix, pp. 216 ff.

1936) it looked as if Italy was determined to make an unusually high degree of economic autarchy the principal future goal of her economic policy. Mussolini repeatedly announced that, after the lesson taught the country by the sanctionist episode, Italy's principal future economic objective must be the achievement, "within the least possible time, of a maximum of economic independence." [11]

Negotiations of new trade treaties with former sanctionist countries were based upon principles of strict reciprocity. Trade debts owed by Italy when sanctions went into effect were liquidated only gradually through the proceeds of trade balances in Italy's favor which creditor countries were asked to maintain if they wished to be paid. Enterprises created during the period of the sanctions for the domestic production of former imports continued to operate and to enjoy the fullest protection of the government. Colonization of the new African empire was limited, in the main, to Italian labor and to Italian capital. Immediately after the sanctions Italy seemed more determined than ever before in her history to seek at all cost a maximum of economic self-sufficiency, military preparedness, and political independence.

1936–1937: CURRENCY DEVALUATION AND THE RESUMPTION OF INTERNATIONAL ECONOMIC ACTIVITY

As the months went by and the resentment at sanctions subsided, the policy of extreme economic isolation described in the preceding pages was gradually modified. Even though economic self-sufficiency and military preparedness continued to be important national objectives, Italy came to realize more and more that she could not afford to live as a hermit nation. On October 5, 1936, following the example of France and the

---

[11] In a formal address made before the Second Assembly of Corporations on March 23, 1936, Mussolini said that the sanctionist episode had taught the Italian people a lesson which they would never forget: the lesson that political autonomy and an independent foreign policy cannot be achieved without a corresponding degree of economic independence. "November 18, 1935," the Fascist leader proclaimed, "is a date which will mark the beginning of a new phase in Italian history, a phase dominated by the fundamental postulate of seeking to achieve, in the least possible time, the maximum possible amount of economic autonomy." See *Sindacato e corporazione*, March 1936, p. 289.

other European go!.1 bloc countries, the gold content of the lira was reduced by about 40 per cent, thus bringing the exchange parity between the lira, the pound, and the dollar back to the parities of 19 and 92.46 respectively, at which rates they had been fixed when the currency was stabilized in 1927. This devaluation of the lira was accompanied by a series of measures designed to liberalize foreign trade and to prevent a rise in the domestic cost of living. The most important among them were tariff reductions on such commodities as wheat and flour, cattle and meat, eggs, coal, coke, fat, bacon, lard, and raw cotton, and the conclusion of a number of important trade agreements. The devaluation of the currency, the new trade treaties, and the previously mentioned reduction of important import duties have already had and will undoubtedly continue to have a stimulating effect upon the development of Italy's international trade and will gradually make unnecessary some of the rigid import and exchange controls which at this time (February 1938) are still in force.

With her national economy relieved of the pressure of war and sanctions and her foreign trade in process of being reestablished, one of the leading economic problems confronting Italy at present is that of the adjustment of her internal economic structure to the devaluation of the lira. To benefit most from her recent monetary reform the country must succeed, on the one hand, in keeping the domestic cost of living from rising unduly and, on the other, in expanding her sales on foreign markets under the stimulus of the lower price of her currency.

Recent developments show that the government and the Italian business classes understand the problem confronting them and are attempting to act accordingly. To offset the rise in prices which occurred as a consequence of the African war and the sanctions (estimated by official Italian sources at 8 per cent on the average) a series of wage increases, ranging from 5 to 11 per cent, were granted to workers in the fall of 1936; [12]

---

[12] On October 18 of the same year the Minister of Corporations reported that through recent changes in existing collective labor agreements the wages of

to prevent further rapid increases in the domestic cost of living, a number of import duties were, as we have seen, lowered or removed altogether; the system of domestic price controls adopted during the sanctions was temporarily maintained and the country's foreign trade stimulated by the conclusion of new trade treaties and the recently completed governmental reorganization of the merchant marine. With industry and trade gradually turning into more normal channels, with the home market enlarged by the acquisition of new colonial domains, with the currency adjusted to a more satisfactory international level and the worst clouds overhanging government finances gradually lifting, it may well be said that the outlook for Italy's economic future, barring too rash a program of government expenditure and fresh international complications, appears, on the whole, better now (February 1938) than it has been at any time during the recent past.

6,347,814 workers in industry, agriculture, commerce, and banking had been increased by an average of 9 per cent. Cf. Fascist Confederation of Industrialists, *Business and Financial Report* (Rome), November 1936.

CHAPTER VIII

POPULATION, AGRICULTURE, INDUSTRY, AND TRADE

As THE survey just concluded shows, radical changes in economic conditions and policy have occurred under Fascism in Italy. Throughout this development, the constant endeavor of the Fascist government has been to stress those policies which would most effectively serve the two fundamental ideological principles of the regime: population growth and economic independence. Through the speeches of Fascist leaders and through the Fascist press these two principles have been kept constantly in the forefront of public attention. Only recently, after devoting one of its meetings to a discussion of a sweeping seven-point program for population increase, the Fascist Grand Council described population as "the problem of problems" because, "without life there is neither youth, nor military power, nor economic expansion, nor a secure future for the fatherland." [1]

THE PROBLEM OF POPULATION

The arguments offered by the Fascists to justify their policy on population are comparatively simple. There is, first of all, the purely political argument. The ultimate goal of their movement, Fascists say, is the building of a strong and powerful Italian commonwealth. But the indispensable basis for political power is a numerous, healthy, and virile population; Italy must consequently increase in numbers. A more refined scientific justification, based upon recent trends in the demographic development of the Italian people, is then added to this essentially political argument. Population, Fascist demographers maintain, follows a cyclical movement of rise and fall, of youth, maturity, and old age, similar to that of the individual. In the case of the white race, the apex of demographic development,

[1] *New York Times*, March 4, 1937, p. 1.

they believe, has been reached, and the trend in the future, for the majority of white nations, will be definitely downward.[2] Some leading non-Fascist students of population have of late supported Fascist demographers in this view. In the introduction to his well-known book, *The Balance of Births and Deaths*, Dr. Robert R. Kuczynski of the London School of Economics writes:

. . . we are ready to characterize as foolish any person who would pretend that a nation with a large excess of births over deaths may still be dying out. Yet such an assertion would not only not be foolish but would even be much to the point today.

It has indeed not been sufficiently realized so far that, however low may be the number of deaths, there must be a definite and rather considerable number of births in order to insure the reproduction of the population. . . . Let us, for a moment, consider England, which in 1927 had 655,000 births and 485,000 deaths. It may seem at first sight that an excess of 170,000 births is a proof of considerable vitality and it may even be assumed that by further improvements in public health the number of deaths might still be reduced. Yet, incredible as it may sound, those 655,000 births of 1927 mean that on the average each woman during her lifetime gives birth to but two children, and that if the population is to hold its own not one of the children thus born may die before attaining parenthood. In case then that natality does not again increase, the population of England is bound to die out no matter how low mortality may be reduced. And this state of affairs is by no means confined to England. Conditions are about the same in Germany and only slightly better in France.[3]

In his recent monograph, *Population Movements*, Dr. Kuczynski restates his earlier views even more forcefully:

If fertility and mortality remain in western and northern Europe what they were in 1933, the population which now is about 193 millions would reach its maximum of 196 or 197 millions in the late 1940's, and by the year 2000 would be reduced to about 150 millions. . . .

With the fertility of 1934 . . . the populations of western and

[2] Cf., especially on this point, Corrado Gini, "The Cyclical Rise and Fall of Population," *Population* (Chicago, 1930), and "The Italian Demographic Problem and the Fascist Policy on Population," *What is Fascism and Why?* Tomaso Sillani, ed. (New York, 1931).

[3] I (New York, 1928), pp. 1 ff. Reprinted here by permission of the Brookings Institution, Washington, D. C.

northern Europe as a whole are doomed to die out even if every newly born girl reached the age of 50.[4]

The fundamental fact upon which these views are based is the recent sharp and continuous decline in birth rates in all the larger countries of the white race. Table 19 gives a graphic statistical account of this movement. The number of births per 1,000 of population fell in the United Kingdom from 24.2 in 1913 to a low of 14.9 in 1933, in France from 18.8 in 1913 to 14.7 in 1937; in Germany from 27.5 in 1913 to 14.7 in 1933, and in the United States from 24.7 in 1913 to 16.7 in 1936. The death rate also declined, but not in the same proportion as the birth rate. The excess of births over deaths per 1,000 of population fell in the United Kingdom from 9.9 in 1913 to 3.0 in 1936, in France from 1.1 in 1913 to −0.5 in 1935, in the United States from 10.6 in 1913 to 5.2 in 1936, and in Germany from 12.5 in 1913 to a low of 3.5 in 1933.

Although Italy has experienced a less drastic fall in the rate of births than other European countries, the trend toward a declining birth rate is clearly evident. According to official data, the Italian birth rate fell from 39.3 per 1,000 in 1876 to 31.7 in 1913 and from there to a low of 22.4 in 1936. The death rate, too, fell during the closing years of the last century, at an even faster pace. The rate of natural increase (excess of births over deaths) therefore continued to rise until the first decade of the present century. Since then that rate also has fallen, from a high of 14.2 in 1912 to a low of 8.7 in 1937.

THE "BATTLE OF BIRTHS" AND EMIGRATION

These unfavorable demographic trends and the aforementioned political considerations have led to what is known in Italy as the "Battle of Births," the campaign for the preservation and increase of the country's demographic resources. Briefly stated, the three major objectives of this campaign are to check the decline in the birth rate, to prevent demographic losses through migration from country districts to the cities or through emi-

---

[4] Oxford, 1936, pp. 49 and 43. Reprinted here by permission of the Oxford University Press.

TABLE 19

BIRTH AND DEATH RATES IN ITALY, THE UNITED KINGDOM, FRANCE, GERMANY, AND THE UNITED STATES, BY YEARS, 1913, 1920–1937 *

(*Number of cases per 1,000 members of population*)

Year	ITALY			UNITED KINGDOM			FRANCE			GERMANY			UNITED STATES		
	Births	Deaths	Excess	Births	Deaths	Excess	Births	Deaths	Excess	Births	Deaths	Excess	Births	Deaths	Excess
1913	31.7	18.7	13.0	24.2	14.3	9.9	18.8	17.7	1.1	27.5	15.0	12.5	24.7	14.1	10.6
1920	31.8	18.7	13.1	25.4	12.9	12.5	21.4	17.2	4.2	25.9	15.1	10.8	23.7	13.1	10.6
1921	29.2	16.8	12.4	22.6	12.5	10.1	20.7	17.7	3.0	25.3	13.9	11.4	24.2	11.7	12.5
1922	30.8	18.1	12.7	20.9	13.1	7.8	19.3	17.5	1.8	23.0	14.4	8.6	22.3	11.8	10.5
1923	30.0	17.0	13.0	20.2	11.8	8.4	19.1	16.7	2.4	21.1	13.9	7.2	22.2	12.3	9.9
1924	29.0	17.1	11.9	19.3	12.6	6.7	18.7	16.9	1.8	20.5	12.3	8.2	22.4	11.7	10.7
1925	28.3	17.1	11.2	18.7	12.4	6.3	19.0	17.4	1.6	20.7	11.9	8.8	21.5	11.8	9.7
1926	27.7	17.2	10.5	18.3	11.9	6.4	18.8	17.4	1.4	19.5	11.7	7.8	20.7	12.2	8.5
1927	27.5	16.1	11.4	17.1	12.5	4.6	18.2	16.5	1.7	18.4	12.0	6.4	20.6	11.4	9.2
1928	26.7	16.1	10.6	17.2	11.9	5.3	18.3	16.4	1.9	18.6	11.6	7.0	19.8	12.0	7.8
1929	25.6	16.5	9.1	16.7	13.6	3.1	17.7	17.9	-0.2	17.9	12.6	5.3	18.9	11.9	7.0
1930	26.7	14.1	12.6	16.8	11.7	5.1	18.0	15.6	2.4	17.5	11.1	6.4	18.9	11.3	7.6
1931	24.9	14.8	10.1	16.3	12.5	3.8	17.5	16.2	1.3	16.0	11.2	4.8	18.0	11.1	6.9
1932	23.8	14.7	9.1	15.8	12.3	3.5	17.3	15.8	1.5	15.1	10.8	4.3	17.4	10.9	6.5
1933	23.7	13.7	10.0	14.9	12.5	2.4	16.3	15.8	0.5	14.7	11.2	3.5	16.6	10.7	5.9
1934	23.4	13.3	10.1	15.2	12.0	3.2	16.1	15.1	1.0	18.0	10.9	7.1	17.1	11.0	6.1
1935	23.3	13.9	9.4	15.2	12.0	3.2	15.2	15.7	-0.5	18.9	11.8	7.1	16.9	10.9	6.0
1936	22.4	13.7	8.7	15.3	12.3	3.0	15.0	15.3	-0.3	19.0	11.8	7.2	16.7	11.5	5.2
1937†	22.9	14.2	8.7	..	..	..	14.7	15.0	-0.3	18.8	11.7	7.1	17.0	11.2	5.8

* Compiled from various issues of *Annuario statistico italiano* and *Bolletino mensile di statistica*, *Statistical Abstract for the United Kingdom* and *Quarterly Return of the Registrar General*, *Annuaire statistique de la France* and *Bulletin de la statistique générale de la France*, *Statistisches Jahrbuch für das Deutsche Reich und Wirtschaft und Statistik*, *Statistical Abstract of the United States* and *U. S. Bureau of the Census Releases*.
† Figures are provisional.

gration, and to provide adequate and independent means of subsistence for the Italian people.

In 1926, in order to achieve the first objective, a flat tax (now equal to 100 lire a year — approximately $5.00 — for men aged 35 to 40 years) was imposed upon all bachelors; at the same time income taxes on bachelors and heads of small families were increased, special family allowances and awards in cash and important tax exemptions to heads of large households were provided for, and special preferences in public employment and apartment space in houses built with government aid were given to married people with dependent children. Stringent laws were also passed against birth control propaganda, the sale of contraceptives, and abortion. Through the royal decree-law of August 21, 1937, a number of further measures favoring large families were adopted. According to this law, loans ranging from 1,000 to 3,000 lire may be granted to newly married couples whose combined annual income is less than 12,000 lire. The loans are to be repaid in full if the marriage remains childless after four years. If children are born, the amounts to be repaid are gradually scaled down and the time limit for repayment extended. Upon the birth of the fourth child the loan is written off altogether, and the amount originally received becomes the property of the new family. The same law also provides for further important tax reductions for heads of large families and for special benefits to be accorded expectant mothers who are government employees.[5]

In December 1925, as we have noted, the Opera Nazionale per la Protezione della Maternità e dell' Infanzia (the National Institute for the Protection of Motherhood and Infancy) was established to give protection and assistance to women during pregnancy (especially to needy and abandoned mothers), to act as a center for the dissemination of information on prenatal and infant hygiene, and to care for babies of poor families and children who are needy, abnormal, orphaned, or abandoned.

[5] *Sindacato e corporazione*, September 1937, p. 553. For a somewhat more detailed discussion of the measures for population growth adopted in Italy and of similar measures taken in Germany and in some other European countries, see D. V. Glass, *The Struggle for Population* (Oxford, 1936).

The Opera Nazionale also coöperates with local authorities in combating infant diseases and in organizing maternity clinics and training courses to take care of young children. The magnitude of its work may be indicated by the fact that in 1936 it gave assistance to over 1,600,000 persons. The figures given in Table 20 of the Opera's annual expenditures (now met, in large part, with the income derived from the tax imposed upon Italian bachelors) shed additional light upon the importance of its activities.

TABLE 20

ANNUAL EXPENDITURE OF THE NATIONAL INSTITUTE FOR THE PROTECTION OF MOTHERHOOD AND INFANCY (OPERA NAZIONALE PER LA PROTEZIONE DELLA MATERNITÀ E DELL' INFANZIA), BY YEARS, 1928–1935 *

Year	Annual Expenditure (*million lire*)	Year	Annual Expenditure (*million lire*)
1928	79.9	1933	137.9
1929	100.0	1934	157.9
1930	121.3	1935	152.9
1931	110.4		
1932	114.3		

* Data compiled from various issues of *Annuario statistico italiano*.

To prevent demographic losses through migration from the country districts to the cities, a law was passed in December 1928 conferring upon the prefects of all Italian provinces the right to regulate migration to urban centers. Under this law all persons arriving in cities without proper means of support and remaining unemployed are sent back to their places of origin and warned not to return to the city under similar circumstances. Agricultural communities, on the other hand, are encouraged to check the exodus to the cities by improving general living conditions through such means as the construction of modern houses and the improvement of communication with the larger urban centers of the region.

The effects of urbanism upon Italian population growth are illustrated by Table 21, which gives the birth, death, and natural increase rates in eleven large Italian cities. The table reveals a striking difference between birth rates in the larger

TABLE 21

BIRTH RATES, DEATH RATES, AND RATES OF NATURAL INCREASE IN POPULATION IN ELEVEN LARGE ITALIAN CITIES, BY YEARS, 1910–1937 *

(Per 1,000 inhabitants)

	BIRTH RATE						DEATH RATE						RATE OF NATURAL INCREASE					
	1910–14	1929	1931	1933	1935	1937	1910–14	1929	1931	1933	1935	1937	1910–14	1929	1931	1933	1935	1937
Northern Italy																		
Turin	17.6	15.0	14.2	11.9	13.1	14.9	16.7	15.3	13.7	13.1	13.0	14.0	0.9	−0.3	0.5	−1.2	0.1	0.9
Genoa	21.1	15.4	14.0	12.7	12.3	13.7	18.4	13.6	12.9	12.3	12.7	12.9	2.7	1.8	1.1	0.4	−0.4	0.8
Bologna	21.9	14.7	14.6	14.2	14.3	15.2	19.3	16.5	15.9	14.2	14.1	15.2	2.6	−1.8	−1.3	0.0	0.2	0.0
Milan	22.7	15.4	15.4	14.4	14.9	15.8	17.1	12.2	11.7	11.5	12.0	12.4	5.6	3.2	3.7	2.9	2.9	3.4
Venice	25.6	20.8	19.3	17.6	18.3	19.2	20.7	16.7	13.2	12.4	12.2	12.6	4.9	4.1	6.1	5.2	6.1	6.6
Central Italy																		
Florence ...	20.9	14.3	14.0	13.0	13.0	14.2	19.9	16.4	13.6	13.3	13.3	14.5	1.0	−2.1	0.4	−0.3	−0.3	−0.3
Rome	26.4	22.4	22.3	20.8	21.2	23.1	18.5	14.3	12.2	11.6	12.3	12.3	7.9	8.1	10.1	9.2	8.9	10.8
Southern Italy																		
Naples	27.5	26.6	26.7	25.6	24.7	25.8	22.2	20.1	17.4	16.1	17.9	17.4	5.3	6.5	9.3	9.5	6.8	8.4
Catania ...	30.8	29.2	28.3	28.8	27.7	25.8	20.1	19.6	17.2	15.4	14.4	17.5	10.7	9.6	11.1	13.4	13.3	8.3
Palermo ...	31.3	27.2	27.6	27.1	25.8	25.4	23.3	18.8	22.8	15.1	15.8	17.0	8.0	8.4	4.8	12.0	10.0	8.4
Messina ...	37.8	26.3	24.9	24.7	22.2	23.1	21.4	18.0	15.7	14.5	13.8	15.0	16.4	8.3	9.2	10.2	8.4	8.1
Italian Kingdom ..	..	25.6	24.9	23.7	23.3	22.9	..	16.5	14.8	13.7	13.9	14.2	..	9.1	10.1	10.0	9.4	8.7

* Compiled from various issues of *Compendio statistico italiano, Annuario statistico italiano,* and *Bollettino mensile di statistica.*

cities and in the country as a whole, an amazing disparity in these rates for the northern and southern centers of the Peninsula, and, for all cities, a notable decline in the rate of births. Internal migration, encouraged and supervised by the newly created office of the Commissioner for Internal Migration and Colonization, has also recently been used as a means of reducing unemployment and achieving a more even spatial distribution of the population. From 1929 to 1934 more than two million workers were moved from their original residences to areas of more intensive industrial or agricultural development. In 1933, under the guidance and with help of the office of the Commissioner for Internal Migration and Colonization, 1,963 families, or a total of 15,936 persons, were moved to the African colonies and the sparsely settled districts of Sardinia.[6] In 1935 over 293,000 workers migrated within the confines of the kingdom: 239,000 to do work in agriculture and over 53,000 to be employed in industry.[7]

As we have noted, the Fascist government has strictly regulated emigration also. In pre-Fascist days emigration was regarded as a necessary and unavoidable means of relief from domestic population pressure. Now it is viewed as a national loss and an evil which must, whenever possible, be checked. A succession of restrictive measures has consequently been adopted by the government, until, for certain classes of persons, emigration has been made practically impossible. Although in 1930 a more liberal policy was instituted because of growing unemployment, Italian emigration remains at a minimum. The reduction, however, is due also, in part, to the stringent immigration restrictions adopted before and during the depression by the principal immigrant-receiving countries of the world.

The combined effect of the restrictions placed upon Italian emigration is shown by the data in Table 22.

What have been the results of these population policies adopted by the Fascist regime? An objective analysis of avail-

---

[6] *Sindacato e corporazione,* February 1935, p. 519.
[7] *Annuario statistico italiano,* 1937, p. 174.

able statistical data leads to the conclusion that the results have been, from a Fascist point of view, definitely disappointing. Neither marriage nor birth rates have been noticeably affected. Apparently, in so delicate a matter as that of a country's demographic development, government action is of little avail. Italy's birth rate has, on the whole, continued in its

TABLE 22

EMIGRATION OF ITALIAN WORKERS, BY YEARS, 1913, 1921–1937 *

(*In thousands*)

	EMIGRANTS TO			EMIGRANTS RETURNING FROM			
Year	Europe and Mediterranean Basin	Trans-oceanic Countries	Total	Europe and Mediterranean Basin	Trans-oceanic Countries	Total	NET EMIGRATION
1913	313	559	872	..	..	..	..
1921	84	117	201	30	94	124	77
1922	155	126	281	56	55	111	170
1923	205	184	389	79	40	119	270
1924	239	125	364	107	65	172	192
1925	177	102	279	122	67	189	90
1926	140	122	262	106	71	177	85
1927	86	132	218	67	73	140	78
1928	79	71	150	49	50	99	51
1929	88	62	150	72	43	115	34
1930	221	59	280	82	47	129	151
1931	125	41	166	64	43	107	59
1932	58	25	83	39	34	73	10
1933	61	22	83	40	26	66	17
1934	42	26	68	29	21	50	18
1935	30	27	57	27	12	39	18
1936	22	20	42	20	13	32	10
1937	29	30	59	21	15	36	23

* Compiled from various issues of *Annuario statistico italiano* and *Bollettino mensile di statistica*, April 1938, p. 280.

downward trend, although the years 1930 and 1937 show a slight upswing. The most that can be said, consequently, for the population policies of the Italian government is that, had they not been adopted, the birth rate would probably have fallen still more rapidly.[8]

[8] In passing judgment upon Italian population policies it should be recognized, however, that these policies are of comparatively recent origin and that their efficacy probably has been handicapped by the recent severe economic

These rather disappointing results notwithstanding, Fascist leaders are prone to dismiss curtly all criticism of their population policies. Italy, they maintain, must grow in strength and power and must ultimately obtain her just share in the world's colonial domains. To achieve these objectives, growth in numbers is essential.

According to the Fascist view, such growth does not necessarily entail unemployment and starvation. Unemployment and a low standard of living are not caused by an excess of population. If the national economy be properly arranged, there are in Italy and in the country's colonial domains enough work and food for everyone. The fundamental problem is to find the proper arrangement. "In a Fascist Italy in which land has been reclaimed, cultivated, irrigated, in which discipline and order prevail," writes Mussolini, "there is room and bread for an additional ten million people." [9]

But if it be true, as some authorities believe,[10] that Italy is even now overpopulated, it is difficult to see how a continued increase in population can fail in the long run to affect the country's standard of living if no outside relief is provided. As the pressure of numbers grows (as Table 23 indicates, the Italian population grows at the rate of almost half a million a year) Italy's demands for additional colonial territories are likely to become more and more insistent, and it hardly seems

---

depression. Furthermore, even though no tangible results were obtained, it must be recognized that the demographic campaign has drawn the population problem to the attention of the Italian public. As for the question whether laws and regulations can have any practical effect on population growth, Mussolini himself believes that this is highly debatable. But when a responsible statesman sees an evil ahead — and according to Mussolini no one who cannot see at least fifty years ahead has the right to rule a nation — he must do his best to check it in time. "Even if the laws are of no avail," Mussolini writes, "my conviction is that it is necessary to try them, just as medicines are tried when, and particularly when the case is a desperate one." Finally, however, "in these matters the moral custom and, above all, the religious conscience of the individual prevail rather than formal laws. If a man does not feel the joy and the pride of being continued as a family and as a people . . . then laws, and even Draconian laws, cannot help." Preface to Riccardo Korherr, *Regresso delle nascite — morte dei popoli*, Rome, 1928.

[9] Preface to Korherr, *Regresso delle nascite*.
[10] Cf. A. M. Carr-Saunders, *World Population* (Oxford, 1936), p. 144.

probable that her claims will be heard with much sympathy as long as her own government contributes through its population policies to increase the difficulties which it will be asking other nations to aid in solving.

Yet the thought that growing population pressure might involve the nation in war does not greatly disturb Fascist leaders.

Fascism [Mussolini writes], the more it considers and observes the future and the development of humanity quite apart from political considerations of the moment, believes neither in the possibility

TABLE 23

THE ITALIAN POPULATION AT FIVE–YEAR INTERVALS, 1885–1935 *

Year (Jan. 1)	Population (in thousands)	Population Density: Inhabitants per Square Kilometer
1885	29,090.2	101.5
1890	30,140.9	105.2
1895	31,191.5	108.8
1900	32,242.2	112.5
1905	33,138.0	115.6
1910	34,205.7	119.3
1915	36,120.1	126.0
1920	36,147.4	126.1
1925†	38,973.6	125.7
1930	40,762.7	131.4
1935	43,009.0	138.6

* *Annuario statistico italiano*, 1932, p. 580, and 1937, p. 5.

† From 1925 on data are for population within the post-war territory of the kingdom.

The census of April 21, 1936, showed a total population of 42,993,602 or 136.8 inhabitants per square kilometer. An official estimate based upon these figures places the Italian population in March 1938 at 43,667,000 or 139.0 people per square kilometer. Cf. *Bollettino mensile di statistica*, April 1938, p. 271.

nor the utility of perpetual peace. . . . War alone brings up to its highest tension all human energy and puts the stamp of nobility upon the peoples who have the courage to meet it.[11]

That Fascism is ready to live up to the letter of this belligerent maxim, the recent Italo-Ethiopian conflict has only too clearly shown.

It is in the light of these doctrines on population that the

[11] In *International Conciliation*, January 1935, p. 7.

significance of many of the novel elements in Fascist political and economic policy becomes clear. In its very essence that policy consists but in a series of attempts to provide economic independence, "room and bread," for the Italian people. This is made particularly evident by the Fascist policies relating to agriculture.

AGRICULTURE: LAND RECLAMATION AND THE "BATTLE OF WHEAT"

Soon after the advent of the Fascist regime an ambitious scheme of land reclamation, aimed at utilizing every available square mile of Italian soil, was launched. While land reclamation in Italy was begun long before the coming of Fascism, it was the Fascist government that gave it a new impetus and made of it one of the cornerstones of its agricultural policy.

The fundamental legal enactment upon which the Fascist program of land reclamation is based is the "Mussolini Act" of December 24, 1928. This law, which is perhaps among the most important of the Fascist regime, provides for the completion (during a period varying from seven to fourteen years) of a number of land reclamation projects at a total cost of 6,823 million lire, 4,010 million of which are to come directly from the government. The magnitude of these reclamation operations may be indicated by a few figures. Out of a total area of about 31 million hectares, over 2,300,000 (or about 7 per cent of the country's total area) were originally too swampy for cultivation. Of these 2,300,000 hectares, 700,000 have been subjected to extensive drainage operations and are already reclaimed. Similar work is now in progress on another 1,200,000 hectares, while work on the remaining 400,000 hectares is still to be begun. On about half of the reclaimed area, however, the building of roads and aqueducts is still necessary before useful cultivation can be started.

What has so far been accomplished by the regime in this field is shown by the data in Table 24, which give the cost of land reclamation from the unification of the kingdom to July 1, 1936. Under Fascism the expenditures for reclamation works

TABLE 24
COST OF ITALIAN LAND RECLAMATION, 1870 TO JULY 1, 1936 *
(In millions of "1927" gold lire)

Type of Works	Works Authorized	Works Completed	Works in Progress
I. PRE-FASCIST PERIOD: 1870 to 1921–22			
A. Government Projects			
1. Reclamation Work Proper and Allied Projects of Land Transformation and Road Building	3,001.3	1,720.5	1,280.8
2. Reclamation Projects in Mountainous Areas	70.3	62.2	8.1
B. Private Works Subsidized by the State			
Irrigation Works, Farm Roads, Rural Aqueducts, etc.	....	....	....
Total Cost	3,071.6	1,782.7	1,288.9
II. FASCIST PERIOD: 1921–22 to July 1, 1936			
A. Government Projects			
1. Reclamation Work Proper and Allied Projects of Land Transformation and Road Building	5,832.6	5,177.3	655.3
2. Reclamation Projects in Mountainous Areas	497.8	442.5	55.3
B. Private Works Subsidized by the State			
Irrigation Works, Farm Roads, Rural Aqueducts, etc.	2,366.7	2,366.7	....
Total Cost	8,697.1	7,986.5	710.6
III. TOTAL, PRE-FASCIST AND FASCIST PERIOD: 1870 to July 1, 1936			
A. Government Projects			
1. Reclamation Work Proper and Allied Projects of Land Transformation and Road Building	8,833.9	6,897.8	1,936.1
2. Reclamation Projects in Mountainous Areas	568.1	504.7	63.4
B. Private Works Subsidized by the State			
Irrigation Works, Farm Roads, Rural Aqueducts, etc.	2,366.7	2,366.7	....
Total Cost	11,768.7	9,769.2	1,999.5

* *Annuario statistico italiano*, 1937, p. 63.

have been over three times as large as those sustained by all previous administrations since 1870; thousands of square miles of formerly useless marshland have been brought under cultivation, and new homesteads, villages, and towns have risen on them.[12]

In addition to its intensive campaign for the reclamation of the soil, the Fascist government has launched a vast program of agricultural education and instruction, intended to improve and intensify agricultural production. The Cattedre Ambulanti d'Agricoltura, traveling agricultural lectureships, have been established to bring agricultural education to the farmers' doors. Agricultural schools and colleges, scientific and research stations, and an extensive system of agrarian credit have been instituted. Vast propaganda campaigns for the preservation of national forests and for increases in the leading types of agricultural production have been put into effect.[13] Finally, the *Battaglia del Grano*, the "Battle of Wheat," was launched, as Mussolini dramatically put it, "to free the Italian people from the slavery of foreign bread."

Strange as it may seem, Italy, a country whose main activity is agriculture, has until recently imported a large part of the wheat consumed by her people. To diminish that importation and to make the country independent of foreign grain, a "battle" for the intensification of domestic wheat production was launched. Frequent prize competitions have been held among farmers, and every possible means to extend wheat cultivation and increase the yield per cultivated unit (such as the establishment of research stations, the use of carefully selected seeds, motorized plowing, large use of modern agricultural machinery in cultivating and harvesting, etc.) have been adopted. The results of this campaign, from a strictly

[12] Cf. for additional details the chapter on integral land reclamation in *Annuario statistico italiano*, 1937, and Cesare Longobardi, *Land-Reclamation in Italy* (London, 1936). For a critique of the Fascist program of land reclamation, see Carl T. Schmidt, *The Plough and the Sword* (New York, 1938).

[13] Cf. in this connection the National Forest Act of 1923 providing for the preservation and extension of national forests, the law of July 29, 1927, on the reform of agrarian credit and the establishment of the National Consortium for Agrarian Credit, and the Act of December 13, 1928, on agrarian education.

technical point of view, have been rather gratifying. As the figures in Table 26 indicate, the importation of foreign wheat has been reduced to a minimum of late, while domestic production, though sometimes disturbed in its regularity by changing harvest conditions, has shown, on the whole, a steady rise. This increase in production has been due not only to the extension of cultivated areas but also, as the data in Table 25 show, to the notable increase in the yield per cultivated unit.

As these figures show, the "Battle of Wheat" may be said, on the whole, to have been definitely won. With the exception

TABLE 25

YIELD OF WHEAT PRODUCTION IN ITALY (QUINTALS PER HECTARE), BY YEARS, 1909–1914, 1920–1936*

Year	Quintals Produced	Year	Quintals Produced
1909–14†	10.4	1928	12.5
1920	8.4	1929	14.8
1921	11.0	1930	11.9
1922	9.5	1931	13.8
1923	13.1	1932	15.3
1924	10.1	1933	15.9
1925	13.9	1934	12.8
1926	12.2	1935	15.4
1927	10.7	1937	15.5

* Compiled from various issues of *Annuario statistico italiano*.
† Annual average for five-year period.

of years of unusually poor harvests, when importation is still necessary, independence of foreign sources of supply may be said to have been achieved — at the cost, of course, of much higher bread prices at home.[14]

While the regime's program of land reclamation and its "Battle of Wheat" have, on the whole, been technically successful, progress in the remaining branches of agriculture has been

[14] Latest data on Italian wheat production and importation show that, the harvest of 1936 having been poor, wheat imports for 1937 rose considerably. The harvest of 1937, however, was good, and the yield of domestic production is deemed sufficient to satisfy the country's needs. It is expected therefore that in 1937–38 foreign imports will again be dispensed with almost entirely. See *Economist* (London), June 26, 1937, p. 732, and Oct. 30, 1937, p. 212.

much less conspicuous. The figures on the development of other leading agricultural products during the years of the Fascist regime given in Table 27 show some increase for citrus fruits and sugar beets, no significant change in the production of olives, and a definite decrease in the production of grapes.

INDUSTRY: EXPANSION, CRISIS, DEPRESSION

We turn now to a brief analysis of the development of some of the principal individual components of Italy's industrial sys-

TABLE 26

PRODUCTION, IMPORTATION, AND CONSUMPTION OF WHEAT IN ITALY, BY YEARS, 1909–1913, 1921–1935 *

Year†	PRODUCTION Millions Quintals	PRODUCTION Index No.	NET IMPORTATION Millions Quintals	NET IMPORTATION Index No.	CONSUMPTION‡ Millions Quintals	CONSUMPTION‡ Index No.	POPULATION Millions	POPULATION Index No.
1909–13§	49.9	100.2	13.2	100.0	57.6	100.0	34.7	100.0
1921–22	52.5	105.2	26.3	199.6	73.2	127.1	38.0	109.7
1922–23	43.9	88.2	31.4	238.1	69.8	121.1	38.4	110.7
1923–24	61.2	122.6	20.9	158.6	76.6	133.0	38.6	111.4
1924–25	46.3	92.8	25.7	195.0	66.4	115.2	38.9	112.3
1925–26	65.5	131.4	16.3	123.4	75.4	130.9	39.3	113.3
1926–27	60.1	120.4	20.9	158.7	74.5	129.3	39.6	114.3
1927–28	53.3	106.8	22.8	172.8	69.6	120.9	40.0	115.4
1928–29	62.2	124.7	22.9	173.5	78.9	136.9	40.4	116.5
1929–30	70.8	141.9	10.0	76.0	74.5	129.4	40.7	117.4
1930–31	57.2	114.6	20.7	157.0	71.4	123.9	41.1	118.5
1931–32	66.5	133.3	6.4	48.6	66.3	115.0	41.4	119.5
1932–33	75.4	151.0	1.8	14.0	70.3	122.1	41.8	120.6
1933–34	81.1	162.5	0.3	2.6	74.5	129.3	42.2	121.8
1934–35	63.4	127.1	1.4	10.7	57.9	101.6	42.6	122.9

* *Compendio statistico italiano*, 1935, p. 75.

† Population figures are those calculated for December 31, of the first of the years given.

‡ Consumption data were arrived at by subtracting the quantity needed for seeding from Production and adding Net Importation.

Production and Importation figures run from August 1 to July 31.

§ Annual average for five-year period.

tem. The figures included in Tables 28–29 provide a convenient summary view of this development. They show, in brief, a steady growth of the different industries until 1926, a mild recession followed by the severe depression beginning in 1929, and eventually a partial recovery after 1932.

TABLE 27

Production of Principal Agricultural Commodities in Italy, by Years, 1909–1914, 1920–1937 *

I. Quantities Produced

Year	Wheat	Rice	Corn	Sugar Beets	Potatoes	Citrus Fruits	Wine (thousands of hectoliters)	Olive Oil (thousands of hectoliters)
			(thousands of quintals)					
1909–14	49,273	4,867	25,683	17,238	16,562	7,888	45,522	1,809
1920	38,466	4,512	22,683	11,999	14,223	6,293	42,294	2,039
1921	52,482	4,713	23,452	17,513	18,027	6,193	31,908	1,615
1922†	43,992	4,644	19,507	22,557	14,612	6,774	35,585	2,843
1923	61,191	5,209	22,659	26,994	17,958	6,181	53,948	1,978
1924	46,306	5,909	26,844	32,209	19,580	6,343	44,714	2,320
1925	65,548	6,294	27,932	15,744	21,577	6,311	45,367	1,490
1926	60,050	6,800	29,996	22,969	23,110	7,873	37,076	1,883
1927	53,291	6,961	22,195	20,154	19,453	6,621	35,650	1,602
1928	62,215	6,316	16,508	28,613	14,899	6,633	46,823	2,400
1929	70,795	6,737	25,306	29,242	20,077	8,075	41,050	3,113
1930	57,173	6,501	29,862	30,490	19,539	8,695	36,333	1,344
1931	66,520	6,621	19,462	24,732	19,646	7,259	36,332	2,428
1932	75,367	6,566	30,156	24,943	28,369	11,637	45,412	2,260
1933	81,252	6,915	25,906	21,436	23,741	7,905	33,035	1,761
1934	63,430	6,730	32,009	26,520	27,117	7,824	30,873	2,332
1935	76,955	7,352	24,961	23,247	21,591	7,009	46,658	2,337
1936	61,038	7,339	30,447	26,318	26,052	7,315	33,644	1,691
1937	80,562	7,402	30,722	33,144	28,718	6,754	34,001	2,980

II. PRODUCTION INDEXES: 1922 = 100 ‡

Year	Wheat	Rice	Corn	Sugar Beets	Wine Grapes	Olives	Total Volume of Agricultural Production	Population Growth
1923	139.1	112.2	116.2	119.7	148.8	71.8	122.7	100.8
1924	105.3	127.2	137.6	165.0	126.2	85.2	121.5	101.5
1925	149.0	135.5	143.2	69.8	127.0	55.0	129.1	102.4
1926	136.5	146.4	153.8	101.8	106.0	78.9	127.1	103.3
1927	121.1	149.9	113.8	89.3	102.9	63.3	111.9	104.2
1928	141.4	136.0	84.6	126.8	133.2	88.9	119.8	105.2
1929	160.9	145.1	129.7	129.6	112.7	108.1	138.3	106.2
1930	130.0	140.0	153.1	135.2	102.6	49.8	129.8	107.1
1931	151.2	142.6	99.8	109.6	105.9	88.0	123.4	108.1
1932	171.3	141.4	154.6	110.6	127.6	81.6	162.5	108.9
1933	184.7	148.9	132.7	95.0	93.3	73.8	147.9	110.0
1934	144.2	132.9	132.8	117.6	86.6	84.1	147.8	111.1

* Compiled from various issues of *Annuario statistico italiano, Compendio statistico italiano,* and *Bollettino mensile di statistica.*

† After 1922 data includes new provinces.

‡ The series of indexes given in this and the following tables were computed by the Central Institute of Statistics in Rome. They were not carried beyond 1934 here, since that is the last year for which comparable official index numbers were published.

TABLE 28

PRODUCTION OF PRINCIPAL INDUSTRIAL COMMODITIES IN ITALY, BY YEARS, 1913, 1920–1937 *

I. QUANTITIES PRODUCED (THOUSANDS OF TONS)

Year	Iron and Steel	Perphosphates	Sulphuric Acid†	Raw Silk (1000 kg.)	Rayon (1000 kg.)	Cotton Yarn	Cotton Cloth
1913	988.9	972.5	644.7	4,702.0	?	?	?
1920	773.8	?	352.0	3,781.0	720	?	?
1921	700.4	858.9	420.0	3,477.5	1,480	136.9	94.0
1922	1,046.0	947.6	485.4	3,989.8	2,593	154.3	100.9
1923	1,219.5	1,227.3	620.5	5,223.1	4,830	160.7	105.3
1924	1,458.1	1,241.6	632.0	5,592.3	10,450	174.8	121.8
1925	1,891.7	1,528.8	800.0	5,097.5	13,850	202.6	117.0
1926	1,883.8	1,474.7	822.9	4,365.8	17,060	195.8	129.7
1927	1,721.8	1,371.5	820.0	5,009.8	24,406	?	116.0
1928	2,097.2	1,151.1	704.1	5,567.7	25,949	202.2	125.0
1929	2,253.0	1,314.3	834.5	5,520.6	32,342	219.8	99.3
1930	1,867.4	1,383.0	831.2	5,289.1	30,139	184.0	81.6
1931	1,525.9	792.4	632.5	3,660.4	36,128	153.4	71.7
1932	1,497.1	661.6	562.0	3,927.0	34,038	169.1	73.2
1933	1,882.6	1,006.9	678.3	3,543.0	40,242	190.8	85.0
1934	1,932.8	1,090.6	1,238.7†	3,124.0	51,047	173.1	83.5
1935	2,247.2	1,049.2	1,286.7†	2,982.0	72,356	171.2	87.6
1936	2,031.0	1,365.9	1,531.7†	2,812.0	92,242	170.4	79.6
1937	2,086.9	1,333.2	1,642.1†	2,861.0	124,388	..	..

II. PRODUCTION INDEXES: 1922 = 100

Year	Iron and Steel	Perphosphates	Sulphuric Acid	Raw Silk	Rayon	Cotton Yarn	Cotton Cloth
1923	116.6	130.6	' 127.8	130.9	165.5	104.2	103.0
1924	139.4	131.1	130.2	140.2	362.1	113.3	120.4
1925	180.9	161.7	164.8	127.8	482.8	133.2	115.7
1926	180.1	158.0	169.5	109.4	575.9	134.9	133.6
1927	164.6	154.5	168.9	125.6	841.4	117.7	115.8
1928	200.5	126.1	145.1	139.5	896.6	131.0	126.0
1929	215.4	157.9	171.9	138.4	1,113.2	142.5	136.3
1930	178.5	170.1	171.2	132.6	1,162.3	119.2	110.0
1931	145.9	106.5	130.3	91.7	1,333.8	99.4	95.0
1932	143.1	94.8	115.8	98.4	1,236.8	109.6	95.4
1933	180.0	138.0	139.7	88.8	1,432.9	123.6	109.6
1934	184.8	151.5	....	78.5	1,860.8	112.2	105.5

* Compiled from various issues of *Annuario statistico italiano, Compendio statistico italiano,* and *Bollettino mensile di statistica.*

† Computed as 66° Bé acid up to 1934; as 50° Bé after that date.

TABLE 29

Indexes of Industrial Production in Italy, by Groups of Industries and Years, 1923–1934*

(Indexes: 1922 = 100)

Year	General Index	Mines and Quarries	Metal Working	Textiles	Paper	Gas and Electricity	Building	Food-stuffs	Chemicals
1923	116.0	120.6	118.8	111.6	70.1	116.6	146.9	103.6	116.9
1924	137.5	128.0	143.3	128.7	99.4	134.6	190.5	118.8	134.8
1925	156.6	149.4	193.3	139.8	150.9	151.0	240.5	83.2	146.9
1926	165.0	155.6	189.6	145.1	128.5	173.0	262.7	108.7	155.0
1927	162.4	159.1	169.6	152.9	112.7	180.0	248.7	106.3	155.7
1928	180.7	151.8	205.8	159.2	122.3	196.8	324.0	120.1	152.9
1929	201.8	161.5	225.5	175.8	130.0	211.5	439.9	127.6	152.8
1930	183.1	156.6	192.5	160.2	129.1	219.0	378.6	114.6	149.6
1931	156.3	128.4	160.4	144.5	122.0	216.0	262.0	105.7	124.7
1932	145.9	110.7	148.5	137.2	125.3	218.2	233.7	95.7	118.9
1933	167.3	110.9	174.2	161.7	136.3	236.6	279.4	93.9	150.0
1934	182.2	126.2	180.2	160.7	155.1	250.1	410.5	100.1	167.8

* *Compendio statistico italiano*, 1935, p. 285.

As these figures indicate, Italy has made considerable progress in the expansion of some of her industries during the last fifteen years. The metallurgical and the textile industries, the backbone of the country's industrial system, have shown, even in the face of the world depression, surprising elements of strength. The iron and steel industry — upon which rest the automobile, the electrical and mechanical, and a variety of

TABLE 30

PRODUCTION OF HYDROELECTRIC POWER IN ITALY AND OTHER COUNTRIES,
BY YEARS, 1925–1937 *

(*In billions of KWH*)

Year	Italy	France	Germany	Canada	United States
1925	6.9	4.0	2.9	9.9	22.4
1926	8.0	4.7	3.3	11.9	26.2
1927	8.4	5.1	3.8	14.3	29.9
1928	9.4	5.6	3.6	16.1	34.7
1929	10.0	6.1	3.6	17.7	34.6
1930	10.4	6.9	4.0	17.8	33.0
1931	10.2	6.1	4.3	16.1	30.6
1932	10.3	5.9	4.0	15.6	34.1
1933	11.2	6.7	4.1	17.0	34.7
1934	12.1	7.2	4.6	20.8	34.1
1935	12.8	8.2	5.8	22.9	40.0
1936	13.2	..	..	25.4	40.9
1937	14.4	..	..	27.0	43.4

* Compiled from various issues of Giorgio Mortara, *Prospettive economiche, Annuario statistico italiano*, and *Bollettino mensile di statistica*.

Note: Data for the U. S. include only the production of plants which sell power to the public; private plants are not included. For Canada and France private plants are included in part.

other industries — has more than doubled its output since 1913. The development of the chemical industry (one of the most important in the country) is shown by the growth in the production of sulphuric acid and perphosphates (chemical fertilizer). The growth of the textile industry is represented by production data on cotton yarn, cotton cloth, and the truly remarkable figures on the production of artificial silk (rayon).

Yet, while the textile, the chemical, and the metallurgical industries are among Italy's largest, the most important in the Italian industrial system, if the amount of capital invested be taken as a measure, is the hydroelectric industry. It is through this industry that the waters of Italy's lakes and rivers are converted into *carbone bianco*, the "white coal" which is more and more taking the place of British coal in supplying the power for the country's factories and railroads. In conformity with the regime's encouragement of activities that tend to free the country from dependence upon foreign supplies, hydroelectric power production has been greatly stimulated by the government. Its rapid growth is illustrated by Table 30.

TRANSPORTATION: ROADS, RAILROADS, AND SHIPPING

To complete this sketch of the recent development of Italy's industries, some mention must be made of road building, rail-

TABLE 31

DEVELOPMENT OF ITALIAN STATE HIGHWAYS, JUNE 30, 1935 *

		WORK OF THE AZIENDA AUTONOMA STATALE DELLA STRADA (FROM JULY 1, 1928 TO JUNE 30, 1935)			
Total Length of Italian State Roads	Ordinary Macadam Surface or Other Old Surfaces	New, Protected Macadam Surface		Special Surfaces	
		Completed	In Process of Completion	Completed	In Process of Completion
20,644 Km.†	9,343 Km.	9,771 Km.	1,027 Km.	499 Km.	4 Km.

* *Compendio statistico italiano*, 1935, p. 120.
† 1 Km. (kilometer) is equal to 0.62137 miles.

roads, and shipping. In 1928, in order to remedy the deplorable condition of many of Italy's roads, the Azienda Autonoma Statale della Strada (the State Highways Corporation), an independently managed government organization for the building and the maintenance of highways, was created. Through the work of the Azienda, many of the proverbially bad roads have of late been transformed into excellent modern highways, or into the splendid *autostrade*, especially built speedways for rapid communication, which now connect many of the most important centers on the Peninsula. The present condition of Italian state highways and the work of the Azienda Autonoma Statale della Strada are interestingly illustrated by the figures in Table 31. The development of the Italian railroad system, particularly its rapid electrification in recent years, is shown

TABLE 32

LENGTH (IN KILOMETERS) AND DEGREE OF ELECTRIFICATION OF ITALIAN RAILROAD AND TRAMWAY LINES, JANUARY 1, 1933*

Type of Traction	Gauge	RAILROADS		TRAMWAYS		Total
		State	Private	Extra Urban	Urban	
Steam	Standard	14.181	1.954	1.510	....	17.645
	Narrow	704	2.192	458	....	3.354
Electric	Standard	1.973	633	1.247	999	4.852
	Narrow	60	1.110	605	720	2.495
Internal Combustion	Narrow	....	11	....	....	11
Total (kilometers)	....	16.918	5.900	3.820	1.719	28.357

* G. Mortara, *Prospettive economiche*, 1934, p. 191.

by Tables 32 and 33. The development of Italian shipping is shown by Table 34.

TABLE 33

INDEXES OF RAILROAD ELECTRIFICATION AND TRAFFIC IN ITALY, BY YEARS,
1923–1934*

(*1922 = 100*)

| | | ALL STATE RAILROADS | |
Year	Growth of Electri- fied Lines	Goods Carried	Passengers Carried
1923	101.7	115.7	105.8
1924	111.9	135.0	103.8
1925	121.6	148.3	113.7
1926	129.3	149.8	120.8
1927	148.5	143.9	122.1
1928	177.6	144.9	117.7
1929	212.4	154.2	116.7
1930	212.4	137.0	110.2
1931	236.3	112.9	93.2
1932	265.8	94.7	84.8
1933	273.3	86.3	84.5
1934	285.2	85.4	85.5

* Compiled from various issues of *Compendio statistico italiano*.

TABLE 34

NUMBER OF VESSELS AND TONNAGE OF THE ITALIAN MERCANTILE MARINE,
BY YEARS, 1913, 1920–1937 *

Year	Number of Steam and Motor Vessels	Net Tonnage (*in thousands of tons*)
1913	931	876.8
1920	495	835.0
1921	603	1,075.2
1922	856	1,508.7
1923	880	1,635.9
1924	1,304	1,588.6
1925	1,370	1,763.9
1926	1,410	1,877.3
1927	1,424	1,946.2
1928	1,454	2,009.7
1929	1,396	1,918.1
1930	1,434	1,990.4
1931	1,443	2,043.3
1932	1,407	2,051.0
1933	1,342	1,868.0
1934	1,301	1,775.7
1935	1,295	1,847.7
1936	1,284	1,832.5
1937	1,335	1,771.5

* Compiled from various issues of *Annuario statistico italiano* and from
Bollettino mensile di statistica, January 1938, p. 56.

While the Italian merchant marine has made some progress during the last decade and a half, and the quality of the equipment and the organization of shipping services have greatly improved, this has been made possible not through the profit-

TABLE 35

VALUES OF ITALIAN IMPORTS AND EXPORTS, BY YEARS, 1909–1913, 1920–1937 *

(*In millions of lire*)

Year	Imports	Exports	Balance
1909–13†	12,474	8,877	3,597
1920†	16,276	7,859	8,417
1921†	13,868	7,487	6,381
1922†	14,141	9,596	4,545
1923†	15,006	11,137	3,869
1924†	16,009	13,653	2,356
1925†	19,833	15,908	3,925
1926†	19,124	15,648	3,476
1927†	19,641	15,071	4,570
1928	21,920	14,559	7,361
1929	21,303	14,884	6,419
1930	17,347	12,119	5,228
1931	11,643	10,210	1,433
1932	8,268	6,812	1,456
1933	7,432	5,991	1,441
1934	7,675	5,224	2,451
1935	7,790	5,238	2,552
1936	5,994	5,454	540‡
1937	13,837	10,429	3,408

* Compiled from various issues of *Compendio statistico italiano, Annuario statistico italiano,* and *Bollettino mensile di statistica.*

† Values converted into post-war gold standard lire for purposes of comparison.

‡ In 1935 and 1936, the years of the Ethiopian campaign, exports to the Italian colonies (included in the figures for total exports given above) were unusually large. While in 1934 and in previous years these exports amounted to about 250 million lire per annum, they grew to 750 million in 1935 and to 1690 million lire in 1936. Imports from the colonies (included in the data for total imports) grew from 93 million lire in 1934 to 128 million in 1935 and to 156 million in 1936. Provisional figures for 1937 show that in that year exports to the colonies amounted to 2,580 million lire, while imports from them were equal to 348 million.

ableness of the shipping industry itself but rather through continued government assistance. An outstanding example of the work carried on under the aegis of the government is the consolidation in 1931, after a period of intensive and destructive competition, of the three main Italian steamship lines into the powerful Italian Line, which now occupies fifth place among the world's shipping concerns.

THE TARIFF, FOREIGN TRADE, AND THE BALANCE OF INTERNATIONAL PAYMENTS

We must now turn — before we proceed to a final evaluation of Italy's economic development under the Fascist regime — to an analysis of the country's international economic position and to a brief examination of her monetary and fiscal problems. It is in the course of this analysis that some of the weakest links in the Italian economic organism will be encountered.

In Italy, as in most other countries, the world depression caused a drastic decline in the volume of foreign trade and a growing deficit in the commercial balance.[15] The extent of the decline is indicated by Table 35, showing the course of Italy's imports and exports in recent years and the condition of the country's balance of trade.

Under normal circumstances a large trade deficit is not a cause for alarm in Italy. Because of her lack of raw materials and basic natural resources, Italy has usually had an "unfavorable" balance of trade, the country's imports exceeding the exports. Through the "invisible" items of her balance of international payments, particularly through expenditures of foreign tourists and the remittances of Italian emigrants, these deficits were, in the past, made up without undue difficulty. During the recent depression, however, automatic adjustments failed to take place. Commodity exports as well as invisible exports were severely reduced.[16] But for a time imports also declined con-

---

[15] Cf. chap. vii, p. 172.

[16] The extent of the reduction of some of the most important "invisible" credit items in Italy's balance of international payments in recent years is shown by the following table (giving data in millions of lire):

Year	Freight and Shipping Services	Tourist Trade	Emigrant Remittances
1929	1,135	2,102	2,120
1930	995	1,930	1,820
1931	700	1,185	1,570
1932	500	830	910

Source: Computed from data on the Italian balance of international payments given by Professor Gino Borgatta in his *Trattato elementare di statistica* (Milan, 1933).

siderably, so that for a while the country was able to maintain the equilibrium in her international accounts. In 1931, however, a slow but progressive widening of the gap between commodity exports and imports began to take place. Imports did not decrease sufficiently to keep pace with the fall in exports. In 1931 exports paid for 88 per cent of imports; in 1933 exports paid for only 80 per cent of imports; in 1934 and 1935 imports increased while exports continued to decline; in 1935 the country's exports paid for only 67 per cent of the imports. The remainder, amounting in that year to over 2,500 million lire, had to be paid for by other means.[17] The absence or insufficiency of these means caused a gradually increasing strain on the foreign exchange markets, frequent outflows of gold, and a consequent noticeable pressure upon the country's gold reserves.

This situation and the inherent threat to the stability of the currency led Italy to a complete reversal of her hitherto comparatively liberal commercial policy and to the adoption of the same elaborate system of import quotas, import licenses, and restrictions which had been in use for some years in other European countries. Till April 1934, when the first important restrictive measures were adopted, Italy's commercial policy had been a comparatively liberal one. The trade treaties which had been concluded with other nations had been based in the main upon the traditional principles of the most-favored-nations

[17] The following table, obtained in part from Francesco Saccà, "Sulla nostra bilancia commerciale," *Economia*, April 1935, clearly shows the progressive widening of the gap between Italian imports and exports in recent years (*data in millions of lire*):

Year	Imports	Index (1929 = 100)	Exports	Index (1929 = 100)	Deficit	Index (1929 = 100)	Exports in Per Cent of Imports
1929	21,303	100	14,884	100	6,419	100	70
1930	17,347	81	12,119	80	5,228	81	70
1931	11,643	55	10,210	67	1,433	22	88
1932	8,268	39	6,812	46	1,456	22	82
1933	7,432	35	5,991	40	1,441	22	80
1934	7,675	36	5,224	35	2,451	38	68
1935	7,790	37	5,238	35	2,552	40	67

clause. This is particularly true of the period immediately preceding 1927, when every effort was made to repair the economic ravages of the World War and to resume normal trade relations. During these years the trade treaties negotiated on the basis of Italy's 1921 tariff act followed in the main the liberal principles of the country's pre-war trade policy. The only exception — though a notable one, for it became the basis for most later restrictions — consisted in the provision in the new treaties that Italy reserved to herself the right to adopt import restrictions and to prohibit certain imports altogether whenever she saw fit against those countries which had adopted import restrictions against Italian commodities.[18]

After the unsuccessful outcome of the Geneva International Economic Conference in 1927, at which the hoped-for world tariff truce and general reduction of tariff barriers failed to materialize, the pursuit of a liberal commercial policy became more and more difficult. Protectionism, extended by many countries to the field of agriculture, made rapid progress. The situation became critical after 1929, when the cessation of American loans and the devaluation of the pound and of other currencies made it extremely difficult, if not impossible, for most countries of continental Europe, still in need of raw materials but suddenly deprived of important export markets, to balance their commercial accounts. The adoption of restrictive measures, of import quotas and licenses, of exchange controls and barter agreements was begun on an unprecedented scale. In most commercial treaties the most-favored-nations clause was replaced by the application of the reciprocity principle, through which restrictive measures adopted by foreign countries were answered with even more stringent restrictions at home. A situation revealing an unusual state of economic nervousness and tension, and not conducive to a widening but to a progressive shrinkage of the volume of world trade, gradually developed.

Italy, as indicated above, was one of the last countries to

---

[18] Cf. Angelo Di Nola, "L'Evoluzione della politica economica internazionale con particolare riguardo all'Italia," *Rassegna di politica internazionale*, November 1935.

succumb to the general trend. When France in the summer of 1931 adopted a rigid system of import limitations and quotas, Italy saw herself forced to reply in kind and to adopt a series of import restrictions against French commodities, formally defined in a reciprocity agreement concluded with France in February 1932. The harmful effects of these restrictive policies were soon apparent: in 1932 Italo-French trade declined by almost 50 per cent as compared with 1931. Apart from this important exception, however, Italy's foreign trade policy remained fundamentally unchanged till 1934. Then the effects of the world depression, of the world-wide currency devaluations, and of the restrictive measures adopted by almost all other countries forced a drastic change in Italy's policy. On April 14, 1934, the importation of four important staple commodities — wool, copper, oil seeds and coffee — was prohibited except under a special import license. During the first eight months of 1934 reciprocal trade treaties based on mutual compensation agreements were concluded with seventeen countries.[19] On December 8, 1934, all Italian exporters were commanded, under a decree, to sell to the National Foreign Exchange Institute all the foreign exchange received and all the foreign credits granted to them in payment of their exports. Through the royal decrees of February 16 and March 30, 1935, the importation of a wide variety of commodities was placed under definite license and quota restrictions. Some commodities could be imported only if the Ministry of Finance granted a special import permit for that purpose; a large number of others was admitted without ministerial license, but the amounts which could be so imported were limited to a percentage (ranging from 10 to 70 per cent) of the amounts imported in 1934.[20] On July 28, 1935, the importation of coal,

---

[19] Cf. speech made at the Bari Fair, September 1934, by Alberto Asquini, then Undersecretary of Corporations.

[20] Imports from countries with which "clearing agreements" had been concluded were admitted up to 100 per cent of their 1934 amounts.

On April 1, 1935, "clearing agreements" under which no payments in actual foreign exchange need be made were in force with Bulgaria, Czechoslovakia, Germany, Yugoslavia, Roumania, Turkey, and Hungary. Because of special accords, importations up to 100 per cent of 1934 imports were also permitted from

coke, tin, nickel, and copper was placed under a special government monopoly.

When, therefore, the League of Nations' economic sanctions were applied against Italy on November 18, 1935, and fifty-two nations suddenly ceased their purchases of Italian commodities, the country already had at her disposal a well-developed machinery for the control of her foreign trade.[21] This machinery, as we have observed, was used to curtail Italy's imports still further, on the one hand to retaliate against the policy of restrictions adopted by the sanctionist countries and on the other to protect her own balance of trade.

It is significant to note what the practical effects of the severe trade restrictions adopted by the Italian government were and whether they achieved their main objective of avoiding increasing trade deficits. On May 19, 1936, in a speech made before the Italian Chamber Paolo Thaon de Revel, the Minister of Finance, announced that during the months of December 1935 and January, February, and March 1936 the total deficit of the country's balance of trade, even disregarding exports to her African possessions, was actually less than it was during the corresponding months of the previous year — a result achieved primarily through the intensive use of the machinery for the curtailment of imports described in the foregoing pages.

The effectiveness of the machinery for import curtailment devised by the Italian government appears in a less favorable light, however, if one proceeds to analyze, with the aid of the official statistics recently made available, the course of Italy's foreign trade during the period of the sanctions taken as a whole. From December 1, 1935, to July 31, 1936 (the period to which all the following figures refer), the total value of Italy's import and export trade (excluding the trade with Italian colonies) was equal to 5.5 billion lire. During the corresponding period in the preceding year (December 1, 1934, to July

---

Albania, Austria, the Netherlands, Switzerland, and Hungary. For France the corresponding percentage was 85 and for Great Britain 80.

[21] For a more complete discussion of Italian import restrictions during this period see William G. Welk, "League Sanctions and Foreign Trade Restrictions in Italy," *American Economic Review*, March 1937, pp. 96–107.

31, 1935) the total value of Italy's foreign trade was equal to 8.0 billion lire, the decrease during the period of the sanctions consequently amounting to 2.5 billion, or about 32 per cent.[22] During the sanctions the total value of Italy's exports was equal to 1.7 billion lire; during the pre-sanctionist period exports were equal to 3.0 billion; the total reduction in exports which Italy suffered because of sanctions amounted, consequently, to 1.3 billion lire, or 44 per cent. Imports, which had been equal to 5.0 billion lire in the pre-sanctionist period, were reduced to 3.8 billion, the reduction amounting to 1.2 billion lire or 25 per cent of the total.

Thus while during the sanctions Italian exports were reduced by 44 per cent, imports were reduced by only 25 per cent. These figures show clearly that while the absolute increase in Italy's "unfavorable" balance of trade during sanctions was comparatively small (from 2.0 billion to 2.1 billion lire) the country's relative trade position was weakened materially. By expressing exports as a percentage of imports one finds, in fact, that while before the sanctions exports paid for 60 per cent of imports, during their duration exports paid for only 45 per cent of imports. "Invisible" exports having been greatly reduced and the concession of foreign credits suspended by all sanctionist nations, the growing trade deficit had to be met in large part by exports of gold. A careful estimate of the shrinkage of Italy's gold reserve during the period under consideration in fact reveals that Italy's losses of gold during the sanctions amounted to 1.45 billion lire.[23]

A somewhat more detailed analysis of the nature and direction of Italy's trade during sanctions throws further light upon the effects of the sanctionist experiment on Italy's international economic position. While the country's total trade with sanctionist nations diminished by 65.0 per cent, trade with all non-

[22] These figures and the data which follow are taken from a study of the effects of the League of Nations' sanctions on Italy's foreign trade recently made by an Italian economist and based upon official Italian statistical sources. Cf. Alberto Campolongo, "Il Commercio italiano con l'estero durante le sanzioni," *Giornale degli economisti*, May 1937, p. 326.
[23] Campolongo, p. 327. Cf. also chap. ix, pp. 214 ff.

sanctionist countries increased by only 4.4 per cent. While exports to sanctionist countries were reduced by 87.8 per cent and imports from sanctionist countries by 51.3 per cent, exports to non-sanctionist countries increased by only 5 per cent and imports from these countries by only 4 per cent. It is interesting to note, furthermore, that during sanctions, non-sanctionist countries bought 88.7 per cent of Italy's total exports (37 per cent of this total going to Germany and 17 per cent to the United States) and sold her 66.4 per cent of her

TABLE 36

VALUE OF IMPORTS OF OTHER COUNTRIES FROM ITALY DURING LEAGUE OF NATIONS' SANCTIONS*

(Thousands of "old" gold dollars)

Month	1934–35	1935–36
November (58 countries)	21,550	25,808
December (57 countries)	21,521	17,155
January (66 countries)	19,661	10,158
February (61 countries)	19,190	8,649
March (37 countries)	17,570	9,281

* *Economist* (London), June 6, 1936, p. 542.

total imports (29 per cent being sold by Germany and 13 per cent by the United States). These figures show clearly that, had Italy not had the support of the non-sanctionist countries (the trade with whom amounted, even before the sanctions, to about 48 per cent of her total foreign commerce), her foreign trade would in all probability have been almost completely paralyzed by the sanctionist measures.

The drastic reduction in exports which Italy suffered during the first five months of the sanctions is interestingly illustrated by the summary data of Table 36, computed from League of Nations' reports. The detrimental effect of the Italian restrictions upon the export trade of some of the leading sanctionist countries, on the other hand, is shown by the numerical data reported in Table 37.

What of the future outlook for Italy's international trade? Despite the tariff reductions made in October 1936 and the several trade agreements concluded since then, an early return to traditional modes of international commerce seems, at least for the immediate future, rather remote. While it is true that the measures designed to liberalize foreign trade (tariff reductions and the stipulation of a number of new trade treaties) which accompanied the recent devaluation of the lira have had a stimulating effect upon Italy's international commerce and will gradu-

TABLE 37

INDEXES OF VALUE OF EXPORTS INTO ITALY AND ITALIAN COLONIES DURING
LEAGUE OF NATIONS' SANCTIONS, BY COUNTRIES OF EXPORT*
(*Percentages calculated from values in "old" gold dollars given in League
of Nations' reports*)

Country	1934–35 Nov.–Feb.	1935–36 Nov.–Feb.	March 1935	March 1936†
Great Britain	100	14.05	100	10.10
Australia	100	14.81	...	....
New Zealand	100	14.81	...	....
Denmark	100	15.25	...	....
Union of So. Africa	100	22.30	...	....
India	100	24.84	100	25.26
Canada	100	28.22	...	....
Greece	100	31.59	...	....
Jugoslavia	100	32.62	100	10.97
Portugal	100	33.06	...	....
Norway	100	35.28	...	92.20
Czechoslovakia	100	45.76	100	....
Spain	100	52.38	...	....
Poland	100	55.10	100	46.79
Belgium-Luxemburg	100	57.64	100	57.58
Holland	100	63.92	100	51.29
France	100	69.62	100	22.67
Russia	100	81.16	100	62.63

* Giuseppe Parenti, "L'Efficacia delle controsanzioni italiane," *Rivista internazionale di scienze sociali* (Milan), July 1936, pp. 355–365.

† Data for a number of countries not available for March 1936.

ally make unnecessary some of the more rigid import and exchange controls now in force, it is also true that currents favoring pronounced economic self-sufficiency are strong in Italy, that the country's international economic position is still far from favorable, and that, therefore, an early return to a regime of unrestricted dealings in the foreign exchanges and of importations controlled solely by the traditional tariff system does not as yet appear to be in sight.

CHAPTER IX

FINANCE, EMPLOYMENT, PRICES, WAGES, AND THE STANDARD OF LIVING

RECENT MONETARY POLICIES OF THE FASCIST STATE

As OUR discussion so far has shown, the coming of the world depression caused a material curtailment of Italy's international trade and a serious weakening of the country's international economic position. This soon resulted in a severe threat to the stability of Italian exchange. After its stabilization in December 1927 the lira can hardly be said to have been on a true gold standard. Except for a brief interval in 1930–31, some degree of control over the country's currency has in fact been maintained ever since June 1926, when speculative foreign exchange transactions were prohibited and dealings in foreign currencies permitted only if undertaken to meet legitimate business needs.

When the depression came and exports began to dwindle at an unprecedented rate, the exchange situation rapidly went from bad to worse, until, early in 1934, the lira moved to a discount of 2 to 4 per cent on the Paris Bourse and a serious outward movement of gold began. As a result, in May 1934 a series of stringent measures of exchange control was adopted by the Italian government. Banks and foreign exchange dealers were required by law to inform the Bank of Italy of their foreign exchange holdings, and foreign securities owned by Italian nationals were subjected to registration. The exportation of Italian currency and the purchase of foreign securities by Italian citizens were prohibited. Only travelers were allowed to export currency, but in amounts not exceeding 5,000 lire.

Though drastic, these measures failed to check the pressure upon the country's balance of international payments. The gold reserves of the Bank of Italy, which stood at 7,091 million in December 31, 1933, declined to 5,811 million in December 1934.

The ratio of gold and foreign exchange reserves to note circulation declined, as the data in Table 38 indicates, from 55.9 per cent in December 1933 to 44.8 per cent in December 1934.

In an attempt to stop the outflow of gold, the Bank of Italy in November 1934 raised its discount rate from 3 to 4 per cent. On December 8 bankers and merchants were ordered to sell their foreign exchange holdings to the National Exchange Institute within ten days, and all citizens were ordered to declare to the Bank of Italy any foreign credits and securities which they might own. On December 19 all exports of lira bonds, bills, drafts, checks, etc., were prohibited. Persons leaving the country were not permitted to carry with them sums in excess of 2,000 lire. Although it was becoming more and more clearly apparent that the threatening monetary crisis could not be permanently averted by these restrictions, their immediate effect was, as had been hoped, to check the heavy outflow of gold.

In February 1935, as we have seen, a number of drastic new import bans were put into effect. On May 9 owners of foreign securities were compelled to deposit these in a special dossier at the Bank of Italy and to receive their dividend, interest, and amortization payments in lire. On May 20 a superintendent of foreign exchange, reporting directly to the Prime Minister, was entrusted with the allocation of available foreign exchange to industry and trade and with the control of exports and imports. In June a decree was passed authorizing the withdrawal from circulation of all silver coins.

When, in the late spring of 1935, the new burden of large raw material imports needed for the impending war with Ethiopia was added to the existing difficulties, the strain on the gold reserves became acute, and the struggle for the stability of the currency had to be definitely abandoned. At the end of July the law prescribing a 40 per cent gold and foreign exchange reserve for the note liabilities of the Bank of Italy was suspended and recourse to the gold reserve for the settlement of outstanding foreign commercial obligations was allowed. The effect of the suspension was an appreciable fall in the external

TABLE 38

ITALIAN NOTE CIRCULATION AND CENTRAL BANK RESERVES, BY YEARS, 1913, 1920–1936*

(*In million lire*)

Year (Dec. 31)	Total Note Circulation	Note Circulation Index† (1928 = 100)	CENTRAL BANK RESERVES			Per Cent of Gold Reserves to Note Circulation	Per Cent of Total Reserves to Note Circulation
			Gold	Foreign Exchange	Total		
1913	2,783	...	1,491	170	1,661	...	59.7
1920	22,000	...	1,593	484	2,077	...	9.4
1921	21,475	...	1,625	373	1,998	...	9.3
1922	20,279	...	1,660	380	2,041	...	10.1
1923	19,674	...	1,662	185	1,847	...	9.4
1924	20,514	...	1,675	150	1,826	...	8.9
1925	21,449	...	1,677	363	2,040	...	9.5
1926	20,133	...	1,668	810	2,478	...	12.3
1927	18,774	...	4,547	7,558	12,105	...	64.5
1928	17,456	100.0	5,051	6,018	11,070	29.2†	64.0†
1929	16,854	97.0	5,190	5,151	10,341	30.9†	61.6†
1930	15,680	90.7	5,296	4,327	9,624	33.8	61.4
1931	14,294	82.7	5,626	2,170	7,796	39.4	54.5
1932	13,672	79.0	5,839	1,304	7,144	42.7	52.3
1933	13,243	76.6	7,091	305	7,396	53.5	55.9
1934	13,145	76.0	5,811	72	5,883	44.2	44.8
1935	16,297	94.2	3,027	367	3,394	18.6	20.8
1936	16,525	95.6	3,959‡	63‡	4,022‡	23.9‡	24.3‡

* Compiled from various issues of *Compendio statistico italiano*, *Bollettino mensile di statistica* and *Annuario statistico italiano*.
† In the computation of the note circulation index and reserve percentages, 161 million state bank notes circulating in 1928 and 80 million still circulating in 1929 were not included.
‡ Figures are given in "new" gold lire, in circulation after the devaluation of the lira in October 1936 and containing 40.94 per cent less gold than the "old" 1927 gold lira. Expressed in "old" gold lire, total central bank reserves on December 31, 1936, were equal to 2,376 million, and the ratio of total reserves to note circulation to about 15 per cent.

value of the lira and a further large gold outflow. The gold reserve of the Bank of Italy, which had stood at 5,829 million in May 1935, declined to 4,704 million in August, while during the same period the percentage of total reserves to note circulation dropped from 45.7 to 36.5 per cent.

To avoid further losses of gold and to replenish its depleted reserves, the government on August 28, 1935, compelled the sale of all credits abroad to the National Foreign Exchange Institute and the exchange of all foreign securities held by Italians for 5 per cent nine-year Treasury bonds. These purchases and the gold obtained from the Italian people at the time of the sanctions are estimated to have yielded the Treasury an added reserve of several billion lire.

On October 3, 1935, restrictive measures were enlarged with the prohibition of the importation of lira bank notes. Only foreign travelers were permitted to import currency, and this in amounts not in excess of 2,000 lire. On November 11 the National Foreign Exchange Institute was given a monopoly for the purchase of gold abroad and was empowered to purchase domestic gold at the price current on the international markets.[1] Finally, on December 29, 1935, the Undersecretaryship for Trade and Exchange, a new government department possessing a complete monopoly on all foreign exchange transactions within the kingdom, was established. This department, recently transformed into an independent ministry, is today the supreme authority in all matters of foreign trade control and exchange regulation in Italy.

Because of the drastic decline in exports and the large purchases of foreign raw materials during the first months of the sanctions the gold reserves of the Bank of Italy declined still further. During the period from October 20 to December 31, 1935, they fell from 3.936 to 3.027 million lire — a decline which was, however, compensated probably more than threefold by the new reserves which accrued to the Treasury through its

---

[1] Gold was received on deposit at 5 per cent interest by the Bank of Italy and was purchased from the public at 15.50 lire per gram, as compared with 12.62 lire, the official gold parity.

purchases of foreign securities and through the gold donated to it by the Italian people.

Since December 1935 no detailed statistics on gold and foreign exchange reserves have been made public. In a speech made on November 28, 1936, however, Mussolini stated that during the seven preceding months the drain on the gold reserves of the Bank of Italy had ceased.[2] The Bank of Italy itself, on December 31, 1936, published a statement showing a total gold and foreign exchange reserve of 4,022 million lire. These, however, are the "new" gold lire in circulation after the devaluation of the currency in October 1936 and contain 40.94 per cent less gold than the "old" gold lira of 1927. Expressed in "old" gold lire, the Bank of Italy's total reserves on December 31, 1936, amounted to only 2,376 million, and the ratio of reserves to note circulation was about 15 per cent. A computation of the Bank of Italy's loss of reserves during 1936, based upon this figure, reveals a total net loss of 1,018 million lire; during 1935 the bank's loss of reserves amounted to 2,489 million, and during 1934 to 2,513 million lire. In estimating the country's total gold and foreign exchange reserves after 1935 it must be remembered, however, that the figures just given do not include the reserves which accrued to the Treasury through the forced sale to it of the foreign securities held by Italian nationals and the gold donated by the Italian people. Figures on the magnitude of these reserves, which are said to amount to several billion lire, have never been made public.

On October 5, 1936, as we have noted, Italian currency was devalued with the French franc and other gold bloc exchanges, and its gold content reduced by 40.94 per cent. The considerable gain in reserves which accrued to the Treasury through the devaluation and through the improvement in the country's international position following the monetary realignment has since made it possible for the government to maintain the lira at its new parity without undue effort. Barring fresh inter-

[2] Speech before the National Foreign Trade Institute, summarized in Fascist Confederation of Industrialists, *Business and Financial Report* (Rome), December 1936.

national complications and too rash a program of government spending it is not unlikely that Italian currency will remain at its present level without undue difficulty.

THE BANKING REFORM OF 1936

In maintaining the stability of the currency, the government will be aided materially by the important reforms which have recently been made in the country's banking system. On March 12, 1936, a decree containing elaborate provisions for "the protection of savings and the regulation of credit" was promulgated. Through this decree, an office of inspection, headed by the governor of the Bank of Italy, was established and given wide powers of supervision over all banks and savings institutions of the kingdom. The office was also empowered to supervise the issue of bonds and shares whenever offered for sale by credit institutions under its control, to authorize the listing of bonds and stocks on Italian stock exchanges, and to control interest rates on deposits and advances, the investment policies and practices of the banks subjected to its supervision, and the extension of long- and short-term credit.

Through the same decree the Bank of Italy was transformed into a public institution (Istituto di Diritto Pubblico) and (after June 30, 1936) forced to give up its commercial business and to confine its rediscount operations exclusively to banks. (Advances on securities may, however, continue to be made by the Bank of Italy, both to the banks and to the public.) The decree provided further that the capital of the bank be repaid to its private shareholders and that the new shares, for a total of 300,000,000 lire, be subscribed to and held exclusively by the country's savings banks and insurance companies. At the same time, Italy's three largest private banks, the Banca Commerciale Italiana, the Credito Italiano, and the Banco di Roma were transformed into public institutions whose stock must now be registered and may be owned by Italian citizens or Italian firms only.

Through these sweeping reforms the Bank of Italy becomes a true "bankers' bank" and the acknowledged leader of the country's credit system, a position similar, in many respects, to that now occupied by the Federal Reserve System in the United States. Although the Italian banking reform is as yet too recent to permit an exhaustive appraisal of its effects, the changes which it has already brought about give every promise of being beneficial and will in all probability contribute to the strengthening of Italy's financial system.

FISCAL POLICY, THE BUDGET, AND THE NATIONAL DEBT

While, then, barring unforeseen difficulties, the currency question may, for the time being, at least, be regarded as solved, another perplexing financial problem at present confronts the Fascist state: that of the budget and of the rapidly growing national debt. We turn now to a brief discussion of that problem.

Any inquiry into Fascist budgetary and fiscal policy must begin with a word of caution as to the interpretation of official statistical materials available on the subject of Italian public finance. The Italian government's accounting methods are extremely complex and changes in accounting procedure, which sometimes impair seriously the comparability of statistical data, are relatively frequent. Total revenues and expenditures, for example, have at times been swelled or diminished by the inclusion, or non-inclusion, in the national budget of more or less complete budgetary data of autonomous bodies, such as the state railways, the postal, telegraph, and telephone services, the autonomous fund for internal debt amortization, etc., and by the varying accounting procedures followed in the treatment of war debts, reparations, and certain classes of public loans and expenditures. Even though of late an effort has been made to render figures for the years since 1922 strictly comparable, Professor Rèpaci, one of the leading authorities in the field of Italian public finance, shows that complete accuracy has not yet been achieved and that official budget figures must be further rectified whenever the data for successive years are compared.[3]

[3] See F. A. Rèpaci, *La Finanza italiana nel ventennio 1914–1932* (Turin, 1934). Cf. also more recent articles in *La Riforma sociale* (Turin), May, June 1934, and March, April 1935.

In Table 39, official figures on the total annual revenues and expenditures of the government during the last two decades are reported.

As these data indicate, the advent of the Fascist regime

TABLE 39

TOTAL ANNUAL REVENUES AND EXPENDITURES OF THE ITALIAN GOVERNMENT, BY YEARS, 1918–1937 *

(*In million lire*)

Year	Receipts	Expenditures	Surplus Deficit (−)
1918–19	9,676	32,452	−22,776
1919–20	15,207	23,093	− 7,886
1920–21	18,820	36,229	−17,409
1921–22	19,701	35,461	−15,760
1922–23	18,804	21,832	− 3,028
1923–24	20,581	21,000	− 419
1924–25	20,440	20,023	417
1925–26	21,044	20,575	469
1926–27	21,450	21,014	436
1927–28	20,072	19,574	497
1928–29	20,201	19,646	555
1929–30	19,838	19,668	170
1930–31	20,387	20,891	− 504
1931–32	19,324	23,191	− 3,867
1932–33	18,217	21,766	− 3,549
1933–34	18,057	24,434	− 6,377†
1934–35	18,818	20,847	− 2,029‡
1935–36	20,371	33,057	−12,686‡
1936–37§	24,702	40,932	−16,230‡

* Compiled from various issues of *Compendio statistico italiano* and *Annuario statistico italiano*.

† From this figure there must be deducted 2,757 million lire expended by the government in converting its 5 per cent Consols into new 3.5 per cent redeemable bonds. The actual deficit for the year is thus reduced to 4,062 million lire. For further details on this conversion, cf. the discussion on pp. 225 ff.

‡ Deficits include expenditures for the Ethiopian campaign and the rearmament program. Cf. the more detailed discussion of recent government finance on pp. 227 ff.

§ Data made public by the Minister of Finance in December 1937. Cf. Fascist Confederation of Industrialists, *Business and Financial Report*, January 1938.

brought about a decided improvement in governmental finances. For the years 1924 to 1930 the budget showed a surplus; it was only with the coming of the depression that, as in other countries, this surplus was replaced by a series of rapidly growing deficits. Yet, while other countries attempted, on the whole not unsuccessfully, to improve their financial and general economic position through monetary devaluation, Italy has until recently maintained the stability of her currency, leaving to the rest of the country's financial and economic machinery the task of bearing the burden of the vast nation and world-wide deflationary process. The effect of that process upon her fiscal position is clearly revealed in the budgetary data for the years of the depression.

TABLE 40

INDEXES OF REVENUES AND EXPENDITURES OF THE ITALIAN GOVERNMENT IN "CURRENT," "GOLD," AND "COMMODITY" LIRE, BY YEARS, 1925–1934*

Fiscal Year	"CURRENT" LIRE		"1927" GOLD LIRE		"COMMODITY" LIRE	
	Revenues	Expenditures	Revenues	Expenditures	Revenues	Expenditures
1925–26 ..	100	100	100	100	100	100
1926–27 ..	102	102	110	110	110	109
1927–28 ..	96	95	131	130	129	128
1928–29 ..	100	99	135	134	135	134
1929–30 ..	98	100	132	135	144	147
1930–31 ..	101	106	136	143	180	189
1931–32 ..	96	118	126	155	199	244
1932–33 ..	91	110	119	144	208	253
1933–34 ..	89	125	118	166	214	301

* G. Mortara, *Prospettive economiche*, 1934, p. 565.

To increase the comparability of these data, Dr. Mortara, one of the best-known students of Italian economic affairs, translated the official figures on the budget given in "current" lire (greatly fluctuating in value before the stabilization in 1927) into "actual" lire (post-war gold standard lire) of a constant gold value, and into "commodity" lire, viz., monetary units of a constant purchasing power. In this recomputation, allowance was also made for changes in budgetary procedure which had precluded the absolute comparability of the data. The indexes which Dr. Mortara obtained are given in Table 40.

These figures reveal some very interesting facts. The data expressed in "1927 gold lire" show that, if translated into a stable monetary unit, the percentage increase in expenditures is much larger than that shown by expenditures expressed in "current" lire. A still clearer indication of the real significance of Italy's budgetary data is given by the figures in the last two columns. They show that, measured in actual purchasing power, expenditures were three times as large and revenues over twice as large in 1933–34 as in 1925–26. While revenue shows a fall if expressed in "current" and "1927 gold" lire, it shows a continuous increase if expressed in "commodity" currency. This indicates clearly that the real burden upon Italian taxpayers has been increasing constantly from year to year.

The considerable increase in some important items of expenditure during the depression, notably those for national defense, road building and public works, interest on the public

TABLE 41

DISTRIBUTION OF ITALIAN GOVERNMENTAL EXPENDITURES, BY FISCAL YEARS, 1928–1934*

(*In million lire*)

	1928–29	1929–30	1930–31	1931–32	1932–33	1933–34
Interest on Public Debt	4,449	4,514	4,603	4,781	5,193	4,609
General Government Services	382	395	410	1,722	1,313	1,362
Financial Services	1,995	2,014	2,380	2,081	1,945	5,519
Justice	495	521	508	502	511	509
War Pensions, Indemnities, etc.	1,362	1,343	1,258	1,230	1,195	1,166
Military Defense	4,289	4,376	5,013	4,890	4,882	4,301
Public Works	1,676	1,841	1,900	2,877	1,621	1,785
Railroad Building	275	335	300	641	226	216
Education	1,394	1,441	1,495	1,597	1,760	1,764
Colonies	494	526	490	441	464	456
Social Welfare and Assistance	166	167	162	167	182	212
Religion	825	213	207	82	76	80
Police	1,009	1,073	1,060	951	949	928
Furthering of National Economy†	653	732	865	1,033	1,243	1,344
Foreign Service	182	177	240	196	206	183
Total	19,646	19,668	20,891	23,191	21,766	24,434

* Compiled from various issues of *Compendio statistico italiano*.

† This includes improvement of and subsidies for railroad, maritime, and air transportation. For these three items a total sum of about 633 million lire was spent.

debt, and those classified under the catchall headings of "general government services" and "expenditures incurred for the furthering of the national economy," is shown by Tables 41 and 42.

In Italy, as in most other countries, large depression deficits were met through borrowing and a consequent increase in the national indebtedness. The strongest feature of this indebtedness is unquestionably the almost negligible amount of Italy's foreign debt. Disregarding the country's war debt obligations to the United States and Great Britain, which are exceeded by her credits on reparation account, her only direct foreign obligations are the 100 million dollar 7 per cent "Morgan" loan floated in 1926 (now reduced to less than 82,000,000 dollars)

TABLE 42

PERCENTAGE DISTRIBUTION OF ITALIAN GOVERNMENTAL EXPENDITURES,
BY FISCAL YEARS, 1928–1934*

	1928–29	1929–30	1930–31	1931–32	1932–33	1933–34
Interest on Public Debt	22.7	23.0	22.0	20.6	23.9	18.8
General Government Services	1.9	2.0	2.0	7.4	6.0	5.6
Financial Services	10.2	10.2	11.4	9.0	8.9	22.6
Justice	2.5	2.7	2.4	2.2	2.4	2.1
War Pensions, Indemnities, etc.	6.9	6.8	6.0	5.3	5.5	4.8
Military Defense	21.8	22.2	24.0	21.1	22.4	17.6
Public Works	8.5	9.4	9.1	12.4	7.5	7.3
Railroad Building	1.4	1.7	1.4	2.8	1.0	0.9
Education	7.1	7.3	7.2	6.9	8.1	7.2
Colonies	2.5	2.7	2.4	1.9	2.1	1.9
Social Welfare and Assistance	0.9	0.8	0.8	0.7	0.8	0.9
Religion	4.2	1.1	1.0	0.3	0.4	0.3
Police	5.2	5.5	5.1	4.1	4.4	3.8
Furthering of National Economy†	3.3	3.7	4.1	4.5	5.7	5.5
Foreign Service	0.9	0.9	1.1	0.8	0.9	0.7
Total	100.0	100.0	100.0	100.0	100.0	100.0

* Compiled from various issues of *Compendio statistico italiano.*

† This includes improvement of and subsidies for railroad, maritime, and air transportation. For these three items a total sum of about 633 million lire was spent.

and an old sterling loan of 1861, of which only a negligible amount is still outstanding.[4]

While, then, Italy's foreign debt is unusually small, her internal indebtedness is large, and, as is indicated by the figures in Table 43, it has been increasing rapidly in recent years.

TABLE 43

ITALY'S INTERNAL PUBLIC DEBT, BY YEARS, 1913, 1922–1935 *

(*In million lire*)

Year (June 30)	Funded Debt	Floating Debt	Total Debt	Total Debt Converted into 1927 Gold Lire
1913	14,285	840	15,125	55,448
1922	56,600	36,256	92,856	83,292
1923	60,058	35,486	95,544	83,410
1924	60,468	32,695	93,163	76,953
1925	63,258	27,589	90,847	68,771
1926	63,453	27,856	91,309	67,477
1927	62,699	20,976	83,675	80,663
1928	84,828	1,618	86,446	86,446
1929	84,624	2,510	87,134	87,134
1930	84,431	3,671	88,102	88,102
1931	85,950	5,492	91,442	91,442
1932	88,925	6,647	95,572	95,572
1933	88,303	8,912	97,215	97,215
1934	91,997	10,625	102,622	102,622
1935	93,827	11,883	105,710	105,710

* Compiled from various issues of *Compendio statistico italiano* and *Annuario statistico italiano*.

In interpreting the figures in Table 43 it must be noted that while, as the data in the last column indicate, the real debt burden was greatly reduced by the depreciation of the lira in 1924, 1925, and 1926, it was notably increased again by the revaluation of the currency in 1927 and even more so by the growth in the value of the monetary unit in terms of commodities, which took place during the depression. The figures given in Table 43, moreover, do not represent Italy's total

[4] After the devaluation of the pound sterling and the dollar, and during the severe decline in the price of Italian bonds during the Ethiopian campaign, a not indifferent share of these loans was bought back by Italians at very advantageous prices, thus reducing still further the total of the country's foreign obligations.

national debt. Various other liabilities must be added to them and these, according to a recent estimate of the London *Economist*, would increase the total by about 50 per cent. According to these computations, Italy's indebtedness at the beginning of 1935 was as shown in Table 44.

In these estimates the largest and most uncertain item is that referred to as "Deferred Payments' Present Value." This item represents the present value of promises of the government to make annuity payments to extinguish debts incurred in

TABLE 44

Estimate of Italy's Total State Liabilities, 1935*

(*In million lire*)

Type of Liability	Amount
I. Consols	9,892
Redeemable debt	82,099
Floating debt	11,285
	103,276
II. Treasury Current Liabilities	798
III. Bank of Italy's Credit	1,773
IV. Morgan Loan	960
V. Miscellaneous Liabilities	8,370
VI. Excess of Overdue Payments over Overdue Revenue	5,987
VII. Autonomous Authorities' Debt	1,184
VIII. Deferred Payments' Present Value	30,000 to 32,000
Total	152,348 to 154,348

* Cf. *Economist* (London), February 23, 1935, p. 414, May 25, 1935, p. 1187.

financing public works and other government enterprises. The somewhat liberal use made by the government of these "deferred payments" is, according to the *Economist*, the main reason for the growth of the public debt since 1922. This is shown by the figures in Table 45.

In studying the statistical data on Italy's public debt given in official Italian sources, one is struck by the sudden contraction of Italy's consolidated debt in 1934 and the notable expansion of the redeemable debt in the same year — a change brought about by a great debt-conversion operation successfully carried through during that period. In February 1934, 61,269 million lire of Italian 5 per cent Consols (*Consolidato*) were in fact converted into 3.5 per cent redeemable bonds. It was hoped that this huge operation, made possible by the decline in interest rates during the depression, would result in a considerable saving to the Italian Treasury.[5]

TABLE 45

COMPARISON OF ITALY'S ESTIMATED TOTAL STATE LIABILITIES, 1922 AND 1934*

(*In billion lire*)

Type of Liability	1922	1934
Other Debts	97 to 101	122.3
Deferred Payments' Present Value	3 to 4	30 to 32
	100 to 105	152.3 to 154.3

* As was pointed out by the Minister of Finance in his speech to the Chamber on May 18, 1935, however, the expansion of Italy's public debt was accompanied by a material increase in the public assets. While the increase in the public debt since 1922 amounted to 31,295 million lire, that increase, the Minister stated, was almost. balanced by 29,126 million lire of state capital expenditures made during that period. But, as the *Economist* points out, this fails to take into account the considerable fall in prices since 1926, which increased the burden of the debt while lowering the money value of the state's assets. A fair estimate of the value of these assets can hardly be obtained on the basis of their cost. See London *Economist*, May 25, 1935, p. 1187; also quoted in Royal Institute of International Affairs, *The Economic and Financial Position of Italy* (New York, 1935), p. 59. In arriving at the total of 31,295 million lire, representing the increase in Italy's public debt since 1922, the *Report* of the Institute points out, the Minister of Finance estimated the present value of deferred payments at 24,000 million lire, and overlooked the other items which according to the *Economist's* estimate are to be added to the official figures of Italy's national debt.

Only a year after the successful completion of this conversion operation, however, the conditions of the Italian capital and money market were radically altered. When, in the spring of 1935, the African war began to appear inevitable, quotations of Italian government securities showed a decided tendency to sag. The new 3.5 per cent loan which reached a maximum

[5] Cf. Mortara, *Prospettive economiche*, 1934, p. 568. To make the conversion operation successful, considerable inducements were offered by the government. In April 1934 a payment of 4.50 lire for every 100 lire of principal was made as a compensation to the holders of Consols for a three-year loss in interest (the difference between the interest of 5 per cent and that of 3.5 per cent paid on the new bonds for a three-year period). The total payment made on that account by the Treasury during 1934 amounted, as we have noted, to 2,757 million lire. In addition, in December 1934, for every 1,000 million lire of converted bonds, 10 million lire were distributed among holders in prizes drawn by lot.

price of 83.60 in January 1935, declined to a low of 64.85 in July of the same year. When, in the summer of 1935, the government was impelled to borrow heavily to meet the growing expenditures for the impending campaign, it had to offer 4 and later (after June, 1935) 5 per cent interest on short-term Treasury bills. When a new, long-term national loan was floated on September 20, 1935, the interest on the new bonds had to be fixed at 5 per cent and the selling price at 95, the yield being consequently equal to 5.26 per cent.

To indemnify, in part at least, the holders of the 3.5 per cent redeemable bonds, which had been issued only a year and a half earlier, and which were now quoted at 68, the government agreed to reconvert the 3.5 per cent bonds into the new 5 per cent bonds at 80 against payment by the bondholders of a cash premium of 15 lire for each 100 lire par value. Besides benefiting the holders of the 3.5 per cent loan, this conversion operation had the advantage of supplying the Treasury (through the 15 lire cash equalization payments) with several billion lire of new funds which could be used to meet the mounting costs of the Ethiopian campaign.

What was the total cost of this campaign and how did the Italian Treasury meet it? An official answer to this important question was given in an address made on May 21, 1937, by the Italian Minister of Finance, Thaon de Revel, before the Chamber of Deputies.[6] In that address the Minister declared that up to June 30, 1936, expenditures for the conquest of Ethiopia had amounted to 12,111 million lire, 975 million of which were expended during 1934–35 and 11,136 million during 1935–36. These expenditures, added to "ordinary" budget deficits, give a total deficit of 14,716 million lire for the two years from June 30, 1934, to June 30, 1936.

These huge expenditures and the equally large outlays made after June 30, 1936, were met by the Treasury with funds procured entirely through internal borrowing, increased taxation, and a number of "extraordinary" Treasury operations. The first among these was the debt conversion previously referred

---

[6] For an English translation of this speech, see Fascist Confederation of Industrialists, *Business and Financial Report*, June 1937.

to, which, up to April 30, 1937, netted the government about six billion lire in new funds.[7] Other sources of "extraordinary" income were the proceeds from sales of the gold and foreign securities surrendered to the Treasury by Italian nationals during the Ethiopian war and the transfer to the Exchequer of the profit made by the Bank of Italy from the revaluation of its gold reserve after the devaluation of the lira in October 1936.

Besides these "extraordinary" revenues, new income was provided by drastic new tax legislation.

When on October 5, 1936, the lira was devaluated, the government passed a decree requiring all owners of real estate to subscribe, for not less than 5 per cent of the value of their properties, to a new 5 per cent loan redeemable in twenty-five years, and to pay, for the same period, an annual 3.5 per mil tax on the capital value of their properties to meet the cost of the service and redemption of the loan. The purpose of this new loan, as officially stated, was to provide funds for "the consolidation of the East African victory and the guarantee of national security."

The yield of the new 3.5 per mil tax on real estate may be estimated with a fair degree of accuracy. As the Minister of Finance revealed, the rolls of the Italian real estate tax include over 2,500,000 owners with land holdings valued at 110,340 million lire and buildings valued at 65,000 million. On a total valuation of approximately 175,000 million the 5 per cent compulsory loan would yield a total of about 8,750 million and the annual 3.5 per mil tax approximately 612.5 million lire per annum.

This sacrifice demanded of Italian real estate owners, the government pointed out, will be compensated for, in part, by the higher values of land and other real property expected as a result of the recent lira devaluation and, in part, by the higher rents which real estate owners will be permitted to charge after the expiration of the two-year limit on rent increases decreed in October 1936.

[7] Up to that date subscriptions to the new 5 per cent funded loan amounted to 43,121 million lire, of which 42,030 million were paid for through conversion of the bonds of the 3.5 per cent redeemable loan of 1934 and payment of the 15 lire equalization premium in cash.

To provide further revenue enabling the government to meet the mounting costs of the occupation of Ethiopia and of the current rearmament program, the Council of Ministers approved, on October 23, 1937, a decree-law levying an emergency tax of 10 per cent on the paid up capital and surplus of all Italian joint stock companies and partnerships. Payment of the new tax is to be made in fifteen bi-monthly instalments beginning March 10, 1938. The yield from this new tax may be estimated roughly at about 5,000 million lire. In 1936 the total capital and surplus of Italian business corporations stood at about 63,000 million lire; allowable exemptions and deductions will, it is estimated, reduce this figure to a taxable total of about 50,000 million lire.[8]

The amounts which accrued to the Treasury from July 1, 1934, to April 30, 1937, as a result of the Treasury operations described above and which were used to meet the deficit of 14,716 million lire for the fiscal years 1934-35 and 1935-36 (and, in part, the new deficit of 16.230 million for the fiscal year 1936-37) were as follows:

	Million Lire
Nine-year 4 per cent 1943 Treasury bonds issued in 1934 ..	2,000.0
Cash premium paid by holders of 3.5 per cent 1934 redeemable loan for conversion into new 5 per cent loan and cash subscriptions to about 1,000 million lire of new 5 per cent loan	6,804.6
Sums paid on account, on the compulsory 5 per cent real estate loan of 1936	5,389.0
Treasury bills	4,713.0
Interest bearing accounts with:	
Cassa Depositi e Prestiti and National Social Insurance Institute	2,442.0
Bank of Naples and other banks	1,285.0
Bank of Italy	448.0
Proceeds from sales of foreign securities and Italian securities issued abroad surrendered to the Treasury by Italian nationals, and other "extraordinary" income	2,206.6
Total	25,288.2

[8] Fascist Confederation of Industrialists, *Business and Financial Report*, November 1937. From a more detailed study of the new law one learns that

The foregoing discussion of Italy's recent financial history shows that through a series of daring and determined financial operations the Fascist government has thus far succeeded in obtaining at home the huge funds needed for the occupation of Ethiopia and the current rearmament program. The question which naturally arises is how long Italy can continue to borrow and to tax her people without serious impairment of the national credit. The answer to this fundamental question can hardly be optimistic. If it is true, on the one hand, that the Treasury has not so far encountered serious difficulty in raising the funds which it has needed and that serious inflation has been avoided, it is equally true, on the other hand, that to raise these funds at all the Treasury has had to resort to a series of very extraordinary measures and that the burden now placed upon Italian taxpayers is such that much additional taxation could hardly be imposed upon them without danger of severe hardships and a material impairment of productive efficiency. It is well to remember that Mussolini himself recognized this over three years ago when, on May 26, 1934, he said, in a speech before the Italian Chamber: "I am the first to proclaim that fiscal pressure has reached its final limit and that the Italian taxpayer must be left, for some time at least, absolutely alone; if possible we must even endeavor to lighten his load if we do not wish to find him crushed under his heavy burden." [9]

---

the 10 per cent emergency tax will be levied on the total obtained by adding together the value of the paid-up capital and surplus of Italian corporations and partnerships on October 5, 1936. Should the total value of the shares computed at the average prices quoted in 1936 differ from the total above referred to, the tax will be levied as follows: (1) if the average market value of the shares in 1936 exceeds the total paid-up capital and reserves by not more than 20 per cent no change will be made; (2) if that value exceeds the total by more than 20 per cent, the increased value will be taken into account up to an amount not exceeding 160 per cent of the total obtained by adding capital and surplus; (3) should the market value in 1936 be less than the said total, that market value will be accepted for taxation. In no case, however, may the taxable valuation be less than two-thirds of the paid-up capital.

The law provides, further, that companies in liquidation shall pay the tax on their undistributed assets and that the tax shall not be levied on banks and coöperative societies with a capital of less than 20,000 lire.

[9] Mortara, *Prospettive economiche*, 1934, p. 577.

EMPLOYMENT AND THE LABOR MARKET

The final question to which we must turn before bringing this discussion of Fascist economic policy to a close is that of whether or not the economic position of the Italian laboring classes has been improved under the Fascist regime. Unfortunately, the question, which is one of the most crucial in our whole analysis, cannot be answered fully and satisfactorily at the present time. If it is true that the wages of Italian labor are among the lowest in Europe, it is equally true that wages

TABLE 46

UNEMPLOYMENT IN ITALY: NUMBER OF PERSONS TOTALLY UNEMPLOYED, BY YEARS, 1922–1935*

(Yearly averages)

Year	Number of Unemployed
1922	407,364
1923	246,396
1924	164,853
1925	110,298
1926	113,901
1927	278,484
1928	324,422
1929	300,787
1930	425,437
1931	734,454
1932	1,006,441
1933	1,018,953
1934	963,677
May 1935	755,344

* Compiled from various issues of *Sindacato e corporazione*.

have always been relatively low in Italy and that many of the present difficulties of the Italian wage earner are caused, in large measure, by factors of a transitory nature, such as the effects of the monetary stabilization and the world depression. However, even though no conclusive answer to our main problem can be given at this time, it is of interest to scrutinize carefully available Italian statistics on unemployment, prices, and wages, and to attempt to draw such conclusions as the existing data may warrant.

We begin, then, with unemployment. An analysis of the figures on total annual unemployment given in Table 46 shows a relatively sharp decline in the total number of the unemployed between 1922 and 1926. During the period of economic stagnation produced by the revaluation of the lira, there was a rapid expansion in total unemployment. When the world depression began to make its effects felt, unemployment increased further, reaching the unprecedented total of 1,018,953 in 1933. After that year conditions gradually improved. The improvement became marked during the spring of 1935, when a million men were mobilized for military duty and the pressing demands of the impending Ethiopian campaign upon the country's industrial system began to make themselves felt.

Another factor which contributed materially to the reduction of unemployment in the early part of 1935 was the conclusion on October 11, 1934, of an agreement among workers' and employers' organizations for the introduction of a forty-hour week in industry. Because of that agreement, up to January 26, 1935, a total of 191,305 workers were reëmployed: 152,359 in industry, 17,932 in agriculture, 19,759 in commerce, and 1,345 in credit and insurance.[10] Although the publication of official unemployment statistics of the sort here given was not resumed after 1935, some further indication of the course of unemployment in recent years is given by official figures on unemployment insurance. As Table 10 shows, the number of persons receiving unemployment subsidies was 774,583 in 1934, 644,406 in 1935, and 858,419 in 1936, unemployment thus showing a marked increase during the last of the years for which data are available.

As we have noted, unemployed workers in Italy are helped through unemployment insurance (which is compulsory for agricultural laborers working with machines and for factory workers), through public works, and through occasional relief grants made by the government, the Fascist party, and the syndical and corporate organizations. In addition, there is indirect unemployment relief consisting of measures taken by the government to prevent and reduce unemployment. These measures include prevention of seasonal unemployment through a government-supervised policy of internal migration (particularly

[10] *Sindacato e corporazione*, January 1935, p. 64.

effective at harvest time), the aforementioned introduction of the forty-hour week in industry, and a system of minimum employment (employment of a certain minimum number of hands on each farm) in agriculture.

THE COURSE OF WHOLESALE AND RETAIL PRICES, MONEY WAGES, REAL WAGES, AND THE STANDARD OF LIVING

If, as the foregoing discussion shows, the employment situation in Italy in recent years has been affected in no small degree by the vicissitudes of Italian currency, even a cursory analysis of prices and money wages under the Fascist regime reveals clearly that the course of wages and prices has also been determined in no small part by the government's monetary policy. As the data given in Table 47 show, in Italy both prices and the cost of living rose gradually up to 1926, declined after the revaluation of the lira in 1927, and then fell rapidly during the depression, reaching their low point in 1934. Since that year the gradual recovery in world prices, the special situation created by the Ethiopian campaign, and, more recently, the devaluation of the currency have tended to reverse the earlier trend.

After 1927 the rigorous policy of deflation pursued by the regime in an attempt to defend the stability of the lira found expression, as we have noted, in repeated and drastic cuts in wages, rents, and prices. With the coöperation of the Fascist party and the Fascist syndical system, these government-decreed reductions were enforced everywhere with rapidity and thoroughness. After 1930, in fact, two major salary and wage reductions were put into effect. On November 18, 1930, the government decreed a 12 per cent reduction of the wages and salaries of all persons in the employ of the state and of other public and semi-public bodies. Private employers soon followed suit, and after that date reductions of varying magnitude were applied everywhere. On April 14, 1934, a further reduction of government wages and salaries, ranging from 20 per cent in the highest grades to 6 per cent in the lowest, was decreed by the government.

TABLE 47

INDEXES OF PRICES AND COST OF LIVING IN ITALY, BY YEARS,
1913–1914, 1922–1937

A. INDEXES WITH PRE-WAR BASE *

Year	Wholesale† Price Index	Retail Price‡ Index	National§ Cost of Living Index
1913	100	100	...
1st Sem 1914	...	...	100
1922	529	545	414
1923	536	525	412
1924	553	544	426
1925	646	621	479
1926	654	648	517
1927	527	568	472
1928	491	531	438
1929	481	559	446
1930	411	515	430
1931	341	446	389
1932	310	425	370
1933	283	399	354
1934	276	376	336
1935	318	387	341

B. NEWLY CALCULATED POST-WAR INDEXES, 1928 = 100 §§

Year	Wholesale Price Index	Retail Price Index of Twenty Important Foodstuffs	National Cost of Living Index
1928	100	100	...
June 1, 1928	...	...	100
1929	95.4	105.4	101.15
1930	85.4	96.9	97.73
1931	74.5	83.1	88.26
1932	69.6	79.7	84.10
1933	63.4	75.5	80.50
1934	62.0	71.0	76.39
1935	68.2	73.4	77.48
1936	76.4	80.9	83.52
1937	89.1	90.4	91.74
March 1938	93.8	94.4	99.25

* Compiled from various issues of *Annuario statistico italiano* and *Bollettino mensile di statistica.*

† Compiled by the Consiglio Provinciale dell' Economia (Chamber of Commerce) of Milan. Index includes 125 commodities.

‡ Index of retail prices of 21 important consumption goods (mainly foodstuffs) in the principal cities of the kingdom.

§ Based upon family budgets in the various provinces of the kingdom.

§§ All indexes were computed by the Istituto Centrale di Statistica. They were compiled from various issues of *Annuario statistico italiano, Bollettino dei prezzi,* and *Bollettino mensile di statistica.*

Yet, while these drastic reductions were made in wages and salaries, the regime endeavored to bring about corresponding reductions of other fixed money charges (notably rents and retail prices) through energetic price controls exercised by local government authorities, the police, and the Fascist syndical and party organizations.

TABLE 48

INDEXES OF "NOMINAL" AGRICULTURAL WAGES IN ITALY, FOR MEN, WOMEN, AND BOYS, BY YEARS, 1922–1934*

(*1929 = 100*)

	MEN		WOMEN		BOYS	
Year	Daily Wages	Hourly Wages	Daily Wages	Hourly Wages	Daily Wages	Hourly Wages
1922	98.8	96.9	97.4	95	93.4	90.1
1923	100.5	97.6	99.5	97.6	95.4	92.3
1924	102	98.5	101.7	99.6	98.9	94.7
1925	108.4	105.2	106.5	104.2	104.3	98.1
1926	112	110.1	111.5	110.3	109.8	109.3
1927	109.2	108.2	107.7	108.6	109.3	109.3
1928	102.1	101.5	101.8	101.5	101.4	101
1929	100	100	100	100	100	100
1930	94.6	94.8	92.6	93.7	92.7	92.6
1931	85.1	85.1	81	81.5	80.9	81
1932	80.3	77.1	76.9	77.2	76.6	76.4
1933	77.7	74.7	76	75.1	72.9	68.4
1934	74.9	72.3	75.8	74.3	70.8	67.1

* These indexes were calculated by Dr. Pier Lodovico Bertani of the Royal University of Bologna, mainly from data gathered and elaborated by Dr. Paola Maria Arcari and published in her exhaustive and authoritative study: *I Salari agricoli in Italia dal 1905 al 1933* (Rome, 1934). The main results of Dr. Arcari's work were published by the Central Institute of Statistics, Rome, in the official *Compendio statistico italiano*. Dr. Bertani's indexes appear in his article: "Il Salario corporativo nell' agricoltura e nell' industria," *Economia* (Rome), May 1936, pp. 374–394.

An accurate evaluation of the effects of the rise in prices before 1926 and the subsequent deflationary action upon the economic position of Italy's working population presupposes a detailed study of the statistical materials relating to prices and wages under the Fascist regime. Unfortunately no exhaustive and really conclusive study of this sort can be undertaken, for comparable official wage statistics for the period since 1922 are not available. Such data as are extant, however, are sufficient to throw some significant light upon the conditions of the Italian working classes under the Fascist regime.

Tables 48 to 51 give a detailed account of the movement of "nominal" and "real" wages in Italian agriculture since 1922. The indexes for "nominal" wages were computed by taking into account actual daily and hourly money wages paid; the indexes for "real" wages were obtained by applying to the "nominal" wage indexes the national cost of living index computed by the Central Institute of Statistics in Rome.

TABLE 49

INDEXES OF "REAL" AGRICULTURAL WAGES IN ITALY, FOR MEN, WOMEN, AND BOYS, BY YEARS, 1922–1934*

(*1929 = 100*)

Year	MEN		WOMEN		BOYS	
	Daily Wages	Hourly Wages	Daily Wages	Hourly Wages	Daily Wages	Hourly Wages
1922	106.5	103.9	105.4	102.5	100.6	96.6
1923	108.7	105.9	108.1	106.2	103.2	100
1924	106.5	103.3	106.8	104.3	103.2	98.3
1925	100.7	98	99.3	96.9	96.8	90.3
1926	96.4	94.7	96.6	95.1	94.9	94.3
1927	102.9	102	102	102.5	103.2	102.9
1928	103.6	103.3	104.1	103.7	103.2	102.9
1929	100	100	100	100	100	100
1930	97.8	98	95.9	97.5	96.2	96
1931	97.8	97.4	92.2	93.8	93	92.5
1932	96.4	92.8	92.6	93.2	92.4	92
1933	97.8	94.1	95.9	94.4	91.8	92.5
1934	98	95.8	98.9	97.5	92.9	94.8

* Bertani, in *Economia*, May, 1936, p. 382.

Even a cursory analysis of these tables reveals some extremely interesting facts. Before the World War nominal and real wages in Italian agriculture showed a pronounced tendency to rise; during the post-war period money wages rose somewhat from 1922 to 1926 and declined thereafter, while real wages fell from a peak in 1923 to a low in 1926, rose somewhat during 1927 and 1928, and then declined consistently to a new low point in 1932.

While, then, agricultural laborers received in 1923 real wages which were about 50 per cent higher than those obtained in 1913, on the whole their real wages did not increase under Fascism but declined on the average by about 8 per cent.[11]

What were the causes of this situation? One of the fundamental reasons for the marked rise in agricultural wages before
the war and their failure to improve during the post-war period
undoubtedly lies in emigration. During the decade before the
war an average of about 700,000 Italians left the country every

TABLE 50

AVERAGE HOURLY WAGES FOR COMMON ITALIAN AGRICULTURAL MALE
LABORERS, BY FIVE-YEAR AVERAGES AND YEARS, 1905–1934*

Year	Hourly Wages Lire	WAGE INDEXES (1913–14 = 100) Nominal Wages	Real Wages
1905–09†	0.18	81	95
1910–14†	0.22	97	98
1915–19†	0.56	259	?
1920–24†	1.40	630	157
1925–29†	1.59	706	151
1930	1.45	637	149
1931	1.26	572	148
1932	1.15	518	141
1933	1.08	502	143
1934	1.05	487	145

* *Compendio statistico italiano*, 1935, p. 147. (Data obtained from the study
on *Agricultural Wages in Italy from 1905 to 1933*, by Dr. Paola Maria Arcari.)
† Five-year averages.

[11] In interpreting the "real" wage figures upon which this conclusion is based,
some allowance must be made for the fact that they were obtained through the
use of a national cost of living index, a composite index which does not portray
with complete accuracy the cost of living of the agricultural classes. If, instead
of applying this general index to nominal wage data, the national index of the
cost of food were used for the years for which such an index is available, the
results shown in column II below would be obtained:

Year	Real Wages I	Wages in Terms of Cost of Food II
1928	103.6	104.1
1929	100	100
1930	97.8	99.5
1931	97.8	101.8
1932	96.4	102.3
1933	97.8	105.2
1934	98	107.3

Cf. P. L. Bertani, "Il Salario corporativo," *Economia*, May 1936, p. 381.

year. Such emigration took place mostly from overpopulated agricultural districts, with evident beneficial effects upon wages and employment conditions in those districts. After the advent of the Fascist regime, emigration was reduced to less than 200,000 persons per year on the average, and during the worst years of the depression to a yearly average of less than 70,000.[12] The results were overpopulation in the districts which had formerly benefited most by emigration and, consequently, re-

TABLE 51

INDEXES OF THE VOLUME OF PRODUCTION, UNEMPLOYMENT, AND DAILY REAL WAGES IN ITALIAN AGRICULTURE, BY YEARS, 1922–1934*

(*1929 = 100*)

Year	Production	Unemployment	Real Wages
1922	72.3	112.3	106.4
1923	88.8	53.4	108.4
1924	87.4	39.8	106.5
1925	93.9	23.1	100.4
1926	91.1	27.3	96.5
1927	80.9	84.5	102.8
1928	86.2	80.5	103.7
1929	100	100	100
1930	93.8	115.5	97.6
1931	89.2	185.3	97.4
1932	117.5	225.7	96.3
1933	106.9	243.5	97.7
1934	101.2	221.3	97.9

* Bertani, in *Economia*, May 1936, p. 383.

duced opportunities for employment and lower wages. Another factor which contributed during the recent depression to cause lower agricultural wages was the almost total lack of employment opportunities for farm youths in industrial centers, an avenue of employment which ordinarily helps to relieve agricultural unemployment and to raise wages in overcrowded agricultural areas.

Table 51 compares trends in agricultural production, unemployment, and real wages since 1922. These data show that, even though agricultural production increased materially

[12] Cf. the detailed statistics on emigration given in chap. viii, p. 188.

during the period, real wages declined and agricultural unemployment increased sharply after 1926.

Judging by such statistical data as are available, conditions in Italian industry were, on the whole, not very much better. Although many specialized studies and monographs for individual industrial wage groups exist, no complete set of comparable data is available for the period since 1922 for Italian industry as a whole. Comparable statistical information on a national scale goes back only to 1928; our general analysis must therefore be limited to the years from 1928 to 1934.

TABLE 52

INDEXES OF NOMINAL WAGES AND AVERAGE MONTHLY WORKING HOURS IN
ITALIAN INDUSTRY, BY YEARS, 1928–1934*

(*1929 = 100*)

Year	Monthly Wages	Hourly Wages	Monthly Working Hours
1928	100.4	101.6	99.1
1929	100	100	100
1930	96.5	100.4	96
1931	88	93.7	93.9
1932	85.6	92.6	92.2
1933	85.6	89.9	95.5
1934	82	87.2	94.4

* Bertani, in *Economia*, May 1936, p. 390.

Table 52 gives an account of average nominal monthly and hourly wages and the average number of working hours per month since 1928. Table 53 sets forth monthly and hourly real wages (obtained by applying the national cost of living index to nominal wage data) and the volume of industrial production and unemployment. An analysis of the data in both tables shows that, though nominal wages during the depression declined on the average by about 15 per cent (monthly wages fell more than hourly wages because of the reduced number of working hours per month), monthly real wages for industrial workers increased from 100 in 1929 to 108.5 in 1934. This increase is explained by the well-known fact that the price of labor tends to change less rapidly than other prices and that laborers (when they are fully employed) stand to gain in times of depression and to lose in purchasing power whenever a pronounced upward movement of prices occurs. That Italian industrial laborers as a group were not better off during the depression becomes more than evident after a glance at the indexes of unemployment. While agricultural unemployment indexes increased from 100 in 1929 to 221.3 in 1934, industrial unemployment rose from 100 to 357.6 during the same period.

As to the position of Italian labor since 1934, an objective estimate can hardly be made at this time, for complete statistics on wages and unemployment are not yet available.[13] From such information as is available, however, it appears that, while there has been a constant upward trend in prices (caused by the general upward movement in world prices, the Ethiopian war, the sanctions, and the recent devaluation of the currency), wages, fixed by collective agreements, so far (February 1938) have been increased only twice.[14] As is always the case during

[13] While no recent data are available on wages in agriculture, the Central Statistical Office has of late published a series of wage data for industrial workers which takes the place of the fragmentary information previously in existence. This series is as follows:

AVERAGE HOURLY WAGES PAID TO ITALIAN INDUSTRIAL WORKERS, BY YEARS, 1928–1937.

Year	Average Hourly Wage (*In lire*)	Index of Average Hourly Wage (*1928 = 100*)
1928	2.10	100.0
1929	2.09	99.5
1930	2.07	98.6
1931	1.95	92.9
1932	1.91	90.9
1933	1.86	88.6
1934	1.80	85.7
1935	1.77	84.3
1936	1.88	89.5
1937	2.11	100.5

Published in: Istituto Centrale di Statistica, *Bollettino dei prezzi*, April 15, 1938, p. 284. This series was recalculated in March 1938. For a detailed explanation of the reasons for the abandonment of the older series and its recomputation, see *Bollettino dei prezzi*, March 15, 1938, Appendix II.

[14] At the meeting held by the Central Corporate Committee on April 30, 1937, the Minister of Corporations discussed the price situation stressing the price rise on international markets since 1932 and the rising tendencies of Italian prices, particularly since the devaluation of the currency on October 5, 1936. He praised

periods of rising prices, prices and the cost of living rose first (though they rose under the watchful eye and the restraining influence of special party price control committees), and wages were adjusted afterwards, a procedure which entails obvious drawbacks from the standpoint of the wage-earning and the salaried classes.

TABLE 53

INDEXES OF REAL WAGES, PRODUCTION, AND UNEMPLOYMENT IN ITALIAN
INDUSTRY, BY YEARS, 1922–1934*

(*1929 = 100*)

Year	Real Monthly Wages	Real Hourly Wages	Production	Unemployment
1922	....	....	43.9	144.2
1923	....	....	52.9	89.2
1924	....	....	67.9	55.1
1925	....	....	75.3	36.8
1926	....	....	78.3	39
1927	....	....	77.6	95.6
1928	102.2	103.4	89.2	115.7
1929	100	100	100	100
1930	99.8	103.9	89.4	153.3
1931	100.9	107.4	75.1	269.7
1932	103	111.5	69	378.1
1933	107.7	113.1	79	369.3
1934	108.5	115.4	82.6	357.6

* Bertani, in *Economia*, May 1936, pp. 392, 393. The indexes shown above were computed by Dr. Bertani from the comprehensive wage statistics published by the Confederation of Italian Industry, the most reliable and complete source now available.

What, then, has been the economic position of the Italian laboring classes under Fascism? Disregarding such benefits as are implied in extended social insurance and the social welfare activities of the regime, our general conclusion about the condition of Italian labor under Fascism as measured by prevailing

the action of price control until then undertaken by the Fascist Party and proposed that a general wage and salary increase ranging from 10 to 12 per cent be granted to workers in industry, agriculture, commerce, and credit and insurance, this increase to include, however, the wage increases already given some groups of workers since the summer of 1936. The committee voted that the wage increases (to be granted by the various confederations) be made effective on May 9, the first anniversary of the foundation of the Italian Empire. *Sindacato e corporazione*, April 1937, p. 579.

wage and employment conditions must be that on the whole it has not only failed of improvement but has been made worse — certainly in agriculture, and most probably in industry. How much of this has been due to the actions of the regime itself, such as restriction of emigration and the 1927 devaluation of the currency, and how much to the repercussions of the world-wide economic crisis upon Italian economy, it is difficult to tell.[15]

[15] In discussing the present wage and general economic conditions of the Italian worker, attention must be called to the *assegni familiari*, the system of special "family allowances" recently established by the regime for the benefit of workers who are heads of families. The *assegni familiari* were first originated through the collective labor agreement concluded between the Confederation of Industrialists and the Confederation of Workers in Industry on December 1, 1934. At that time a national fund for family allowances to workers in industry was established and its administration entrusted to the National Fascist Institute for Social Insurance. After October 5, 1936, all private contractual agreements were replaced by the provisions of the decree-law on "family allowances" of August 21, 1936. This decree provides that family allowances of 4 lire per week for each dependent child under 14 years of age are to be paid to all workers in industry who are heads of families.

The fund from which the allowances are to be paid is made up of contributions by the workers (1.0 per cent of their weekly wages), by the employer (2.5 per cent of the weekly payroll), and by the state (0.50 lire for each weekly allowance paid). During 1936 a total of 241,346,400 lire (corresponding to 60,366,000 weekly grants of 4 lire each) was paid to 702,039 industrial workers. In December 1936 and throughout 1937 the system of family allowances was gradually extended to workers in commercial and credit and insurance enterprises and to other occupational groups, including, most recently, workers in agriculture. Although allowances granted under the system are in the average case very small, they represent nevertheless a considerable aid to heads of large families; it was these that the government intended primarily to favor through the new law. See *Sindacato e corporazione*, September 1936, p. 244, and November 1937, p. 1069.

CHAPTER X

CONCLUSION

GAINS AND LOSSES OF FASCISM

THE analysis of the principal aspects of Fascist economic policy is now complete. We may proceed, therefore, to draw some general conclusions. As the preceding discussion has shown, Fascism arose as a movement of reaction among the Italian middle classes against the bitter aftermath of the World War, the ineptitude of post-war political regimes, and the dangers of a socialist and communist *coup d'état*. From its inception the movement was fervidly nationalistic. Italians, united by Fascism, would, it was hoped, rouse themselves from the torpor into which they had been plunged by centuries of political servitude and strive for the attainment of a strong, respected, and well-ordered Italian commonwealth. The bygone days of power and prestige would thus be recreated, and Italy would establish, in the briefest time possible, her own rightful "place in the sun."

All other Fascist doctrines have sprung from this creed of fervid, passionate nationalism. The need for unity and strength in the struggle for these ideals has supplied the Fascist movement with its fundamental doctrinal cornerstone: the theory of an authoritarian national state, a state which, in return for the surrender of political freedom and submission to strict party discipline, would furnish the Italian people with able and aggressive government in the national interest.

This intensely nationalistic creed has exerted and still exerts a strong fascination upon the Italian people. After careful inquiries during several visits to Italy, I am convinced that the mass of Italians sympathize with Fascism and, on the whole, support the regime. The situation in Italy was well appraised by the American journalist who in the summer of 1934 described Italian political and economic conditions for the read-ers of the magazine *Fortune*. To the question, "Do they like it?" he gave the following answer:

There is no free press in Italy, so it is impossible to tell by reading the newspapers. There are also no riots, no strikes. There is no evidence of the existence of any "underground" opposition of any importance whatever. As a *bon mot* Il Duce once remarked that the Italian people now possess the *Jus Murmurandi* or right to grumble. They grumble indeed. But no amount of private conversation with Italians will evoke any more "dislike" of the regime than may be conveyed by a good-natured shrug of the shoulders. The inescapable conclusion of all impartial observers is that the Italians *do* like it — and that they like it quite as much as any Socialist or Democrat is ever likely to like any socialistic or democratic state of which he may ever be a part. Which is not to say that any man who really loves liberty could ever endure the Fascist State. But in this connection the interesting point is not that Mussolini calls liberty "a putrid corpse" and despises democracy. The interesting point (and a point that is invariably missed by all off-hand anti-Fascists) is that in this new kind of autocratic state, the autocrat actually seeks the consent of his people. Far from "not giving a damn" whether the Italian people like Fascism, Mussolini is passionately desirous that his people should like Fascism and he has worked for twelve years to build up their liking in his own dictatorial way.[1]

This description of the situation is, I believe, substantially accurate today. On the whole, the Italian people do support Fascism, not, as is generally believed, because they have been bludgeoned into submission, but rather because somehow they have been made to feel that Fascism is "their" government, a patriotic, deeply nationalistic, eminently "Italian" regime, which is able and willing to look after the national interest in a novel, vigorous, and, they are convinced, very efficient way.[2] Though Fascism makes no extraordinary demands upon the average Italian, the intense nationalism of the movement stirs him and makes him feel, as no other movement has done in the past, that he is a living part of the national community.

[1] *Fortune*, July 1934, p. 55, reprinted here by permission of the editors of *Fortune*.

[2] This was written before the recent discrimination against Italian Jews began — a policy of which, I am sure, large sections of the Italian population will heartily disapprove.

For Italian youth, in particular, Fascism has the charm of restless, energetic activity; it gives it something to live up to and continually inspires it to new deeds for the advancement of the Fatherland.

Moreover, during the first years of the regime most Italians felt that important changes for the better were being made. For the democratic political regimes of the past, which had plainly shown their inadequacy during the immediate post-war period, there was substituted a strong national government based upon novel ideals of national unity and solidarity. Dirt, thievery, the *maffia*, the *lazzaroni*, the old-time *dolce far niente* tended to disappear, and cleanliness, order, and efficiency were established in their place. Industry and trade were expanded, splendid new roads built, millions of square miles of marsh-land reclaimed, and an imposing commercial fleet, including, at one time, the fastest liner afloat, was made to carry the Italian flag to the four corners of the globe. All this, it is true, might have been accomplished under a different political regime, yet under the circumstances the presumption of credit for what was achieved was clearly in favor of Fascism. The average Italian, aroused by the constant appeal which the regime makes to his patriotism and flattered in his national pride by the vigor with which the new government pursues its nationalistic objectives, did not appear to see — and does not seem to see today — the drawbacks inherent in the new governmental system.

As we have repeatedly noted, with the advent of Fascism the traditional liberties which Italians had enjoyed since the foundation of the kingdom were definitely lost. Political parties have ceased to exist; freedom of speech, of the press, and of assembly have been barred; newspapers, the radio, the cinema have been placed under strict governmental control. Grouped into semi-military youth organizations, the country's young people have been subjected to strict party discipline, while employers and workers, organized into an all-embracing system of syndical associations, have been subordinated to the state and have been made to serve its interests as interpreted by the

Fascist regime. Besides the power of wholesale endorsement or rejection of the present regime through periodic plebiscites, the people at large have at present little or no direct part in the government. There is, consequently, little encouragement under the present political regime for the mass of Italians to think independently or to strive earnestly after truth. No one in Italy may safely speak his mind with frankness or attempt to win others to his views. Enlightenment of the people through free discussion and argument is utterly impossible.

The intellectual stagnation born of these conditions is already apparent. Since open expression of disagreement with the fundamental ideas of the ruling party is not tolerated, there is little stimulus for original and creative thought in the social and political sphere. Why, indeed, should Italians make any effort to think when independent thinking is dangerous and all that is needed is to have "faith"? Is it not easier to react emotionally and to join, without much thought, the official parades, shouts, songs, and salutes? At the universities students and teachers alike are anxious to comment upon the achievements of the regime, to justify, to defend, but never to criticize. The legal and the social sciences in Italy are gradually losing their originality and are becoming mere commentaries on official doctrine. While hundreds of apologias of the corporate system have been printed in Italy and countless controversies and discussions have been carried on on points of detail, not one serious attack on the system as a whole has as yet been published. For all practical purposes, economic liberalism, socialism, and social Catholicism are dead.

This serious limitation of intellectual freedom is bound in time to affect the quality of the Italian governing class. The opportunity to discover and train real leaders who will champion new ideas, fight for them, and win adherents to them is absolutely lost. For example, duplication of Mussolini's own career, the development of his qualities for leadership through years of political strife and battle, would now be utterly impossible. In Fascist Italy leaders are in large part appointed from above; they do not emerge, in competition with others, from below.

The chances for real talent to assert itself are lessened, and opportunities for the discovery and the most useful employment of the available intellectual resources are clearly diminished. Appointments are made dependent — and to preserve the system must be made dependent — upon political "conformity" rather than upon technical ability and intellectual capacity. Thus the best men or even the good men may never reach the posts where they might make their greatest contribution or where their abilities might be most advantageously and effectively utilized.

Another serious defect of the system is the total absence of criticism by able and honest opponents. No one in Italy may speak his mind freely unless he belongs to the limited inner circle of party leaders. And, as numerous examples show, even these may fall from grace if they speak their minds too openly or too forcefully. The result is that all important decisions ultimately rest with the party leader and head of the government alone — that is, with Mussolini. Though because of his genius for leadership and his intimate knowledge of the Italian people and of their problems he is often right, he too is liable to make, and has made, mistakes. Had there been an open forum in Italy in which opponents of the government could have been heard, mistakes such as the revaluation of the lira, for example, might well have been avoided.

Even though Mussolini calls liberty a "putrid corpse" and despises democracy, it is upon their return that in the long run, I am convinced, the future and real progress of Italy will depend.

THE FRUITS OF FASCIST ECONOMIC POLICY

We turn now to a more detailed summary of the achievements of the regime in the economic sphere. As our previous discussion has shown, the economic policy of Fascism is in its essentials the product of the nationalistic philosophy of the Fascist regime. The Italian nation, Fascists contend, must be made "strong" and "powerful": for power the essential prerequisites, they assert, are population growth and economic independence. The attainment of the former is sought through the Fascist "Battle of Births"; that of the latter through the stupendous Fascist program of land reclamation, the imposing "Battle of Wheat," an intensely nationalistic monetary policy, and the recent successful attempt to expand the country's colonial domain and to lay the foundations for a vast colonial empire.

What have been the results of these policies? Thus far the results of some of them, as we have seen, have been definitely disappointing. Despite the "Battle of Births" Italy's birth rate on the whole has continued in its downward trend, and all that may safely be said for the government's efforts is that without them birth rates might possibly have fallen even more rapidly. Italian emigration has been greatly reduced (in part because of the stringent restrictions applied at home, in part because of the restrictive legislation passed by most immigration countries during the depression), the reduction having so far been effected, as we have shown, at the expense of the standard of living of Italy's working population. The Fascist "Battle of Wheat" as such has been technically successful; but success has been achieved at the cost of higher bread prices at home. Again, the revaluation of the lira and the subsequent staunch maintenance of the stability of a currency of high intrinsic gold value in a period of world-wide deflation may have benefited Italian capitalists and savers for a while, and increased Italy's political prestige; yet these apparent advantages have been achieved at the cost of a substantial decline in exports and an extremely painful and long-drawn-out readjustment of domestic prices, wages, and costs.

Though I do not share the pessimism of some observers, who maintain that Italy is verging on bankruptcy because of the Ethiopian campaign, I do think that the colonial venture and its aftermath, in conjunction with the heavy costs of the current rearmament program, will mean the continuance of very heavy burdens upon Italian taxpayers for a long time to come. A long time too, at best, will elapse before the new colonies can be turned into economic assets able to repay the nation for the economic sacrifices which their conquest and their occupation have entailed.

While, then, the leading economic policies adopted by the Fascist regime may have served to increase the country's economic independence and political prestige, they cannot be said, so far at least, to have contributed to her economic advancement or to an increase in the economic well-being of the Italian people. Population growth, economic independence, and colonial expansion are being paid for by the mass of Italians through a lowered standard of living.

A FINAL ESTIMATE OF THE ITALIAN CORPORATE STATE

What of the Italian corporate state?

What role has it played and what role is it likely to play in Italy in the future? What lessons, if any, does it teach which might find application under a different political regime?

A detailed critical evaluation of the Fascist syndical and corporate system as a whole and of the individual organs of the corporate state has already been presented in Chapter VI and needs no repetition here. While, as that discussion has shown, the Italian worker may have gained a new group consciousness under Fascism and greater economic security through the Fascist syndical organizations, such gains have been achieved at the price of the monopolization of the labor movement by one political party and at the price of a system of associations from which genuine freedom of opinion, discussion, and criticism are definitely excluded.

As to the work of the higher organs of economic coördination (thoroughly controlled, as are the syndicates, by the party and the government), little detailed criticism can as yet be made. As has already been pointed out, even though the higher organs of the *stato corporativo* may have interesting possibilities as organs of national economic control, they have played a comparatively minor role in the actual conduct of Italian economic affairs. Economic activity in Italy has been managed, on the whole, as it is managed in other western European countries: whatever positive action there has been, has been taken primarily upon the initiative and through the direct intervention of the central government. To be sure, a new syndical and corporate structure has been created and under strict government control has contributed to the coördination of economic activity; some economic policies favored by the central government for political reasons have been strongly pursued; fundamentally, however, Italian economic life has gone on as yet but little changed. The twenty-two category corporations were established so recently and their action has been of so cautious a nature that the scope of their work remains at the present time comparatively limited. Independent economic planning, coördination of the national economy through the action of autonomous syndical groups and corporations, has not as yet been attempted on any significant scale. The role of the Corporate Chamber and of the National Council of Corporations, the highest organs in the Fascist corporate state, has been limited almost exclusively to putting the stamp of approval upon whatever measures the Fascist government has chosen to propose.

Although the evolution of the Fascist corporate system is not complete and its ultimate merits and shortcomings cannot, therefore, be finally evaluated, it seems safe to conclude that the system has been and is likely to continue to be in the future not an agency for the economic self-government of the Italian people but an instrument of economic control used by the totalitarian Fascist state for the achievement of its ultimate economic and political ends.

APPENDICES

APPENDIX I

LAWS OF THE CORPORATE STATE: SUMMARIES AND EXCERPTS

(The Italian text is not always literally rendered; involved sentences have been simplified, and unessential passages omitted.)

LAW ON THE CORPORATE ORGANIZATION OF THE STATE AS PROPOSED BY THE COMMISSION OF EIGHTEEN

(Published as an appendix to the final report of the Commission, in: Presidenza del Consiglio dei Ministri, *Relazioni e proposte della commissione presidenziale per lo studio delle riforme costituzionali*, Rome, 1925)

(Condensed Version)

PART I.   ORGANIZATION OF SOCIAL ACTIVITIES

Section I.   On Orders

ARTICLE 2.   All social and economic activities (professions, industries, trades, etc.), for the purposes of the present law, shall be classified into three Orders, the Order of liberal professions, the arts, and public employment; the Order of agriculture and agricultural industry; and the Order of industry, commerce, and real and personal property. Within these Orders the various classes of activities shall then be subdivided into categories and the categories shall in turn be classified into sections.

ARTICLE 3.   Within the first Order categories shall be formed corresponding to the principal liberal professions, arts, and public employments. Ministers of religion, retired public employees, and journalists shall also be assigned to the first Order.

ARTICLE 4.   The second Order shall include proprietors of landed estates, farmers, and agricultural workers of every description, divided into categories according to local exigencies.

ARTICLE 5.   The third Order shall be divided into three fundamental sections: namely, industry, commerce, and real and personal property. The owners of shares in industrial and commercial enterprises shall be included in the sections of industry and commerce. Whenever necessary the following sections shall be distinguished within the different categories: entrepreneurs, technical and administrative employees, and workmen. The category of workmen shall be subdivided into skilled and unskilled workmen. Artisans, small industrialists, and small merchants shall form separate categories.

ARTICLE 6. In every province the division of citizens into Orders shall be made by Royal Decree on the proposal of the president of the Council of Ministers. This Decree shall be issued after an advisory opinion has been obtained from the Provincial Councils for the first two Orders and from the Chambers of Commerce for the third. The divisions shall be revised every six years.

Section II. On the Electorate

ARTICLE 7. In every municipality registers for the enrollment of citizens according to their professional categories and sections shall be established.

ARTICLE 8. Citizens performing various kinds of activities simultaneously shall be assigned to the category corresponding to their main occupation. The minimum amount of shares required for enrollment in the third Order shall be defined later.

ARTICLE 9. All citizens of full age shall be included in the municipal registers. Women shall also be registered if they perform an economic or social activity autonomously and continuously.

ARTICLE 10. Foreigners shall be registered, provided they have performed an economic activity within the Italian kingdom for at least ten years without interruption.

ARTICLE 11. In every province there shall be formed three Chambers corresponding to the three Orders described in Art. 2. Two provinces may be united to form one joint Chamber. Chambers shall be divided into sections corresponding to those of the professional Orders which they include.

ARTICLE 12. The Chambers shall be composed of the representatives of the citizens included in the various professional categories. Such representatives shall be elected by the citizens registered in municipal registers and grouped according to professional categories.

ARTICLE 13. The number of representatives shall be proportionate to that of the citizens registered. This proportion shall be greater in the first Chamber than in the others and such as to insure to it a number of components of not less than one-fourth of the total number of components of the three Chambers of the province. Detailed provisions for the determination of the number of representatives shall be made by special law. In no province shall the number of representatives in one Chamber exceed five hundred.

ARTICLE 14. In the first Chamber one-half of the number of representatives shall be allotted in equal parts to all professional categories represented in it. The other half shall then be distributed among the various categories in proportion to the number of citizens registered.

ARTICLE 15. In the second Chamber representatives shall be divided into categories corresponding to the various agricultural interests of the province. In this division, however, due attention shall be paid to the number of citizens included in each category and to the amount of taxes paid to the State. Agricultural laborers shall be separately represented whenever they shall constitute an essential factor in the agricultural enterprise. The number of their representatives, however, shall never exceed the number of representatives assigned to proprietors and to other agricultural entrepreneurs.

ARTICLE 16. In the third Chamber representatives shall be distributed among the three sections of industry, commerce, and real estate ownership in proportion both to the number of citizens registered in each section and to the amount of the taxes paid. In the industrial section representatives shall be divided so as to allot two-fifths of the total number to employers, one-fifth to technical and administrative employees, and two-fifths to the workers. Workers' representatives may in turn be divided into representatives of skilled and unskilled workmen. In the commercial section a part of the total number of representatives varying according to the various professional categories shall be allotted to commercial employees, reserving one-half of the total number to skilled employees. In the third section the distribution of representatives shall take place on the basis of taxes paid.

ARTICLE 17. Every three years the Chamber shall be entirely renewed.

Section III. On the Organs of the Corporate System

ARTICLE 18. Every Chamber shall elect a Council and a Directorate. The Council shall in turn elect its president.

Besides electing the Council, the Chambers divided according to categories shall give opinions on all questions of interest to the respective category which might be placed before them by members of the Council.

ARTICLE 19. The three Chambers of each province shall constitute the Provincial Corporate College, which shall also have a Council and a Directorate. The Council shall be elected by the representatives of the Councils of the various provincial Chambers. The Directorate shall be elected by the Council of the Corporate college of the province.

ARTICLE 20. Corporate Provincial Colleges shall elect representatives for the National Corporate Council to be formed at Rome. The

National Corporate Council shall be divided into three Committees corresponding to the three Orders represented by the three provincial Chambers. Each committee shall have a directorate.

The president of the National Corporate Council shall be elected by the Council by a three-fourths majority. The election shall be submitted to the Government for approval.

ARTICLE 21. The Presidents of the various Provincial Chambers shall take the oath of office before the Prefect of the Province. The President of the National Corporate Council shall take the oath before the President of the Council of Ministers.

ARTICLE 22. The Prefects of the various Provinces shall have the right to attend the meetings of Provincial Chambers. A member of the government shall have the right to attend the meetings of the National Corporate Council.

ARTICLE 23. Corporate organs shall be entrusted with the official representation of the interests of which they are the expression. They shall perform their functions distinctly or jointly and shall seek to insure the collaboration of all national interests in the solution of their respective problems.

ARTICLE 24. The functions of the organs of the Corporate system shall relate to discipline, arbitration, and administration.

ARTICLE 25. Corporate organs shall have disciplinary power in all matters pertaining to the professional activity of citizens enrolled with their respective Orders.

Corporate organs shall also:

(1) Solve labor conflicts in public services through compulsory arbitration;

(2) Prevent collective labor conflicts not within the class of public services, by offers of conciliation and solve them by means of arbitration whenever asked to do so by both parties involved;

(3) Express their opinion, through specially appointed commissions, on collective labor disputes mentioned in subdivision 2, whenever the parties involved should not have consented to submit to arbitration and whenever such advisory opinion should have been requested by public authorities, or when the disputes in question should involve serious danger to the national economy and to public order;

(4) Sanction collective labor agreements stipulated by legally recognized syndicates;

(5) Supervise the work of provincial professional colleges and of private employment bureaus.

ARTICLE 26. Corporate organs shall within the limits determined by existing laws and regulations be empowered to publish rules regulating the economic and social activities of the groups which they represent. They shall also be empowered to levy a contribution from the members in the different corporate Orders; such rules and regulations, however, shall be approved by the competent government authorities.

ARTICLE 27. Corporate organs shall give their advice and opinion in all cases in which they shall be required to do so by government authorities and whenever such opinions shall be required by the laws in force. They shall be obliged always to advise upon the legal recognition of syndicates.

ARTICLE 28. The main administrative functions of Corporate organs shall be: formation of the rolls of authorized professional men; registration of legally recognized syndicates; registration of commercial and industrial firms; gathering, elaboration, and publication of statistical data; preparing records of commercial usages; general control on the observance of laws and regulations referring to hours and conditions of work; coördination of the various forms of economic and professional activity tending to bring about a reduction in production costs; industrial specialization and standardization of industrial products; employment of labor and provisions against unemployment; professional instruction, industrial apprenticeship; social insurance; internal migration, and assistance to temporary or permanent emigrants; propaganda for and promotion of savings and private insurance; sanitation and social relief activities.

ARTICLE 29. In addition to those named the second and third Chambers shall exercise all the attributions now within the province of agricultural councils and chambers of commerce which shall be replaced by them.

The rules necessary for the coördination of the activities of the first Chamber with those of the Orders of legally recognized professions now in existence shall be separately determined. All other professional orders shall be absorbed by the first Chamber.

ARTICLE 30. Legally recognized syndicates shall have the right to be heard by corporate organs whenever regulations pertaining to the interests for the defense of which they were constituted shall be passed.

Syndicates may, under the supervision of Corporate organs, be entrusted with the placement of unemployed workers.

ARTICLE 31. After hearing the State Council and whenever the preservation of public order or other reasons should require it, the government shall always have the right to dissolve Corporate organs.

Dissolved organs shall, however, be reconstituted within six months.

PART II. CORPORATE AND POLITICAL REPRESENTATION

ARTICLE 32. After the formation of the corporate system a political representation shall be instituted on its basis and half the number of deputies shall be elected through its organs. The designation of deputies shall take place by an election made by the members of the provincial Chambers then holding office.

LAW OF APRIL 3, 1926, NO. 563
ON THE LEGAL DISCIPLINE OF COLLECTIVE
LABOR RELATIONS

(Published in the *Gazzetta ufficiale* of April 14, 1926, no. 87)

(Condensed Version)

Section I. Legal Recognition of Syndicates and of Collective Labor Agreements

ARTICLE 1. Syndical associations of employers and workers, both intellectual and manual, may be legally recognized provided they satisfy the following conditions:

(1) *For employers' associations:* that employers who have voluntarily enrolled employ at least one-tenth of the total number of workmen working for enterprises of that kind located within the district in which the association is operating.

For workers' associations: that workers who have voluntarily enrolled represent at least one-tenth of the total number of the workers of the industry within the district in which the association is operating.

(2) That beside the protection of their economic and moral interests the associations shall also aim to promote and shall effectively promote the welfare, instruction, and moral and national education of their members.

(3) That the directors of the associations give evidence of competence, of good moral character, and of strong national convictions.

ARTICLE 2. Associations of independent artists, of artisans, and of professional men may be legally recognized, provided the requirements set forth in the preceding article are satisfied.

Orders and associations of independent artists, of artisans, and of professional men at present existing and legally recognized shall continue to be governed by the laws and regulations in force. Such laws and regulations shall be revised and harmonized with the provisions of the present law.

ARTICLE 3. Associations mentioned in the preceding articles shall include in their membership either employers or workers exclusively.

Associations of employers and workers may be connected through central connecting organizations of a higher order. The representation of employers and employees shall, however, always remain distinct. For associations representing several classes of workers, each class shall be separately represented.

ARTICLE 4. Legal recognition of an association shall be granted by royal decree, on proposal of the competent minister in agreement with the Minister of the Interior and after an opinion from the State Council. The decree granting the recognition shall also approve the association's by-laws to be published at its expense in the *Gazzetta ufficiale* of the kingdom.

The by-laws shall give exact information on the aims of the association, on the appointment of administrative officers and on the requirements for the admission of members. One of the requirements shall be good political conduct from a national point of view.

The by-laws may provide for the establishment of professional schools, institutions of financial assistance and of moral and national education, and institutes for the advancement and the refinement of production and of national culture and art.

ARTICLE 5. Legally recognized associations shall possess legal personality and shall be empowered legally to represent all employers, employees, artisans, and professional men of the class for which they are organized, regardless of whether or not the latter are members of the association, within the district in which they operate.

Legally recognized associations shall be empowered to impose annual dues not to exceed one day's compensation for each employee in the case of employers, and the compensation received for one working day in the case of workers, artists, and professional men, on all the employers, employees, artists, and professional men whom they represent, whether or not they are enrolled members. At least one-tenth of the income of these contributions shall be deducted annually for the formation of a fund securing the obligations assumed by the associations in their collective agreements. This fund shall be administered in accordance with the provisions of the special regulation.

Employers shall report the number of their employees to their associations not later than March 31 of each year. Failure to report or the filing of a false or incomplete statement shall be punishable by a fine not to exceed 2,000 lire.

These contributions shall be collected in accordance with the regulations contained in the laws on the collection of municipal taxes.

Contributions of employees shall be deducted from their wages or salaries and turned over to the associations.

Members only shall participate in the activities of the association and in the election or nomination of administrative officers.

Only the legally recognized associations of employers and employees shall send representatives to councils, organizations, or associations for which such representation is prescribed by laws and regulations.

ARTICLE 6. Associations may be municipal, territorial, provincial, regional, inter-regional, and national.

Federations or unions of several associations and confederations of several federations may be legally recognized in accordance with the conditions of the present law. The recognition of these federations or confederations carries with it the recognition of each affiliated association or federation. Federations or confederations shall have disciplinary powers over affiliated associations and their individual members, which, however, they shall exercise in accordance with the provisions of their by-laws.

Only one association for each class of employers, or workers, or artists and professional men shall be recognized by law. Within the limits of its territorial jurisdiction only one federation or confederation of employers, employees, or artists and professional men shall be recognized by law for each class of employers and employees represented.

Whenever a national confederation of all classes of employers or employees in agriculture, industry, commerce, or artists and professional men shall have been recognized, the recognition of federations or of associations not included in the confederation shall be prohibited.

Associations which, without the consent of the Government, have become affiliated with international organizations shall in no case be recognized.

ARTICLE 7. Every association shall be managed and represented by a responsible president or secretary. The president or secretary shall be nominated or elected in accordance with the rules contained in the constitution and in the by-laws.

Appointments or elections of presidents or secretaries of national, inter-regional, and regional associations shall not be valid unless approved by royal decree on proposal of the competent Minister in agreement with the Minister of the Interior. The approval may at any time be revoked.

Appointments or elections of presidents or secretaries of provincial, territorial, or municipal associations shall not be valid unless approved by a decree of the competent Minister, in agreement with the Minister of the Interior. The approval may at any time be revoked.

The by-laws of the association shall designate the committee holding powers of discipline and possessing authority to expel members on account of moral and political misconduct.

ARTICLE 8. Presidents or secretaries shall be assisted by a board of directors elected by the members of the association in accordance with the provisions contained in the by-laws.

Municipal, territorial, and provincial associations shall be subject to the supervision of the prefect of the province and of the Provincial Administrative Board. They shall exercise their respective powers in accordance with the provisions to be determined by special regulation. The regional, inter-regional, and national associations shall be supervised by the competent Minister.

The competent Minister in agreement with the Minister of the Interior may dissolve the associations' boards of directors and entrust all powers to the president or the secretary for a period not exceeding one year. In special cases he may appoint a commissioner to take charge of the administration.

For associations affiliated with a federation or confederation, the decree recognizing the federation or confederation and approving its constitution may provide that powers of supervision be given in whole or in part to such federation or confederation.

ARTICLE 9. In exceptional cases and whenever the conditions required for recognition and described in the preceding articles shall not have been observed, a royal decree, to be issued on the proposal of the competent Minister in agreement with the Minister of the Interior and after hearing the Council of State, may revoke the recognition.

ARTICLE 10. Collective labor agreements, negotiated by legally recognized associations of employers, employees, artists or professional men shall apply to all the employers, employees, artists or professional men of the professional class to which the collective agreement refers and whom such associations represent in accordance with the provisions of Art. 5.

Collective labor agreements shall be made in writing, under penalty of voidance. They shall also, under penalty of voidance, specify the period of duration of the agreements.

The central connecting organizations of a higher order described in Art. 3 may issue general regulations on the conditions of labor upon agreement with the representatives of both employers and employees. These regulations shall apply to all employers and employees within the class to which the regulations refer and whom the grouped associations represent in accordance with Art. 5.

For municipal, territorial, or provincial associations, a copy of the collective labor agreements negotiated and of the general regulations established in accordance with the provisions of the preceding paragraphs shall be filed at the local prefecture and published in the official bulletin of the province. For regional, inter-regional, or national associations, such a copy shall be filed at the Ministry of National Economy and published in the *Gazzetta ufficiale* of the kingdom.

Employers and employees failing to observe collective agreements and the general regulations referring thereto shall be civilly liable both to the association of employers and to the association of employees by which the agreement has been negotiated.

Further regulations relating to the negotiation and application of collective labor agreements shall be issued by royal decree, on the proposal of the Minister of Justice.

ARTICLE 11. The provisions of the present law on the judicial recognition of syndical associations shall not be applicable to associations of state, provincial, and municipal employees or to employees of public welfare institutions, for which special regulations shall be provided.

Associations of officers, non-commissioned officers, and soldiers of the Royal Army, the Royal Navy, the Royal Air force, and the other armed corps of the State, provinces, and municipalities, as well as associations of magistrates, associations of professors of secondary schools and of institutions of higher learning, associations of officers and employees of the Ministries of the Interior, Foreign Affairs, and the Colonies shall be prohibited under penalty of demotion, removal from rank or dismissal.

ARTICLE 12. Associations of employers, employees, artists or professional men not legally recognized shall continue to exist as *de facto* associations in accordance with existing legislation. This provision shall not affect the second paragraph of the preceding article.

In such cases the provisions of the Royal Decree of January 24, 1924, no. 64, shall be applicable.

Section II. On Labor Courts

ARTICLE 13. All controversies on collective labor relations, whether arising in connection with the application of existing regulations or collective labor agreements or in connection with requests for new working conditions, shall come under the jurisdiction of the Courts of Appeal of the Kingdom, functioning as Labor Courts.

Before a judicial decision is arrived at, the president of the Court must attempt conciliation of the parties.

Controversies described in the preceding section may be submitted to arbiters, in accordance with the provisions of Articles 8 and following, of the Code of Civil Procedure.

Appeals against decisions of arbiters, arbitration commissions, or other legal organizations concerning labor contracts shall be referred to the Court of Appeals, functioning as a Labor Court.

ARTICLE 14. A special Section shall be organized at each one of the sixteen Courts of Appeal of the Kingdom to perform the work of a Labor Court. Each Section shall be composed of three magistrates, viz., a Section president and two counsellors of the Court of Appeals. Two citizens, experts in the problems of production and labor and selected by the first president of the Court in accordance with the regulations of the following article, shall be added to this body from time to time.

To give effect to the foregoing provisions, the personnel of the Court and of the judiciary chanceries shall be revised by royal decree to be issued on proposal of the Minister of Justice in agreement with the Minister of Finance.

ARTICLE 15. At each Court of Appeals there shall be kept a list of experts in the problems of production and labor, classified into groups and subgroups in accordance with the various kinds of business enterprises existing within the jurisdiction of the Court. The list shall be bi-annually revised.

The regulations for the preparation and for the revision of the lists and for the daily compensation and other indemnities to be paid to persons called upon to exercise judicial functions shall be determined by separate Royal Decree.

The first president of the Court shall designate each year, and for each group and subgroup, the persons who shall be called upon to act as expert advisers in cases affecting the enterprises included in the group or subgroup in question. Persons directly or indirectly interested in the controversy shall not be included in this body.

ARTICLE 16. The judgment of the Court of Appeals, functioning as a Labor Court shall be rendered in accordance with the law of contracts in cases involving existing agreements. In cases involving the determination of new labor conditions the judgment shall be rendered in accordance with equity, and with a view to harmonizing the interests of employers with those of employees and protecting the higher interests of production.

In the determination of new labor conditions the period of their duration, usually the same as the one determined by freely negotiated agreements, shall always be specified.

The decision of the Labor Court shall be made after hearing the verbal opinion of the public prosecutor.

From the decisions of the Labor Courts appeals to the Supreme

Court of the Kingdom (Corte di Cassazione) may be made for the reasons specified in Article 517 of the Code of Civil Procedure.

ARTICLE 17. Legal action for controversies on collective labor relations shall be initiated solely by the legally recognized associations and shall be applicable to the legally recognized associations where they exist; otherwise such actions shall be argued by a special attorney appointed by the president of the Court of Appeals. In the latter case the voluntary interpleading of the interested parties shall be permitted.

No legal action may be taken by associations of employers and employees, members of federations or confederations, by associations for which central connecting organizations exist unless it be shown that the federation or confederation, or the central organization has endeavored to bring about an amicable solution of the controversy and that its efforts have been unsuccessful.

Only legally recognized associations shall be empowered to represent in court within their territorial jurisdiction all employers and employees of the professional class for which they were organized.

Decisions made by the Courts shall apply to all interested parties and shall be published, for communal, territorial, and provincial associations in the official legal bulletin of the province, and for regional, inter-regional or national associations in the *Gazzetta ufficiale* of the kingdom.

All memoranda and documents relating to the proceedings of the Court of Appeals as a Labor Court, and all judgments issued by it shall be exempt from registration fees and stamp taxes.

Section III. On Strikes and Lockouts

ARTICLE 18. Lockouts and strikes are prohibited. Employers who shall close their factories, their enterprises, or offices without justifiable reasons and for the sole object of compelling their employees to modify existing labor agreements shall be punished by a fine of from ten thousand to one hundred thousand lire.

Employees and laborers who, in groups of three or more, shall cease work by agreement, or shall work in such a manner as to disturb its continuity or regularity, in order to compel employers to change existing labor agreements, shall be punishable by a fine of from one hundred to one thousand lire. In the ensuing judicial proceedings the regulations of Article 298 et seq. of the Code of Criminal Procedure shall be applicable.

Leaders, promoters, and organizers of the crimes mentioned in the preceding paragraphs shall be punishable by imprisonment for not less than one year, nor more than two years, and by the fine provided for in the same paragraphs.

ARTICLE 19. Employees of the State and of other public organizations and employees of public service and public utility enterprises who in groups of three or more shall cease work by agreement or perform it in such a manner as to disturb its continuity or regularity shall be punishable by imprisonment from one to six months, and shall be barred from public office for six months.

The regulations of Article 298 et seq. of the Code of Criminal Procedure shall be applicable in the ensuing judicial proceedings.

Leaders, promoters, and organizers shall be punishable by imprisonment of from six months to two years and shall be barred from public office for not less than three years.

Administrators of public service or of public utility enterprises who without justifiable reason shall suspend work in their establishments, in their enterprises, or offices shall be punished by imprisonment of from six months to a year and by a fine of from five thousand to one hundred thousand lire, in addition to being temporarily barred from public office.

When, in accordance with the provisions of the present article, the safety of the public should be endangered, persons found guilty shall be imprisoned for a term of not less than one year. If the death of one or more persons should result, the term of imprisonment shall not be less than three years.

ARTICLE 20. Employees of State and other public enterprises and administrators and employees of public service or public utility enterprises failing, in case of strikes or lockouts, to do all that lies within their power to restore or continue the regular work of their enterprises shall be punishable by imprisonment of from one to six months.

ARTICLE 21. When employers or employees suspend work or work at irregular periods in order to coerce or influence the decisions of State, provincial, or municipal authorities or of a public official, the leaders, promoters, and organizers of the movement shall be punishable by imprisonment of from three to seven years, and by being permanently barred from public office. Other participants shall be punishable by imprisonment of from one to three years and by being barred temporarily from public office.

ARTICLE 22. Employers and employees refusing to obey the decisions of a Labor Magistrate shall be punishable by imprisonment of from one month to one year and by a fine of from one hundred to five thousand lire.

The directors of legally recognized associations refusing to carry out the decisions of labor magistrates shall be removed from office and punishable by imprisonment of from six months to two years and by a fine of from two thousand to ten thousand lire.

If, in addition to failure to carry out the decision of a labor magistrate, the defendant shall be found guilty of having caused a lockout or a strike, the provisions of the Criminal Code shall be applicable.

ARTICLE 23. All regulations contrary to the present law shall be revoked.

ROYAL DECREE OF JULY 1, 1926, NO. 1130, CONTAINING THE REGULATIONS FOR THE ENFORCEMENT OF THE LAW OF APRIL 3, 1926, NO. 563, ON THE LEGAL DISCIPLINE OF COLLECTIVE LABOR RELATIONS

(Published in the *Gazzetta ufficiale* of July 7, 1926, no. 155)

(Condensed Version)

PART I.   UNITARY OR FIRST DEGREE ASSOCIATIONS

Section I.   Establishment and Legal Recognition of Syndical Associations

ARTICLE 1. Admission to syndical associations shall be open to Italian citizens of both sexes who have reached the age of eighteen, and who, in addition to possessing the other requirements prescribed by law and by the by-laws of the associations, are of good moral and political character from a national point of view.

Admission shall also be open to legally established commercial companies and to other legal persons of Italian nationality, the directors and administrators of which are of good moral and political character from a national point of view.

ARTICLE 2. Admission to legally recognized syndical associations shall also be open to foreigners who have resided in Italy for at least ten years. Such persons, however, shall not be eligible for appointment or election to any administrative position or to the office of director.

ARTICLE 3. State, provincial, and municipal administrators and administrators of public welfare institutions shall not be permitted legally to join syndical associations of employers in accordance with the Law of April 3, 1926, no. 563, nor shall they be subjected to the provisions of the same law, dealing with collective labor agreements and the jurisdiction of the labor courts.

The same rule shall apply to the autonomous administration of the state railroads, to the postal, telegraph, and telephone administration, to the savings and loan fund, to the bank of issue, to the banks of Naples and Sicily, to savings banks and to other semi-official institutions and organizations. Associations formed by employees of such enterprises cannot be legally recognized.

Autonomous enterprises under municipal control and their personnel shall be subject to the provisions of the Law of April 3, 1926, no. 563.

ARTICLE 4. When their members are neither employers nor employees, associations aiming to protect the material and moral interest of their members shall not be legally recognized in accordance with the Law of April 3, 1926, nor shall they be subject to the provisions of the law dealing with collective labor agreements and the jurisdiction of the labor courts.

Owners of rural properties who have leased their estates shall be allowed to join the legally recognized associations of agricultural employers, shall be organized into a separate section, and shall be separately represented in the associations' administrative organization.

Such representation, however, shall not imply participation in the negotiation of collective agricultural labor agreements.

ARTICLE 5. Separate associations shall be formed by artisans working in their personally owned shops, small business men and traders, brokers, commission agents, independent farmers, lease holders and metayers.[1]

ARTICLE 6. Even if employed in the same type of enterprise, intellectual and manual workers shall not be members of the same association.

Technicians and administrative employees may be grouped into the same association, but shall constitute a separate section with direct representation.

Technical and administrative managers, heads of departments, agents, and, in general, employees with a power of attorney shall be grouped into separate associations.

ARTICLE 7. Employers and employees belonging, because of the character of their occupation, simultaneously and in a stable and permanent manner to different classes of employers and of employees shall be permitted to join several syndical associations simultaneously.

A person combining the capacity of employer and employee in a stable and permanent manner shall be permitted to join employers' and employees' associations simultaneously.

In accordance with the provisions of Art. 12 of the Law of April 3, 1926, members of legally recognized associations shall not, under penalty of expulsion, join *de facto* associations established for the pursuit of the same syndical aims.

ARTICLE 8. Coöperative enterprises shall, for syndical purposes,

[1] As corrected in the *Gazzetta ufficiale*, no. 161, of July 14, 1926.

organize themselves into special associations, different from the associations of similar capitalistic enterprises and the associations of workmen therein employed.

ARTICLE 9. If a person be expelled or excluded from a legally recognized association or if admittance be refused him, an appeal to the Minister of Corporations shall be permitted as a last resort.

ARTICLE 10. To ascertain the existence of the conditions of Art. 1, Number 1, of the Law of April 3, 1926, the lists of workmen compiled in accordance with the compulsory notification provision of Art. 5, third paragraph, of the same law, shall be used. After consultation with the Provincial Economic Council, these lists shall be compiled by the prefects to whom the information in question, received by syndical associations, shall be immediately transmitted.

For independent artists or professional men, there shall be used the lists compiled by the prefectures on the basis of information to be supplied by the municipalities.

All persons practicing an art or a profession in a municipality shall register at the municipality within three months, under penalty of a fine of one hundred lire.

ARTICLE 11. Whenever, in order to practice an art or a profession, registration with a professional order or college is necessary, in accordance with the present laws, a syndical association for the profession may also be recognized. Such syndical association shall then be subject to the regulations of the Law of April 3, 1926.

Syndical associations and not professional orders or colleges shall be empowered to protect the moral and material interests of their members and shall have the duty to give assistance and instruction in accordance with the law. They shall have the exclusive power to designate representatives in the political, administrative, and technical organizations of the State and in other public bodies whenever such designation shall be provided for by the existing laws and regulations.

Professional men and artists employed by industrial, agricultural, commercial, transportation, or banking concerns shall, for the purposes of collective labor agreements, form a part of the syndical association of employees existing within these fields. They shall, however, be admitted to membership, in separate sections and with direct personal representation, in associations of independent professional men or of artists.

ARTICLE 12. Professional orders or colleges existing and legally recognized when the Law of April 3, 1926 shall take effect shall continue to operate. New orders or colleges shall, however, not be recognized even though their establishment may have been provided for by previous laws.

Whenever registration with a professional order be necessary in order to practice an art or a profession for which no legally recognized order or college exists, all duties and powers incumbent upon orders or colleges concerning membership and disciplinary measures shall be exercised by syndical associations. If there be no legally recognized syndical associations such duties and powers shall be entrusted to the president of the tribunal.

ARTICLE 13. Recognition of syndical associations shall be denied whenever the conditions prescribed by law have not been complied with and whenever recognition is not advisable for political, economic, or social reasons.

The granting of legal recognition may be made subject to modifications in the association's by-laws.

ARTICLE 14. To obtain legal recognition, associations shall furnish, besides their by-laws, a report on their origin and on their activities since the date of their establishment, as well as a list of members and of persons holding administrative offices.

The by-laws shall indicate the aims of the association, its territorial jurisdiction, the location of its headquarters, its relation with other associations, the conditions for admission and dismissal of members, the procedure for the determination of dues, according to the provisions of Art. 5 of the Law of April 3, 1926, the modalities for the appointment or election and the powers of the directing organs, the reasons for exclusion from the association, the modalities for the administration of income and endowment, and the percentage of income to be used for the compulsory expenditures of the association.

ARTICLE 15. The Government shall be empowered to encourage, and, if necessary, to decree ex officio, the revision of the by-laws of legally recognized associations.

Section II. Organization and Administration of Syndical Associations

ARTICLE 16. The powers of the administrative boards of syndical associations, established by Art. 8 of the Law of April 3, 1926, shall be specified by the by-laws of the association.

The administrative board shall be presided over by a president or secretary, who shall manage and represent the associations.

ARTICLE 17. The same requirements of moral and political fitness as are demanded of the leaders of legally recognized syndical associations shall also be demanded of their employees.

ARTICLE 18. Expenditures of legally recognized syndical associations shall be classified into compulsory and optional expenditures.

Expenditures in connection with syndical organization, economic and social welfare activities, moral and religious assistance, national education and professional instruction shall be compulsory.

The following expenditures, the proportion of which shall be determined by decree of the Minister of Corporations after hearing the opinion of the legally recognized organizations of higher rank with which the association is affiliated, namely, contributions to the National Dopolavoro organization, the National Association for Maternal and Infant Welfare, the National Balilla Organization and the National Welfare Fund established by the decree of the Minister of National Economy dated June 26, 1925, shall be compulsory.

The establishment of the guarantee fund provided for by Art. 5 of the Law of April 3, 1926, shall also be compulsory. The funds used for this purpose shall be invested in bonded government securities.

All other expenditures shall be optional.

ARTICLE 19. Regulations for the coördination of the activities of syndical associations with those of the National Dopolavoro Organization, the National Association for Maternal and Infant Welfare, the National Balilla Organization, and the National Welfare fund, shall be issued by royal decree.

ARTICLE 20. Whenever the recognition of an association shall be withdrawn or revoked, a receiver shall be appointed by the Prefect, for provincial associations, and by the Minister of Corporations, for inter-provincial associations. The receiver shall dispose of the assets and pay off the liabilities.

The net capital remaining after this settlement shall be turned over, by royal decree, to the legally recognized association of higher rank with which the association in question was affiliated. In the absence of such an association the remaining funds shall be spent for welfare and educational work among the members of the association of employers and of employees of that professional class.

ARTICLE 21. Any property belonging to syndical associations prior to their legal recognition, regardless of who shall be holding or administering it on behalf of the association, shall become by law part of the endowment of legally recognized associations.

All property belonging to associations partially or fully organized for objectives provided for by the Law of April 3, 1926, shall be turned over by law to the syndical association organized for the same objectives and for the same classes of employers and workers. This provision shall be applicable whenever the majority of the members of the preëxisting association shall have joined the legally recognized syndical association.

By a decree the prefect may order, even prior to the granting of recognition to the association, that the property referred to in the two preceding paragraphs be turned over to one of his commissioners. As soon as the association shall become legally recognized, the property shall then be turned over to its legal representatives. Whenever the recognition shall not be granted within six months of the issuance of the decree, the property shall be returned to the person who formerly held or administered it.

ARTICLE 22. Syndical associations shall not be permitted to interfere with the administration nor with the technical and commercial management of the enterprises of their members, without their consent and unless labor relations are involved.

Excepting the case of labor relations, no compulsory regulations for non-members may be issued by syndical associations.

Syndical associations shall not be permitted to engage in commercial enterprises.

Section III. Syndical Dues

ARTICLE 23. Decisions for the levying of syndical dues as provided for by Art. 5 of the Law of April 3, 1926, shall be approved by the Provincial Administrative Board for provincial associations and by the Minister of Corporations for inter-provincial associations.

The approved decision shall be published at the association's expense, in the official bulletin of the province in the first case, and in the *Gazzetta ufficiale* in the latter.

Appeals against the decisions of the Provincial Administrative Board or the decree of the Minister may be made to the Government within fifteen days of publication.

ARTICLE 24. The Minister of Corporations shall establish regulations for the levying of dues also in cases in which, because of the nature of the work or the character of the enterprise, determination of the rate on the basis of one day's compensation is not possible.

ARTICLE 25. Every association shall compile registers of its contributors classified according to residence.

The registers shall be posted in the town halls of the various communities for at least one month from the date of the decree.

During the following month each contributor shall have the right to file a protest against his enrollment in these lists. Such protests shall be filed with the Provincial Administrative Board for provincial associations and with the Minister of Corporations for inter-provincial associations.

The decisions of the Provincial Administrative Board and of the Minister shall be final, but recourse may be had to the judiciary authorities in cases in which such recourse shall be permitted for the levying of taxes.

The final registers shall be compiled on the basis of uncontested entries and of those for which protests were disposed of. They shall be made valid by a decree of the prefect. Appeal to the prefect shall be allowed only for error of fact.

ARTICLE 26. The collection of syndical dues shall be entrusted to the ordinary tax collectors. They shall possess fiscal powers and shall be responsible for uncollected assessments.

In accordance with the terms and conditions established by Art. 80 of the laws on the collection of direct taxes, approved by the Royal Decree of October 17, 1922, no. 1401, amounts collected through these lists shall be deposited in the special account of the prefecture, at the Royal Treasury office of the respective provinces.

The prefect shall in turn authorize payment to the unitary associations and to the associations of higher rank with which they are affiliated. The amounts of these contributions shall be determined in each case by a decree of the Minister of Corporations, to be issued on the proposal of the organization of the highest rank with which the unitary association shall be affiliated.

Ten per cent of the collected amounts shall in any case be turned over to the State and placed in a special account of the Ministry of Corporations at the Royal Treasury in Rome.

ARTICLE 27. The associations' by-laws may provide for supplementary dues applying to members of the association. Such supplementary dues shall be collected directly by the associations.

ARTICLE 28. By decree, the Minister of Corporations may order that compulsory dues shall be collected by the individual associations. This shall not alter the method of distribution of the funds collected, in accordance with the provisions of the last two paragraphs of Art. 26.

Section IV. Supervision and Control

ARTICLE 29. The prefect, for provincial associations, and the Minister, for inter-provincial associations, may request the filing of documents and other information and may order inspections and investigations of the activities of the associations.

At any time, upon complaint or ex officio, the Minister of Corporations may annul the decisions of the various organs of legally recognized associations whenever they are contrary to laws, regulations, and by-laws or contrary to the essential aims of the organizations.

ARTICLE 30. The following shall be subject to approval by the Provincial Administrative Board, or by the Minister of Corporations:

    (a) Budgets;
    (b) Actions involving changes in assets;

(c) Expenditures to be carried in the budget for more than five years;

(d) Regulations for lists of personnel;

(e) Regulations for collection of dues;

(f) Payments to be made from the fund constituted in accordance with the provisions of Art. 5 of the Law of April 3, 1926.

Whenever the proper organs of an association shall omit to do what they are bound to do by law, regulation, or by-laws, the Prefect or the Minister may order the performance of the necessary acts, including the budgeting and payment of the association's expenses.

Within fifteen days after the decisions of the Provincial Administrative Board, the Prefect, or the Minister have been rendered, an appeal against them may be made to the Government.

ARTICLE 31. When functioning as an organ controlling syndical associations, the Provincial Administrative Board shall be composed of the prefect (as its presiding officer), two counselors of the prefecture, and four members designated biennially by the Provincial Economic Council.

PART II. SYNDICAL ASSOCIATIONS OF HIGHER RANK (FEDERATIONS AND CONFEDERATIONS)

ARTICLE 32. Legally recognized syndical associations of higher rank (federations and confederations) shall have legal personality.

ARTICLE 33. In addition to the recourse provided for by the by-laws an appeal to the Minister of Corporations shall be permitted as a measure of last resort whenever an association of lower rank is refused admission to or membership in an association of higher rank.

An appeal to the Minister shall also be made in the case of exclusion of an association of lower rank by one of higher rank, regardless of the form in which such exclusion shall be made.

ARTICLE 34. Syndical associations of technical and administrative managers, heads of departments, special agents, and employees with a power of attorney shall join federations of employers' associations.

Associations of coöperative enterprises shall join the syndical association of higher rank of employers or of employees, depending upon the nature of their activities. They shall also be permitted to join a central bureau or other legally recognized institution aiming at the promotion and encouragement of coöperation. Such affiliation shall not entail interference with the administrative, technical, and commercial management of the coöperatives belonging to the association with the exception of cases in which such right of interference shall have been granted to the association and expressly stated at the time of affiliation.

Associations of artisans, small merchants, commercial agents, and small landowners cultivating their own lands, organized in accordance with the provisions of Art. 5 shall join employers' associations of higher rank.

Associations of metayers, organized in accordance with the provisions of Art. 5, shall join associations of higher rank of agricultural laborers.

ARTICLE 35. Orders and colleges of independent professional men retained in accordance with the provisions of the second paragraph of Art. 2 of the Law of April 3, 1926, shall neither constitute federations or other organizations of higher rank nor join such organizations.

ARTICLE 36. All regulations on the recognition of unitary associations given in Arts. 13, 14, and 15 of Part I shall be applicable to the legal recognition of associations of higher rank (federations and confederations) with the following modifications:

In order to be legally recognized, associations of higher rank shall present, in addition to the by-laws and the report described in Art. 14, a list of the affiliated syndical associations of lower rank and also of the other associations and institutions organized for the purposes described in the last paragraph of Art. 4 of the Law of April 3, 1926. They shall also present an authentic copy of the affiliation act, the by-laws of each organization, and a certificate, issued by the prefecture in whose district the individual associations are located, testifying that the conditions prescribed in Arts. 1 and 2 of the Law of April 3, 1926, have been fulfilled. For national associations the fulfillment of these requirements shall be ascertained directly by the Minister of Corporations.

The list of all syndical associations of lower rank and of all other associations and institutions affiliated with it shall be approved with the by-laws of the association of higher rank. Later changes in the list shall be approved by royal decree.

The decree granting legal recognition to the syndical association of higher rank shall also automatically grant legal recognition to all syndical associations of lower rank affiliated with it. It shall also grant recognition to the other affiliated associations and institutions organized for the purposes described in the last paragraph of Art. 4 of the Law of April 3, 1926. Associations and organizations so recognized shall acquire legal personality. If affiliation takes place after recognition has been granted to the association of higher rank, legal recognition shall be granted to the associations of lower rank and to the other organizations mentioned above by means of a special decree and at the request of the recognized association of higher rank.

ARTICLE 37. If the royal decree approving the by-laws of an association of higher rank (federation or confederation) prescribes that it shall be the duty of such association to supervise and control the affiliated associations of lower rank, the former shall be vested with all the powers which the law and the regulation grant to the prefect, to the Provincial Administrative Board, and to the Minister, with the exception of those specifically omitted.

After hearing the State Council these powers may at any time be revoked by royal decree.

The delegation of their powers notwithstanding, the Minister of Corporations and the prefect shall always have the right to request associations subject to the control of a higher organization to present documents and other information and to submit to direct investigations and inspections. This right shall be exercised whenever requests made to higher organizations shall not have been carried out.

ARTICLE 38. All provisions contained in Arts. 16, 17, 18, first, second, fourth, and fifth paragraphs, and in Arts. 19, 20, 21, and 22 of Part I, shall be also applicable to syndical associations of higher rank (federations and confederations).

Associations of higher rank shall not be permitted to interfere with the administrative, the technical, and the commercial management of enterprises affiliated with the unitary or first degree associations excepting the case in which such interference shall be permitted them.

ARTICLE 39. Syndical associations of higher rank shall not be permitted to impose dues on individual employers or employees.

The amount of supplementary assessments to be levied from affiliated associations in addition to those established by the Minister of Corporations in accordance with Art. 26 shall be established by the by-laws.

ARTICLE 40. All regulations on supervision and control contained in Arts. 29, 30, and 31 of Part I shall be applicable to syndical associations of higher rank (federations and confederations).

Such regulations shall also be applicable to associations and institutions organized for the purposes referred to in the last paragraph of Art. 4 of the Law of April 3, 1926.

ARTICLE 41. The following national confederations, comprising several national federations, national associations, or local federations or confederations of syndical associations, shall be recognized:

(a) For employers: a national confederation of industrialists; a national confederation of farmers; a national confederation of merchants; a national confederation of enterprises of maritime and air transportation; a national confederation of enterprises of land transportation and internal navigation; a national confederation of banking.

(b) For employees: a national confederation of industrial employees and laborers; a national confederation of agricultural employees and laborers; a national confederation of commercial employees and laborers; a national confederation of employees and laborers of enterprises of maritime and air transportation; a national confederation of employees and laborers of enterprises of land transportation and internal navigation; a national confederation of banking employees.

(c) For independent professions: a national confederation of independent artists, artisans, and professional men.

Two general confederations, one for employers and the other for employees and professional men, may also be recognized.

After hearing the Council of Ministers and the National Council of Corporations, there may be authorized, whenever necessary, by royal decree, the recognition of other national and general Confederations.

PART III. CENTRAL CONNECTING OR CORPORATE ORGANIZATIONS

ARTICLE 42. The central connecting organizations provided for by Art. 3 of the Law of April 3, 1926, shall be national in scope. They shall connect the national syndical organizations existing within the various branches of production and including employers and intellectual and manual workers devoted to a given kind of productive activity or belonging to one or several groups of enterprises.

Organizations thus united shall constitute a corporation.

A corporation shall be established by a decree of the Minister of Corporations.

ARTICLE 43. The corporation shall not possess legal personality, but shall constitute an administrative organ of the State.

The decree establishing a corporation shall determine its powers and duties, its organization, and the jurisdiction of its central and local bureaus.

Expenses arising in connection with the work of corporate organs shall be met by the State from the share in syndical dues received by it.

ARTICLE 44. In the carrying out of their aims corporate organs shall have the power:

(a) To conciliate controversies arising among affiliated organizations and to issue the regulations provided for by Art. 10 of the Law of April 3, 1926;

(b) To promote, encourage, and subsidize all efforts aiming at the coördination and improvement of production;

(c) To establish employment offices wherever their need shall be felt. Where such offices shall exist a royal decree may prohibit free mediation and the establishment of other employment agencies, the special legal provisions and regulations existing on the subject, however, remaining unchanged;

(d) To regulate technical training and apprenticeship by issuing general compulsory regulations on the subject and by supervising their observance. To these regulations all provisions regarding collective labor agreements shall be applicable.

ARTICLE 45. Associations affiliated with corporate organs shall be autonomous in all matters concerning the negotiation of collective labor agreements. Corporate organs shall, however, be required to make an effort at conciliation in accordance with Art. 17 of the Law of April 3, 1926, and shall have the right to issue the regulations provided for in Art. 3 of the law.

ARTICLE 46. Presidents of corporations shall be appointed and removed by decree of the Minister of Corporations. Each corporation shall have a Council composed of delegates from the various organizations connected through the Council. The representation of employers' organizations within the Council shall be equal to that of the workers, intellectual and manual combined.

The procedure for the appointment of these delegates, the duties of the Council, and the powers of the presidents shall be determined in the decree establishing the corporations.

The latter shall for all purposes be placed under the direct control of the Minister of Corporations.

PART IV. COLLECTIVE LABOR AGREEMENTS AND REGULATIONS RELATING THERETO

ARTICLE 47. Legally recognized syndical associations shall be empowered to stipulate collective labor agreements.

Collective labor agreements not stipulated by legally recognized syndical associations shall be void.

ARTICLE 48. Collective agreements shall specify the enterprise or enterprises, or the class of enterprises and workers to which they apply, as well as the territory of jurisdiction.

In the absence of this information collective agreements shall apply to all employers and workers legally represented by the negotiating associations in accordance with the provisions of Art. 5 of the Law of April 3, 1926.

ARTICLE 49. Collective agreements shall, under penalty of voidance, be signed by the legal representatives of the contracting associations or by other specially authorized persons.

In accordance with the provisions of the by-laws, collective agreements may be stipulated subject to the approval of the competent organs of the respective associations.

In such cases the agreement shall not be valid until such approval shall have been obtained.

Article 50.   The by-laws of associations of higher rank (federations and confederations) may require that collective labor agreements negotiated by affiliated associations shall be previously authorized by them.

In such cases agreements negotiated without proper authorization may be declared void.

Authorization may be given in general terms for a definite period of time and for several classes of employers and of employees.

Article 51.   Collective labor agreements shall be void unless filed and published in accordance with Art. 10 of the law of April 3, 1926. Agreements negotiated by inter-provincial associations shall be filed both with the Ministry of National Economy and with that of Corporations.

Agreements declared void on account of substance or form shall not be published. An appeal may be made to the labor court against refusal of publication of such contracts.

Arbitrative sentences pronounced in collective labor controversies shall be void unless filed and published in accordance with the provisions of the preceding paragraph.

Article 52.   No collective labor agreements shall be stipulated concerning labor relations regulated by acts of public authority in accordance with existing laws, regulations, or special agreements.

No collective labor agreements shall be stipulated for personal or domestic services.

Collective agreements stipulated in violation of these provisions shall be void.

Article 53.   At the end of the term of its duration a collective agreement shall be automatically renewed for an equal period unless notice shall have been filed by one of the contracting parties within the period provided for in the agreement or, in its absence, within two months of the date of expiration. Unless a similar notice shall have been filed the agreement shall be automatically renewed at the date of expiration of the new period of duration and so forth.

The notice shall be communicated to the other party and published in the bulletin of judicial announcements for provincial agreements and in the *Gazzetta ufficiale* for all others.

Article 54.   Individual labor agreements negotiated by employers and workers, and subject to a collective agreement, shall be made to harmonize with the regulations of the collective agreement.

Clauses of individual agreements, stipulated prior to or after collective agreements with the provisions of which they are at variance, shall be automatically replaced by those of the collective agreement, excepting cases in which such original clauses are to the advantage of the workers.

Collective agreements shall have the same efficacy with regard to factory regulations.

ARTICLE 55. Associations having negotiated a collective labor agreement shall be liable for damages resulting from failure to fulfill the obligations therein assumed.

Associations shall be responsible for non-fulfillment of contractual obligations by persons bound by the agreement, whether members or non-members only when they shall have failed to do everything within their power in order to bring about the fulfillment of such obligations. With regard to members, associations shall be obliged to use the disciplinary powers granted to them by their by-laws.

If it be explicitly stipulated in the collective agreement that its execution shall be guaranteed by the association, the latter shall be responsible for the failure of persons bound by the agreement to fulfill their obligations as a guarantor in solidarity.

ARTICLE 56. To enable central corporate organs to issue general regulations on labor conditions in accordance with the provisions of Art. 10 of the Law of April 3, 1926, it shall be necessary for each affiliated association to grant them the necessary power. Such power may, however, be granted generically in the associations' by-laws.

Corporate organs shall issue such regulations on an equitable basis, harmonizing the interests of employers with those of employees and both of them with the higher interests of national production.

Regulations issued by corporate organs shall retain their validity, although affiliated associations may bring their efficacy to an end by negotiating direct collective labor agreements.

ARTICLE 57. Regulations of corporate organs shall have the validity of a collective labor agreement negotiated between affiliated associations and all legal provisions for collective agreements shall be applicable to them.

Whenever such regulations are issued, the collective agreements existing between the affiliated associations shall be abrogated or modified insofar as they are entirely or partially incompatible with them.

ARTICLE 58. Collective labor agreements, regulations having equal validity, and all documents necessary for their negotiation shall be exempt from stamp and registration taxes.

ARTICLE 59. If the legal recognition granted to any negotiating association be withdrawn or revoked, its endowment shall be subject to legal control and may be used to fulfill the obligations the association had assumed in the collective agreement during the entire duration of the agreement and for a year thereafter.

Withdrawal or revocation of legal recognition shall not affect the rights granted by legally valid collective labor agreements.

ARTICLE 60. The provisions of common law shall be applicable to cases dealing with collective labor agreements to which the Law of April 3, 1926, and the present regulations do not apply.

PART V. COLLECTIVE LABOR CONTROVERSIES

Section I. Organization of the Labor Courts

ARTICLE 61. Each Provincial Economic Council shall propose the names of citizens qualified to act as expert advisers in the labor courts. Citizens whose names shall be so proposed shall be divided into groups and sub-groups according to the various classes of business enterprises existing within the jurisdiction of the court.

The lists of the names of these citizens shall be transmitted to the competent central corporate organizations, which, after securing the necessary information, shall be empowered to make changes or additions.

If no corporate organization should exist, the lists proposed by provincial economic councils shall be transmitted directly to the Court of Appeals.

ARTICLE 62. Upon receipt of these lists, and after hearing the opinion of the President of the Labor Court, the First President of the Court of Appeals shall select the names of the persons who shall act as expert advisers.

The final list shall be posted at the Court of Appeals and at the prefectures of all the provinces included in the district. Legally recognized associations may, within fifteen days from the posting of the list, file exceptions as to the composition of these lists.

Such exceptions shall be brought to the attention of all persons interested in the matter, and shall be decided by the Court of Appeals in united sections.

For this purpose, the united sections of the Court of Appeals shall consist of the First President, of the President of the special section acting as the labor court, and of five counsellors of the court, designated by the First President, two of whom shall be attached to the labor court, and three to the first section of the Court of Appeals.

The decision shall be rendered in Council Chamber, after presentation of written arguments by the interested parties.

Within fifteen days, such decisions may be appealed for violation of law, to the Supreme Court (*Corte di Cassazione*).

ARTICLE 63. The regulations contained in the two preceding articles shall also be applicable to the biennial revision of the lists in question.

ARTICLE 64. No person shall be included in the list who is not an Italian citizen, twenty-five years of age, of honest and irreproachable moral and political conduct, and who does not possess a university degree or its equivalent.

As for the educational requirement, an exception shall be permissible for persons who shall have acquired exceptional skill in the practice of an art or a profession.

In such cases a person may be included in the lists by order of the First President of the Court, who shall give the reasons for his decision.

Employees of the State and of other public organizations may be included in these lists.

ARTICLE 65. A person called upon to exercise judiciary functions as an expert adviser of the labor court shall be entitled to a fee of one hundred lire for each day of service; he shall, in addition, be entitled to the traveling and maintenance expenses allowed to counsellors of the Court of Appeals.

ARTICLE 66. The roll of expert advisers attached to the labor courts shall be compiled every year by the first president after hearing the President of the Labor Court, from the list of names prepared in accordance with the provisions of the preceding articles.

Expert advisers of the labor courts shall be appointed for each case by the Presidents of these Courts.

The President of the Labor Court may always request the First President to appoint as members of the Court one or more experts not included in the roll of persons attached to the section. The selection shall be made by the First President from among the names contained in the general list.

In exceptional cases, and with the consent of the parties concerned, the First President may select persons not included in such lists.

ARTICLE 67. The regulations of the Code of Civil Procedure shall be applied whenever magistrates shall refuse to serve in the special labor courts of the Court of Appeals.

All questions relating thereto shall be disposed of by the Court of Appeals. The regulations of the Code of Civil Procedure shall also be applicable whenever expert advisers shall refuse to serve. Appeals relating thereto shall be disposed of by the college of magistrates. Whenever expert advisers shall refuse to serve for reasons other than those permitted by law, appeals relating thereto shall be disposed of by the college composed in accordance with the preceding paragraph.

Section II.   Action and Jurisdiction

ARTICLE 68.   Legally recognized first degree associations, as well as associations of higher rank, shall have the power to bring action in controversies concerning collective labor relations.

The public prosecutor shall also have the right to act whenever the interest of the public shall demand it. In such cases the syndical association concerned shall be allowed to take part in the proceedings.

A syndical association of higher rank having a direct interest in the issue may participate in the proceedings instituted by the association of lower rank, and vice versa.

ARTICLE 69.   Syndical associations shall be represented in the legal proceedings by their president or secretary, who shall represent them in accordance with the provisions of Art. 7 of the Law of April 3, 1926, or by a special attorney.

ARTICLE 70.   The special attorney referred to in Art. 17 of the Law of April 3, 1926, shall be selected, whenever possible, from among the interested employers or employees possessing the requirements prescribed in Art. 1 of the law.

ARTICLE 71.   In controversies arising from the application of collective agreements and of other existing regulations, action shall be taken against the legally recognized association representing the employers or employees subject to such agreements and responsible for their execution. In controversies arising from the formulation of new labor conditions legal action shall be taken against the legally recognized association representing the employers or the employees to whom such new labor conditions shall apply.

Legal action intended to bring about the formulation of new labor conditions may be taken even when a collective agreement exists, and before the end of its period of duration, whenever significant changes have taken place in the conditions existing when the contract was negotiated.

ARTICLE 72.   The legal action shall be brought before the Court of Appeals having jurisdiction within the districts in which the labor agreement to which the controversy refers is in force. If the controversy shall fall within the jurisdiction of two or more Courts of Appeals, the legal action shall be taken before the Court of Appeals in Rome.

Section III.   Judicial Procedure

(*Note:* The version of this and the following section, containing detailed rules of judicial procedure, has been greatly condensed.)

ARTICLE 73.   In the judicial proceedings, the parties may appear personally or be represented by an attorney.

The magistrate may order the personal appearance of the parties at any time during the proceedings.

ARTICLE 75. The brief, and all documents on which it is based, shall be filed at the chancery of the Court of Appeals. After affixing the date of receipt, the chancellor shall immediately transmit it to the President of the Labor Court.

ARTICLE 76. Within twenty-four hours of its receipt, the President of the Court shall determine the date of the hearing.

Notice of the action shall immediately be given to the interested parties and published in the journal of judicial announcements of the province, or in the *Gazzetta ufficiale* of the kingdom.

ARTICLE 80. It shall be the duty of the president to try at all times to bring about a just settlement of the controversy. To that effect he shall make continued attempts during the proceedings, whenever the opportunity shall present itself.

If a settlement be reached, it shall be recorded in the minutes of the Court and shall take the place of a collective agreement.

If no settlement is reached, the president shall provide within ten days for a hearing of the parties before the Court.

ARTICLE 81. Decisions of the Court are to be taken in Council Chamber. The final sentence shall be read at a public hearing.

Section IV. Sentences and Appeals

ARTICLE 87. Sentences pronounced by a magistrate on subjects concerned with collective labor relations shall have the force of collective labor agreements.

ARTICLE 88. Sentences of the labor court shall be subject to annulment, to revision, and to appeal to the Supreme Court (*Corte di Cassazione*).

They may be revoked in accordance with the provisions of the Code of Civil Procedure, the request for revocation to be made within fifteen days.

PART VI. ASSOCIATIONS OF GOVERNMENT EMPLOYEES AND OF EMPLOYEES OF OTHER PUBLIC INSTITUTIONS

ARTICLE 92. Associations of state, provincial, and municipal employees, and of employees of public welfare institutions and of other organizations mentioned in the second paragraph of Art. 3 of the present decree, shall have to be authorized as follows: Associations of government employees shall be authorized by a decree of the Head of the Government; associations of employees of interprovincial organizations shall be authorized by a decree of the Minister of the Interior; associations of employees of local and provincial organizations shall be authorized by a decree of the prefect of the province. These provisions shall apply only when such organizations shall be allowed by law and when the requirements prescribed in Art. 1 of the Law of April 3, 1926, shall have been satisfied.

Associations of lowest and of higher rank including employees of the government and of other public administrations and organizations shall be authorized by decree of the Head of the Government acting in agreement with the Minister of the Interior and with the other interested ministers.

Authorization shall not imply legal recognition in accordance with the provisions of the Law of April 3, 1926, nor shall it confer legal personality.

Authorization may at any time be revoked.

ARTICLE 93. The Head of the Government may order the dissolution of the associations of state, provincial, and municipal employees, as well as of employees of public welfare institutions and of the other organizations mentioned in Art. 3, whenever their activities shall be incompatible with good order and the discipline of public service.

ARTICLE 94. Associations for the protection of alleged educational or professional interests of students in educational institutions of whatever nature shall be prohibited.

Organization of and membership in similar associations shall be considered a serious disciplinary infraction and shall be punishable by exclusion from all schools and educational institutions of the kingdom.

PART VII. CRIMINAL OFFENSES AND PENALTIES

ARTICLE 95. When lockouts, strikes, and irregular work occur because of objectives other than those mentioned in Art. 18 of the Law of April 3, 1926, the penalties established in Art. 235, first paragraph, and in Art. 236 of the Criminal Code may be imposed, and regular ex officio measures taken.

ARTICLE 96. When lockouts, strikes, and irregular work shall be accompanied by threats of violence, the penalties established in Arts. 166 and 167 of the Criminal Code shall be imposed.

ARTICLE 97. For the application of Arts. 19 and 20 of the Law of April 3, 1926, the Minister of Corporations shall determine by decree what classes of enterprises shall be considered as enterprises of public utility. On the basis of this decree, municipalities shall then compile a list of enterprises of public utility operating within their jurisdiction.

After a hearing of possible exceptions, the prefect of the province shall approve the final list of public utility enterprises existing within each municipality. This final list shall be published in the journal of provincial announcements.

ARTICLE 98. The services of medical practitioners, lawyers, attorneys, notaries, engineers, architects, surveyors, and technical agriculturalists shall always be considered as of public utility.

PART VIII. TRANSITORY AND FINAL PROVISIONS

ARTICLE 101. In matters of collective labor relations the Code of Civil Procedure shall be applied in all cases in which the Law of April 3, 1926, and the present regulations shall not be applicable.

ROYAL DECREE OF JULY 2, 1926, NO. 1131, ON THE ESTABLISHMENT OF THE MINISTRY OF CORPORATIONS

(Published in the *Gazzetta ufficiale* of July 7, 1926, no. 155)

(Condensed Version)

ARTICLE 1. The Ministry of Corporations is established.

The Minister of Corporations and, under his direction, the prefects of the provinces shall exercise all the activities of organization, coordination, and control entrusted to the government by the Law of April 3, 1926, no. 563, and by the regulations relating to its application.

ARTICLE 4. The National Council of Corporations is organized and attached to the Ministry of Corporations.

The Council shall be composed of: the Minister of Corporations, who shall preside over it; the Under Secretary of State in the Ministry of Corporations; the director general of the Bureau of Labor of the Ministry of National Economy; two representatives of the Ministry of National Economy and a representative of each of the other ministries holding a position not inferior to director general; two representatives of each of the legally recognized national syndical confederations of industry and agriculture, a representative of each of the other legally recognized syndical confederations; a representative of each of the legally recognized general confederations of employees and employers; a representative of the National Dopolavoro Organization; a representative of the National Balilla Organization; a representative of the National Organization for Motherhood and Infant Welfare. Appointments shall be by royal decree and members of the Council shall hold office for four years and be subject to reappointment.

The Council shall be called upon to express its opinion on questions affecting the various organizations and associations belonging to the different corporations as well as on any other matter that may be submitted to it by the Minister of Corporations.

ROYAL DECREE OF MARCH 17, 1927, NO. 401, ON THE ORGANIZATION OF THE MINISTRY OF CORPORATIONS

(Published in the *Gazzetta ufficiale* of April 4, 1927, no. 78)

(Condensed Version)

ARTICLE 1. The Ministry of Corporations shall have two divisions, a division of corporations and a division for professional associations.

The organizations connected with the Ministry of Corporations shall be:

(a) The National Council of Corporations, established by royal decree of July 2, 1926, no. 1131;

(b) The Corporations to be established by ministerial decree in accordance with the provisions of Art. 42 of the Royal decree of July 1, 1926, no. 1130.

By decree, the Ministry of Corporations may provide for the establishment of special permanent advisory commissions for the study of definite problems or for the publication of reviews and periodicals dealing with questions connected with the duties of the ministry.

ARTICLE 2. The presidency of corporate organs shall be entrusted to citizens who have distinguished themselves notably in production, labor, or the direction of public offices.

The office of president of corporate organs shall not entitle the incumbent to a salary or to other fixed remuneration, but merely to an indemnity and to daily fees to be determined by ministerial decree in accordance with the provisions of Art. 4 of this decree and to be paid from a special fund of the ministry formed by the contributions provided for in Article 26 of the royal decree of July 1, 1926, no. 1130.

The powers of the two ministerial divisions shall be defined by decree of the Ministry of Corporations.

ARTICLE 3. In every province the work of the Ministry of Corporations shall be entrusted to an officer of the prefecture or of the provincial bureaus of the Ministry of National Economy.

In addition to his ordinary duties, this officer shall coöperate with the prefect in the performance of the tasks prescribed by the Law of April 3, 1926, no. 563, and by the regulation pertaining thereto, approved by the Royal Decree of July 1, 1926, no. 1130; he shall supervise the work of the local bureaus of the corporate organs established by Art. 43 of the Royal Decree of July 1, 1926; he shall receive and preserve the records pertaining to collective labor agreements, to be deposited at the local prefecture in accordance with Art. 10 of the Law of April 3, 1926, and shall authorize their publication. This officer shall be entitled, ex officio, to membership in the provincial administrative board acting as an organ for the protection of the interests of syndical associations and in the provincial economic council. He shall be dependent upon the prefect of the province and shall communicate through him with the Minister of Corporations.

For matters pertaining to seamen and to dock workers, all duties described in this article shall be entrusted to the commanders of the various maritime departments.

ARTICLE 4. The expenses for the personnel, the buildings, and the supplies needed by the bureaus of the Ministry of Corporations and by the various corporate organs shall be charged to the general budget of the state.

The expenses represented by indemnities, daily remunerations, and other fees paid to members of the National Council of Corporations, as well as to members of other commissions of the Ministry of Corporations and the expenses paid for other purposes stated in the Law of April 3, 1926, and in the Royal Decree of July 2, 1926, no. 1131, shall be charged to the special fund formed by the state's share in syndical contributions.

THE CHARTER OF LABOR

(Published in the *Gazzetta ufficiale* of April 30, 1927, no. 100)

THE CORPORATE STATE AND ITS ORGANIZATION

I. The Italian nation is an organism endowed with purposes, a life, and means of action transcending in power and duration, those of the separate individuals or groups of individuals which compose it. It is a moral, political, and economic unity which realizes itself completely in the Fascist state.

II. Labor in all its forms, intellectual, technical, and manual, is a social duty. As such and only as such is it safeguarded by the state.

From a national point of view the productive process is unitary; its ultimate aims coincide with individual well-being and the development of national power.

III. Professional and syndical organization is free. But only a syndicate legally recognized and subject to the control of the state has the right legally to represent the entire class of employers or workers for which it has been formed, to protect their interests against other professional organizations and the state, to negotiate collective labor agreements binding upon all members of that class, to levy contributions and to exercise such functions of public interest as may be delegated to it.

IV. In the collective labor agreement the solidarity of the various factors of production finds its concrete expression through the reconciliation of the conflicting interests of employers and workers and through their subordination to the higher interests of production.

V. The Labor Court is the organ through which the state intervenes in settling labor disputes whether arising from the application of existing contracts and agreements, or occurring in the determination of new labor conditions.

VI. Legally recognized professional associations assure legal equality between employers and workers and maintain and improve the efficiency of production and the discipline of labor.

The corporation constitutes the unit of organization of one field of production and represents its interests as a whole.

By virtue of this integral representation and because of the national character of production corporations are recognized by law as organs of the state.

As unitary representatives of the interests of production, corporations are authorized to make compulsory regulations concerning labor relations or the coördination of production whenever the necessary power is delegated to them by the affiliated associations.

VII. The corporate state considers private enterprise in the field of production as the most efficacious and useful instrument for the furthering of the nation's interests.

Private organization of production being a function of national interest, the entrepreneur is responsible to the state for the direction of the productive process. Reciprocity of rights and duties results from the coöperation of productive forces. The employee, whether a technical expert, a clerk, or a laborer, is an active collaborator in the economic undertaking, the direction of which belongs to the employer who is responsible for it.

VIII. Professional associations of employers are obliged to promote and improve production and to seek the reduction of costs. The representatives of the liberal professions and the associations of public employees coöperate in safeguarding the interests of the arts, letters, and the sciences, in the development and refinement of national production, and in the attainment of the ideals of the corporate state.

IX. The state intervenes in economic production only when private initiative is lacking or insufficient, or when the political interests of the state are at stake. Such intervention may take the form of encouragement, regulation, or direct management.

X. In labor disputes judicial action cannot be started until the competent corporation has made an attempt at conciliation.

In individual controversies concerning the application or interpretation of collective agreements, professional associations may offer their good offices to effect conciliation.

Jurisdiction in such disputes belongs to the ordinary magistrates, assisted by referees appointed by the respective professional associations.

COLLECTIVE LABOR CONTRACTS AND LABOR GUARANTEES

XI. Professional associations are required to regulate relations between the employers and the workers whom they represent by means of collective labor agreements.

The collective labor agreement is made between first degree associations under the guidance and supervision of the central organizations except for the power of substitution granted to the associations of higher rank by laws and statutes.

All collective labor agreements must contain under penalty of nullity precise regulations on disciplinary matters, on trial periods, on the amount and payment of wages, and on working hours.

XII. The action of syndicates, the conciliatory efforts of the corporate organs, and the decisions of the labor courts insure the adjustment of wages to the normal requirements of life, the possibilities of production, and the productivity of labor.

Wages are not to be fixed according to a general standard, but are determined by agreement between the parties in collective labor agreements.

XIII. Statistical data on the conditions of production and labor, the situation of the money market, and the variation in the standard of living of the working classes as compiled by the various governmental departments, the Central Institute of Statistics, and the legally recognized professional associations, and as elaborated and coördinated by the Ministry of Corporations shall determine the criteria to be followed in conciliating the interest of the different categories and classes with each other and with the superior interests of national production.

XIV. Wages must be paid in the form best suited to the exigencies of the worker and of the enterprise.

When wages are based on piece work and settlement is made at longer than bi-weekly intervals suitable bi-weekly or weekly advances must be provided for.

Compensation for night work not included in regular shifts must be at a rate above that which is normal for day work.

When remuneration is based upon piece work, piece rates must be so constructed that an industrious worker of average ability may earn a minimum over and above the basic wage.

XV.   The employee is entitled to a weekly holiday falling on Sunday.

Collective agreements will apply this principle insofar as it is compatible with existing laws and the technical requirements of the enterprise in question. Within the same limits they shall aim to keep civil and religious holidays in accord with local traditions. Working hours must be scrupulously and intensively observed by the employee.

XVI.   After a year of uninterrupted service the employee of enterprises whose work is continuous is entitled to an annual vacation with pay.

XVII.   In concerns whose work is continuous the employee is entitled, in case of discharge through no fault of his own, to an indemnity proportioned to his years of service. Such an indemnity must also be paid in case of the worker's death.

XVIII.   Transfers of ownership of concerns whose work is continuous do not affect labor contracts; employees of such concerns retain all their rights and claims toward the new employers. Illness of an employee not exceeding a specified period likewise does not lead to cancellation of the labor contract. A call to arms or to service in the Fascist militia is no valid cause for dismissal.

XIX.   Infractions of discipline and acts which disturb the normal functioning of the enterprise, committed by workers, are punishable, according to the gravity of the offense, by a fine, by suspension from work, or, in serious cases, by immediate dismissal without indemnity.

The cases in which the employer may impose fines, suspensions, or immediate dismissal without indemnity must be specified.

XX.   A new employee is subject to a trial period during which mutual right to cancellation of the labor contract exists and during which wages are paid only for the time of actual service.

XXI.   The benefits and the discipline of collective labor agreements also apply to workers in the domestic trades. Special regulations shall be passed by the state to assure proper control and hygienic conditions for such domestic workers.

EMPLOYMENT OFFICES

XXII.   The state ascertains and supervises the phenomenon of employment and unemployment: a comprehensive indicator of the general conditions of production and labor.

XXIII. Employment offices are organized on the basis of equal representation for employers and employees and are to be operated under the control of the corporate organs of the state. Employers must select their workers from among those enrolled in these offices. While they have the right of selection from among the registered applicants, preference must be given to members of the Fascist party and of the Fascist syndicates according to priority of registration.

XXIV. Professional associations of workers must exercise selection among workmen with a view to the constant improvement of their technical skill and moral character.

XXV. The corporate organs shall supervise the observance of the laws on accident prevention and sanitation by individual members of their affiliated associations.

Social Insurance and Assistance, Education and Professional Instruction

XXVI. Social insurance being another instance of the principle of class collaboration, employers and employees must proportionately share in its cost. Through the corporate organs and professional associations the state undertakes to coördinate and unify the various agencies and systems of social insurance.

XXVII. The Fascist state proposes to achieve:

(1) The improvement of accident insurance;

(2) The improvement and extension of maternity insurance;

(3) The institution of insurance against occupational diseases and tuberculosis as an approach to a general system of health insurance;

(4) The improvement of unemployment insurance;

(5) The adoption of special forms of dowry insurance (*dotalizie*) for young workers.

XXVIII. The professional associations representing employees are entrusted with the protection of their interests in legal and administrative cases arising in connection with accident and other forms of social insurance.

Collective labor agreements shall provide, as far as technically possible, for the establishment of mutual sickness insurance funds contributed to both by employers and employees and administered by representatives of both classes under the general supervision of corporate organs.

XXIX. It is the right and duty of professional associations to render aid to those whom they represent whether they are members of the association or not. Such aid must be given directly by the associations themselves and cannot be delegated to other institutions except for purposes of a general character transcending the particular interests of the individual professional groups.

XXX. Education and instruction, and particularly the professional education of the workers they represent, whether members or non-members, is one of the principal duties of professional associations. They must support national recreational institutions and other activities in the field of education.

ROYAL DECREE OF MARCH 29, 1928, NO. 1003, ON THE NATIONAL REGULATION OF THE DEMAND AND SUPPLY OF LABOR

(Published in the *Gazzetta ufficiale* of May 18, 1928, no. 116)

(The following text contains the modifications to the above decree made by the Royal Decree of December 9, 1929, no. 2333, published in the *Gazzetta ufficiale* of January 31, 1930, no. 25)

(Condensed Version)

Employment Offices and Their Coördination and Supervision

ARTICLE 1. Free employment offices for the benefit of the various classes of unemployed workers shall be created, as the need arises and after hearing the competent corporations, by means of royal decrees of the Minister of Corporations, in agreement with the Minister of National Economy.

The offices shall be located at the workers' syndicates and the decree creating each individual office shall determine its territorial competence as well as its competence as to professional classes and kinds of production.

ARTICLE 2. Each employment office shall be headed by a Commission, presided over by the Secretary of the National Fascist Party and composed of an equal number of representatives of the interested syndicates of employers and employees, the exact number to be determined by the decree instituting the employment office.

The nomination of these representatives, made directly by the respective syndicates, shall be ratified by the competent corporations where they exist.

ARTICLE 3. The commissions described in Art. 2 shall direct the activities of the individual offices and control their functioning in harmony with ministerial directions and with the directions issued by the Section of Labor and Social Welfare of the competent Provincial Economic Council. They shall make recommendations to the competent ministers on questions pertaining to the labor market and shall fulfill all other tasks attributed to them by means of special regulations.

ARTICLE 4. The administrative commissions of the various employment offices shall select employing agents from among the officers of the workers' syndical organizations.

Employing agents shall be responsible to the Commission for the fulfillment of their tasks, and the Commission shall be empowered to arrange for their replacement.

ARTICLE 5. Employment offices shall be exempt from all stamp and registration taxes, including those on documents and on advertisements dealing with their activity and with the demand and supply of labor.

ARTICLE 6. Control over employment offices and their coördination as to unity of policy shall be entrusted, within the various provinces, to the Section of Labor and Social Welfare of the Provincial Economic Council.

Within the limits of ministerial regulations, this Section shall also issue rules for the organization, the functioning, and the reciprocal relations of newly created employment offices.

The supervision of the activities of employment offices shall rest with the President, who may request the assistance of other members of the Section.

ARTICLE 7. The Sections of Labor and Social Welfare of the Provincial Economic Councils shall be presided over by a delegate of the Ministry of Corporations and shall be composed of:

(a) Representatives of syndical organizations of employers (selected among the components of other Sections of the Provincial Economic Councils), and an equal number of representatives of the syndical organizations of workers;

(b) The inspector of industry and labor;

(c) The director of the Institute of Social Welfare;

(d) The director of public works or his representative.

ARTICLE 8. The regional and national coördination of employment offices, in relation to internal migration and emigration, shall be entrusted to the Ministry of Corporations, acting in agreement with the ministries of National Economy and Finance and with the other interested ministries.

ARTICLE 9. In the case of irregular functioning of an employment office the Minister of Corporations, in agreement with the Minister of National Economy, shall be empowered, after hearing the section of labor and social welfare of the competent Provincial Economic Council, to dissolve the administrative commission and to name a special Commissioner.

The Demand and Supply of Labor and Duties Relating Thereto

Article 10. Mediation for the employment of idle workers, by private persons, associations, or organizations, even though made free of charge, shall be forbidden for all categories of employers and employees for which employment offices, as described in Art. 1 of the present decree, have been created.

Article 11. Employers shall hire unemployed workmen through the employment offices mentioned in Art. 1 of the present decree. They shall have free choice among the registered applicants. Preference, however, shall be given to members of the National Fascist Party, the members of Fascist syndicates, and to ex-service men.

The preceding provisions shall also be applicable, for the employment of manual labor, to public institutions, with the exception, however, of the personnel of state administrations.

Unemployed workmen, in ways to be determined by the regulation for the application of the present decree, shall apply for the inclusion of their names in the registers of the employment office of the district in which they reside and the jurisdiction of which extends to their professional class, or kind of productive activity. Registration by the employment offices shall be made according to the order of presentation of the individual requests.

Article 13. With the exception of state administrations, employers shall, within five days, indicate the names of workers who, on whatever ground, have been dismissed or have left their employ to the employment office at which they are registered, stating the kind of activity in which these workers were engaged and the duration of their services.

Penalties

Article 14. Whoever shall accomplish acts of mediation in violation of the provisions of the present decree shall be punishable by a fine not exceeding 5,000 lire. In cases of special gravity or of second offense and when the act of mediation has been accomplished for a gainful purpose, the offender may, in addition to the fine, be imprisoned for a term not exceeding one month.

Employers who do not hire unemployed workers through employment offices or who employ them through mediators, shall be punishable by a fine of from 50 to 300 lire for each worker illegally employed, the maximum fine not to exceed 3,000 lire.

Employers omitting to report the discharge made, according to the provisions of Art. 13 of the present decree, shall be fined from 50 to 200 lire for each discharged worker, the maximum fine not to exceed 4,000 lire.

Unemployed workers accepting employment without previous registration at the employment office shall be punishable with a fine not to exceed 300 lire.

LAW OF MAY 17, 1928, NO. 1019, ON THE REFORM OF POLITICAL REPRESENTATION IN THE ITALIAN KINGDOM

(Published in the *Gazzetta ufficiale* of May 21, 1928, no. 118)

(Condensed Version)

ARTICLE 1. The number of deputies for the entire kingdom shall be four hundred. The kingdom shall form one electoral district.

ARTICLE 2. The election of deputies shall be made:

(a) On proposal of the institutions named in Arts. 3 and 4;
(b) By designation of the National Fascist Grand Council;
(c) By approval of the electorate.

ARTICLE 3. The right to propose candidates shall rest primarily with the legally recognized National Confederations of Syndicates according to the provisions of the royal decree of July 1, 1926, no. 1130.

The aforesaid associations shall propose a total number of candidates equal to twice the number of deputies to be elected.

The allocation of this number among the various Confederations shall be made according to the table appended to the present law.

The nomination of candidates shall be made by each Confederation through its general or national council, regularly elected and convened according to statutory provisions.

The meetings called for the purpose of nominating candidates shall be held in Rome. In the balloting those persons shall be elected to whom the greatest number of votes shall have been given.

A royal notary shall draw up the minutes of the meeting and record the votes given.

ARTICLE 4. Other cultural, educational, or welfare institutions of national importance shall also propose candidates up to a total equal to half the number of deputies to be elected, provided the right to do so shall be accorded them by royal decree and upon proposal of a special commission consisting of five senators and five deputies. The decree according the right of nomination shall be subject to revision every three years.

ARTICLE 5. After having received the names of the candidates proposed by the various nominating bodies the secretary of the Grand Council shall form a single alphabetical list of candidates indicating with each name the institution by which it has been proposed.

The Grand Council shall then form the list of the deputies it chooses, selecting them freely from the list of candidates and also outside of that list when it is necessary to include persons distinguished in the arts, letters, sciences, politics, or the army who have not been previously included in the list of candidates.

The list of deputies designated by the Grand Council shall then be published in the *Gazzetta ufficiale* and posted in all the communities of the kingdom.

ARTICLE 6.   The vote for the approval of this list of deputies shall take place on the third Sunday following its publication in *the Gazzetta ufficiale.*

The vote shall be taken by means of ballots bearing the emblem of Fascism and the formula: "Do you approve of the list of deputies designated by the National Grand Council of Fascism?" The vote shall be expressed under this formula by "Yes" or "No."

ARTICLE 7.   The Court of Appeals in Rome shall act as the national electoral office and determine the total number of favorable or unfavorable votes received by the proposed list of deputies.

If half of the votes plus one shall be favorable to the list, the Court of Appeals shall declare it approved and shall proclaim elected all the deputies included in it.

If half the number of votes plus one shall be unfavorable to the list, the Court of Appeals shall declare the list not approved. If exactly half the number of votes shall be cast in favor, the list shall be approved.

ARTICLE 8.   When the list of deputies shall not be approved the Court of Appeals in Rome shall order, by its own decree, the renewal of the election by means of competitive lists, fixing the date of the election at between thirty and forty-five days from the date of the decree.

In the new election, lists of candidates of all associations and organizations including more than five thousand members entitled to vote may be submitted. The list of candidates shall not include more than three-fourths of the number of deputies to be elected.

ARTICLE 9.   After the election is made and the number of votes cast for the individual lists determined, the Court of Appeals of Rome shall declare elected all candidates in the list which shall have obtained the largest number of votes. The remaining one-fourth of the seats, reserved to the minority, shall be subdivided among the other lists in proportion to the number of votes received.

ARTICLE 10.   The right to vote in the elections described in Arts. 6 and 9 shall be given to Italian citizens of more than twenty-one years of age, and to those older than eighteen but less than twenty-one years of age if married and having children. Members of both groups must possess one of the following pre-requisites:

(a) Payment of a syndical contribution according to the Law of April 3, 1926, or a status of partner or administrator of a corporation or firm paying a syndical contribution as provided for by that law. In the case of corporations, only shares inscribed with the name of the shareholder for at least a year shall bestow the right to vote on the holder;

(b) Payment of at least 100 lire in annual taxes to the state, the province or local community, or the ownership of governmental or municipal securities yielding an income of at least 500 lire;

(c) A stipend, pension, or salary continuously received from the state, the province or the local community;

(d) Membership in the Catholic Clergy or the clergy of other religions admitted within the State.

TABLE SHOWING THE NUMBER OF CANDIDATES EACH LEGALLY RECOGNIZED NATIONAL CONFEDERATION OF SYNDICATES MAY PROPOSE FOR EVERY HUNDRED CANDIDATES PRESENTED BY ALL THE CONFEDERATIONS TAKEN TOGETHER

National Confederation of Agriculture	12
National Confederation of Agricultural Employees and Laborers	12
National Confederation of Industry	10
National Confederation of Industrial Employees and Laborers	10
National Confederation of Merchants	6
National Confederation of Commercial Employees and Laborers	6
National Confederation of Maritime and Air Transportation	5
National Confederation of Employees and Laborers in the field of Maritime and Air Transportation	5
National Confederation of Land Transportation and Internal Navigation	4
National Confederation of Employees and Laborers in the field of Land Transportation and Internal Navigation	4
National Confederation of Banking	3
National Confederation of Bank Employees	3
National Confederation of Professional Men and Artists	20

ROYAL DECREE OF DECEMBER 6, 1928, NO. 3222, CONTAINING RULES FOR THE APPLICATION OF THE DECREE OF MARCH 29, 1928, NO. 1003, ON THE NATIONAL REGULATION OF THE DEMAND AND SUPPLY OF LABOR

(Published in the *Gazzetta ufficiale* of January 22, 1929, no. 18)

(The following text contains the modifications to the above decree made by the Royal Decree of December 9, 1929, no. 2393, published in the *Gazzetta ufficiale* of February 25, 1930, no. 46)

(Condensed Version)

Part I. Employment Offices and Their Establishment

Article 1. As to their territorial jurisdiction, employment offices may be: (a) national; (b) interprovincial; (c) provincial. They may deal with the employment of workers of one or more classes.

Article 2. The Ministry of Corporations, with the concurrence of the Ministry of National Economy, may on its own initiative, or upon the proposal of syndical associations, establish employment offices. Decrees establishing new employment offices must be published in the *Gazzetta ufficiale* of the Kingdom.

The establishment of national employment offices may be proposed by national syndical associations of employers and employees; that of other offices by provincial or local associations.

Each proposal must be transmitted to the Ministry of Corporations with the recommendations of the corresponding association of higher rank.

The Ministry of Corporations may, if necessary, instruct the existing offices to establish local branches.

Part II. The Administrative Commission

Article 3. The Commission, established by Art. 2 of the Royal Decree of March 29, 1928, no. 1003, on the national regulation of the demand and supply of labor, is presided over:

(a) For the national employment offices, by the Secretary of the Fascist Party or by his representative;

(b) For inter-provincial offices, by a representative of the Secretaries of the National Fascist Party of the provinces in question;

(c) For provincial offices, by the provincial secretary of the Fascist Party or by his representative.

ARTICLE 4. Members of administrative commissions of inter-provincial or national employment offices, representing syndical associations, shall be nominated by the competent organs of such national syndical associations.

Their term of office shall be two years, at the end of which they may be reappointed.

Members of administrative commissions of provincial employment offices representing syndical associations shall be nominated by the competent organs of the provincial syndical associations or, in their stead, by the competent organs of the respective national federations or confederations.

ARTICLE 5. The ministerial decree establishing individual employment offices shall determine which syndical associations shall be represented on the administrative commission.

The provisions of Art. 2 of the Royal Decree of March 29, 1928, no. 1003, on the parity of representation of employers and employees remaining unchanged, the decree instituting the employment office shall determine the number of representatives which each association of workmen and of employers shall nominate.

ARTICLE 6. The names of these representatives must be transmitted to the Ministry of Corporations for approval by the competent corporations, according to the provision of Art. 2 of the Royal Decree of March 29, 1928, no. 1003.

ARTICLE 8. The administrative commission shall perform the duties assigned to it by the Royal Decree of March 29, 1928, no. 1003. In particular the commission shall:

(a) Administer the funds assigned to the employment office;

(b) Keep up-to-date statistical data on the demand and the supply of labor in the district and in the trades to which its competence extends;

(c) Perform all other tasks entrusted to it by the Ministry of National Economy;

(d) Supply the National Institute for Social Insurance with such statistical data and information concerning unemployment as that Institute may request.

PART III. EMPLOYING AGENTS

ARTICLE 9. When requested to do so the workers' syndical associations shall transmit to the administrative commissions of the employment offices the lists of their managing officers and directors, specifying the aptitude of each to act as an employing agent.

The administrative commission shall then proceed to the nomination of employing agents, making its choice from among the persons included in these lists.

The members of the commission shall not be employing agents. If, within fifteen days of the request, syndical associations should have failed to transmit the lists in question, the commission may name persons of its own choice.

ARTICLE 10. Employing agents shall carry out the orders of the administrative commissions; they shall receive requests and offers of work and enter them in chronological order on special lists divided according to classes of unemployed workmen.

A monthly salary may be paid to employing agents.

PART IV. THE TREASURER

ARTICLE 11. At the beginning of every year the administrative commissions of the various employment offices shall appoint one of their employing agents to the office of treasurer.

ARTICLE 12. The treasurer shall administer the funds, income, and expenditures of the employment office and shall, within a month after the end of the fiscal year, render an account of his administration.

PART V. CONTROL

ARTICLE 13. The section of labor and social welfare of the Provincial Economic Councils shall control provincial employment offices as provided for by Art. 6 of the Royal Decree of March 29, 1928, no. 1003;

This control shall consist of:

(a) An audit of the budget and accounts of the offices which shall then be transmitted to the Ministry of Corporations;

(b) An inspection of the technical and administrative work of the offices.

National and inter-provincial employment offices shall be controlled directly by the Ministry of Corporations.

ARTICLE 17. In providing for transfers of labor between the different provinces of the kingdom or when it shall be necessary to send laborers employed within the kingdom to the colonies or abroad, the Ministry of Corporations must be interpellated and shall be empowered to issue instructions or compulsory regulations as to such transfers.

PART VI. REGISTRATION AT EMPLOYMENT OFFICES

ARTICLE 21. Employers must select unemployed workers from among those registered at the employment offices. Preference shall be given to members of the National Fascist Party, the members of Fascist syndicates, and to ex-service men.

Unemployed workmen shall register with employment offices according to the provisions of Art. 11 of the Royal Decree of March 29, 1928, no. 1003, within five days of the day on which they have ceased to be employed. In case of omission or delay, they shall incur the penalties provided by Art. 14 of that Decree.

The requests for registration by workers according to Art. 11 of the Royal Decree of March 29, 1928, no. 1003, and notifications of employers (Art. 13 of the same Royal Decree) may be made verbally or by registered letter.

ARTICLE 22. The employer shall be relieved of the obligation stated in Art. 2 of the Royal Decree of December 9, 1929, no. 2333, if the employee be employed for less than one week.

If for technical reasons or unforeseen circumstances, work is suspended for a period not exceeding one month, or if production itself is seasonal, employers and employees shall be relieved of their obligation to register or notify employment offices prescribed by Arts. 11 and 13 of the Royal Decree of March 29, 1928, no. 1003, provided the workmen employed are not definitely and finally discharged.

PART VII. APPEALS AND PENALTIES

ARTICLE 23. In the case of non-inclusion or late registration of a worker in the list of unemployed of a provincial employment office, the employer who has made his notification or the worker who has made a request for registration may appeal to the section of labor and social welfare of the Provincial Economic Council.

In the case of non-inclusion of a worker in the list of unemployed of a national or inter-provincial employment office, the worker or the employer may appeal to the Ministry of Corporations.

ARTICLE 24. The employing agent who has refused without justification to register an unemployed workman shall be punishable with a fine not exceeding 500 lire.

The employing agent who delays registration for more than twenty-four hours without justification shall be punishable with a fine not exceeding 300 lire.

LAW OF DECEMBER 9, 1928, NO. 2693, ON THE ORGANI-
ZATION AND POWERS OF THE FASCIST GRAND
COUNCIL

(Published in the *Gazzetta ufficiale* of December 11, 1928, no. 287)

ARTICLE 1. The Fascist Grand Council is the supreme organ which shall coördinate and integrate all activities of the regime created by the revolution of October 1922. The Council decides the matters placed under its jurisdiction by law and gives its advice on all political, social, and economic questions of national interest whenever requested to do so by the Head of the Government.

ARTICLE 2. The Head of the Government, Prime Minister, and Secretary of State is ex officio the president of the Fascist Grand Council. He calls its meetings whenever he deems it necessary and determines their agenda.

ARTICLE 3. The secretary of the National Fascist Party is also secretary of the Fascist Grand Council. The Head of the Government may instruct him to call the meetings of the Grand Council and to preside over them in case of his absence or inability to attend.

ARTICLE 4. The following are members of the Fascist Grand Council for an unlimited period of time:

(1) The "quadrumvirs" of the March on Rome;

(2) All those who in their capacity of members of the government have also been members of the Grand Council during at least 3 years;

(3) The secretaries of the National Fascist Party who have held office since 1922.

ARTICLE 5. By virtue of their office and during its duration the following are also members of the Grand Council:

(1) The president of the Senate and the president of the Chamber of Deputies;

(2) The ministers, secretaries of state;

(3) The under-secretary of state in the department of the president of the Council of Ministers;

(4) The commander in chief of the Voluntary Fascist Militia;

(5) The members of the directorate of the National Fascist Party;

(6) The president of the Italian Academy and the president of the Fascist Cultural Institute;

(7) The president of the National Balilla Institution;

(8) The president of the National Tribunal for the Defense of the State;

(9) The presidents of the National Fascist Confederations of legally recognized syndicates;

(10) The president of the National Institute of Coöperation.

ARTICLE 6. Membership in the Grand Council, of the persons indicated in the three preceding articles, is granted by royal decree on the proposal of the Head of the Government. By the same procedure recognition can at all times be revoked.

ARTICLE 7. By decree of the Head of the Government persons who have rendered distinguished service to the nation and to the cause of the Fascist revolution can also be admitted to membership in the Fascist Grand Council for a period of three years and with the possibility of further confirmation in office. By the same procedure the nomination can at all times be revoked.

The Head of the Government may ask persons of particular competence in the matters under discussion to participate in the work of the Grand Council.

ARTICLE 8. Membership in the Grand Council is compatible with the office of senator or member of the Chamber of Deputies.

ARTICLE 9. No member of the Grand Council can be imprisoned, excepting a case of flagrant crime, or prosecuted or held in police inquiries without the authorization of the Grand Council.

ARTICLE 10. No compensation is allowed for the office of member of the Grand Council and no expense of its operation borne by the government.

The meetings of the Grand Council are secret. The Grand Council establishes the rules for its own procedure.

ARTICLE 11. The Grand Council decides on:

(1) The list of deputies designated according to the provisions of Art. 5 of the Law of March 17, 1928, no. 1019;

(2) The statutes, the regulations, and the political policies of the National Fascist Party;

(3) The nomination and recall of the Secretary, the assistant secretary, the administrative secretary and of the other members of the directorate of the National Fascist party.

ARTICLE 12. The opinion of the Grand Council must be heard in all questions of constitutional character.

Projects of law in the following matters are always considered of constitutional character:

(1) Royal succession and the powers and prerogatives of the Crown;

(2) The composition and the functioning of the Grand Council, the Senate of the kingdom, and the Chamber of Deputies;

(3) The power and prerogatives of the Head of the Government, Prime Minister, Secretary of State;

(4) The power of the executive to promulgate judicial rules;

(5) The syndical and corporate system;

(6) The relations between the state and the Holy See;

(7) International treaties which entail a variation in the territory of the kingdom or the colonies or the renunciation of an acquisition of territory.

ARTICLE 13. On proposal of the Head of the Government the Grand Council prepares and keeps up to date a list of the names to be submitted to the Crown for the nomination of the Head of the Government, Prime Minister, Secretary of State, in case a vacancy should occur in that office.

The powers and prerogatives of the Head of the Government remaining unchanged, the Grand Council prepares and keeps up to date the list of persons whom it deems qualified to take over the functions of government in case of vacancy.

ARTICLE 14. The secretaries, the assistant secretaries, the administrative secretaries, and the other members of the directorate of the National Fascist party are named by decree of the Head of the Government, Prime Minister, Secretary of State, after deliberation of the Grand Council according to the provisions of Art. 11. They remain in office for a period of three years and their nomination is renewable. By the same procedure they can at all times be recalled.

By royal decree and on the proposal of the Head of the Government, the Secretary of the National Fascist party can be called to participate in the meetings of the Council of Ministers.

LAW OF MARCH 20, 1930, NO. 206, ON THE REFORM OF THE NATIONAL COUNCIL OF CORPORATIONS

(Published in the *Gazzetta ufficiale* of March 28, 1930, no. 74)

(The following text contains the modification to the above made by Royal Decree of March 17, 1932, and published in the *Gazzetta ufficiale* of April 13, 1932, no. 86)

(Condensed Version)

ARTICLE 1. The composition and the attributions of the National Council of Corporations, established by the Royal Decrees of July 2, 1926, no. 1131, and July 14, 1927, no. 1347, shall be modified as follows:

ORGANS OF THE NATIONAL COUNCIL OF CORPORATIONS

ARTICLE 2. The organs of the National Council of Corporations shall consist of:

(a) Sections and sub-sections;
(b) Special and permanent commissions;
(c) A general assembly;
(d) A central corporate committee.

ARTICLE 3. The presidency of the National Council of Corporations and of all its organs shall be vested in the Head of the Government, who shall convene the Council according to necessity.

By his delegation, these powers of the Head of the Government may be exercised by the Minister of Corporations.

When not presided over by the Head of the Government or the Minister of Corporations, the meetings of sections and sub-sections and of special permanent commissions shall be presided over by the Under-secretaries of State for Corporations, excepting cases especially dealt with in the regulation for the present law.

The Director General of Corporations shall be the Secretary General of the Council.

ARTICLE 4. The National Council of Corporations shall be composed of seven sections:

(1) The section of Liberal Professions and Arts, divided into two sub-sections, one for professions and one for arts;

(2) The section of Industry and Handicrafts, divided into two sub-sections, one for industry and one for handicrafts;

(3) The section of Agriculture;

(4) The section of Commerce;

(5) The section of Land Transportation and Internal Navigation;

(6) The section of Maritime and Air Transportation, divided into two sub-sections, one for maritime transportation and one for air transportation;

(7) The section of Banking.

The ordinary membership in the various sections shall be determined according to the provisions given in the table appended to the present law. This table may be modified by decree of the Head of the Government on proposal of the Minister for Corporations and after hearing the General Assembly of the Council.

In matters within their exclusive jurisdiction, sub-sections shall have the same powers as sections and shall be entitled to function independently.

Whenever the matters to be discussed shall be of common interest to several sections or sub-sections, such sections or sub-sections may be convened jointly in number of two or more.

In cases specifically dealt with in the Regulation, separate meetings may be called for either the employer or employee representatives of the joint sections of the Council.

ARTICLE 5. Whenever the deliberations of the Council shall refer to the entire syndical and corporate structure of the State, and in cases explicitly stated in the present law, the various sections of the Council shall be convened in a general assembly.

This assembly shall include the Minister for Corporations, the Minister for the Interior, the Minister for Agriculture and Forestry, the Secretary of the National Fascist Party, the Under-secretaries of State for Corporations, as well as all the representatives of the syndical confederations of employers and workers included in the various sections of the Council.

Of the other permanent representatives included in the various sections of the Council, the following will participate in the Assembly:

(a) For the National Confederation of Fascist Syndicates of Professional Men and Artists: the President of the Confederation and representatives of the National Syndicates of Professional Men (ten delegates) and of Artists (four delegates) selected from among those included in the Council's sub-sections of Liberal Professions and Arts, and designated by the aforesaid Confederation;

(b) For the National Institute of Coöperation: the President of the Institute and two other representatives designated by the Institute and belonging to the corresponding section of the Council.

The following shall also be members of the General Assembly:

(1) The Ministers and Under-secretaries of State delegated by the President of the National Council of Corporations to preside at meetings of some of the Council's sections;

(2) The Minister of Justice;

(3) The Minister of Finance;

(4) The Minister of Public Works;

(5) The Minister of Communications;

(6) The presidents of the various National Corporations;

(7) The assistant secretaries of the National Fascist Party;

(8) The general managers of the Ministry of Corporations;

(9) The general managers of the Ministry of Agriculture and Forestry;

(10) The president of the Dopolavoro organization;

(11) The president of the National Institute for Social Assistance;

(12) The president of the Association of Disabled War Veterans;

(13) The president of the National War Veterans' Association;

(14) The commissioner for tourist trade;

(15) The president of the National Institute for Maternal and Infant Welfare;

(16) Two representatives of Italian economic interests abroad, one of whom nominated by the Minister of Foreign Affairs from among the officials of that Ministry and the other one nominated by the Minister of Corporations in agreement with the Minister of Foreign Affairs from among the leaders of Italian Chambers of Commerce abroad;

(17) Three representatives of associations of public employees,

authorized by Art. 92 of the Royal Decree of July 1, 1926, designated by the Secretary of the National Fascist Party;

(18)   Ten persons of particular competence in questions of syndical organization, of corporate law and economics, or in other legal or technical fields directly concerned with production, designated by the Minister of Corporations.

On proposal of the Head of the Government, additions to the list of members indicated in the preceding paragraph may be made by royal decree.

ARTICLE 6.   By decree of the Head of the Government and on proposal of the Minister of Corporations, special permanent commissions composed of members of the General Assembly shall be instituted within the National Council of Corporations for the discussion of special topics of eminently technical character, excluding, however, those indicated in the following Arts. 11 and 12.

The composition of these commissions and the limits of their competence shall be determined by special royal decrees.

ARTICLE 7.   The opinion of the General Assembly may always be heard upon matters already submitted for study to the various sections and special permanent commissions of the National Council.

Regulations and agreements elaborated within the various sections of the Council in accordance with the provisions of Art. 12 shall be communicated to the General Assembly, which shall be empowered to make the changes deemed necessary before any other step shall be taken.

NOMINATION FOR MEMBERSHIP IN THE NATIONAL COUNCIL OF CORPORATIONS

ARTICLE 8.   The designation of representatives in the National Council of Corporations by syndical organizations and other associations and organizations indicated in Art. 5 and in the table appended to the present law shall be made by the higher managerial bodies of such organizations, constituted and convened according to the provisions of their by-laws.

Membership in the National Council of Corporations shall be granted by royal decree on the proposal of the Head of the Government.

Upon taking office, members of the National Council of Corporations shall take the oath of office as described in the Special Regulation.

Members of the National Council of Corporations whose membership in the Council is not due to other public office which they may hold, shall continue in office for three years and be eligible for re-appointment at the end of their term.

ARTICLE 9. All the qualifications necessary for election to Parliament shall be required for eligibility to membership in the National Council of Corporations.

If any one of these qualifications is missing, the mandate shall be revoked.

ATTRIBUTIONS OF THE NATIONAL COUNCIL OF CORPORATIONS

ARTICLE 10. The National Council of Corporations shall be called upon to give opinions on the following subjects:

(1) Application of the principles of the Labor Charter in the development of the corporate system;

(2) Elaboration of new laws and regulations on the discipline of production and labor according to the provisions of the Law of January 31, 1926, no. 100.

(3) Protection of professional interests by syndical associations and performance of the functions of public interest delegated to them by the state in accordance with Declaration III of the Charter of Labor;

(4) Social welfare activities of syndical associations as provided for in Art. 4 of the Law of April 3, 1926, and in Declaration VIII of the Charter of Labor;

(5) Activities of corporate organs and institutions directed toward coördination and improvement of production and the advancement of national culture and art according to Declarations VI and VIII of the Charter of Labor;

(6) Relations between syndical associations and complementary corporate institutions arising out of the activities indicated in the preceding paragraph;

(7) Coördination of the welfare activities of syndical and other organizations;

(8) Questions relating to syndical organization of the various professional groups;

(9) Legal recognition of syndical associations according to the provisions of Art. 4 of the Law of April 3, 1926;

(10) Authorization for the legal recognition of national confederations in addition to those provided for by Art. 41 of the Royal Decree of July 1, 1926;

(11) Appeals to the Ministry of Corporations on the admission of syndical associations to membership in associations of a higher order presented in accordance with the provisions of Art. 9 of the Royal Decree of July 1, 1926;

(12) Regulations concerning annual financial statements and reports required of syndical associations;

(13) National and regional coördination of employment according to the provisions of Art. 8 of the Royal Decree of March 29, 1928;

(14) Constitution of individual corporations, according to the provisions of Art. 42 of the Royal Decree of July 1, 1926;

(15) Diffusion of knowledge concerning the principles underlying the corporate system in popular and scientific circles;

(16) Determination of syndical contributions.

The National Council of Corporations may, in addition, be requested to give opinions on all questions concerning national production. Opinions of the National Council of Corporations shall not, however, supplant those of other competent consulting organs of the state whenever their opinions shall be required by law.

The opinion of the National Council of Corporations shall be required for the subjects described in paragraphs 9, 10, 11, and 14. In such cases the opinion shall always be expressed by the general assembly.

ARTICLE 11. After obtaining authorization from the federations or confederations of which they are members, syndical associations of a given economic category may, unless existing laws provide otherwise, obtain from the National Council of Corporations the right to determine the schedules of fees for the professional services rendered by their members as well as the right to issue professional regulations binding upon all the members of their professional group.

These powers shall be conferred by the general assembly of the National Council of Corporations, upon recommendation by the competent section or sub-section.

ARTICLE 12. In addition to those mentioned, the National Council of Corporations shall perform the following functions:

(1) Formulation of rules for the coördination of welfare activities of syndical and other associations;

(2) Formulation of rules for the coördination of the legislative provisions relating to collective labor agreements;

(3) Formulation of rules on the collective economic relations existing among the various classes of production as represented by legally recognized syndical associations.

ARTICLE 13. By decree of the Head of the Government and on proposal of the Minister of Corporations the attributions and powers of Corporations as described in Art. 3 of the Law of April 3, 1926, may be conferred upon the different sections and sub-sections of the council.

ARTICLE 14. The sections and sub-sections of the Council shall interrelate and coördinate the work of the Confederations established in the different branches of production. The details of this function shall be specifically determined by decree of the Head of the Government.

THE CENTRAL CORPORATE COMMITTEE

ARTICLE 15. Within the National Council of Corporations there shall be established the Central Corporate Committee.

The Central Corporate Committee shall coördinate the activities of the Council, serve in the place of the general assembly between its meetings for all urgent deliberations except those described in Art. 12, and give opinions on questions regarding the political orientation of syndical activity, problems of national production, and the moral ends of the corporate system.

ARTICLE 16. Membership in the Central Corporate Committee shall include the Minister of Corporations, the Minister of the Interior, the Minister of Agriculture and Forestry, the Secretary of the National Fascist Party, the Assistant Secretaries of State for Corporations, the Presidents of the National Confederations of Employers, of Employees, and of Professional Men and Artists, the President of the National Institute of Coöperation, the President of the National Institute of Social Welfare, and the Secretary-General of the National Council of Corporations.

GENERAL PROVISIONS

ARTICLE 17. The Ministers or Under-secretaries of State of the Departments interested in the questions under discussion shall be entitled to participate in the meetings of the various organs of the Council after obtaining authority to do so from the Head of the Government. General Managers of the various governmental departments may also be called on to participate in these meetings upon invitation by the President. Technical consultants and the representatives of syndical associations within a given economic class may also be invited to participate in the work of the Council.

ARTICLE 18. Representatives of permanent international organizations in which Italy participates by means of governmental delegations may also be invited by the Head of the Government to attend the meetings of the various organs of the Council as observers.

TABLE SHOWING THE DISTRIBUTION OF MEMBERSHIP
IN THE VARIOUS SECTIONS OF THE NATIONAL
COUNCIL OF CORPORATIONS

(This table contains the modifications made by the Royal Decree
of December 20, 1931, published in the *Gazzetta ufficiale* of February 13, 1932, no. 36 and by the Royal Decree of February 29, 1932,
published in the *Gazzetta ufficiale* of March 30, 1932, no. 74)

SECTION OF LIBERAL PROFESSIONS AND ARTS

A. *Sub-section of Liberal Professions*

Representatives named by the National Confederation of Fascist
syndicates of Professional Men and Artists:

(1) The President of the National Confederation of Fascist
Syndicates of Professional Men and Artists;

(2) A representative of the National Fascist Syndicate of
Counsellors of Law;

(3) A representative of the National Fascist Syndicate of
Doctors of Economic and Commercial Sciences and of Doctors of
Social Science;

(4) A representative of the National Fascist Syndicate of
Accountants;

(5) A representative of the National Fascist Syndicate of
Engineers;

(6) A representative of the National Fascist Syndicate of
Architects;

(7) A representative of the National Fascist Syndicate of
Chemists;

(8) A representative of the National Fascist Syndicate of
Surveyors;

(9) A representative of the National Fascist Syndicate of
Commercial Experts;

(10) A representative of the National Fascist Syndicate of
Physicians;

(11) A representative of the National Fascist Syndicate of
Veterinarians;

(12) A representative of the National Fascist Syndicate of
Pharmacists;

(13) A representative of the National Fascist Syndicate of
Notaries;

(14) A representative of the National Fascist Syndicate of
Journalists;

(15)   A representative of the National Fascist Syndicate of Obstetricians;

(16)   A representative of the National Fascist Syndicate of Private Teachers;

(17)   A representative of the National Fascist Syndicate of Industrial Experts.

B.   *Sub-section of Arts*

Representatives named by the National Confederation of Fascist Syndicates of Professional Men and Artists:

(1)   The President of the National Confederation of Fascist Syndicates of Professional Men and Artists;

(2)   A representative of the National Fascist Syndicate of Authors and Writers;

(3)   A representative of the National Fascist Syndicate of Fine Arts;

(4)   A representative of the National Fascist Syndicate of Musicians;

(5)   A representative of the National Fascist Syndicate of Architects;

(6)   A representative of the National Fascist Syndicate of Journalists (Artistic).

Representatives named by the General Fascist Confederation of Italian Industry:

(7)   A representative of the National Fascist Federation of the Publishing Industry;

(8)   A representative of the National Fascist Association of Newspaper Editors;

(9)   A representative of the National Fascist Federation of the Stage;

(10)   A representative named by the Autonomous Fascist Federation of Italian Handicraft Associations.

SECTION OF INDUSTRY AND HANDICRAFTS

A.   *Sub-section of Industry*

(1)   The President of the General Fascist Confederation of Italian Industry;

(2)   Seven representatives named by the General Fascist Confederation of Italian Industry, two of them representing Managers of Industrial Enterprises;

(3)   The President of the National Fascist Confederation of Industrial Syndicates;

(4)   Seven representatives of Industrial Clerks and Laborers

named by the National Fascist Confederation of Industrial Syndicates, two of them representing industrial clerks;

(5) Two representatives of the National Institute of Coöperation named by the Institute.

B. *Sub-section of Handicrafts*

(1) The President of the General Fascist Confederation of Italian Industry;

(2) The President of the Autonomous Fascist Federation of Italian Handicraft Associations;

(3) Two representatives of the Autonomous Fascist Federation of Italian Handicraft Associations named by the Federation;

(4) The President of the National Fascist Confederation of Industrial Syndicates;

(5) Three representatives of the National Fascist Confederation of Industrial Syndicates named by the Confederation.

SECTION OF AGRICULTURE

(1) The President of the National Fascist Confederation of Agriculture;

(2) Seven representatives named by the National Fascist Confederation of Agriculture, two of them representing managers of agricultural enterprises;

(3) The President of the National Fascist Confederation of Agricultural Syndicates;

(4) Seven representatives of employees and laborers in agriculture named by the National Fascist Confederation of Agricultural Syndicates, two of them representing agricultural technicians;

(5) Two representatives of the National Institute of Coöperation named by the Institute.

SECTION OF COMMERCE

(1) The President of the National Fascist Confederation of Merchants;

(2) Seven representatives named by the National Fascist Confederation of Merchants, two of them representing managers of commercial enterprises;

(3) The President of the National Confederation of Fascist Syndicates of Commerce;

(4) Seven representatives of commercial employees and laborers named by the National Fascist Confederation of Commercial Syndicates;

(5) Two representatives of the National Institute of Coöperation named by the Institute.

SECTION OF MARITIME AND AIR TRANSPORTATION

A. Sub-section of Maritime Transportation

(1) The President of the National Fascist Confederation of Maritime and Air Transportation;

(2) Four representatives named by the National Fascist Confederation of Maritime and Air Transportation, one of them representing managers of such enterprises;

(3) The President of the National Fascist Confederation of Sea and Air Men;

(4) Four representatives of seamen named by the National Fascist Confederation of Sea and Air Men, one of them representing captains and engineers;

(5) A representative of the National Institute of Coöperation named by the Institute.

B. Sub-section of Air Transportation

(1) The President of the National Fascist Confederation of Maritime and Air Transportation;

(2) Three representatives named by the National Fascist Confederation of Maritime and Air Transportation, one of them representing managers of such enterprises;

(3) The President of the National Fascist Confederation of Sea and Air Men;

(4) Three representatives of Air Men named by the National Fascist Confederation of Sea and Air Men, one of them representing pilots and navigation officers;

(5) A representative of the National Institute of Coöperation named by the Institute.

SECTION OF LAND TRANSPORTATION AND INTERNAL NAVIGATION

(1) The President of the National Fascist Confederation of Land Transportation and Internal Navigation;

(2) Five representatives named by the National Fascist Confederation of Land Transportation and Internal Navigation, one of them representing managers of such enterprises;

(3) The President of the National Confederation of Fascist Syndicates of Land Transportation and Internal Navigation;

(4) Five representatives of employees and laborers in enterprises of land transportation and internal navigation named by their Confederation;

(5) A representative of the National Institute of Coöperation named by the Institute.

SECTION OF CREDIT AND INSURANCE

(1) The President of the General Fascist Confederation of Credit and Insurance;

(2) Six representatives named by the General Fascist Confederation of Insurance, one of them representing officials of Credit and Insurance Institutions;

(3) The President of the National Confederation of Fascist Syndicates of Credit and Insurance Employees;

(4) Six representatives of Credit and Insurance Employees named by the National Confederation of Fascist Syndicates of Credit and Insurance, one of them representing managers.

REGULATION FOR THE APPLICATION OF THE LAW OF MARCH 20, 1930, ON THE NATIONAL COUNCIL OF CORPORATIONS

(Outline of the provisions contained in the Royal Decree of May 12, 1930, no. 908, published in the *Gazzetta ufficiale* of July 9, 1930, no. 159)

PART I (Arts. 1 to 3). Contains regulations on the attributions of the President of the National Council of Corporations.

PART II (Arts. 4 and 5). Contains rules relating to the meetings of the various organs of the Council.

PART III (Arts. 6–14). Contains regulations concerning the work of the General Assembly.

Art. 6. The general assembly of the National Council of Corporations shall normally meet twice a year in ordinary session during the months of March, April, or May and during the months of September, October, or November.

Art. 7. Special sessions of the general assembly of the National Council of Corporations may be called by its President and whenever one-third of its members shall request it in writing.

Art. 10. For the validity of the meetings of the general assembly the participation of at least one-half of its members shall be necessary in first convocation, and at least one-third in second convocation.

Art. 14. The meetings of the general assembly shall be open to the public. The president may, however, if he shall deem it necessary, call secret meetings.

PART IV (Arts. 15 to 19). Contains regulations concerning the Council's sections and sub-sections.

Art. 15. The sections and sub-sections of the National Council of Corporations shall meet whenever the president shall deem it necessary or whenever one-half of the members shall make a written request for a special meeting to be called for the discussion of specific topics.

Art. 18. To the meetings of the sections and sub-sections of the National Council of Corporations the public shall be admitted upon decision of the President.

PARTS V, VI, and VII (Arts. 20 to 27). Contains regulations concerning the special permanent commissions, the Central Corporate Committee, and membership in the National Council of Corporations.

Art. 26. Membership and participation in the work of the National Council of Corporations, or in one of its organs, does not entitle to compensation or indemnity, with the exception of expenses incurred for travel from the residence of the Council's member to the place where the meetings are to be held.

PARTS VIII, IX, and X (Arts. 28 to 39). Contain regulations on the attributions and powers of the National Council of Corporations and of its secretary general.

REGULATIONS ON THE INTERNAL ORGANIZATION OF THE NATIONAL COUNCIL OF CORPORATIONS

(By a decree of the Head of the Government, issued on October 1, 1932, and published in the *Gazzetta ufficiale* of October 5, 1932, no. 231, official approval was given to the detailed regulations on the methods of voting and the internal organization of the National Council of Corporations.)

SECTION 1 (Arts. 1–4). Defines the order of the topics to be brought before the various organs of the Council.

SECTION 2 (Arts. 5–16). Contains rules on the organization of the Council's meetings, the assignment of seats, the admission of representatives of the press to the Council's meetings, the formalities to be observed before the opening of the Council's sessions, such as roll calls, oath of office of new members, etc.

SECTION 3 (Arts. 17–20). Regulates the procedure to be followed during the discussions (timing of speeches, etc.).

SECTION 4 (Arts. 21–36). Divided into four sections, deals with the mechanism of the various systems of voting. Individual voting (Art. 22) is the system normally used by all organs of the Council, with the exception of special cases for which the President may decide on the adoption of a different method.

The various bodies constituted within the Council may vote separately on all questions, with the exception of those involving the regulation of labor relations or those in which there is a conflict of interests between employers and employees.

SECTION 5 (Arts. 37–40). Contains rules on the validity of the decisions taken during the Council's meetings. To be valid, all decisions of the Council must be approved by a majority vote, and in some cases by vote of a two-thirds majority.

SECTIONS 6–9 (Arts. 41–54). Contain detailed provisions on the Council's administrative functions such as the procedures to be followed in the formulation of corporate regulations, in the passing of resolutions, and in a number of other official acts to be performed by the Council.

EXCERPTS FROM THE LAW OF APRIL 18, 1926, NO. 731, ON THE ESTABLISHMENT OF PROVINCIAL ECONOMIC COUNCILS

(Published in the *Gazzetta ufficiale* of May 10, 1926, no. 108)

ARTICLE 1. A provincial economic council shall be established in the capital of each province of the kingdom.

ARTICLE 2. Provincial economic councils shall represent the interests of producers within the different provinces and promote the development of productive activities in harmony with the general economic interests of the nation.

ARTICLE 3. Among other attributions, provincial economic councils shall:

(1) Function as local observers of provincial economic and social life, and collect and elaborate information on agricultural, industrial, and commercial conditions within the province;

(2) Formulate proposals concerning the agricultural, industrial, and commercial development of the province, to be submitted to the Government;

(3) Supervise and administer schools and other institutions for agricultural, industrial, and commercial education;

(4) Keep records of recognized commercial usages existing within the province;

(5) Keep the records required by law on the establishment, the successive modifications, and the cessation of industrial and commercial enterprises;

(6) Supervise and regulate produce and stock exchanges.

ARTICLE 4. Provincial economic councils shall usually have the four following sections:

(1) Agriculture and Forestry;

(2) Industry;

(3) Commerce;

(4) Labor and Social Welfare.

ARTICLE 15. Meetings both of the Council and of its sections shall be open to the public.

ARTICLE 28. Whoever shall, individually or in partnership, engage in industrial, agricultural, or commercial activities shall be required to register with the Provincial Economic Council within fifteen days of the establishment of the new enterprise.

ARTICLE 35. Provincial Economic Councils shall replace all existing Chambers of Commerce, Agriculture, and all other similar institutions.

EXCERPTS FROM THE ROYAL DECREE OF JUNE 16, 1927, NO. 1071, ON PROVINCIAL ECONOMIC COUNCILS AND OFFICES

(Published in the *Gazzetta ufficiale* of July 7, 1927, no. 155)

ARTICLE 1. A Provincial Economic Office shall be established in the capital of each Province. These offices shall be dependent on the Ministry of National Economy. They shall serve as Secretariats for the Provincial Economic Councils, in whose budgets their expenditures shall be included.

ARTICLE 2. The Provincial Economic Offices shall serve as observers of local economic and social life and collect and elaborate statistical and other information pertaining thereto. They shall register new business firms, prepare official market price lists, and collect and elaborate information on the topics to be discussed by the Provincial Economic Councils.

ARTICLE 4. Provincial Economic Councils shall be composed of not less than twelve and not more than twenty-eight elective members.

ARTICLE 10. Employees of Provincial Economic Offices shall be members of the Civil Service.

EXCERPTS FROM THE LAW OF JUNE 18, 1931, NO. 875, ON THE COMPOSITION AND THE ATTRIBUTIONS OF PROVINCIAL COUNCILS OF CORPORATE ECONOMY

(Published in the *Gazzetta ufficiale* of July 14, 1931, no. 160)

ARTICLE 1. The name of Provincial Economic Councils shall be changed to that of Provincial Councils of Corporate Economy, and that of the Provincial Economic Offices to Provincial Offices of Corporate Economy.

ARTICLE 2. The organization of the Provincial Councils of Corporate Economy shall be composed of:

(1) The President, who shall be the Prefect of the Province;

(2) The Vice-President;

(3) The Presidential Committee, composed of the President, the Vice-President, and the presidents and vice-presidents of the various sections of the Council;

(4) The General Council, composed of the presidential committee, of the councilors of the various sections, and of the persons legally entitled to membership according to the provisions of Art. 4;

(5) The Sections;

(6) The Special Commissions.

ARTICLE 3. The Councilors, whose number shall be determined by the Ministry of Corporations, shall be appointed by the legally recognized professional associations of employers, of employees, and of professional men and artists existing within the province.

The number of representatives of employers' associations shall be equal to that of workers' representatives (both intellectual and manual).

The Councilors shall be appointed by decree of the Prefect of the Province.

ARTICLE 6. Among other attributions, Provincial Councils of Corporate Economy shall:

(1) Provide for the coördination, within the province, of the activities of syndical organizations directed, according to Declaration VIII of the Charter of Labor, toward the increase and the improvement of production;

(2) Provide for the coördination of welfare activities of syndical associations;

(3) Exercise control over provincial employment offices.

(The remainder of the decree contains detailed provisions concerning the functions and attributions of the various organs of these Councils.)

LAW OF JUNE 16, 1932, NO. 834, ON THE ESTABLISHMENT OF SPECIAL ASSOCIATIONS (CONSORZI) AMONG CONCERNS ENGAGED IN THE SAME KIND OF ECONOMIC ACTIVITY

(Published in the *Gazzetta ufficiale* of July 25, 1932, no. 170)

(Condensed Version)

ARTICLE 1. For the purpose of regulating production and competition, provision may be made by royal decree, on the recommendation of the Head of the Government, for the establishment of compulsory associations (*consorzi*) among concerns engaged in the same kind of economic activity.

The duration of such associations shall be determined by royal decree and shall not exceed a period of five years.

By an analogous procedure, and after consultation with the competent corporations, compulsory associations (*consorzi*) for the regulation of interrelated economic activities may be established in the interests of national economy.

No modification shall be made to the general attributions conferred upon the National Council of Corporations by Art. 12 of the law of March 20, 1930, concerning the regulation of collective economic relations.

ARTICLE 2. The establishment of a special compulsory association (*consorzio*) among concerns engaged in the same kind of economic activity shall take place:

(a) Whenever a request shall have been made by persons representing at least 70 per cent of the total number of concerns and 70 per cent of the average actual production during the last three years or (in the absence of the required number of concerns) representing 85 per cent of the total production. For the establishment of Consorzi among agriculturalists a request made by persons representing 70 per cent of the total production shall be sufficient.

(b) Whenever the government, after consultation with the competent Corporations, shall deem the establishment of a compulsory Consorzio to be in harmony with the general interests of the country's economic life because of its ability to secure a more rational technical and economic organization of production.

ARTICLE 3. Whenever concerns belonging to the state or concerns in which the state holds 50 per cent of the capital stock shall exist within the branch of production in which a compulsory Consorzio has been formed, and it shall not require governmental concerns to participate in the Consorzio the Government shall take steps to bring about coöperation of such concerns with the policies of the Consorzio.

ARTICLE 4. Requests for the establishment of a compulsory Consorzio shall be made to the competent Minister through the respective Confederations, which shall be required to transmit such requests to the Minister with their own recommendations.

Each request shall be accompanied by a draft of the proposed by-laws and by an explanatory report, indicating the objectives of the proposed Consorzio and the means whereby the attainment of these objectives is sought.

ARTICLE 5. The rules relating to conditions of membership, to penalties for infringement of such rules and to the internal organization of the Consorzio, shall be stated in the by-laws, the provisions of which shall be discussed by the general assembly of all the participants in the Consorzio and accepted by a majority such as is required for the Consorzio's establishment. The by-laws shall be approved by royal decree upon the recommendation of the competent ministers, who shall also ascertain the existence of the aforesaid majority.

The by-laws shall also provide for the establishment of a committee empowered to annul or modify resolutions relating to the assignment of quotas and to other obligations imposed upon individual members. This committee shall consist of three members of whom one shall be nominated by the President of the Consorzio, one by the appellant, and one by agreement among the other two members, or, if no agreement shall be reached, by the President of the Tribunal of the city in which the Consorzio has its headquarters. No appeal shall be permitted in the case of persons or firms having in some manner approved the resolution in question.

For all obligations contracted in its name and through its authorized representatives the Consorzio shall be responsible solely up to the limits of its own capital.

No modification shall be made in the jurisdiction of judicial authorities in disputes arising in connection with employment and working conditions between the Consorzio and its dependents.

ARTICLE 6. The Consorzi shall be required to communicate to the competent Ministers all resolutions relating to their general policies and all other documents which they may be asked to supply.

Whenever the general policies of a Consorzio shall not be found to correspond to its specific objectives the competent Minister shall be empowered formally to request the Consorzio, through the competent Confederation, to modify its course of action.

If this should prove unsuccessful, the Minister may order that within a period determined by ministerial decree the Consorzio's management be relieved of its duties and arrangements be made for its replacement.

The Minister may, on his own initiative or upon the recommendation of the competent Corporation, appoint an official to attend the meetings of the managers of the Consorzio.

A Consorzio may be dissolved before the full expiration of its term by a royal decree issued with the same modalities which were required for its formation, whenever its existence should, in the opinion of the Government, cease to be in harmony with the general interests of the country.

In such cases, the Minister shall nominate a liquidator by means of a decree to be published in the *Gazzetta ufficiale* of the kingdom. The provisions of the Commercial Code for the liquidation of corporations shall, as far as possible, be applied to the procedure of liquidation. The liquidator's services shall be remunerated at the expense of the Consorzio at the rate to be determined by the Ministry.

In the case of bankruptcy, the pertinent provisions of commercial law shall be applied.

ARTICLE 7. The competent Corporations shall keep in close touch with the activities of the Consorzio. They shall analyze its general policies, and communicate their findings to the competent Minister. On the basis of these findings they shall also prepare a report on the activity of· the Consorzio and on the results obtained from the point of view of the general interests of production, and submit the same periodically to the Central Corporate Committee.

ARTICLE 8. Whenever special conditions existing within certain branches of production shall make it necessary, the decree establishing the compulsory Consorzio, or a later one, may subject the building of new factories or the extension of existing ones manufacturing products dealt in by the Consorzio to the previous authorization of the Head of the Government acting in agreement with the other competent Ministers and with the competent Corporation.

All persons engaging, after the formation of a Consorzio, in the branch of production regulated by it shall be subject to its discipline and to its regulation.

The provisions of the Royal Decree of November 18, 1929, no. 2488, on the manufacture of products required for the defense of the State and those of the Royal Decree of November 3, 1927, no. 2107, on the establishment of industrial plants shall remain unchanged.

ARTICLE 9. Upon proposal of the competent Minister and after consultation with the proper Corporations, legislative provisions regulating already existing compulsory Consorzi may be revised by royal decree, and harmonized with the provisions of the present law.

ARTICLE 10. To make possible the coördination of the activities of compulsory Consorzi with those of voluntary ones, voluntary Consorzi of whatever description, proposing to regulate the economic activities of their members, shall as from July 1st, 1932, transmit to the competent Ministers a copy of the by-laws and of the amendments made thereto.

By royal decree, to be issued with the same formalities as those required for the establishment of compulsory Consorzi, the competent Minister may provide that the provisions concerning corporate and governmental supervision be also applied, wholly or partially, to voluntary Consorzi representing in any particular branch of productive activity at least 75 per cent of the total national production during the last three years.

ARTICLE 11. Managers of Consorzi neglecting to communicate resolutions passed on matters of general policy to the competent Minister, as required by the law, within thirty days of their passing, shall be punishable by a fine not exceeding 1,000 lire.

Managers of Consorzi neglecting to follow ministerial directions as to modifications in policy within the required period, shall be punishable by a fine not exceeding 10,000 lire.

The penalty shall be the same for managers of Consorzi who, disregarding ministerial instructions, shall not call within the required period a general meeting of their Consorzio for the purpose of their substitution in office.

ARTICLE 12. The necessary regulations for the application of the present law and in particular, the regulations relating to the general meetings of members of the Consorzi shall be issued by royal decree upon proposal of the Head of the Government, acting in agreement with the competent Ministers and after consultation with the Council of Ministers.

LAW OF FEBRUARY 5, 1934, NO. 163, ON THE ESTABLISHMENT AND FUNCTIONS OF THE CORPORATIONS

(Published in the *Gazzetta ufficiale* of February 20, 1934, no. 42)

(Condensed Version)

ARTICLE 1. The Corporations described in Declaration VI of the Charter of Labor, in the Law of April 3, 1926, and in the Royal Decree of July 1, 1926, shall be established by decree of the Head of the Government, upon the proposal of the Minister for Corporations and after hearing the Central Corporate Committee.

ARTICLE 2. Corporations shall be presided over by a Minister, an Under-secretary of State or by the Secretary of the National Fascist Party, appointed to the office by a decree of the Head of the Government.

ARTICLE 3. The decree establishing a Corporation shall determine the number of members in its Council and also the number of Council members to be appointed by each one of the affiliated associations. These appointments shall be approved by decree of the Head of the Government upon the proposal of the Minister for Corporations.

ARTICLE 4. In the Corporations in which various branches of economic activity are represented, there may be established special sections, the deliberations of which shall be approved by the Corporation.

ARTICLE 5. For matters concerning different branches of economic activity, the Head of the Government may provide for the simultaneous calling into session of two or more Corporations.

ARTICLE 6. Upon the proposal of the Minister of Corporations and after hearing the Central Corporate Committee, the Head of the Government may, by his decree, establish Corporate Committees for the regulation of the economic activities relating to individual products, such committees to be composed of the representatives of the economic groups concerned, the interested government bureaus, and the National Fascist Party.

The deliberations of Corporate Committees shall be subject to the approval of the competent corporations and of the General Assembly of the National Council of Corporations.

ARTICLE 7. The Syndical Associations connected through a Corporation shall become autonomous in the syndical field, but shall continue their membership in the respective Confederations, according to the regulations to be issued by the Ministry of Corporations.

ARTICLE 8. In addition to exercising the attributions and powers described in the Law of April 3, 1926, and in the Royal Decree of July 1, 1926, the Corporations shall elaborate norms for the collective regulation of economic relations and for the unitary discipline of production.

The Corporations shall exercise this function upon the proposal of the competent Ministers or upon request of one of the affiliated Associations, with the consent of the Head of the Government.

ARTICLE 9. The agreements entered into according to Art. 12 of the Law of March 20, 1930, by syndical associations affiliated to a Corporation, must be submitted to the Corporation for an opinion before the approval, provided for in Art. 11 of the present law, is obtained.

ARTICLE 10. Within the field of its competence, a Corporation shall have the right to establish, in the manner described in the second paragraph of Art. 8, the rates of remuneration for all forms of work performed and services rendered, as well as the prices for articles of consumption sold to the public under non-competitive conditions.

ARTICLE 11. All rules and agreements, as well as the rates described in the preceding article, shall be subject to the approval of the General Assembly of the National Council of Corporations and shall become binding when published by a decree of the Head of the Government. In the case of non-observance of such rules, agreements and rates by individuals, the penalties provided for in the laws relating to collective labor agreements shall be applied.

ARTICLE 12. Whenever asked to do so by competent government organs, a Corporation shall express opinions on all matters pertaining to the branch of economic activity within which it is established.

The Head of the Government may, by decree, establish that for certain subjects an opinion must be obtained by government organs from the competent Corporation.

Through the decree establishing the Corporation or through a later one, the Head of the Government may suppress consultive commissions existing within the branch of economic activity within which a Corporation has been established, whatever the nature of the act establishing said commissions.

ARTICLE 13. Attempts at the conciliation of collective labor disputes shall be carried out by the Corporation through a board of arbitration composed of members of the Corporation itself, chosen from time to time by the president, with due regard to the nature of the individual controversies.

ARTICLE 14. All provisions contrary or incompatible with the present law are abrogated. The Government shall have the right to publish regulations in order to coördinate the present law with the laws of April 3, 1926, of March 20, 1930, of June 16, 1932, of January 12, 1933, and with the other laws of the state.

ARTICLE 15. By royal decree and upon the proposal of the Head of the Government after authorization of the Council of Ministers, there shall be modified the composition of the membership in the organs of the National Council of Corporations.

DECREE OF THE HEAD OF THE GOVERNMENT OF MAY 29, 1934, ON THE ESTABLISHMENT OF THE CORPORATION OF GRAINS

(Published in the *Gazzetta ufficiale* of June 5, 1934, no. 131)

(Condensed Version)

ARTICLE 1.   There shall be established a Corporation of Grains. The headquarters of the Corporation shall be in Rome at the Ministry of Corporations.

ARTICLE 2.   The Council of the Corporation shall be composed of a president and thirty-six members, including:

(a)   Three representatives of the National Fascist Party;

(b)   Seven employers' and seven workers' representatives for the grain-growing industry;

(c)   One employers' and one workers' representative for the threshing industry;

(d)   Three employers' and three workers' representatives for the milling, rice, pasta, and sweatmeat industries;

(e)   One employers' and one workers' representative for the bread-making industry;

(f)   Three employers' and three workers' representatives for the trade in grains and the products of other above-named industries;

(g)   One representative of consumers' coöperative societies;

(h)   One representative of agricultural technicians;

(i)   One representative of artisans.

The number of employers' representatives shall include three representatives of business executives, one for agriculture, one for industry, and one for commerce.

ARTICLE 3.   Members of the Council of the Corporation shall be appointed by the following: by the Secretary of the National Fascist Party for the members mentioned under (a) in the preceding article, by the National Fascist Institute of Coöperation for the member mentioned under (g) and by the competent syndical associations for the other members.

The appointments by syndical associations and by the National Institute of Coöperation shall be made by competent organs in accordance with the by-laws or by whoever legally exercises powers of appointment in their place.

ARTICLE 4.   Members of the Council of the Corporation shall possess the qualifications required of syndical officials by Art. 1, no. 3 of the Law of April 3, 1926.

Members appointed by syndical associations must belong to the occupational groups which they are called upon to represent or be qualified syndical officials.

ARTICLE 5. Members of the Council shall be appointed for three years, their appointments to coincide in length with those of the members of the National Council of Corporations.

Members appointed in the course of the three-year period shall not remain in office beyond the end of that period.

ARTICLE 6. The Minister for Corporations shall be the President of the Corporation.

The Members of the Council shall be appointed by royal decree.

By the same decree one of the members named by the Fascist Party shall be appointed as a substitute to the President and empowered to take his place in case of absence.

ARTICLE 7. The President of the Corporation shall prepare the agenda of the matters to be brought before the Council and transmit it to the Secretary General of the National Council of Corporations, who shall in turn submit it to the Ministers concerned.

The agenda and the Ministers' reports shall then be submitted by the Secretary General to the Head of the Government for his assent.

ARTICLE 8. All resolutions adopted by the Corporation shall be transmitted to the office of the Secretary General of the National Council of Corporations, who shall communicate them to all interested government and other authorities.

ARTICLE 9. The President of the Corporation may invite to the sessions of the Council, without the right to a vote, experts in the problems under discussion. With the consent of the respective Ministers, the general managers and division chiefs of the interested government departments may also be invited.

The National Research Council and other technical bodies may be asked by the President for their opinion or for special research work bearing upon the problems under discussion.

The President may, in addition, authorize syndical associations and other bodies represented by the Corporation to send experts to the sessions, the numbers and modalities to be determined from time to time.

ARTICLE 10. The Minister and the Under-secretaries for Agriculture and Forestry, the Under-secretaries for Corporations and the Ministers and Under-secretaries of Government departments directly interested in the discussion shall be always authorized to participate in the sessions.

There may also participate in the sessions, the Presidents of the National Confederations of workers and employers in agriculture, industry, and commerce.

With the authorization of the President of the Corporation, the President of the National Fascist Institute for Coöperation and the presidents of all other Institutes and organizations represented on the National Council of Corporations may participate in the sessions whenever problems of interest to their institutes or organizations are being discussed.

ARTICLE 11. The Arbitration Board, described in Art. 13 of the Law of February 5, 1934, shall be composed of a president, chosen from among members of the Corporation other than those belonging to the occupational categories involved in the dispute, and of two members, one representing employers and one representing the workers, to be named by the President of the Corporation.

The syndical association asking for the intervention of the Board shall deposit with the Secretary General of the National Council of Corporations the minutes proving the negative outcome of the final attempt at conciliation among the competent syndical associations.

ARTICLE 12. The Arbitration Board shall be assisted by an official from the office of the Secretary General of the National Council of Corporations and by an official of the Labor Section of the Ministry of Corporations.

The minutes of the attempt at conciliation shall be drawn up by the representative of the office of the Secretary General of the National Council of Corporations and shall be signed by the contending parties, by the members of the Board, and by the government officials present.

ARTICLE 13. For the internal operation of the Corporation there shall be followed the rules contained in the regulations for voting and for the internal procedure of the National Council of Corporations.

For the voting procedure of the Council of the Corporation the rules contained in the regulations referred to in the preceding paragraph shall be opportunely modified by later decree after hearing the Central Corporate Committee.

ARTICLE 14. The Secretary General of the National Council of Corporations shall provide for the coördination of the work of the Corporations with the work of the various government departments and with the organs of the National Council of Corporations; he shall also provide for the secretarial services required by the Corporations.

ROYAL DECREE OF DECEMBER 27, 1934, ON CHANGES
IN THE MEMBERSHIP OF THE CENTRAL CORPORATE
COMMITTEE

(Published in the *Gazzetta ufficiale* of January 11, 1935, no. 9)

(Condensed Version)

ARTICLE 1. The Central Corporate Committee shall be composed
of:

(a) The Ministers for Corporations, Interior, Justice, Finance,
National Education, Public Works, Agriculture and Forestry, and
Communications, and the Secretary of the National Fascist Party;

(b) The Under-secretaries of State for Corporations;

(c) Such other Ministers and Under-secretaries of State as are
presidents of Corporations;

(d) The Assistant Secretaries and the Administrative Secretary
of the National Fascist Party;

(e) The representatives of the National Fascist Party in the
Councils of the Corporations to whom is entrusted the representation of the presidents in case of absence;

(f) The presidents of the Syndical Confederations of employers, workers, and professional men and artists, and the president of the Fascist Institute of Coöperation;

(g) The Secretary General of the National Council of Corporations.

MEMBERSHIP OF THE FASCIST SYNDICAL SYSTEM: APRIL 1926 TO DECEMBER 31, 1933

NUMBER OF LEGALLY RECOGNIZED SYNDICAL ASSOCIATIONS OF EMPLOYERS, DECEMBER 31, 1931*

National Fascist Confederations (Third Degree Associations)	Second Degree Associations (National Federations)	National Syndical Associations	First Degree Associations				Total
			Other Syndical Associations				
			Inter-provincial		Provincial	Local	
			Mixed	Individual Trades			
Industry	41	6	9	40	68	3	168
Agriculture	..	..	..	..	92	..	93
Commerce	12	1	..	..	92	..	106
Maritime and Air Transportation ...	3	3	3	5	..	..	15
Land Transportation and Internal Navigation	..	4	..	15	..	..	20
Credit and Insurance	..	10	..	..	..	..	11
Total	56	24	12	60	252	3	413

* *Annuario statistico italiano*, 1932, p. 227.

NUMBER OF LEGALLY RECOGNIZED SYNDICAL ASSOCIATIONS OF WORKERS, DECEMBER 31, 1931*

National Confederations of Fascist Syndicates (Third Degree Associations)	SECOND DEGREE ASSOCIATIONS		FIRST DEGREE ASSOCIATIONS			
	Provincial Unions	National Federations of Individual Trade Syndicates	National Associations of Syndicates	Inter-provincial Syndicates	Provincial Syndicates	Total
Industry	92	15	35	162	2096	2401
Agriculture	92	6	..	44	276	419
Commerce	92	7	..	107	370	577
Land Transportation and Internal Navigation	..	6	..	122	...	129
Banking and Insurance	..	4	1	15	...	21
Maritime and Air Transportation	..	..	4	..	...	5
Total	276	38	40	450	2742	3552

* *Annuario statistico italiano*, 1932, p. 227.

NUMBER OF LEGALLY RECOGNIZED SYNDICAL ASSOCIATIONS OF PROFESSIONAL MEN AND ARTISTS, DECEMBER 31, 1931*

National Confederations (Third Degree Associations)	Second Degree Associations (National Syndicates)	FIRST DEGREE SYNDICAL ASSOCIATIONS					
		Provincial	Inter-provincial	Regional	In Court of Appeals District	In Ordinary Court District	Total
National Confederation of Fascist Syndicates of Professional Men and Artists	21	642	12	180	44	126	1026

* *Annuario statistico italiano*, 1932, p. 227.

NUMBER OF LEGALLY RECOGNIZED SYNDICAL ASSOCIATIONS OF EMPLOYERS, DECEMBER 31, 1933*

National Fascist Confederations (Third Degree Associations)	Second Degree Syndical Associations		First Degree Syndical Associations					Total
	National	Inter-provincial	National	Regional	Inter-provincial	Provincial	Local	
Industry	40	..	5	..	47	71	..	164
Agriculture	..	..	..	..	..	92	..	93
Commerce	15	..	1	..	..	92	..	109
Internal Communications	3	..	2	..	15	..	..	21
Maritime and Air Transportation	..	3	3	..	8	..	2	17
Credit and Insurance	..	..	12	..	..	..	..	13
Total	58	3	23	..	70	255	2	417

* Annuario statistico italiano, 1934, p. 151.

National Confederations of Fascist Syndicates (Third Degree Associations)	Second Degree Syndical Associations		First Degree Syndical Associations					Total
	National	Inter-provincial	National	Regional	Inter-provincial	Provincial	Local	
Industry	12	..	5	..	..	92	..	110
Agriculture	5	..	1	..	..	92	..	99
Commerce	6	..	..	..	..	92	..	99
Internal Communications	6	..	..	..	16	..	..	23
Maritime and Air Transportation	..	..	4	..	..	..	..	5
Credit and Insurance	3	..	1	..	14	..	..	19
Total	32	..	11	..	30	276	..	355

Annuario statistico italiano, 1934, p. 151.

NUMBER OF LEGALLY RECOGNIZED SYNDICAL ASSOCIATIONS OF PROFESSIONAL MEN AND ARTISTS, DECEMBER 31, 1933*

National Confederations (Third Degree Associations)	Second Degree Syndical Associations	First Degree Syndical Associations							Total
	National	National	Inter-provincial	Regional	Provincial	Local	Court of Appeals District	Ordinary Court District	
National Confederation of Fascist Syndicates of Professional Men and Artists	22	..	21	180	642	..	44	126	1036

Annuario statistico italiano, 1934, p. 151.

REPRESENTATION AND MEMBERSHIP OF EMPLOYERS IN FAS

(Number of Employers Represented and Number of A

(December 31 of

National Fascist Confederations	1927		1928		1929	
	Total Number Represented	Total Number of Actual Members	Total Number Represented	Total Number of Actual Members	Total Number Represented	T Nu of A Me
Industry	102,453	60,000	120,824	71,453	128,700	7?
Agriculture	3,198,046	221,134	3,203,080	314,639	2,818,238	48?
Commerce	805,661	320,000	805,661	360,000	805,661	44
Land Transportation and Internal Navigation	23,143	7,376	50,301	20,250	40,096	2
Credit and Insurance†	3,748	2,695	3,798	2,874	4,075	
Maritime and Air Transportation	1,820	631	1,820	631	1,256	
Autonomous Fascist Federation of Italian Artisans' Communities	316,009	206,000	422,662	206,000	529,734	15?
Total	4,450,880	817,836	4,608,146	975,847	4,327,760	1,18?

* Compiled from various issues of *Bollettino del lavoro e della previdenza sociale* and *Annuario statistico italiano.*
† Up to 1931, General Fascist Confederation of Banking.

REPRESENTATION AND MEMBERSHIP OF WORKERS AND OF PROFESSIONAL MEN

(Number of Workers and of Professional Men and Artists Represented

(December 31 o

National Confederations of Fascist Syndicates	1927		1928		1929	
	Total Number Represented	Total Number of Actual Members	Total Number Represented	Total Number of Actual Members	Total Number Represented	T Nu of A Me
Industry	2,341,866	1,104,556	2,555,327	1,218,207	2,599,767	1,4?
Agriculture	4,646,558	874,637	4,699,333	1,021,461	3,740,843	1,09?
Commerce	908,400	267,341	908,400	346,931	908,400	2?
Land Transportation and Internal Navigation	208,306	133,532	201,597	157,914	202,800	1?
Credit and Insurance †	55,182	26,804	55,182	33,506	40,514	?
Maritime and Air Transportation	552,841	63,134	552,841	67,387	586,284	4
Total Workers' Representation	8,713,153	2,470,004	8,972,680	2,845,406	8,078,608	3,01?
National Confederation of Fascist Syndicates of Professional Men and Artists	143,940	76,402	143,940	76,402	143,940	7?
Grand Total	8,857,093	2,546,406	9,116,620	2,921,808	8,222,548	3,09?

* Compiled from various issues of *Bollettino del lavoro e della previdenza sociale* and *Annuario statistico italiano*
† Up to 1931, General Fascist Confederation of Banking.

(embers in Fascist Syndical Associations)

ear)

1930		1931		1932		1933	
Total umber resented	Total Number of Actual Members	Total Number Represented	Total Number of Actual Members	Total Number Represented	Total Number of Actual Members	Total Number Represented	Total Number of Actual Members
5,266	75,403	117,293	70,180	117,630	70,044	119,849	69,343
8,238	492,489	2,700,000	464,207	2,800,000	543,486	2,742,764	662,692
6,795	454,088	786,588	454,184	747,884	365,422	722,969	385,483
9,842	18,802	32,609	10,963	29,682	11,576	30,172	12,994
3,998	3,009	4,935	3,052	10,659	3,835	11,436	5,542
1,321	884	1,321	1,089	2,038	1,465	3,838	1,782
4,649	170,671	520,387	159,797	550,000	148,805	520,766	172,819
0,109	1,215,346	4,163,133	1,163,472	4,257,893	1,144,633	4,151,794	1,310,655

umber of Actual Members in Fascist Syndical Associations)

ar)

1930		1931		1932		1933	
Total umber resented	Total Number of Actual Members	Total Number Represented	Total Number of Actual Members	Total Number Represented	Total Number of Actual Members	Total Number Represented	Total Number of Actual Members
5,228	1,632,608	2,428,550	1,661,874	2,160,602	1,654,340	2,194,961	1,813,463
5,690	1,322,700	2,814,102	1,408,607	2,815,778	1,659,011	2,815,778	1,926,931
8,612	287,485	815,397	321,457	650,000	350,632	565,502	368,175
5,000	190,226	250,000	191,883	303,352	194,230	310,507	201,873
4,523	20,315	43,944	21,705	47,996	33,781	48,593	34,791
4,563	15,205	124,563	41,402	124,648	50,772	124,600	24,539
3,616	3,468,539	6,476,556	3,646,928	6,102,376	3,942,766	6,059,941	4,369,772
5,000	92,425	110,910	86,002	120,223	90,277	159,442	105,484
8,616	3,560,964	6,587,466	3,732,930	6,222,599	4,033,043	6,219,383	4,475,256

BIBLIOGRAPHY

The following list of books, documents, and other sources does not constitute an exhaustive bibliography of the writings available on Italian Fascism. It is merely a selection of representative materials of value from the point of view of the present study. Publications used in the preparation of this work but not dealing primarily with Fascism are omitted from the list. Bibliographical descriptions of these will be found in the footnote references given in the text. For a comprehensive and authoritative list of Italian publications on Fascism the reader is referred to the monumental *Bibliografia fascista*.

PUBLICATIONS IN ENGLISH

I. Official Publications

Ministry of Corporations, *News Notes on Fascist Corporations* (Rome, monthly, January 1929-).

II. Unofficial Publications

Ashton, E. B., *The Fascist, His State and His Mind* (New York, 1937).

Baravelli, G. C., *Integral Land-Reclamation in Italy* (Rome, 1935). *Policy of Public Works under the Fascist Regime* (Rome, 1935).

Barnes, James S., *The Universal Aspects of Fascism* (London, 1928).

Bonomi, Ivanoe, *From Socialism to Fascism* (London, 1924).

Borgese, G. A., *Goliath: The March of Fascism* (New York, 1937).

Cippico, Antonio, *Italy, the Central Problem of the Mediterranean* (New Haven, 1926).

Counts, George S., and others, *Bolshevism, Fascism, and Capitalism* (New Haven, 1932).

Davis, Jerome, *Contemporary Social Movements* (New York, 1930).

Einzig, Paul, *The Economic Foundations of Fascism* (London, 1933).

Elliott, W. Y., *The Pragmatic Revolt in Politics* (New York, 1928).

Fascist Confederation of Industrialists, *Business and Financial Report: A Monthly Survey of Italian Trade and Industry* (Rome, monthly, January 1925-).

Finer, Herman, *Mussolini's Italy* (New York, 1935).

Florinsky, Michael T., *Fascism and National Socialism* (New York, 1936).

Fortune, X (1934), pp. 45-172 (July 1934).

Gini, Corrado, "The Italian Demographic Problem and the Fascist Policy on Population," *What is Fascism and Why?* (Tommaso Sillani, ed., London, 1931).

Glass, D. V., *The Struggle for Population* (Oxford, 1936).

Goad, Harold E., *The Making of the Corporate State* (London, 1932).

Gorgolini, Pietro, *The Fascist Movement in Italian Life* (New York, 1923).

Haider, Carmen, *Capital and Labor under Fascism* (New York, 1930).

International Center of Fascist Studies, Yearbook (London).

King, Bolton, *Fascism in Italy* (London, 1931).

Longobardi, Cesare, *Land-Reclamation in Italy* (London, 1936).

Ludwig, Emil, *Talks with Mussolini* (London, 1932).

Marriott, J. A. R., *The Makers of Modern Italy: Napoleon — Mussolini* (Oxford, 1931).

Matteotti, G., *The Fascisti Exposed* (London, 1924).

McClellan, George B., *Modern Italy* (Princeton, 1933).

McGuire, Constantine E., *Italy's International Economic Position* (New York, 1926).

Mussolini, Benito, *Fascism: Doctrine and Institutions* (Rome, 1935).
   Four Speeches on the Corporate State (Rome, 1935).
   "The Political and Social Doctrine of Fascism," *International Conciliation*, Carnegie Endowment for International Peace, January 1935,
   My Autobiography (New York, 1928).

Page, Kirby, ed., *A New Economic Order* (New York, 1930).

Palmieri, Mario, *The Philosophy of Fascism* (Chicago, 1936).

Pennacchio, Alberto, *The Corporative State* (New York, 1927).

Pitigliani, Fausto, *The Italian Corporative State* (London, 1933).

Prezzolini, Giuseppe, *Fascism* (New York, 1927).

Rocco, Alfredo, *The Political Doctrine of Fascism* (Worcester, 1926).

Royal Institute of International Affairs, Information Department Papers.
   No. 15: *The Economic and Financial Position of Italy.* No. 16:
   Abyssinia and Italy. No. 17: *Sanctions* (London, 1935).

Salvemini, Gaetano, *The Fascist Dictatorship in Italy* (New York, 1927).
   Under the Axe of Fascism (New York, 1936).

Schmidt, Carl T., *The Plough and the Sword* (New York, 1938).

Schneider, Herbert W., *The Fascist Government of Italy* (New York, 1936).
   Italy Incorporated (New York, 1928).
   Making Fascists (Chicago, 1929).
   Making the Fascist State (New York, 1928).

Sforza, Carlo, *Makers of Modern Europe* (Indianapolis, 1930).

Sillani, Tommaso, ed., *What is Fascism and Why?* (New York, 1931).

Spencer, Henry Russell, *Government and Politics of Italy* (Yonkers, 1932).

Sturzo, Luigi, *Italy and Fascismo* (New York, 1927).

Trevelyan, George, "The Historical Causes of the Present State of Affairs in Italy," *Barnett House Papers*, No. 8 (Oxford, 1923).

Villari, Luigi, *The Awakening of Italy* (London, 1924).
The Fascist Experiment (London, 1926).
Italy (New York, 1929).
Volpe, Gioacchino, *History of the Fascist Movement* (Rome, 1934).
Welk, William G., "League Sanctions and Foreign Trade Restrictions in Italy," *American Economic Review*, XXVII (1937), pp. 96–107 (March 1937).

PUBLICATIONS IN GERMAN

Andrae, Wilhelm, *Staatssozialismus und Staendestaat — Ihre grundlegenden Ideologien und die juengste Wirklichkeit in Russland und Italien* (Jena, 1931).
Beckerath, Erwin von, *Wesen und Werden des fascistischen Staates* (Berlin, 1927).
Dobbert, Gerhard, *Die fascistische Wirtschaft* (Berlin, 1934).
Eschmann, Ernst Wilhelm, *Der fascistische Staat in Italien* (Breslau, 1930).
Heinrich, Walter, *Der Fascismus: Staat und Wirtschaft im neuen Italien* (Munich, 1932).
Heller, Hermann, *Europa und der Fascismus* (Berlin, 1931).
Hirschberg-Neumeyer, Margherita, *Die italienischen Gewerkschaften* (Jena, 1928).
Koch, Woldemar, *Die Staatswirtschaft des Fascismus* (Jena, 1935).
Mannhardt, J. W., *Der Fascismus* (Munich, 1925).
Michels, Robert, "Der Einfluss der Fascistischen Arbeitsverfassung auf die Weltwirtschaft," *Weltwirtschaftliche Vortraege* (Leipzig, 1929).
Italien von heute . . . 1860 bis 1930 (Leipzig, 1930).
Sozialismus und Fascismus . . . in Italien (Munich, 1925).
Raue, Ernst, *Beitraege zur neuen Staats-und Wirtschaftsauffassung in Deutschland und Italien* (Berlin, 1934).
Reupke, Hans, *Unternehmer und Arbeiter in der fascistischen Wirtschafts-idee* (Berlin, 1931).
Das Wirtschaftssystem des Fascismus (Berlin, 1930).
Schmidt, Emil, *Die Arbeitgeber Organisationen in Italien* (Leipzig, 1927).
Walter, Heinrich, *Die Staats und Wirtschaftsverfassung des Fascismus* (Berlin, 1927).

PUBLICATIONS IN FRENCH

I. Official Publications

Ministère de l'Agriculture et des Forêts, *Le Progrès de l'agriculture italienne en régime fasciste* (Rome, 1934).
Ministère des Corporations, *L'Organisation syndicale et corporative italienne* (Rome, 1935).

II. Unofficial Publications

Agapitidès, Sotiris, *Le Corporatisme en Italie* (Paris, 1935).

Dupeyroux, Henri, *La Charte du travail in Italie* (Paris, 1928).

Ferrari, Francesco L., *Le Régime fasciste italien* (Paris, 1928).

Mitzakis, Marcel, *Les Grands Problèmes italiens: L'économie, les finances et les dettes* (Paris, 1931).

Nitti, Francesco, *Bolscevisme, fascisme et démocratie* (Paris, 1926).

Perroux, François, *Contribution à l'étude de l'économie et des finances publiques de l'Italie depuis la guerre* (Paris, 1929).

Rosenstock-Franck, Louis, *L'Économie corporative fasciste en doctrine et en fait* (Paris, 1934).

Trentin, Silvio, *Antidémocratie* (Paris, 1930).
L'Aventure italienne; légendes et réalités (Paris, 1928).
Les Transformations récentes du droit public italien de la Charte de Charles Albert à la création de l'état fasciste (Paris, 1929).

PUBLICATIONS IN ITALIAN

I. Official Publications

Parlamento Italiano. *Atti. Senato del Regno* (Rome).
Atti. Camera dei Deputati (Rome).

La Gazzetta ufficiale del Regno (Rome; daily).

Ministero dell'Agricoltura e delle Foreste, *La legge sulla bonifica integrale nel quinto anno di applicazione* (Rome, 1935).

Ministero delle Corporazioni, *Atti dei convegni di studi sindacali e corporativi* (Rome, 1930, 1932).

Ministero delle Corporazioni, *Le Corporazioni. Lavori preparatori — Legge e decreti istitutivi — Composizione — Insediamento* (Rome, 1935).

Bollettino del lavoro e della previdenza sociale (Rome, monthly, October 1929–December 1932; discontinued).

Bollettino ufficiale del Ministero delle Corporazioni (Rome).

Contratti collettivi di lavoro (Rome).

Il Diritto del lavoro (Rome).

Sindacato e corporazione (Rome, monthly, January 1933–).

Ministero dell'Economia Nazionale, *Bollettino del lavoro e della previdenza sociale* (Rome; monthly, July, 1923–September, 1929).

Ministero delle Finanze, *Il Bilancio dello stato dal 1913–14 al 1929–30 e la finanza fascista a tutto l'anno VIII* (Rome, 1931).

Il Bilancio e il conto generale del patrimonio dello stato per l'esercizio finanziario 1930–1931 (Rome, 1932).

Il Bilancio e il conto generale del patrimonio dello stato per l'esercizio finanziario 1931–1932 (Rome, 1933).

La Finanza statale dell'anno XI. (Esercizio 1932–1933) (Rome, 1934).

La Finanza statale dell'anno XII. (Esercizio 1933–34) (Rome, 1935).

Istituto Centrale di Statistica del Regno d'Italia, *Annuario statistico italiano* (Rome; annual).
Bollettino dei Prezzi (Rome; monthly, July 1927–).
Bollettino mensile di statistica (Rome; monthly, November 1926–).
Compendio statistico italiano (Rome; annual).

Presidenza del Consiglio dei Ministri, *Relazioni e proposte della commissione presidenziale per lo studio delle riforme costituzionali* (Rome, 1925).

II. Unofficial Publications

Alessio, Giulio, *La Rivalutazione della lira* (Milan, 1926).

Ambrosini, Gaspare, *Sindacati, consigli tecnici e parlamento politico* (Rome, 1925).

Arcari, Paola Maria, *I Salari agricoli in Italia dal 1905 al 1933* (Rome, 1934).

Banca Commerciale Italiana, *Cenni statistici sul movimento economico italiano* (Milan; annual).

Bassani, Gerolamo, "Sviluppi corporativi," *Giornale degli economisti* (Milan), LII (1937), pp. 576–592 (August 1937).

Belluzzo, G., *Economia fascista* (Rome, 1928).

Bernabò-Silorata, Gino, *Le Assicurazioni sociali* (Turin, 1930).

Bertani, Pier Lodovico, "Il Salario corporativo nell'agricoltura e nell'-industria," *Economia* (Rome), XVII (1936), pp. 374–394 (May, 1936).

Biagi, Bruno, *Lineamenti di economia corporativa* (Padua, 1936).

Bortolotto, Guido, *Lo Stato e la dottrina corporativa* (Bologna, 1931).

Bottai, Giuseppe, *Il Consiglio Nazionale delle Corporazioni* (Rome, 1932).
Le Corporazioni (Milan, 1935).
Esperienza corporativa (1929–1935) (Florence, 1935).
Lo Stato corporativo (Rome, 1929).

Bottai, Giuseppe, and Turati, Augusto, *La carta del lavoro illustrata e commentata* (Rome, 1929).

Campese, Ernesto, *Il Fascismo contro la disoccupazione* (Rome, 1929).

Carli, Filippo, *Premesse di economia corporativa* (Pisa, 1929).
Teoria generale della economia politica nazionale (Milan, 1931).

Chiarelli, Giuseppe, *Il Diritto corporativo e le sue fonti* (Perugia, 1930).

Chiurco, G. A., *Storia della rivoluzione fascista* (Florence, 1929).

Confederazione Generale Fascista dell'Industria Italiana, *Annuario* (Rome).

Confederazione Fascista dei Lavoratori del Commercio, *Azione sindacale contro la disoccupazione* (Rome, 1935).

Confederazione Fascista dei Lavoratori dell'Industria, *Convegni nazionali dei dirigenti dei sindacati fascisti dell'Industria* (Rome, 1934).
Organizzazione sindacale e ordinamento corporativo (Rome, 1934).

Costamagna, Carlo, *Diritto corporativo italiano* (Rome, 1934).
Lo Stato corporativo quale stato di diritto (Rome, 1928).

Di Nola, Angelo, "L'Evoluzione della politica economica internazionale con particolare riguardo all'Italia," *Rassegna di politica internazionale* (November, 1935).

Einaudi, Luigi, *Il Sistema tributario italiano* (third ed., Turin, 1935).

Fanno, Marco, *Introduzione allo studio della teoria economica del corporativismo* (Padua, 1936).

Fantini, Oddone, *Stato e lavoro* (Rome, 1928).

Fovel, Natale Massimo, *Politica economica ed economia corporativa* (Rome, 1929).

Gangemi, Lello, *Lineamenti di politica economica corporativa* (Catania, 1932).
La Politica economica e finanziaria del governo fascista nel periodo dei pieni poteri (Bologna, 1924).
Pressione tributaria, produzione e scambi internazionali (Florence, 1935).

Gentile, Giovanni, *Che cosa è il Fascismo* (Florence, 1925).
Origini e dottrina del fascismo (Rome, 1929).

Guidotti, Franco, *Il Contratto collettivo di lavoro nel diritto corporativo* (Rome, 1935).

Istituto Coloniale Fascista, *Annuario delle colonie Italiane e paesi vicini, Anno XIII* (Rome, 1934).

Istituto Nazionale Fascista di Coltura, *Legislazione e ordinamento sindacale corporativo* (Rome, 1934).

Istituto Nazionale Fascista per gli Scambi con l'Estero, *Autorizzazione ad importazioni in compensazione privata* (Rome, 1935).
Dati statistici sul commercio estero italiano nel quinquennio 1930–34 (Rome, 1935).
Nuovo Regime delle importazioni e delle compensazioni private (Rome, 1935).

Korherr, Riccardo, *Regresso delle nascite, morte dei popoli* (with a Preface by Benito Mussolini, Rome, 1928).

Lessona, Alessandro, *Realizzazioni e propositi del colonialismo italiano* (Rome, 1935).

Lojacono, Luigi, ed., *Le Corporazioni fasciste* (Milan, 1935).

Loria, Achille, *Sulla disciplina giuridica dei contratti collettivi del lavoro* (Rome, 1926).

Magri, Francesco, *La Bonifica delle paludi pontine e l'Opera Nazionale per i Combattenti* (Milan, 1933).

Malusardi, Edoardo, *Elementi di storia del sindacalismo fascista* (Turin, 1930).

Marpicati, Arturo, *Il Partito fascista* (Milan, 1935).

Marrani, Pelio, *Il Contratto collettivo di lavoro nella statica e nella dinamica della economia industriale* (Padua, 1935).

Miceli, Giuseppe, *Manuale di norme corporative* (Rome, 1928).

Michelis, Giuseppe de, *La Corporazione nel mondo* (Milan, 1934).

Missiroli, Mario, *L'Italia d'oggi* (Bologna, 1932).

Mortara, Giorgio, *L'Italia e l'economia corporativa di fronte alla crisi economica mondiale* (Rome, 1934).
Prospettive economiche (Milan; annual).
La Realtà economica (second ed., Padua, 1935).

Mussolini, Benito, *Diritti e interessi dell'Italia in Africa Orientale* (Rome, 1935).
I Discorsi della Rivoluzione (Milan, 1927–31; annual).
Scritti e discorsi dal 1932 al 1933 (Milan, 1934).

Napolitano, Gaetano, *Principi di economia corporativa* (Rome, 1930).

Olivetti, A. O., *Il Sindacalismo come filosofia e come politica* (Milan, 1924).

Olivetti, Gino, *Lezioni di diritto corporativo* (Turin, 1929).

Opera Nazionale Balilla, *L'Opera balilla nell'anno XII* (Rome, 1935).

Opera Nazionale per i Combattenti, *La Bonifica e la trasformazione fondiaria dell'agro pontino* (Rome, 1935).
Il Contratto di mezzadria per i coloni dell'agro pontino (Rome, 1933).

Palladino, Giuseppe, *I Maggiori Problemi delle corporazioni a ciclo produttivo* (Rome, 1935).

Panunzio, Sergio, *Stato nazionale e sindacati* (Milan, 1924).

Parenti, Giuseppe, "L'Efficacia delle controsanzioni italiane," *Rivista internazionale di scienze sociali* (Milan), XLIV (1936), pp. 355–365 (July 1936).

Pennacchio, Alberto, *Lo Stato corporativo fascista* (Milan, 1928).

Pighetti, G., *Fascismo, sindacalismo, corporativismo* (Milan, 1930).

Rèpaci, F. A., *La Finanza italiana nel ventennio 1913–1932* (Turin, 1934).

Rivista internazionale di scienze sociali, "L'Economia italiana nel 1936," vol. VIII (1937), July 1937.

Rocco, Alfredo, *La Dottrina del fascismo* (Milan, 1925).
La Trasformazione dello stato: dallo stato liberale allo stato fascista (Rome, 1927).

Ronchi, Ennio, *Economia liberale, economia socialista, economia corporativa* (Rome, 1932).

Rosboch, E., *La Riforma monetaria* (Milan, 1927).

Rossoni, Edmondo, *Le Idee della ricostruzione* (Florence, 1923).

Sarfatti, Margherita, *Dux* (Milan, 1926).

Serpieri, A., *La Legge sulla bonifica integrale nel quinto anno di applicazione* (Rome, 1935).

Spirito, Ugo, *Capitalismo e corporativismo* (Florence, 1933).
La Critica della economia liberale (Milan, 1930).
I Fondamenti della economia corporativa (Milan, 1932).

Squadrilli, Gaspare, *Il Consiglio nazionale delle corporazioni* (Rome, 1930).

Stefani, Alberto de, *L'Ordine economico nazionale* (Bologna, 1935).
La Restaurazione finanziaria, *1922–1925* (Bologna, 1926).

Tassinari, Giuseppe, *Saggio intorno alla distribuzione del reddito nella agricoltura italiana* (Rome, 1935).

Turati, Augusto, *Ragioni ideali di vita fascista* (Rome, 1926).

Turati, Augusto, and Bottai, Giuseppe, *La Carta del lavoro illustrata e commentata* (Rome, 1929).

Valsecchi, Franco, *Le Corporazioni nell'organismo politico del medio evo* (Milan, 1931).

Vito, Francesco, and others, *Economia corporativa* (Milan, 1935).
L'Economia corporativa nazionale nell'ambito del mercato mondiale (Milan, 1935).

Volpe, Gioacchino, *L'Italia in cammino* (Milan, 1927).
Lo Sviluppo storico del fascismo (Palermo, 1928).

Periodicals

Critica fascista, fortnightly, Rome.

Economia, monthly, Rome.

Gerachia, monthly, Milan.

Il Giornale degli economisti, monthly, Rome.

Nuovi Studi, quarterly, Rome.

Politica, quarterly, Rome.

La Riforma sociale, Turin (discontinued, 1935).

Daily Newspapers

Il Corriere della Sera, Milan.

Il Giornale d'Italia, Rome.

Il Messaggero, Rome.

Il Popolo d'Italia, Milan.

INDEX

INDEX

A.A.A. (Agricultural Adjustment Administration), 155

Abortion, laws against, 184

Accident insurance, 291; development of the National Fascist Institute for, by years, 1922–1936, 104

Accidents, prevention of, 291

Agricultural Adjustment Administration (A.A.A.), 155

Agricultural education, promoted by the regime, 193

Agriculture, legally recognized syndical associations in, first organized, 56; representation and membership of these associations, by years, 1927–1933, 334; 1934–1936, 131; their part in national elections, 65; corporations established in, 109 ff; production in, stimulated after 1922, 160, 165; the Fascist program of land reclamation, 191, 192; of agricultural education, 193; the 'Battle of Wheat,' 161, 165, 193, 195, 248; principal agricultural productions, by years, 1909–1914, 1920–1937, 196; production indexes, 197, 238; unemployment in, annual indexes, 1922–1934, 238; nominal and real wages in, by years, 1922–1934, 235–238

Amendola, Giovanni, persecuted as anti-Fascist, 18

Annunzio, Gabriel d', his agitation for Italy's entry into the World War, 6; his occupation of Fiume, 12, 47

Ansaldo, 160

Arbeitsgerichte, 82

Arbitration of collective labor disputes, see Collective labor disputes

Arditi, 11, 13

Artificial silk, see Silk, artificial

Artisans, 168

Artists, see Professional men and artists

Assegni familiari, 242n

Associations, required to submit by-laws and membership lists to the government, 21; of workers and employers in the theories of Léon Duguit, 26; and political pluralism,

28; Fascist, of workers and employers. See also Syndicates, Fascist

Associations of government employees, 283

Associations, syndical, see Syndicates

Autarchy, plans made by corporations for, 147; after League of Nations' sanctions, 177. See also Economic independence

Authoritarian state, 243

Autostrade, 201

Avanti, Mussolini resigns editorship of, 7

Aventino, 'Rival Chamber' on the, 19

Azeglio, Massimo d' (quoted), 5n

Azienda Autonoma Statale della Strada, 201

Azienda Italiana Carboni, 175

Bachelors, tax on, 184, 185

Balance of international payments, 'invisible' items of, reduced by world depression, 172; failure of automatic adustments in, 172; condition of, during world depression, 213; during League of Nations' sanctions, 173. See also Balance of trade

Balance of trade, deficit of, increased during the depression, 172; 205 ff; deficit of, during League of Nations' sanctions, 173, 209; annual data on, 1909–1913, 1920–1937, 204. See also Balance of international payments, Foreign trade

Balbo, Italo, extremist attitude in 1921, 15; his part in the March on Rome, 17

Banca Commerciale Italiana, 169, 218

Banca Italiana di Sconto, 160

Banco di Roma, 218

Bank credit, liberal, after 1922, 161; excessive in 1926, 162; stringent policy adopted by Volpi, 163; foreign, denied by sanctionist countries, 173; legislation passed for the regulation of, in 1926, 218. See also Bank of Italy, Banking reform, Note circulation

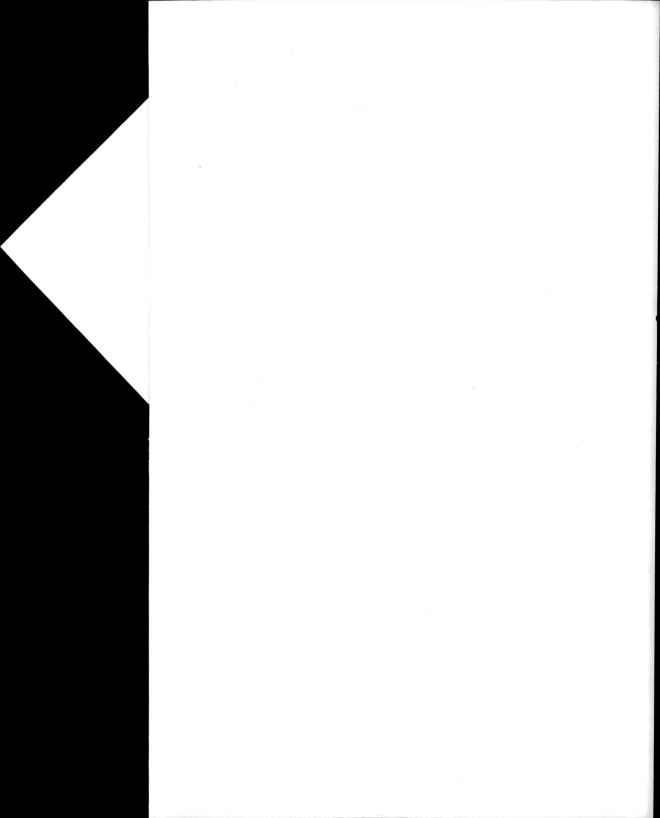

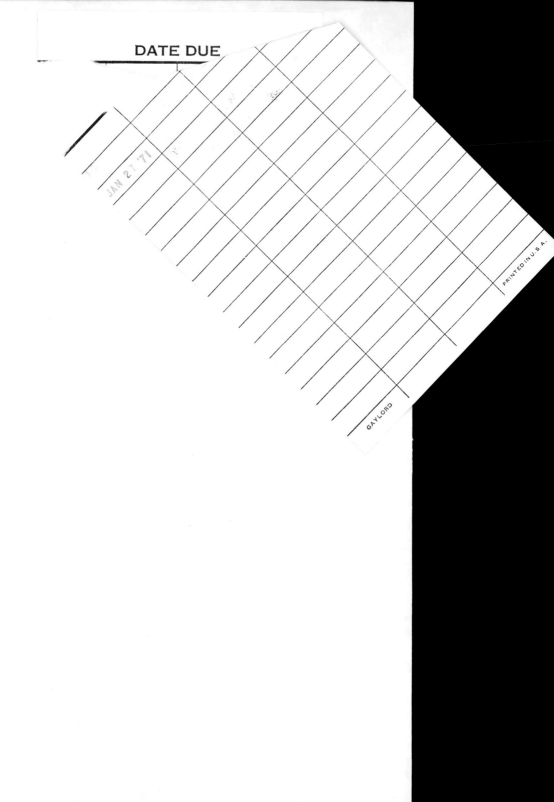

DATE DUE